On a River

A History of North River

Massachusetts

Lyle Nyberg

Copyright © 2025 Lyle Nyberg. All rights reserved.
Article contributed by Thomas Whalen, copyright © 2025 Thomas Whalen
Published by Lyle Nyberg, www.lylenyberg.com
Scituate, Massachusetts, 2025

ISBN: 978-1-7354745-8-8 (paperback)
ISBN: 979-8-9925277-0-4 (Kindle)
ISBN: 978-1-7354745-9-5 (hardcover)
Library of Congress Control Number: 2025901787

Cover: Design by Susannah Green using (1) aerial photo of North River mouth, copyright by G. Banks/W. Richardson (March 14, 2020, IMG_2297), by permission, and (2) "Site of Old Block House Yard and Rocky Reach, North River, Norwell, Mass." postcard (pub. by H. S. Turner & Co., Norwell, Mass.), early 1900s, courtesy of Norwell Historical Society, public domain.

Inside: Photos by Lyle Nyberg, 2024, except as noted. Author photo by Kjeld Mahoney. Most images are edited for clarity and size, and converted to black and white (grayscale).

Editors: Janet Paraschos and Alix Stuart

Special thanks to Bill Keegan for finding and copying old maps and aerial photos, and to John Roman, for making maps and photos look good, www.johnromanillustration.com.

Contents

Preface vii
Maps xi
Introduction 1
    Overview, Towns 1
    Colonial Rivers 4
    English Settlement 5
    A Faire River 6
    Pursuits 9
    Vital Statistics 10
    Fish First 15

1 Shad and Other Fish 17
    Shad Names 18
    Dams, a Brief History 21
    Dam Maps 22
    Dam Laws 24
    Seines 28
    Shad, Dams, and Dam Removal 29
    The State Fish 35
    Salmon and Cod 36
    Herring 36
    Shad Painted 38

2 Salt Haying 41
    Need for Hay 41
    Gathering Hay 45
    Haystacks and Staddles 46
    Transporting Hay 49

    Gundalows 51

3 MEN OF THE RIVER 55

    L. Vernon Briggs, M.D., Historian 55

    Uncle Josh, Salt Hay Mower..56

    Walter Crossley, Storyteller..58

    William Tilden, Fisherman..59

    Jerry Gunderway, Pilot 61

    Tolman Family, Tool Makers (*article contributed by Thomas Whalen*) 62

    Shipbuilders..64

4 IMPROVING THE RIVER: EARLY YEARS..69

    Early Proposals 70

    1839–1841 Federal Petitions..74

    1842–1844 State Petitions 81

    1852 Plan of Harbor and Canal 85

    1854 Report..89

    1850s Pushes to Improving the River 90

    Fourth Cliff House..90

    The *Helen M. Foster*, and Norwell History..93

5 IMPROVING THE RIVER: 1870 PLAN TO RECLAIM THE MARSHES........................101

    1870 Report..101

    1871 Objections..120

    1871 Legislature Authorizes Dam 122

    1872 Further Objections 122

6 IMPROVING THE RIVER: IMPLEMENTING 1870'S PLAN 125

    1872 Reclamation and Development Plan 125

    1873 Proposal to Reclaim the Marshes 127

    Dams Compared 131

    Green Harbor River...134

7 DEVELOPING THE VALLEY 141

    1870s–1880s Developments 141

    A Hill of Dreams...142

    Great Green Island, Flats, and Other Islands 150

    Trouant Island 155

8 1898 Portland Gale and Aftermath 159

    Nature Had Other Plans 159

    Scenic Images 164

9 North River in the 1900s 167

    1915 Report — Overview 167

    1915 Map 167

    1915 Report 169

    1934 and Later Aerial Photos 173

    1966 Report 175

    Environmental Awareness 176

    Frontiers of Environmentalism 178

10 Changing Values 181

11 Climate Change and Recent Studies 183

    Climate Science 183

    Floods 184

    Flooding Research 185

12 Coastal Wetlands Research 187

    Threats to Coastal Wetlands 187

    Benefits of Coastal Wetlands 188

    Sample Projects 190

    English Salt Marsh, Marshfield 192

    2024 NERRS Study 193

    North River Marsh Size 193

    Marshes Compared 195

13 2022 Report 197

14 Values of North River 199

15 Streams, and A Nice Drive in the Country 201

    Hanson 202

    Hanson/Hanover 206

    Hanover/Pembroke, Ludden's Ford 206

    Hanover 209

    Norwell 214

    Scituate 216

CONCLUDING REFLECTIONS 220

NOTES ON SOURCES 223

NOTES 227

INDEX 269

ACKNOWLEDGMENTS 273

ABOUT THE AUTHOR 275

Preface

John Stilgoe of Harvard University, who had written a nice blurb for my earlier book *On a Cliff*, sent me a congratulatory email on the publication of my *Seacoast Scituate by Air* — "excellent." He added, "keep writing . . . the North River awaits."[1]

"No," I thought. How could I add anything worthwhile to the history of the North River here in southeastern Massachusetts? So much has been written, including a history of shipbuilding by Briggs; histories by Deane, Merritt, and Vinal; and a fine historical survey by Galluzzo. This narrow tidal river winds through six towns along the South Shore of Boston, and these towns have their own published histories. In addition, Stilgoe himself has a body of excellent writings about landscapes and maps of the North River valley, among other places.[2]

Besides, I was already deeply at work on a book about Scituate's seashore.

That work led me along the shore, and then – lo and behold – up the river. Like the shad, a fish featured in this book, I found myself going upstream, from salt water to fresh water. Some kind of incoming tide drew me from seashores to riverbanks.

As I was drawn in, against my initial resistance, I found material that earlier writers either overlooked or downplayed. The material seemed worth a fresh look, particularly in light of today's environmental concerns.

This book arises from discovering old scientific reports to state and federal governments. In addition, the reports mentioned some old maps but did not attach them. They languished in archives. Further sleuthing uncovered them. In essence, this is a historical excavation.

Since those reports, people have studied and learned more about this area. We now have access to aerial photos and photogrammetry of the 1900s, recent satellite imaging, expanding digital and archival resources on the internet, layers upon layers of data in Geographic Information Systems (GIS), and continuing scientific study of the river and its marshes.

So this book covers these scientific advances in understanding our environment. That includes tides, floods, weather, and storms. Rising sea levels raise questions about the role and future of tidal estuaries such as those along the North River.

Important figures like John Quincy Adams and Daniel Webster were involved with the river and lived not far from it. Their writings contribute to this book's analysis of local rivalries, along with state and federal politicking, over the river.

In full disclosure, I, too, live not far from the North River. I can see it from my house. I like to walk down to its salt marshes, and I even gathered clams there. The area's beauty and history inspire me, as do talks held by the North and South Rivers Watershed Association (NSRWA). This book includes some of their work and the work of engineers and scientists who have studied this place. I have been driven by a similar curiosity to discover the untold stories of the river and to explain it. It is a deep dive into the history of what was called "a faire river" in 1643.

In this book, you will see many maps. I admit I am a "maphead," a geography nut. But the maps reveal stories that writings alone do not or cannot. They make place names more real. We use these place names all the time without realizing their origins.

The big story explored in this book – and it takes up much of it – is humans' relentless push to "improve" the river in the 1800s. In addition to routine dredging, the improvement plans included adding canals, and cutting through beaches to add new openings to the sea. The early goal was to improve navigability of the river and enhance (or resuscitate) the shipbuilding industry along its shores.

The high-water mark of this push was the 1870 plan, with detailed designs, to reclaim the river's marshes. That would have dammed the tidal river, excluding the ocean's salty water, turning the river into a fresh water stream, and allowing the river's extensive salt marshes to be "reclaimed." That would turn the salt marshes into fresh water meadows, which would support farming crops of higher value than the existing salt hay. That 1870 plan would have had drastic effects on the environment.

The 1870 plan for the North River did not happen. It was a bit early, one might say experimental. It was echoed in similar plans in America into the 1900s. Some happened, some did not. But the 1870 plan had a companion proposal to dam the nearby Green Harbor River in Marshfield and reclaim its marshes. That was adopted. What happened there is explored in this book. It is a lesson in what might have happened to the North River.

The river is an exemplar of colonial American settlement, pressures to "improve" nature, plans and dreams for using this area, conflicts between man and nature, and conflicts among people for use of our environment.

This book explores diverse topics related to the river: fish and fishing, farming and salt haying, industries (particularly shipbuilding) and craftsmen, dams and islands, local characters and storytellers, and grand plans by nationally known engineers and scientists.

This book covers the river's historical, cultural, and geographical landscapes, including its:

- natural environment (river, tributaries, salt marshes), including water, land, and areas in between

- built environment (dams, mills, fishways, weirs, kiddles, roads, bridges, ditches, staddles), including towns developed by English settlers, and

- almost-built environment, mainly the 1870 proposal to dam the North River, as contrasted with 1870s dam of the nearby Green Harbor River.

This is a history of human struggles over the proper uses of the river, man's plans, and nature's designs. Its story has echoes in the history of other rivers.

The book's geographic focus is obvious. Its scope is large. To understand the North River in context, we look at places as remote as Rio de Janeiro, Pakistan, the Netherlands, the Yakima River, and, of course, England. We look beyond these places, as well, to examine emerging global climate science.

The book's time span is long. It covers periods before, during, and after English contact with Native Americans. Many of the pursuits we associate with the river, like shipbuilding and salt marsh haying, lasted from the 1600s well into the 1800s. Engineering plans for the river in the 1870s marked the rise of the scientific field of hydrography in America. A century later marked the rise of the environmental movement in America.

Recent environmental research shows the river and its marshes seem to have recovered well from a devastating storm in 1898 that opened a new mouth of the river and increased its tides and salinity. This may be another big story in this book. It offers hope today as we look to the river's role in an age of rising sea levels.

So my work expanded from a slice of coast to a whole river. It grew from my perch on Third Cliff in Scituate to a whole group of towns on the South Shore of Boston, and a worldwide look at tidal rivers.

This is not just the story of a river, but also the settlement of a place of land and water; claims upon it by humans and by nature; human disputes over its uses; and environmental lessons for its future.

This book is for you if you live in or visit this area, or are interested in tidal rivers or salt marshes, or just love maps. Colorful stories abound. You will also discover more about New England, its colonial history, its coastal rivers, and their place in understanding our world in a time of climate change.

Lyle Nyberg
Third Cliff, Scituate, Massachusetts
March 2025

Maps

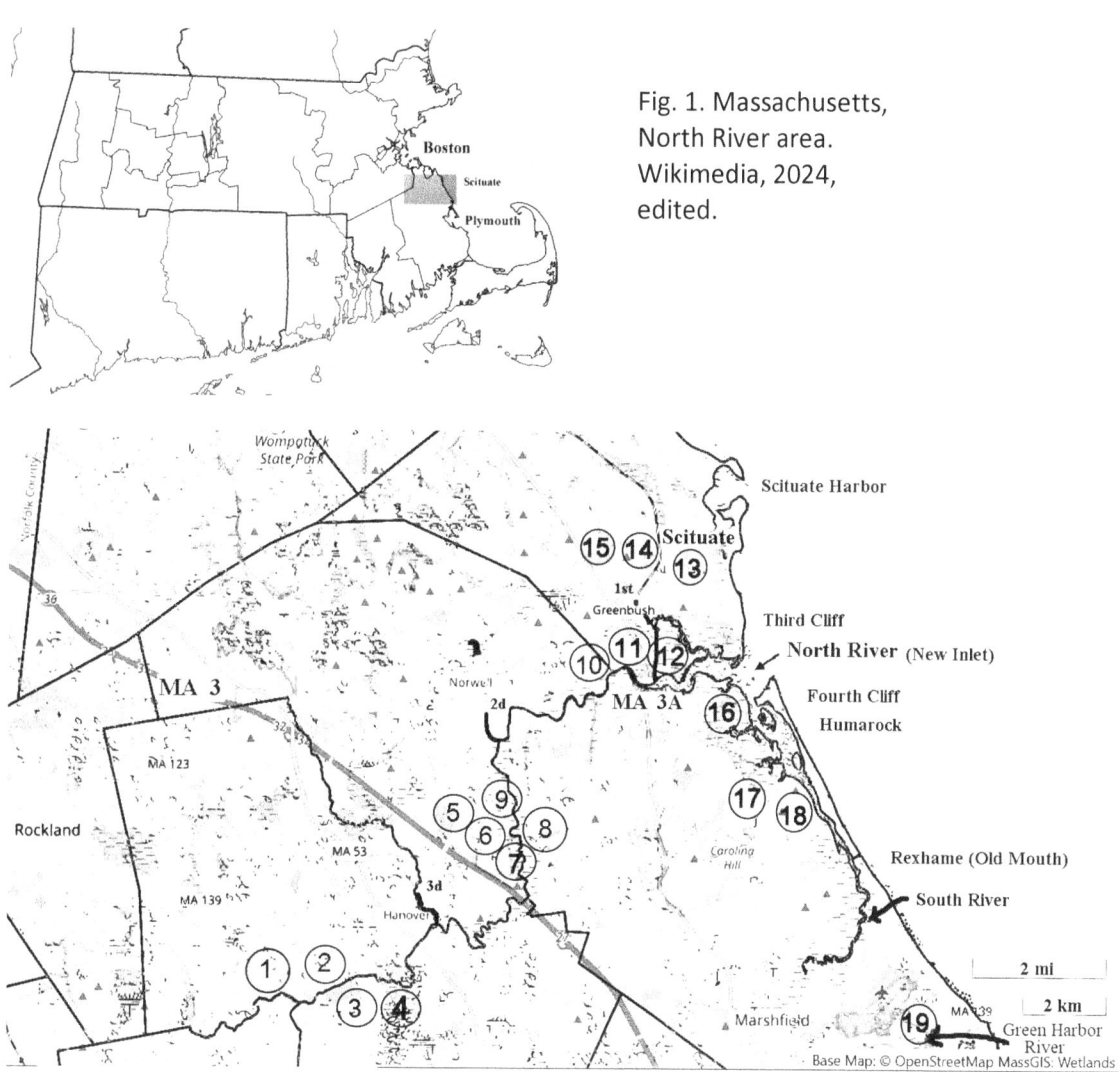

Fig. 1. Massachusetts, North River area. Wikimedia, 2024, edited.

Fig. 2. North River and area. MACRIS Maps, OpenStreetMap, DEP: Wetlands, 2024, edited.

1 Indian Head River
2 Waterman's Tack Factory Dam
3 Ludden's Ford Dam; former Clapp Rubber Mill
4 Herring Brook (Pembroke) at Indian Head River
5 Hanover Four Corners
6 Sylvester Field
7 North River Bridge/Hanover Bridge (1904-)
8 Turner's Shipyard
9 Waterman & Barstow Shipyard
10 Chittenden Shipyard
11 Union Bridge
12 Little's Bridge
13 Driftway
14 Stockbridge Mill
15 Old Oaken Bucket Pond
16 Trouant Island; English Salt Marsh
17 Sea View
18 White's Ferry Shipyard; Roger's Wharf
19 Green Harbor River
   Shown on map: <u>1st,</u> <u>2d,</u> <u>3d</u> Herring Brooks
   Off map to west: Wampatuck Pond,
   Drinkwater River, Forge Pond, Factory Pond

xi

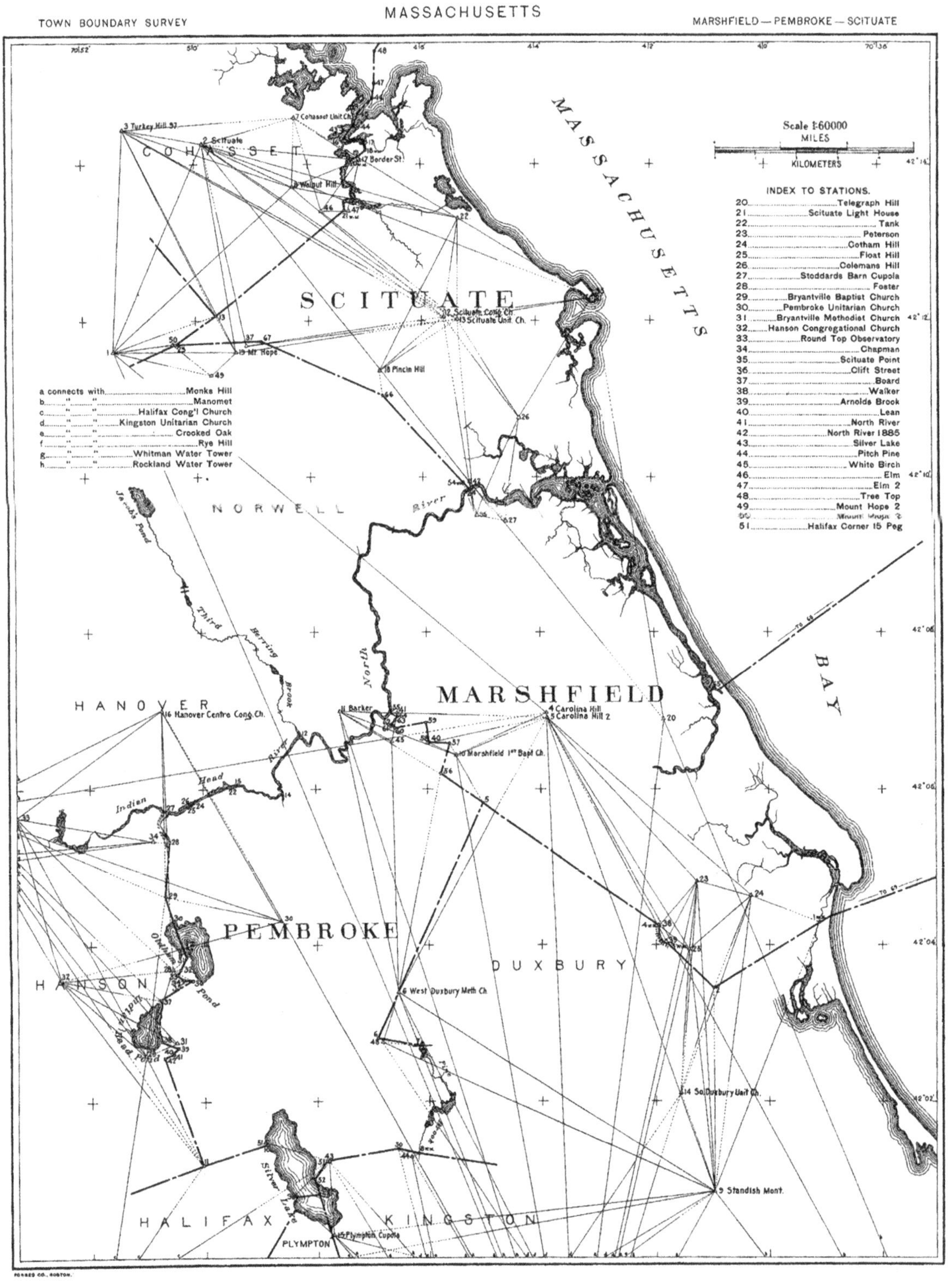

Fig. 3. 1902 atlas of boundaries, sheet 1. Board of Harbor and Land Commissioners of MA, *Atlas of the boundaries of the towns of Marshfield, Pembroke and Scituate, Plymouth County*. Massachusetts State Library, http://hdl.handle.net/2452/47879. North River forms town boundaries across middle of this map. Also shows South River and Green Harbor River.

Introduction

Overview, Towns

The North River area was inhabited by the Massachuset and Wampanoag people before Europeans came to settle.

A network of Native American trails covered the area. A state survey noted:

> The easternmost of the north–south trails ran south from Massachusetts Bay through Norwell, forded the North River in Hanover, continued southeast along Plymouth Bay and on through southern Plymouth to Cape Cod.
>
> … Native trails and ford locations generally survive because of their incorporation into later transportation systems. A number of major native trails have been adapted for use as major highways including Routes 44, 123 and 138. … In turn, most of the important native fords have survived as major bridge sites. Two examples include the Indian head River Bridge in Hanover and Little's Bridge in Scituate.[3]

We travel these trails and bridge sites every day. For example, the Little's Bridge site now has the Route 3A bridge over the North River between Scituate and Marshfield.

The North River is in southeastern Massachusetts (see Fig. 1Fig. 1. Massachusetts, North River area. Wikimedia, 2024, edited., Fig. 2, and Fig. 3). It flows into Massachusetts Bay at Scituate, about halfway between Boston and Plymouth. It is a tidal river. Another way of describing it is "a tidal arm of the sea, an estuary and not a river." We call it a river.[4]

The river rises from marshes and springs in Weymouth, Rockland, and Hanson. Its source is at the confluence of the Indian Head River (Hanover) and Herring Brook (Pembroke).

The river is narrow and it meanders to its mouth, where it widens (see cover and Fig. 4). Its length is about 12 miles, fewer as a crow flies.[5]

Fig. 4. North River, looking west, with Union Bridge at upper center, Marshfield on left, Norwell on right, 2012. Courtesy of Gary Banks/Bill Richardson.

On its winding way, the North River flows past the following towns, all in Plymouth County. They are listed here generally west to east, along with their founding years and 2020 census populations:

- Hanson   1820   10,639
- Pembroke   1712   18,361
- Hanover   1727   14,833
- Norwell   1849   11,351
- Marshfield 1640   25,825
- Scituate   1636   19,063

These towns are considered part of the South Shore of Boston. Most are inland, however, away from the shore. Take Hanover, for example. It is a South Shore town without a seashore. "South Shore" is a nebulous term. But tides, sent from the ocean, reach upriver in Hanover. Hanover and other towns are still North River towns, maybe with a touch of the ocean.[6]

The river supplies town borders, also called "bounds" or boundaries (Fig. 3). Rivers and other natural features make things more difficult than straight lines in delineating, legislating, surveying, mapping, and making borders. The border between Scituate and Marshfield generally runs down the center of the river. The 1902 atlas of boundaries says,

> The line between Scituate and Marshfield was defined as following the main channel of the North river in 1887. The storm of November, 1899 [1898], opened a new mouth to the North river several miles further to the north, but the corner (65) is assumed to be where the old mouth of the river was located.

Scituate may have 1.5 miles of that North River border. Marshfield has those and many more miles because the river provides Marshfield borders with other towns.[7]

More towns than these six contribute to the North River watershed.

Most towns were settled in the 1600s by the English. Some towns broke off from others. For example, Norwell was part of Scituate until 1849, when it separated to become South Scituate, then renamed Norwell in 1888. Settlements and farms expanded along the North River and country roads.[8]

The North River is a small river. Perhaps it is an overachiever among small rivers in the historical record, in environmentalism, and in governmental recognition. The state designated it as the first Scenic Protected River.

The river is particularly noted for its past shipbuilding industry starting in colonial times. In addition, proposed improvements to the river and its marshes led to detailed and comprehensive government reports and maps in the 1800s and early 1900s. That included two key state reports. The 1870 report[9] and the 1915 report[10] are discussed in detail in this book.

The river is affected by ocean tides. It is an estuary because the river's fresh waters meet and mix with the ocean's salt waters. Tides reach far up the river, almost to its source. The salinity reaches more than halfway up the river, to almost seven miles from its mouth.[11]

The mouth of a tidal river is both an exit for the river, and an entrance for the ocean's tides. The storm of 1898 opened a new mouth of the North River about three miles north of its old mouth. After that, maps called it "New Inlet." They still call it that, more than 125 years later.

The maps could have called it "New Outlet." It depends on which force of nature's waters you consider dominant. Or whether you are looking from a ship or from shore. Or whether you are a local or an outsider. Locals who asked state officials for help with the river used the word "entrance," likely considering the outside point of view of their readers up the coast. The state's 1915 report is replete with the word "entrance."[12]

Probably, the word "mouth" better accommodates both exit and entrance, as well as both locals and outsiders.

The nearby South River runs north to meet the North River. After the storm of 1898, their meeting place moved three miles north. Waters of both rivers now reach the ocean between Third Cliff and Fourth Cliff in Scituate. Confused? Just remember the North River is *north* of the South River.

Below, this introduction covers more of the river's geographic details, its vital statistics. But first we turn to history.

Colonial Rivers

Water was a key feature of many New World settlements. There was a pattern of locating them at a bay, harbor, or river, sometimes all of them. Examples include:

- *Rio de Janeiro* (founded 1565). The site was surveyed by a Portuguese explorer on January 1, 1502, at a bay originally thought to have been a river, thus giving the city its name, Rio de Janeiro, or "January River."[13]

- *Jamestown* (1607). This was the first permanent English settlement in the Americas, located on the northeast bank of the James River, named after King James I of England.[14]

- *Plymouth* (1620). The Pilgrims on the *Mayflower* aimed to settle at the mouth of the Hudson River but landed instead at the tip of Cape Cod. After days of scouting the coast, they found a sheltering harbor, with a place to settle. The Patuxet people, decimated by disease, had recently abandoned the site. That left much land cleared, easing agriculture for the English. Fresh water came from Town Brook and Billington Sea.[15]
  Note that the site had already been named "Plymouth" on John Smith's map of 1616 based on his exploring the coast. The map scattered English town names rather arbitrarily across a land named "New England," and years before any English settlements. It was just a coincidence that the *Mayflower* departed from Plymouth (as well as earlier departure points) in England, and later arrived at a map place named Plymouth.[16]

- *New York City* (founded 1624, named New Amsterdam in 1626, chartered as a city in 1653). The site has a huge natural harbor, along with the Hudson River (which the Dutch called the North River) and the East River.[17]

In Plymouth Colony, towns spread along the seacoast and then inland. Scituate and Marshfield, both settled by the early 1630s, led to later towns along the North River.

Rivers were important features attracting early settlers.

English Settlement

The North River's history of English settlement can be briefly traced.

The river was important to English settlers by the early 1630s. Its salt marshes provided hay to feed livestock. It provided a water highway to transport people and goods. The river was the scene of many human pursuits, including fishing and trading. From the 1600s until the 1800s, the North River was a major shipbuilding center. Many writers have told the stories of the North River, highlighting its importance for American shipbuilding.[18]

In recorded history, the river started inland, wandered east, then north, then east along what became the border of Scituate and Marshfield. After meeting a stony shingle beach between Third Cliff and Fourth Cliff, it turned south for three miles between Marshfield's shore and Humarock. Humarock is Scituate's long barrier beach or peninsula that stretches south from Fourth Cliff. Then the river reached the ocean near today's Rexhame. That was the old mouth of the river. A new mouth was created three miles north of Rexhame by the Portland Gale of 1898.

As explored in this book, overlooked documents reveal attempts to improve the river, or what people believed were improvements. They included damming it; straightening it; cutting new channels, ditches, or canals into it; and converting its salt marshes into fresh (salt-free) meadows. These proposed improvements range from 1802 plans for a canal from the North River to Scituate Harbor, to 1915 proposals to dredge the river's channel.

The 1915 report has a helpful overview of previous studies. In addition, it summarizes the river's tides, showing its dynamic effect on the environment:

> Extended tidal observations were not made; but the mean range of tide as determined is 9.4 feet at the entrance, 7.3 feet at Little's bridge [later replaced by the Route 3A bridge] and 3.2 feet at Hanover bridge [the 1904 version on Washington Street]. High water at Hanover bridge is about four

hours later than at the entrance to the river. The tides run very swiftly, with hardly any period of slack water.[19]

Briggs' book, *Shipbuilding on North River*, seems to catalog all the old bridges over the North River and its tributaries.

The efforts to improve the river involved a continual churn of local approaches for help from state and federal governments. They raise questions about how much governments should get involved in some projects that might be better handled by private, entrepreneurial ventures, or by commercial markets. These issues resonate in our times, with our American federal system of government.

In addition, the overlooked documents for improvements provide deeply detailed images of the river.

A Faire River

English settler William Vassall described this area in 1643:

> … our lands reach ten miles or more to the south-westward, by which runneth a faire River navigable for boats ten miles and hay grounds on both sides, and hath an outlet into the sea about four miles from the Meeting-House, with lands sufficient for a Township to settle upon.[20]

This is a great description of the North River, its marshes and lands, and early settlement. Yes, it was and still is "a faire River."

William Vassall (1592–1656) was a wealthy man who helped lead the Massachusetts Bay Colony. He came to Scituate in 1635. "A most beautiful tract of land on the river [North River] was granted him, by far the largest tract allotted to any one settler." The tract was named Belle [beautiful] House Neck. He was, according to one source, the wealthiest man in Plymouth Colony. Yet Vassall wanted more, and he eventually moved to Barbados, where he established a large slaveholding plantation.[21]

Vassall's description of the North River raises many questions.

First, the above quote needs context. It comes in the midst of a contest between Vassall and Timothy Hatherly, a rival leader who was later considered the father of Scituate. The contest was overtly about religious matters. Underneath was Vassall's desire for more land.

In his long letter, Vassall defends criticism by the new minister Chauncy that Vassall is harming the church, including by Vassall's objecting to the location of the existing meeting house. In particular, Vassall complains that Hatherly and his colleagues had already established the meeting house in a place convenient for them, and they owned much land in Scituate, and were muscling in on more. Historian Bangs says, "This is an early and extreme expression of the [land] division that existed within the territory of Scituate township." Historian Valdespino says, "Vassall was primarily concerned with the acquisition of more land."[22]

Second, we need to be clear about who Vassall was speaking for. By "our lands," he meant those of himself and his associates, in contrast to those of Hatherly. He was not speaking for all English colonists.

By "our lands," he certainly was not speaking for the Native Americans who had lived there for centuries, or millennia. Their population had been decimated by illness, probably brought by Europeans. We know little of their presence in Scituate at first contact with the English. We are left with claims by English settlers to title in land, documented in the records of Plymouth Colony. As many others have explained, those claims were based on hypothesized rights of discovery and possession, or royal charters and prerogatives.[23]

Vassall's 1643 quote came before settlers obtained a deed for the land of Scituate from Massachuset leader Josias Wampatuck in 1653.[24]

By "our lands," Vassall implicitly asserted English dominion of the waterways. Since the river ran between the towns of Scituate and Marshfield, they would have to share it. More than that, the river would have been held and shared in common, for use by the public.

Englishmen were accustomed to the common field system of husbandry. This included marshy meadows along rivers. Brian Donahue's splendid book *The Great Meadow* explains the common field system in early Concord, Massachusetts, and its later evolution. It notes that most imported English grasses did not perform well at first. It says, "Converting these wetlands from rough marshes and swamps into productive mowings had absorbed the labor of the first three generations of Concord husbandmen."[25]

In contrast, salt marsh hay did not require fertilizing ("manuring" in Donahue's words). It only needed mowing by the early English settlers. It is noteworthy that Vassall mentioned "hay grounds" on both sides of the river.

Common property did not mean free use. English customs applied and so did English common law. Then there were government regulations, which would grow over the years. That included:

- Orders adopted by Plymouth Colony "freemen" acting through its court, all under authority granted by royal charters.[26] These were as detailed as where and when to gather hay in salt marshes, and where grass could be mowed in 1633. In 1639, the court granted Vassall the liberty to make an oyster bank in the North River near Belle House Neck.[27]

- Royal prerogatives, such as royal forests and royal hunting parks, such as Hyde Park in London though not necessarily in New England.[28]

- Town regulations, including town meeting bylaws and resolutions, delegating authority to individuals, all within the Colony's grants of authority, subject to appeal to the Colony's governance. Examples in Scituate range from the 1668 rules on when and where to cut thatch on the North River flats, to the town's 1679 attempt to bring together two religious societies, including "our nayghtbors up the River."[29]

A notable example of colonial laws still in effect in Massachusetts, and few other states, involves shorefront access. English colonies followed English common law, which had adopted the ancient "public trust" doctrine. That meant "the sovereign state held the sea bed and the land affected by the tides in trust for the benefit of the public." For shorefront property owners, Massachusetts Bay Colony ordinances of 1641–1647 extended ownership from the high tide mark out to the mean low tide mark. This was to encourage construction of wharves, piers, and jetties. The intertidal area was thus generally private. Massachusetts, however, allowed use of that area by the public for fishing, fowling (hunting for birds), and navigation. In addition to oceanfront property, the public trust doctrine might apply to inland lands affected by the tides, such as those on tidal rivers. In sum, in this state there is no general property right of access to the shore.[30]

For English men, these rules were all very orderly, mostly written down, and in English. They might have had a say in adopting them. The bodies that adopted them, however, had small or no places for women, or Native Americans.[31]

For colonists, land was a valuable commodity, to be claimed, owned (mostly by individuals), divided, and subdivided. Plymouth Colony records are full of deeds conveying and re–conveying title to various parcels of land.

Native Americans had different views or interests in the lands and rivers. However, they, too, like the English, valued this "faire river."

The "faire river" is what the English called the North River. Native Americans appear to have called it *Massaugetucket*, "great outlet of a tidal river," with "saugetuck" meaning "mouth of a river."[32]

Pursuits

The river was important to Native Americans and the English settlers and their pursuits. They relied on the river and its marshy banks for travel, fishing, shipbuilding, and farming. These pursuits would come into conflict.

For travel, the river served as a highway connecting the world with inland areas. Packet boats, some of which were built on the North River, provided a trade network along the coast, "carrying farm produce and timber and bringing back items from the China and Mediterranean trade, as well as staple products for the stores along the river towns." The boats stopped at packet landings on the North River. The river trade thrived from colonial times until railroads came to the South Shore in the mid-to-late 1800s.[33]

For fishing, the river served as a source of food for humans and a habitat for fish. We take a look at the river from the point of view of a fish, a fish named shad. Its travels were limited by fishing, of course, and by dams erected along the river's tributaries, dams that provided power to mills and other industries.

For shipbuilding, many books tell the river's stories. The premier example is L. Vernon Briggs' book, *Shipbuilding on North River*. Here, we go beyond those books to examine overlooked federal and state reports and maps. They describe attempts to "improve" the river, originally to help the shipbuilding industry.

For farming, we briefly discuss salt marsh haying, important to the first settlers and for centuries later.

The North River valley has been home to an impressive array of carpenters, craftsmen, salt hayers, river pilots, ministers, doctors, reformers, and storytellers.

This book moves on to the river's salt marshes. Proposals were made, including in 1870, to convert the marshes into fresh-water meadows. That would require damming the river to keep out the salty tides. The proposals produced splendid engineering plans, political maneuvering, and conflicting interests at local, state, and federal levels.

Later, the book discusses Nature's sudden intervention with the Portland Gale of 1898. It opened a new mouth of the North River, three miles north of the old mouth. It marked a change from the older pursuits in the river valley.

The newer pursuits accommodated Americans' developing appetite for summer vacations, especially by the seashore.[34] This could be with quaint cottages, new hotels, or even new housing developments. South Shore towns were easily accessible after the railroad arrived in 1871. Because of this, and because the North River was close to the shore and connected to the sea, its towns attracted vacationers in the late 1800s into the 1900s.

A 1909 MIT student thesis described the charm of Sea View in the town of Marshfield:

> The little village, thirty miles from the noise and bustle of the city, nestling quietly here among the hills, with its neat, well-kept homes dotting the gentle slope to the sea, is a true haven of rest for the scores of vacationists who spend their summers here on the shore.[35]

In addition, the North River has long been the subject of serious scientific examination. Now it is being assessed in light of climate change and rising sea levels. It can provide lessons for our future.

Vital Statistics

Name

What's in a name? There are 26 "North Rivers" in America, according to the federal Geographic Names Information System (GNIS), or 22 if you count only streams. The most noted one, because it is close to New York City, is probably North River (Dutch: Noort Rivier), an alternative name for the southernmost part of the Hudson River. Massachusetts has three rivers named North River. They are in Essex, Franklin, and Plymouth counties. This book deals with the latter one, number 615268 in GNIS.[36]

There are so many geographic names, they have to be numbered.

Area

The North River's watershed drains about 59,000 acres, according to some estimates. Much of that area consists of wetlands.[37]

The watershed of 59,000 acres equals 92 square miles. That is about twice the size of Disney World (47), bigger than Boston (48), larger than eight countries, and almost as large as Martha's Vineyard (96).

The watershed includes salt marshes, covering many acres. The marshes widen significantly along the river's mouth. A 1915 report, discussed in detail below, reported:

There are 1,160 acres of salt marsh on both sides of the river below the Hanover bridge, and between the present outlet and the old outlet there are 830 acres of salt marsh on the west side of the old river. There are also 820 acres of fresh marsh above Hanover bridge.[38]

Much remains of these salt marshes.

Below is an image of the area's marshes (Fig. 5). It comes from the first-ever (2023) analysis of satellite data. It is heavily edited from a screenshot in color that used 2020 data. Marshes appear, enhanced, as light areas that extend well beyond their rivers. The image covers the shoreline from Scituate Harbor (very top) to Brant Rock and Green Harbor in Marshfield (bottom).[39]

Fig. 5. South Shore marshes shown as light on this Global Tidal Marsh Distribution map (which used 2020 satellite data and Earth Engine App) (original in color), https://www.nature.org/en-us/newsroom/tidal-marshes-on-the-map/?vu=marshes. Covers shoreline from Scituate Harbor (very top) to near Brant Rock in Marshfield (bottom). North River marshes with the South River marshes form an upside-down U-shape.

The image above highlights marshes along the North River, as well as those west of Peggotty Beach, and along Indian Head River, South River, and Green Harbor River. All these rivers are discussed in this book. Also discussed is a fine 1870 map covering the same area.[40] At the end of this book, we overlay this image onto the 1870 map to see how this area might have changed.

Length

As to the North River's length, most sources say 12 miles. Its length has changed over time, and it depends on how you measure it. One way is straight as a crow flies, but the river is so crooked that it is much longer. It even turns back west in places, as it generally meanders east. It wiggles and squirms like an earthworm on a fishhook.

As rivers go, the North River is not the longest, nor is it the deepest, by far. It is also not the shortest.[41]

Slope

To say that the river has a gentle slope would be way off. It is almost flat.

"The world average river reach slope," according to a Wikipedia article, "is 2.6 m/km or 0.26%; a slope smaller than 1% and greater than 4% is considered gentle and steep, respectively. Stream gradient may change along the stream course."[42]

Elsewhere, we mention the Boston Marathon course of about 26 miles along the Charles River. With rolling hills such as Heartbreak Hill, the marathon course drops significantly from 490 feet above sea level to 10 feet above. That is 480 feet in 26 miles (137,280 feet), or 1:286 (0.35%). That is a gentle slope, a bit above average if it were a river.[43]

By contrast, the North River starts about 3 to 10 feet above sea level, and it ends at, well, the sea. The river thus has a slope of, say, 10 feet in 12 miles (63,360 feet), or 1:6,336 (0.0016%). That is far below a 1% gentle slope, and well below an average 0.26% slope. It is a very lazy river.[44]

One wonders how all that water even finds its way to the sea, particularly when the tide is rising. Yet the river runs.

Tides

Tides and water levels are complex.

Tides are caused or affected by the moon, sun, and earth, as well as their relative distances and positions. In addition, tides are affected by the shape of the shoreline and, for tidal rivers, the narrowness of the opening. Tides are further affected by winds, other weather conditions, and ocean conditions. Tides can have all kinds of names: strong, weak, spring, neap, king, flood, half, ordinary, extreme, high, and low. A particularly high tide is called a perigean spring tide, or maybe a "king tide" (not a technical term), or a "wicked high tide" (in Massachusetts). Some places, such as Hawaii, have no tides. It is all very cosmic.[45]

The 1915 report's data on tides at the North River seem to provide decent baselines to compare with present tides.

Today, times and heights of tides at Boston seem close to those in Scituate Harbor near the mouth of the North River. The advice is to add 20–30 minutes to the Boston times to get times near the river's mouth.[46]

In the 1915 report, at the mouth of the river the mean tidal range, between low and high tides, was 9.4 feet. In December 2024, the range seemed closer to 10 or 11 feet. Perhaps the increase reflects a general sea level rise. All these numbers, old and new, seemed alarmingly large to me at first. Then I took a tape measure to the boardwalk leading to The Spit at the river's mouth, and confirmed it. NOAA tide information for Scituate Harbor agrees.[47]

The tidal range diminishes going up the river. The 1915 report said the mean tidal range at the Hanover bridge was 3.2 feet. In December 2024, the mouth's range was somewhat higher. I could find no good data for the Hanover bridge area.[48]

So I asked NSRWA's Brian Taylor, who has spent time on the river. He said, "after tons of paddling up there, I have only seen what seems like around a 4ft high/low differential. But that is only an estimation." He referred me to a USGS website, which reports data from a gauge below Ludden's Ford dam (Fig. 6). That is about 1.6 miles upstream from the Hanover bridge on Washington Street in Hanover.[49]

Brian's link to the USGS website was like opening the door to a secret garden, a garden of water data. The data at Ludden's Ford is mostly outflow amounts (fresh water from the Indian Head River), but it seems to reflect tidal influence. This place seems to be, and was historically recognized, as the head of the tide.[50]

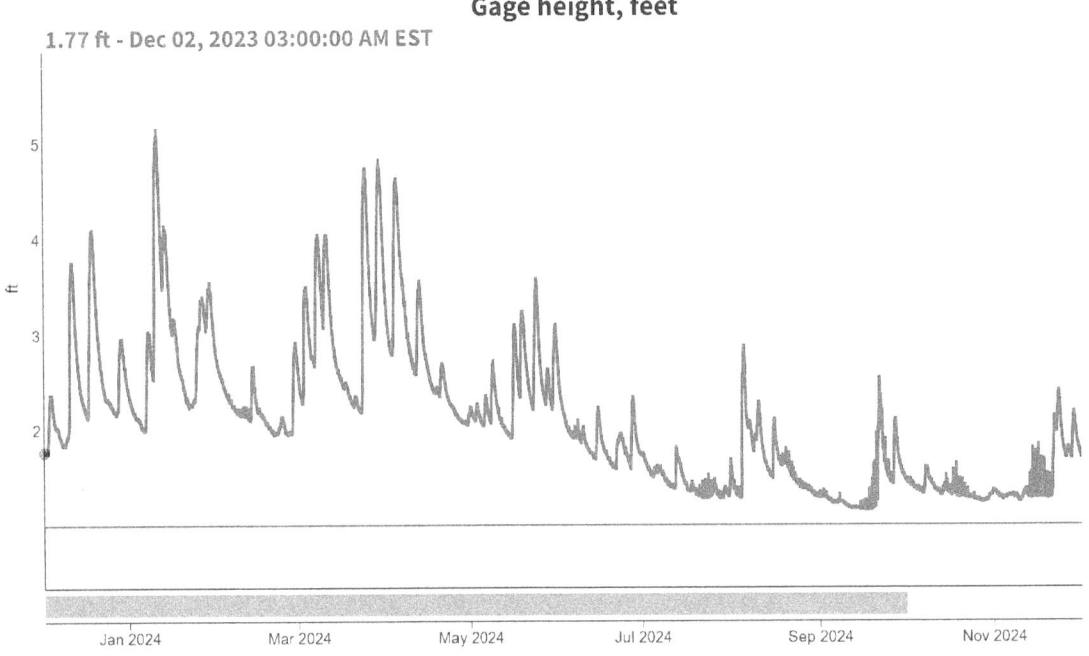

Fig. 6. Water gauge heights at Ludden's Ford dam, 2024. Water Data For the Nation (WDFN), USGS website, accessed 12/2/24.

This USGS chart shows data for the past year (2024) at Ludden's Ford dam. Over the year, the tide ranged from about 1.5 feet to 5 feet, a 3.5-foot difference. That is a bit higher than the 3.2 feet reported in 1915 at the Hanover bridge as the mean tidal range. (I did not calculate a mean or median tidal range for the year 2024.) A January surge ranged from 2 feet to 5 feet, a 3-foot difference.

Thus, Brian's estimate of 4 feet was good. The lesson here is if you want to know the river, ask a paddler.

It takes time for the tide to reach up the river. The 1915 report said, "High water at Hanover bridge is about four hours later than at the entrance to the river." Today, the tide delay is said to be about 3 ½ hours.[51]

Tidal data can be even more complicated than this, and sometimes fascinating. For example, a coastal earth observation scientist recently posted a 30-second clip that visualized one week of tides across Australasia. A reader of that post then posted a NASA visualization of tides across the globe. It compresses slightly more than one day of data into a 2-minute, 13-second clip. It shows how the tides vary around the world (Fig. 7).[52]

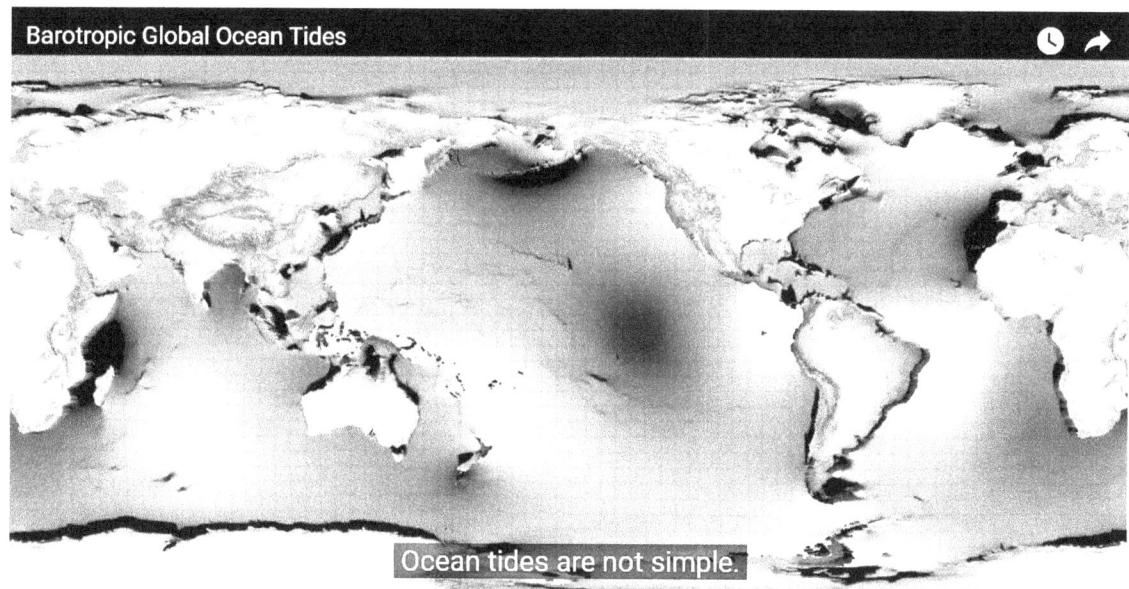

Fig. 7. Global tides, with high tides in dark. Screenshot of simulation in color covering one day. Greg Shirah, NASA Scientific Visualization Studio, November 5, 2020, updated October 10, 2024, https://www.youtube.com/watch?v=u6ZNnGnc-cQ, and https://svs.gsfc.nasa.gov/4821.

Unlike a century ago, we now have satellites with remote sensors to collect petabytes of ocean and earth data, and computers to process the data. It would be easy to get lost in all this data. But it is useful if properly analyzed and visualized.

We grapple with more tidal data later on. For now, it seems fair to say the tides on the North River are higher than in 1915. As we shall see, they are much higher than before the storm of 1898.

Fish First

Before the English settlers came, there were fish in the North River.

Native Americans called this area Mattakeeset, "place of many fish." They used fishing gear, some of which has survived. For example, according to the Norwell Historical Society,

> Nancy Joseph, a 4th generation Norwellian, generously donated a collection of Native artifacts which were found on her ancestors' property. Her grandfather, Harry P. Henderson, and her father, Lloyd B. Henderson, collected these items between 1890 and 1965 on their farm and near their home at the end of Block House Lane (at the bend of the North River) — a popular Native fishing and home site. Found in fields and in the roots of uprooted trees, they collected spear heads (used for fishing), arrowheads, tool heads, hoes, and decorative stones.[53]

Native American artifacts were also found in 1966 where Scituate's sewage treatment plant was being constructed near the North River. Archeologist Donald G. Scothorne of Pembroke excavated 30 pits before remaining pits were bulldozed in the construction. The pits produced stone implements, knives, scrapers, mortar, pestle, and clam shells. It appeared to have been the site of a fishing settlement.[54]

Scothorne also excavated "The Oak Island Site" on a bluff overlooking the North River. It revealed stone hearths and many other artifacts from the early Archaic period through the 17th century.[55]

Native Americans also built weirs. They were enclosures like fences set in a stream to trap fish. They could be staked out at low tide, to trap fish at higher tides (say, up to 2 to 3 feet). Then, at low tide, the stranded fish could be collected easily by persons walking or wading out to the weirs. Weirs were built for thousands of years, and in many places. Remains of weirs were found under Boston's man made land — land made by filling tidal flats — including the Back Bay.[56]

In southeast Massachusetts, the Taunton River had weirs at two major fords, according to a state survey of historic and archaeological resources. Walter Crossley (1898–1991) mentioned a weir in his reminiscence of fishing as a boy at a North River brook.[57]

Fish fed the early English settlers in Plymouth. Fish fertilized their crops of corn, after Squanto and other Native Americans taught the settlers how. Fish were there in the North River valley when humans started fishing, made settlements, built ships, established industries, built dams, built bridges, and populated the area. Fish had to deal with all this and with government regulations about fishing, which were supposedly meant to protect fish. Human history here intertwines with the history of fish.[58]

So we start with fish, and we focus on a fish named shad. We follow its journey to and from the ocean, up and down the river, and its encounters with fishermen and dams.

1

Shad and Other Fish

Fig. 8. Sherman F. Denton, "The Shad," in First Annual Report of the Commissioners of Fisheries, Game and Forests of the State of New York [report to Hon. Hamilton Fish, Speaker of the Assembly] (New York, 1896), 130 (original in color), https://babel.hathitrust.org/cgi/pt?id=hvd.32044106352289&view=2up&seq=6. Current name for the fish is *Alosa sapidissima*. Common length for female adult shad is 24.3 inches, about four times as wide as the image on this page.

"What do you know about shad?" I asked my neighbor Skip DeBrusk. I knew he fished. He wrote a book, *Codfish, Dogfish, Mermaids and Frank*. (Only one of those subjects lived on land, I think.) Recently he was writing a book with the working title, *Tales of Territory, Tuna and Tomatoes*. I thought he might know about fish, maybe even shad.[59]

"Shad is a spectacular sport fish," Skip said. He mentioned the Connecticut River, a good place to fish for shad. He has fished shad, but not really eaten them because they are so bony. Perhaps a better game fish is striped bass (called "stripers" around here), but shad is right up there.

Except for Skip, John McPhee, and what seems to be a small group of others, shad is an overlooked fish. Yet it is a part of American history and North River history. So we start discussing the history of the North River from the shad's point of view.

Shad populate the Atlantic coast and its rivers. In 1871, Seth Green took four milk cans of baby shad from the Hudson River and carefully transported them by train to Sacramento, where he let them loose. They wound up populating America's West coast.[60]

Shad is the largest member of the herring family and considered the tastiest. Its name, *Alosa sapidissima*, means "most savory." It is quite bony. It is anadromous. This means it is born in fresh water, lives in salt water for most of its life, and returns to its fresh water origins to spawn. That makes it uncommon. It comprises less than 1% of the fish on the planet. It may swim over 12,000 miles during its lifetime. Shad migrate up and down the mid-Atlantic, with primary summer feeding grounds in the Bay of Fundy in Canada. The Atlantic shad was abundant in Massachusetts waters in colonial times, but its numbers sharply declined. However, it still spawns and swims in North River tributaries.[61]

Below we discuss the shad, its history, how it has been frustrated or threatened by dams, and how it is doing today.

We focus on the Atlantic shad, *Alosa sapidissima*, of the clupeid family. Its relative, the hickory shad, also appears in these waters. The hickory shad is named *Alosa mediocris*. If I were a fish, I would not like to be called mediocre. It might make me fight harder if caught.[62]

If you want a superb visual display about shad, check out this Pennsylvania StoryMap. It says, "While there are no mainstem dams on the Delaware River today, there are over 1,400 dams on tributaries throughout the Delaware basin. These dams, many of which no longer serve their intended purpose, fragment habitat and inhibit access to vital spawning and rearing habitat for American Shad and other migratory fish."[63]

Shad Names

In the mid-1600s, according to tradition, Dutch colonists of New Netherland (New York) "knew only ten kinds of fish and that when the shad came they called it the eleventh kind (*Elft*)."[64]

English settlers in Massachusetts would have already known about shad, and feasted on them. It has been called America's "founding fish" by John McPhee, one of America's best writers and a shad fisherman. His excellent book, *The Founding Fish*, is all about shad.[65]

English colonists might use the names shad, herring, and alewife (all in the herring family) almost interchangeably. For example, in the earliest days of Plymouth colony, according to *Mourt's Relation* in 1622:

> You shall understand, that in this little time, that a few of us have been here, we have built seven dwelling-houses, and four for the use of the plantation, and have made preparation for divers others. We set the last spring some twenty acres of Indian corn, and sowed some six acres of barley and peas, and according to the manner of the Indians, we manured our ground with *herrings or rather shads*, which we have in great abundance, and take with great ease at our doors. [emphasis added][66]

Again, in 1633, the Plymouth Colony General Court passed an act with these words:

> That whereas God, by his providence, hath cast the fish called alewives or herrings in the midst of the place appointed for the town of Plymouth, and that the ground thereabout hath been worn out by the whole, to the damage of those that inhabit the same, that therefore the said *herring, alewives, or shads* commonly used in the setting of corn be appropriated to such as do or shall inhabit the town of Plymouth … [words modernized, emphasis added][67]

As noted, the fish were used to fertilize the growing of corn. Native Americans including Squanto showed them how.

By then, English had settled neighboring areas, notably Marshfield and Scituate to the north of Plymouth, two towns on either side of the North River. In Scituate, the English settlers named brooks entering the North River as Herring Brooks. Starting from the east in Scituate, there was Herring Brook (also known as First Herring Brook), Second Herring Brook (now in Norwell), Third Herring Brook (now in Hanover), and Herring Brook (now in Pembroke).

Herring was a popular name for a brook. It far outranked shad as a fish name, according to a Google Books Ngram Viewer (Fig. 9), which illustrates the frequency of words in books. That is, except that short time when shad surpassed herring, about 1634 to 1650. Perhaps the colonists who named the brooks before 1634 were "old school," using the briefly more popular term shad, or used herring as an overall term to include shad, or were just able and willing to distinguish shad from herring and preferred the name herring.[68]

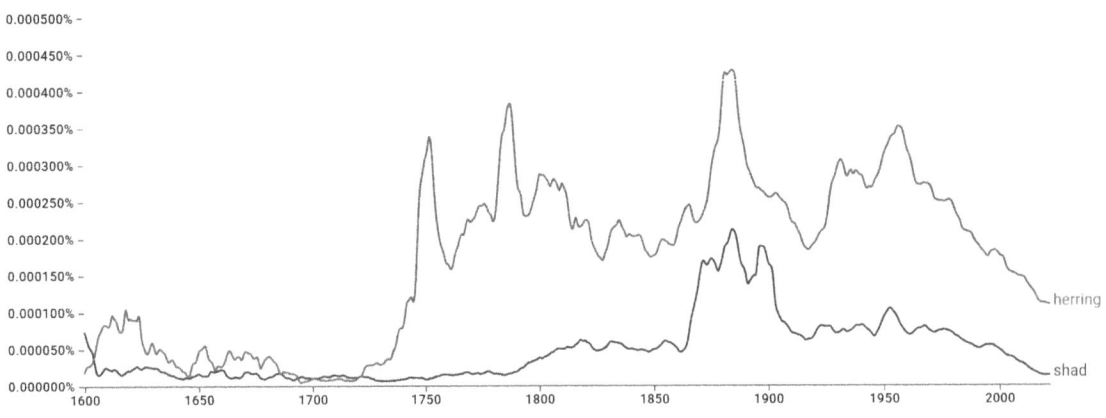

Fig. 9. Google Books Ngram Viewer for "shad,herring" for 1600–2022. Accessed 2025.

After all these years, Herring Brook is a much more common term for a brook. Shad Brook is archaic. A rare survivor is in Philadelphia, where:

> A narrow creek that still winds in an "S" pattern through the Meadows area of FDR Park and flows into Hollander's Creek was called "Ship Brook" until the end of the 18th century. Possibly — this is my own conjecture — the name is derived from the English transliteration of the Lenape word for creek, "sipu." Some later maps called it "Shad Brook" (probably for the fish that spawned in its shallows), and finally, "Shedbrook Creek."[69]

In addition, there seems to be a Shad Creek in Salisbury, Essex County, Massachusetts, according to the US Board on Geographic Names (BGN).[70]

John Quincy Adams (1767–1848) kept extensive diaries, now transcribed and digitized. He had little to say specifically about shad, but he enjoyed catching and eating fish, and going on fishing parties. For example, on Friday, August 2, 1839, he went on a fishing party to Hingham and Cohasset:

> We dined [in the morning] at a small shed [at Cohasset] built by several of Hingham for the sole purpose of accommodating fishing parties. We went out in small row boats about two miles from the shore. Mr Stearns who is now preaching at the Church where Mr Charles Brooks was lately settled. Mr Baker, and Mr Morse all persons with whom I had no previous acquaintance were in the same boat with me. We changed our fishing ground three times with little success, but caught a few haddocks and perch — my portion was one hake, and one small cod. Mr Baker took the largest that was caught — a cat fish weighing perhaps ten pounds — black, goggle eyed and with a dorsal fin six inches high — Our boatman cautioned us not to approach too near his jaw, or he might take off one of our fingers — We returned to land between one and two O Clock, and dined upon Chowder, Claret and Champagne — After dinner we went upon the rocks, and fished again, with Poles, for perch with no better fortune — In the space of an

hour and a half I took only two — At 4. P.M. the tide was up and the perch ceased to bite — We took a second dinner of fried perch: and at the earnest invitation of Mr Loring most of the company repaired to his house at Hingham, where we had tea, and coffee, and conversation till past 8 O'Clock — I had a dark ride home, not without danger of running foul of Chaises and Carryalls travelling the other way. The Quincy Curfew Bell of 9 P.M struck as we were approaching it, and when I reached home I found Charles and his wife there — Happy that the day had passed off without other accident than getting Sun burnt — The day had been calm and cool.[71]

Two months later, Adams became enmeshed in competing proposals from his South Shore constituents to improve the North River, proposals that would later include damming the river. They are discussed later in this book.

Brooks, creeks, and rivers, whether named Herring or Shad, would have their dams. They appear in historical records, in legislative records, and on maps.

Dams, a Brief History

Settlers built mill dams along tributaries of the North River early on. Records of the seventeenth century often mention mill dams along the First, Second, and Third Herring Brooks. Historians and writers mention the following:[72]

- Between 1637 and 1640, Isaac Stedman dammed the First Herring Brook and established a sawmill. Alongside the sawmill, John Stockbridge built a water-driven gristmill about 1650 to grind corn. The gristmill remains today, and is, according to many sources, the oldest mill of its kind in America.[73]

- Coons (1979): "The Cornet [Robert Stetson] led a group who built what seems to have been the first Norwell mill – 1656 [at Third Herring Brook]."[74]

- Merritt (1938): "About the year 1690 John Bryant built a grist mill on the Second Herring Brook about ten rods west of his house, in what is now Norwell village. From that time until January 24, 1927, there has been a mill at this location and, in fact, certain portions of the original structure were still standing."[75]

- NSRWA: "Col. Thomas completed the work the beavers had begun and constructed a dam here [in Hanson, at Indian Head Brook] in 1694–1695 — the first dam in Plymouth Colony to power a water wheel. Shortly thereafter Nathaniel's son Isaac built a sawmill there."[76]

- Bacon (2008): "The first mill dam in Hanover was on the Indian Head River at Luddam's Ford, erected by Thomas Bardin in 1704."[77]

Later, we return to discussing dams on tributaries of the North River.

Dams on large American rivers appeared later. The first dam in the Connecticut River was built in 1798, the Schuylkill at Philadelphia in 1822, the Susquehanna in 1830 and 1839, the Concord by 1839, and the Hudson at Troy in the early 1900s. No dams appeared on the Delaware. Or, on the North River, just its tributaries.[78]

Dams supplied water power to mills, whether for grinding corn or sawing lumber or running machinery. While there were windmills (the first one in Plymouth Colony was Gilson's on Third Cliff), and tidemills (at least one in Scituate Harbor), the preferred sources of power were streams and rivers. Some were better than others. A 1794 map of Marshfield says, "There are seven corn mills and one cloth mill in Marshfield, but two corn mills with a good supply of water would do the work they all seven do." An 1838 map of Marshfield marked a Satinett Factory, Box Board Mill, Grist Mill, Saw Mill, Nail Factory, and Littles Mill, all on streams.[79]

Dams stopped or limited the migration of shad. By 1849, Henry David Thoreau was distressed:

> Shad are still taken in the basin of Concord River at Lowell ... . Still patiently, almost pathetically, with instinct not to be discouraged, not to be reasoned with, revisiting their old haunts, as if their stern fates would relent, and still met by the Corporation with its dam. Poor shad! where is thy redress? When Nature gave thee instinct, gave she thee the heart to bear thy fate? Still wandering the sea in thy scaly armor to inquire humbly at the mouths of rivers if man has perchance left them free for thee to enter.[80]

Dam Maps

Dams appear often on old maps, mainly the state-required maps of 1795 and 1831. Just follow the thread of a waterway and look for a swelling, sometimes almost triangular. Many of these dams were set up to power mills. You can see them on Charles Turner's 1795 map of Scituate. Details below show mills on the herring brooks from west (left) to east (right) (Fig. 10, Fig. 11, and Fig. 12).[81]

Starting from the east, Fig. 12 shows First Herring Brook with a grist mill at today's Old Oaken Bucket Pond. This is probably the historic Stockbridge Mill, one of the Scituate Historical Society's premier historic sites. Moving west, Fig. 11 shows Second Herring Brook (now in Norwell), with a sawmill on a large pond and a gristmill on a smaller pond opposite the South Precinct Meetinghouse. The meetinghouse is perhaps the site of today's First Parish Church of Norwell Unitarian Universalist Church, established in 1642. The meetinghouse and a windmill are at today's Norwell Center.

The windmill is perhaps where one still exists behind Rev. Samuel Deane's house. Moving farther west, Fig. 10 shows Third Herring Brook with a pond and gristmill just west of an Episcopalian church, almost certainly St. Andrew's that stood from 1731 to 1810 on Church Hill along today's River Street in Norwell.[82]

Fig. 10. Third Herring Brook, Turner's 1795 map of Scituate

Fig. 11. Second Herring Brook, Turner's 1795 map of Scituate

Fig. 12. First Herring Brook, Turner's 1795 map of Scituate

Farther upstream on Third Herring Brook (but not shown here), Turner's 1795 map depicts two more gristmills, then a large gristmill and sawmill opposite a meetinghouse. All these mills have triangular ponds, indicating the presence of dams.[83]

Third Herring Brook again appears on a 1794–1795 map of Hanover. The brook had a sawmill and two gristmills, presumably powered by water from dams. And west of that brook's flow into the North River, the North River or its tributaries already had (going west and upstream from the North River Bridge), a forge and anchor shop, a gristmill, a forge, and another gristmill. These, too, were presumably powered by dams. At the top of the map was a note: "[There] are no ponds in the Town of Hanover but such as are made by erecting Dams across the several Streams."[84]

An 1801 map of Scituate then shows Third Herring Brook with a dam close to the North River and close to the North River Bridge. It shows no other herring brooks, with "Rocky Island" and "Rocky Reach" at the places where Second Herring Brook entered the river south of Norwell Center. Otherwise, it is an excellent map.[85]

Third Herring Brook again appears on an 1812 map of the North River's western parts. The map indicates a "seine" (a long net) attached to the Hanover side of the second curve in the river west of the North River Bridge, west of Third Herring Brook. It does not specifically mention shad, but it says, "no place below this in Hanover to Draw a Seine." Seines were used to catch herring, or possibly shad.[86]

The otherwise excellent map of Scituate in 1831 was reticent. Along with brooks, it showed mills only by a double asterisk (**), with no mention of dams.[87]

A map of Pembroke in 1831 shows swellings along the Indian Head River, indicating dams, and showing that river's connecting with the North River (Fig. 13).

Fig. 13. John Groves Hales, "Map of the town of Pembroke in the county of Plymouth, from survey made in 1831," (Boston: Pendleton's Lith., [1831]), detail showing at lower left the swellings of Indian Head River, probably due to mill dams. *Digital Commonwealth*, https://ark.digitalcommonwealth.org/ark:/50959/x059cb52d.

Dam Laws

The acts of provincial Massachusetts were fundamentally protective of fisheries, although not necessarily the fish. They regulated fishing or delegated authority to towns to regulate fishing.

Let's go back to the royal Charter of the Province of the Massachusetts Bay, issued by William & Mary on October 17 of the third year of their reign, 1692. The charter is long, but at the end it says the charter:

> shall not in any manner Enure or be taken to abridge bar or hinder any of Our loveing Subjects whatsoever to use and exercise the Trade of Fishing upon the Coasts of New England but that they and every of them shall have full and free power and Libertie to continue and use their said Trade of Fishing upon the said Coasts in any of the seas thereunto adjoining or any Arms of the said Seas or Salt Water Rivers where they have been wont to fish …[88]

The royal Charter's mention of salt water rivers would include the North River. The Charter, however, did not mean that anyone was free to fish there or on Scituate's coast. In fact, the government would restrict fishing, if only to maintain the stock in the fishing areas, or fisheries.

Even today, restrictions on lobster fishing and cod fisheries are disputed and contentious. Those in Scituate, where the Massachusetts Lobstermen's Association is located, would know.[89]

From colonial times, the state legislature's duties included protecting fisheries, establishing corporations, and authorizing dams. These three subjects sometimes clashed and sometimes meshed. For example, an 1813 act said:

> The time for the passage way or ways to be kept open, for the fish to pass and repass through any mill dam or dams now erected, or to be hereafter erected on the stream running from Humphrey's pond, so called, into said Ipswich river, shall be from the tenth day of May to the tenth day of June annually, … . [And] the agent appointed by The Danvers Cotton Factory Company shall always be one of the fish committee provided for in the acts to which this is in addition and amendment.[90]

The act did not provide for representation of fish on the fish committee.

Below, we discuss how the state protected fish and fisheries by limiting obstructions in the water and restricting the use of seines to catch fish. Then the state regulated the owners of dams and enterprises that built them and provided mill power. The state would allow dams, but require their owners to build fishways (fish sluices) so fish could travel and spawn, and to keep the fishways in good repair.

An act in 1709–1710 prohibited obstacles to the passage of fish in rivers. That included weirs (called "wears" in the act), which are fences or (alternatively) low dams. Native Americans established them to trap fish in places like the North River. In fact, they are mentioned in the Pilgrim journal *Mourt's Relation* in 1622, saying "we found many of the Namascheucks (they so calling the men of Nemasket) fishing upon a weir which they had made on a river which belonged to them, where they caught abundance of bass." Later, a Namascheuck "had shot a shad in the water, and a small squirrel as big as a rat, called a neuxis; the one half of either he gave us, and after went to the weir to fish."[91]

The 1709–1710 act said:

> That no wears [weirs], hedges, fish-garths, stakes, kiddles or other disturbance or incumbrance shall be set, erected or made on or across any

river, to the stopping, obstructing or straightning of the natural or usual course and passage of fish, in their seasons, or spring of the year, without the approbation and allowance first had and obtained from the general sessions of the peace in the same county .... [If not, then they] are declared to be a common nusance, and shall be demolished and pulled down, not to be again repaired or amended.[92]

An ancient herring fish weir gave its name to the Weir River, which empties into Hingham Bay. At one time, the river had a source in Accord Pond. The pond is about six miles south of Hingham Bay at the opposite end of Hingham. As a tidal river, the Weir River has one of the most extensive salt marsh systems in the greater Boston metropolitan area.[93]

An act in 1761–1762 was intended to protect fish, saying:

> Whereas the said town of Hingham has been at great expence in purchasing and opening a water-passage, for the fish called alewives, from the sea, into the pond called Accord Pond, being wholly within the bounds of the said town, and it appears just that the sole ordering, taking, and disposing the fish, when taken, should be vested in the said town; [then authorizing the town for three years to regulate the time and manner of such actions, and imposing fines and jail terms of up to five days for violations].[94]

A later map, from 1795 (Fig. 14), shows the Weir River with two sawmills and three gristmills along its way from Accord Pond to Hingham Bay.[95] The mills may have obstructed alewives, and one wonders if the act in 1761–1762 was still effective in protecting the fish.

A 1765 act used strong language, noting that existing laws "do not, in diverse circumstances, reach the case of divers rivers and ponds where said fish usually go to cast their spawn, so that great waste is made of them by *ill-minded persons*, to the great damage of the publick." (Emphasis added.)[96]

This act empowered towns to "see that the passage-ways are open, pursuant to said act, and that said fish may not be obstructed in their usual passing up and down stream," and to regulate the time, place, and manner of fishing.[97]

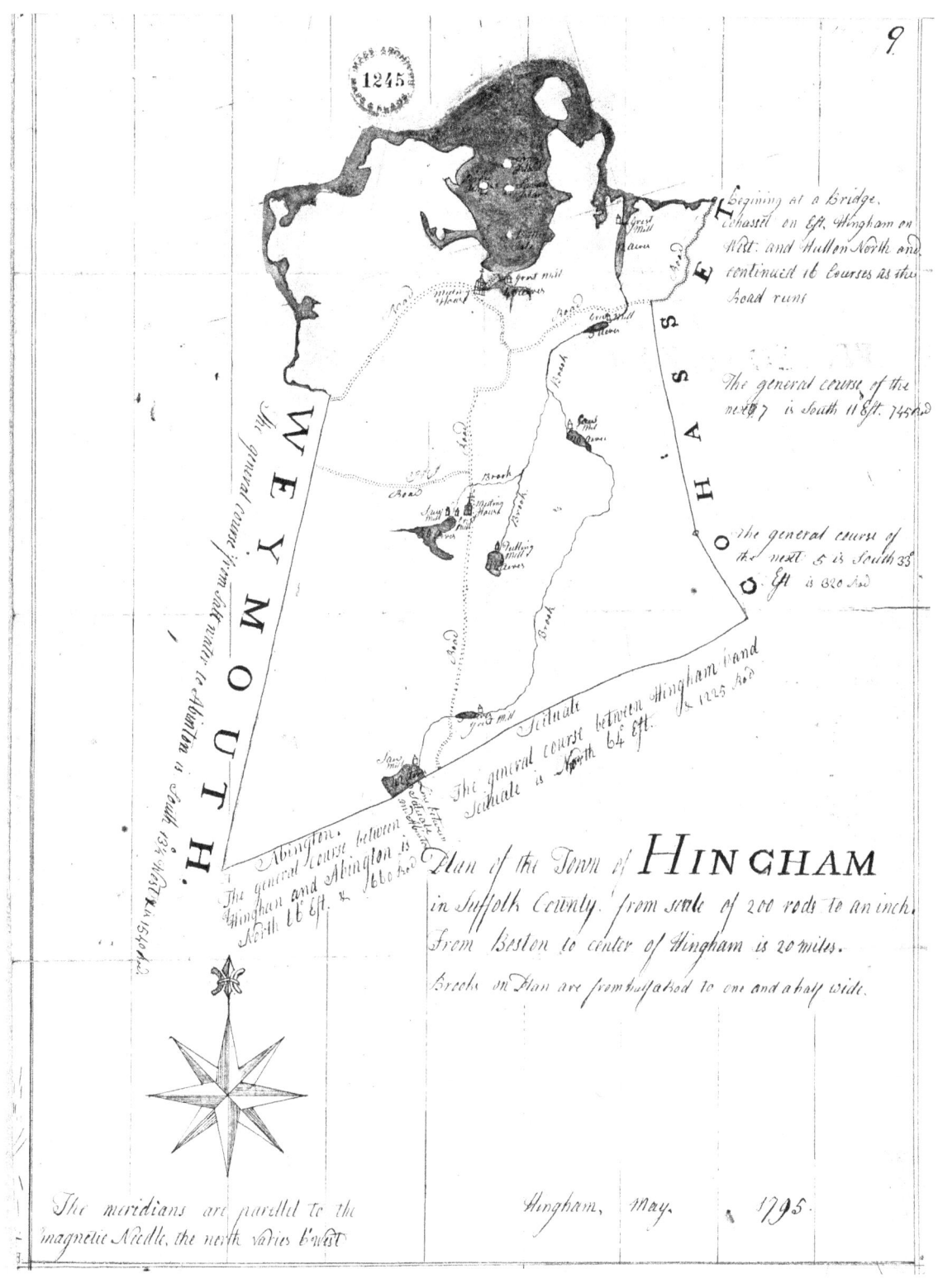

Fig. 14. "Plan of Hingham, surveyor's name not given, dated May, 1795," Massachusetts State Archives #1245, *Digital Commonwealth*. Weir River (called "brook" here) runs north and south in center.

The 1765 act went even further. Section 6 said:

> That all tide-mills that have been erected across any such rivers or streams since the making of the aforesaid act, or that shall hereafter be so erected, shall be understood to be comprehended in said act, and the owners and occupants, and all others concerned, shall conform thereto accordingly, and be subject to the same penalties, for their neglect, as if tide-mills had particularly been named in said act.[98]

In other words, dams, tide mills, and their owners and operators, had a duty to not obstruct the fish runs.

That 1765 act also penalized using seines or "drag-nets" to catch fish; that prohibition also went back to earlier times.

Seines

Shad and alewives were important to the first colonists of Plymouth in the 1620s, and later provincial laws aimed to protect the fisheries. A 1758 act had this preamble, reiterating a past prohibition:

> that no person or persons whatsoever, shall, on any pretence, presume to stretch, set or draw any siene [sic] or drag-net, or set up any wares [weirs] or other fishing engines, in any parts of the rivers within this province, or ponds adjacent thereto, Merrimack and Connecticut rivers only excepted, where the fish usually spawn, or use any other instruments for catching alewives but by dip-nets or scoop-nets, on penalty of a fine of five pounds for each offence" [then mentioned "catching of shadd or alewives" in excepted rivers][99]

Early on, the government prohibited using seines to take alewives and other fish from rivers. Deane's history reports that a 1761 act permitted seines to be drawn in the North River, when Massachusetts was a province. As far back as the 1750s, the provincial government of Massachusetts Bay passed similar acts. They made exceptions for certain rivers, then abounding in fish, including the Merrimack, the Charles, and the Connecticut. (So, my neighbor Skip was right to mention shad on the Connecticut River.) These exceptions came with conditions. For example, fish could be taken only on certain days of the week. Doubtless, the North River also had a conditional exception, as Deane reported in 1831.[100]

In 1821, Scituate appointed Capt. William Peakes as "agent to defend Town's rights to Shad and Alewife fishery by Seines in North River in said Town."[101]

In 1822, the town of Scituate chose Charles Turner (perhaps the author of the 1795 map of Scituate) as "agent to meet with those from Marshfield, Hanover, & Pembroke on Alewife fishery in North River," and later, "to oppose Pembrok's [sic] petition on Alewife fishery in North River." Then, in 1829, the town instructed its representatives in the legislature "to oppose Pembroke's petition concerning Shad and Alewife fishery in the North River." Perhaps that 1812 map discussed above was useful in these inter-town disputes.[102]

In 1848, Scituate chose agents to aid a petition for the alewife fishery. In 1855, the town petitioned the legislature to revise statutes regulating alewife or herring fishery.[103]

Laws and regulations continued to be added to regulate fishing. According to one historical summary, "In 1854, a law was passed by the Massachusetts Legislature permitting the towns along the river to use ten seines on the North river to catch herring and other fish. Marshfield had four of these privileges and Scituate, Pembroke, and South Scituate had two apiece." Towns then sold these privileges to private parties.[104]

Notwithstanding all these regulations, presumably a person was allowed to fish with a pole and hook.

Shad, Dams, and Dam Removal

Shad travel thousands of miles in the Atlantic Ocean and then on American rivers.

For example, according to an 1897 bulletin, "On the North Branch [of the Susquehanna River], American shad ranged as far north as Binghamton, N.Y., 318 miles from the mouth of the river and 513 miles from the sea."[105]

Even in our time, you can fish for shad at the Delaware Water Gap, where the Delaware River still has 200 miles more to run to Delaware Bay and the Atlantic Ocean. Shad and herring return from the ocean and swim up rivers and streams against the current in "runs" in spring and early summer. They try to run as far as they can up the stream where they were born. That's where they aim to spawn.[106]

Shad have some things in common with humans. They have skeletons. They feel pain and stress. In addition,

> The bright-red copious blood of a shad looks like human blood and has in it about the same level of salt as there is in human blood – roughly a third as much as in sea water. The fresh water in a river will have salt in it, too, but precious little – about a thousandth of what is in the sea. Since the salt

in a fish's blood is drawn and replenished from the fish's environment, a fish in fresh water has to hoard the salt it takes up, while a fish in the ocean must get rid of more salt than it keeps.[107]

In addition, shad are like salt marsh hay, a familiar feature of shad's early and late environment, in this respect:

> *Spartina*'s flooded roots draw the brackish water up into its cells; the cells concentrate the salt; glands on the surface of the grass then extract the excess salt and expel it. The matted, swirling cord grass of a high marsh often glistens with tiny salt crystals, until they're washed off with the tide.[108]

In other words, they not only tolerate salt but require it. Salt was necessary for shad and salt hay, and both were important to early European settlers.

Like the shad, early European settlers traveled across salty oceans and up rivers — such as the Hudson, Delaware, Potomac, and James — as far as they could go, until reaching rapids, rocky areas, shallow water, or waterfalls. That was the so-called head of navigation. There, shad spawned and returned down the river. Unlike shad, settlers stayed and raised families, establishing towns on land and dams on the water to power industries.[109]

Dams limited the range and population of shad. In his 1831 history, Deane reported that in the North River, "Shad and alewives are still taken, but they are gradually diminishing." The fishery, he said, was "long a subject of controversy between Scituate and Pembroke," suggesting the mill dams in Pembroke might be causing the reduction of fish. These dams are upstream along the North River and its tributaries.[110]

By 1889, according to Briggs:

> The alewives and shad ascend the different herring brooks and the main stream now to some extent, and are taken in fairly large quantities; but each year they come in diminished numbers. The dams prevent their ascending to their old spawning grounds, and the refuse of the mills, especially the rubber mill, so impregnates the waters and fills up the smaller streams, that they cannot and will not go up, and without some decided steps are soon taken, all fish will become as much strangers to the river as the bass and salmon have already.[111]

Briggs mentions the refuse of the mills. Today we would call it pollution. The Indian Head River had two main mill sites with dams: Clapp and Waterman. Their industrial uses go back to colonial times. For example, the Clapp Rubber Mill site was noted for its anchor industry since before 1760.[112]

Both mill sites appear on the 1902 atlas (Fig. 15) and a 1917 map.[113]

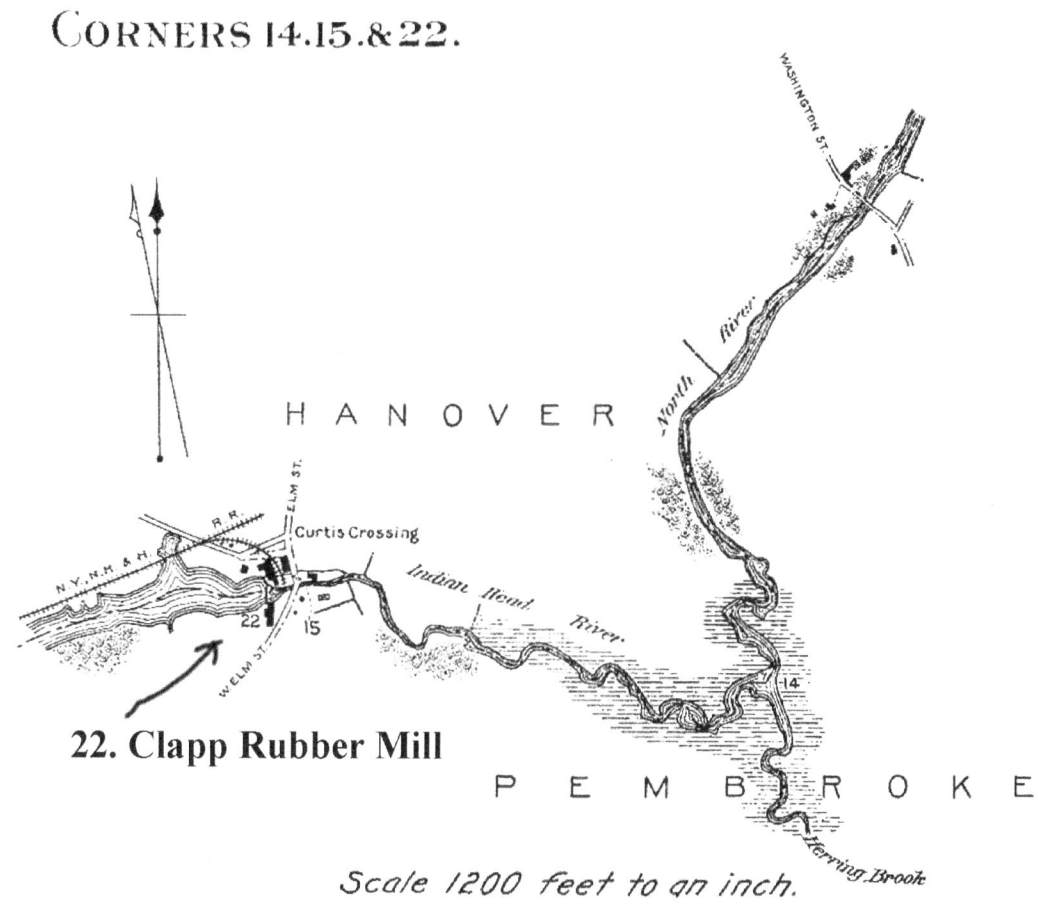

Fig. 15. 1902 atlas of boundaries, sheet 14, detail, showing corner 22, site of dam and Clapp rubber mill (note added). Also shows origin of North River at confluence of Indian Head River and Herring Brook. Rubber mill is also shown on 1917 Sanborn Map, sheet 3 of 6.

The rubber mill that Briggs mentioned was owned by the E. H. Clapp Rubber Company. According to the NSRWA, "Eugene H. Clapp, a native of South Scituate (Norwell), invented a method for removing the fiber from old rubber and preparing it so it could be used again for new goods." Starting in Roxbury, the company relocated to Ludden's Ford about 1873. It started on the Hanover side of the Indian Head River, and expanded to the Pembroke side of the river.[114]

In 1889, Briggs' book said that the mill employed as many as 100 men, "is doing two or three times as much work as any of his competitors, and is handling more than one half of this business in the United States."[115]

In 1911, a history of Hanover told about the Clapp Rubber Company and its site, with a wonderful photo (Fig. 16).[116]

Fig. 16. Clapp Rubber Mill. Dwelley and Simmons, *History of Hanover*, 204–205 (1911). View from upstream looking east, Hanover on left, Pembroke on right.

On the 1917 Sanborn map, detail below, the entire Clapp mill was called "Clapp Rubber Co Reclaiming Rubber" (Fig. 17). It comprised about two dozen buildings, including a "devulcanizing storage" room.

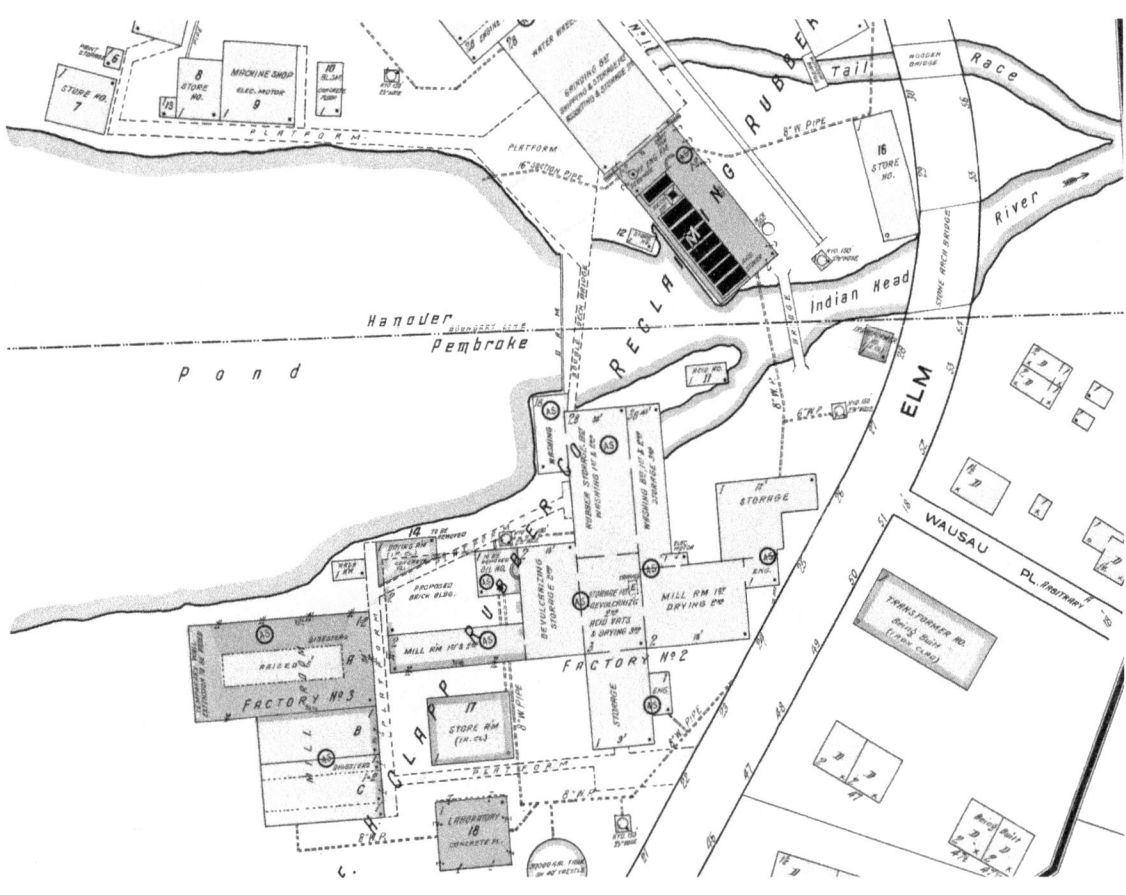

Fig. 17. Clapp Rubber Mill, 1917 Sanborn Map, sheet 3 of 6, detail, with dam in center. Library of Congress, Geography and Map Division, Sanborn Maps Collection, public domain.

None of this remains, except for a dam or dams. The Clapp Rubber Company went bankrupt in 1934.[117]

Ludden's Ford now has scenic town parks on both sides of the river. We explore them at the end of this book in presenting a nice drive in the country.

Farther upstream from the Clapp Rubber Mill dam was the dam of R. C. Waterman & Son's tack factory in Hanover (Fig. 18). Industry use of the site goes back to the 1700s. An old dam there was damaged extensively over the years. Its remains were finally removed in 2017.[118]

Kezia Bacon described an interesting walking tour of this area. It covers the Clapp and Waterman sites.[119]

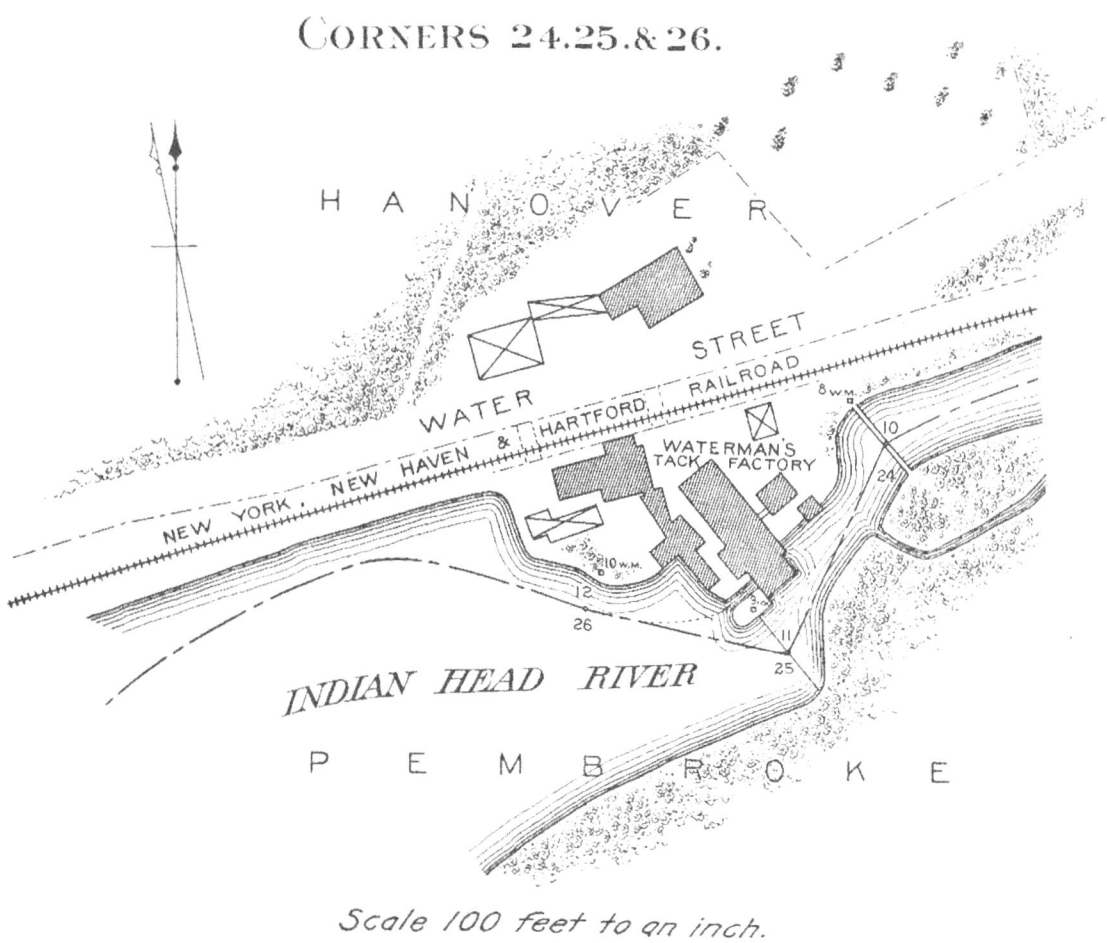

Fig. 18. 1902 atlas of boundaries, sheet 14, detail, showing Waterman's Tack Factory and dam. The "rolling-dam" is at corner 25 (where water depth is 11). Water Street runs next to the Indian Head River, as did railroad. Factory is also shown on 1917 Sanborn Map, inset.

Besides those dams on the Indian Head River, others in the North River valley obstructed fish. Briggs said that First Herring Brook's "whole length is scarcely three miles. Until mills were erected on this Herring Brook [probably mid-1600s], alewives ascended as far as George Moore's Pond [now Old Oaken Bucket Pond in Scituate], and, as the stream was narrow, they were easily taken with nets."[120]

Dams on these waterways provoked the following response by Prof. Baird in the late 1800s:

> As is well known, the erection of impassable dams across the streams, by preventing the ascent of the species just mentioned [alewives, shad, and salmon] to their spawning grounds, produced a very great diminution, and almost the extermination of their numbers; … Unfortunately, however, the lumbering interest in Maine and the manufacturing in New Hampshire and Massachusetts, are so powerful as to render it extremely difficult to carry out any measures which in any way interfere with their convenience or profits; and notwithstanding the passage of laws requiring the construction of fishways through the dams, these have either been neglected altogether, or are of such a character as not to answer their purpose.[121]

Fishways were supposed to allow fish passage up and over the top of the dams. They were often not a good solution. In his book on shad, John McPhee wrote about a dam on the Kennebec River in Maine, at the state capital of Augusta. It was built for the Augusta Power Company to serve several industries, in 1837. It had a fishway. In 1838, the fishway disappeared in a flood. It was never replaced. It stopped shad for 161 years.[122]

In 1999, the Kennebec dam was demolished. Then the river subsided to its former condition. Upstream at Six-Mile Falls, in a remarkable description of this transformation, McPhee wrote, "The place was making scenery lifted from the dead."[123]

Today, along the North River tributaries, shad fishing continues. A prime spot during shad runs is near Ludden's Ford Dam, at the Hanover–Pembroke line. The dam is properly called a weir, since in one sense of the word, it lets water flow over its crest (top). It is about 10 to 15 miles from the Atlantic Ocean. So are the shad who gather there.[124]

Ludden's Ford Dam has a fishway that theoretically allows fish to swim upstream beyond the dam. In the 1970s, the towns of Hanover and Pembroke repaired the dam and installed a concrete Denil fishway. It is 109 feet long, and 4 feet wide, with 33 baffles. The fishway does not seem to be very effective in allowing fish to bypass the dam.[125]

Dams act as a physical barrier to fish passage. They can also act as a thermal barrier, raising water temperatures. This can make places along a waterway inhospitable to fish, like shad and trout, which are sensitive to water temperature.[126]

The American shad is the Olympic athlete fish, according to McPhee, recognizing its determination and length of its journey to spawn. It seems a shame that obsolete dams stop its runs upriver just before the finish line.[127]

McPhee wrote, "Toward the end of the twentieth century, the once unthinkable notion of destroying dams went through a surprisingly swift trajectory from the quixotic to the feasible." And then to the actual.[128]

The world's largest dam-removal project was completed October 2, 2024, at the Klamath River in northern California. The first of four dams demolished was 17 stories tall, and nearly four times as wide. After demolition, work continues to restore the former dam sites and the river, which once had the third-largest salmon runs in the continental US. Early reports are promising. "Now, less than a month after those dams came down in the largest dam removal project in U.S. history, salmon are once more returning to spawn in cool creeks that have been cut off to them for generations."[129]

At a Hudson River watershed, Prof. Karin Limburg of SUNY College of Environmental Science & Forestry, along with others are working on a project to explore community acceptance of removing dams. Dams in the watershed have proliferated wildly since 1850.[130]

Locally, removals or planned removals of dams include the obsolete Ludden's Ford Dam at the Hanover–Pembroke line. A recent report said the North River system:

> contains the largest remaining shad populations in coastal MA rivers and supports ongoing sportfisheries. Two dams appear to limit upstream access for shad in the Indian Head and South rivers. Therefore, Barriers to Migration are an ongoing threat to shad in this river system.[131]

Perhaps the dam's removal and river restoration will help return this area to what Native Americans named Mattakeeset, "place of many fish."[132]

The State Fish

My neighbor Skip was right to mention the Connecticut River. It flows through Massachusetts and Connecticut. It is a great place for shad.

Massachusetts is where shad are studied, as McPhee's book discussed, at the "S. O. Conte Anadromous Fish Research Center in Turners Falls. It is a small community in northern Massachusetts" near the Connecticut River. The Conte center of the US Geological Survey has a fitting street address of 1 Migratory Way, perhaps a nod to the fish that migrates so far. The Conte center is associated with UMass Amherst, whose scientists worked there and were sources for McPhee's book about this "founding fish."[133]

Shad could have been the Massachusetts state fish. Except that is the cod. Cod gets all the attention. It was a big fish in its day, the old colonial days, and it gave its name by the early 1600s to the state's Cape Cod. It has been a symbol of Massachusetts for more than 200 years. Cod was not officially named the state fish until 1974.[134]

A carving of a "sacred cod" hangs in the House of Representatives in Boston. The Senate has a figure of a "holy mackerel." There are no more legislative branches that could honor the shad.[135]

However, Connecticut named the American shad as its state fish in 2003. It has a good part of the Connecticut River, and it has the shad. The state celebrates this overlooked fish.[136]

Salmon and Cod

Salmon disappeared from the North River by 1889, as Briggs noted. In the 1940s, Atlantic salmon were stocked in the river at its headwaters in Hanover/Pembroke. The stocking program was not successful. Undeterred, the Massachusetts Division of Marine Fisheries stocked the North River with Pacific coast "Cohoe" salmon starting in 1971. It seems to have achieved some success as a trial, at the time.[137]

In late spring or early summer, probably in 1974, Walter Crossley caught codfish in the mouth of the river.[138]

Herring

Dams stop shad, one of the largest members of the herring family. They also stop the smaller herrings. But herrings get all the attention, often for their runs at spawning time.

Herring runs are mentioned in old Scituate town records. In 1794, the town tried to make "better accommodations for the herring run at the Lincoln Mill stream [in North Scituate at Mordecai Lincoln Road]." They agreed with Cohasset that "there being no natural obstructions it was recommended that all sluice ways be opened on April 20 and be kept open until June 5, annually, and fishing be restricted to one day each week, namely Thursday, with proper penalties for transgressions. No fishing at all to be allowed below Lincoln's Mill." Governments were protective of herring and their habitat to reproduce.[139]

Pembroke gained a lasting reputation for its herring runs on Herring Brook. Early postcards and photos captured the annual event (Fig. 19).[140]

Fig. 19. "Herring Run, Pembroke, Mass." Postcard (Bryantville, MA: George E. Lewis). Author's collection. Same image in *Pembroke 1712-2012* captioned "Herring commissioners, c. 1900. Photo by George Edward Lewis."

In 1938, a newspaper reported:

> The Pembroke herring run rarely saw as many people as it did last Sunday. And the novelty and wonder of seeing these slender, intelligent creatures trying to reach Nature's nursery, the place in the Pembroke Ponds which is to be the breeding place of the replacements in the alewive family.[141]

In 1996, another newspaper report said:

> Protection of the herring population continues today. In Mashpee, Plymouth and Brewster, among the oldest herring runs in the state, the public can no longer take the little fish.

> And in Pembroke, herring are only taken from the picturesque herring run on Route 14 one day a year – the annual fish fry sponsored by the local historical society, held last Sunday.[142]

Writers struggle between singular (herring) and plural (herring or herrings). The collective term for a herring run is an army of herrings, like a flock of chickens. The army goes upstream to spawn, to procreate. (The army does not actually march, run, or walk; it swims fast and occasionally jumps.) There are other collective nouns for herrings.[143]

Once caught and landed, a group of fresh herrings can be called a "mess" of fish (colloquially). A "cran" of them is an old unit of measure in the North Sea fishing industry, equivalent to one standard box of about 37.5 imperial gallons. It comes from Scottish Gaelic "crann."[144]

The North and South Rivers Watershed Association (NSRWA) published a handy map and guide to herring runs in South Shore towns of Weymouth, Hingham, Pembroke, Hanover, Marshfield, Norwell, Cohasset, and Scituate; plus (farther south) in Kingston, Bournedale, and Plymouth.[145]

The NSRWA annually seeks volunteers – they call them "citizen-scientists" – to count the herring in local streams. Counts have been low in a number of North River tributaries. However, three dams and two weirs have been removed on Third Herring Brook. That opened up 9.7 miles of stream for spawning fish. Counts were broadly up in 2023:

> Last year was a heartening one for local fisheries scientists. After several years of declining river herring numbers, 2023 saw a significant uptick throughout many Massachusetts rivers. Our own Herring Brook in Pembroke was one of five rivers in the state that recorded its highest ever count in 2023. In fact, Herring Brook was the largest herring run in the state with a total run estimate of 570,000 fish! Other notable runs in 2023 included the Parker River in Newbury, Town River in Plymouth, Herring River in Wellfleet, and the Marston Mills River in Barnstable. Each of these rivers saw the highest numbers in the history of their counting programs (27 years for the Parker!).[146]

Shad Painted

Nobody pictured shad better than Massachusetts artist Sherman Foote Denton (1856–1937). His painting starts this chapter (Fig. 8) and appears on the cover of McPhee's book, *Founding Fish*. That is like appearing on the cover of *Sports Illustrated's* swimsuit edition.[147]

Denton was born in Dayton, Ohio. His family moved to Wellesley, Massachusetts, in the 1860s. He attended the Wellesley Public Schools, Allen School in West Newton, and the Academy of Art in Boston. From an early age, he was interested in depicting the natural world, and made a living from his drawings and painting as early as age 17.

From about 1886 until 1900, he was the official artist to the US Commission of Fish & Fisheries, and lived in Washington, DC. The agency commissioned him to create taxidermy specimens of fish. His painting skills were put to excellent use as the skin of a fish loses its coloration as it dries. To record the natural shape and color of the freshly caught fish, Sherman painted detailed watercolors of the specimen which he then referenced to create the mounted and painted fish.

Denton is perhaps best known for the chromo-lithographic prints of his fish illustrations that were published by the State of New York Fisheries, Game and Forest Commission at the turn of the twentieth century. These prints proved to be collectible and continue to be popular.

Denton lived with his wife and two children in Wellesley for several years, then moved to Weston. He died at his home and is buried at the Woodlawn Cemetery in Wellesley.[148]

His image of a shad appears at the beginning of this chapter.

2

SALT HAYING

Fig. 20. Salt hay, or cordgrass, *Spartina patens*. It is matted and swirling, growing in the high marsh. Source: Dana Filippini, National Park Service, via Wikimedia, public domain. Original in color.

Need for Hay

The first English settlers in New England arrived in desperate circumstances.

The *Mayflower* departed late from England. It was further delayed by bad weather.

The *Mayflower* arrived at Cape Cod. After scouting sites to settle, it eventually anchored near the abandoned Native American village of Patuxet, the place we call Plymouth.

It was the middle of winter, 1620–1621. Half the *Mayflower*'s passengers died on the voyage or in the early months of settlement. Ship supplies were exhausted. The earth was bare or fallow. Settlers found and took Native American stores of corn. (A kindly view is that they borrowed them, planning to replace them later.) Fish and game were available, but settlers could not live on them alone. Clearing land and planting crops would take years.[149]

Settlers looked to the salt marshes. They were abundant along the coast of what became Plymouth Colony, and abundant along the North River (as Vassall noted in 1643). The salt marshes provided grasses of the *Spartina* family to feed their cattle and other farm animals, thatch to roof their dwellings, and hay to insulate their dwellings. *Spartina* included *Spartina alterniflora* (smooth cordgrass in the low marsh), and *Spartina patens* (saltmeadow cordgrass — "salt hay" — in the high marsh) (Fig. 20). Later, settlers would develop fresh meadows of English hay. But salt hay continued to be important well into the 1800s.[150]

The early settlers were accustomed to the milder climate of England. Their experience was described in an 1857 report by the Massachusetts Board of Agriculture:

> The climate of England, on the other hand, admitted a greater degree of reliance on the wild luxuriance of nature, and this mode of management was brought over by the first settlers and attempted for some years, the few cattle they had being kept on poor and miserable swale hay, or often upon the hay obtained from the salt marshes. The death of their cattle from starvation and exposure was of very common occurrence, and not unfrequently the farmer lost his entire herd.[151]

The colonial Boston area had salt marshes. Settlers collected hay from mainland marshes, and some from marshes on Boston harbor islands, as early as 1634.[152]

Salt marshes were an important feature of early New York City, also, but that is a story for another time and place.[153]

Salt marshes appear in a delightful view of Boston looking north from Dorchester in 1776 (Fig. 21). On the left is the estate of William Shirley (1694–1771), Massachusetts Colony's governor from 1741 to 1749 and 1753 to 1756. A flock of sheep grazes on the hilly meadow in the center. A hay wagon, accompanied by a horse and rider, traverses the bottom right (Fig. 22). The wagon is likely bringing a load of salt hay to the estate.[154]

Fig. 21. James Newton, "A view of Boston taken on the road to Dorchester" (London: J.F.W. Des Barres, 1776). Shirley estate at left. Reproduction courtesy of Norman B. Leventhal Map & Education Center at Boston Public Library.

Fig. 22. Hay wagon, lower right, followed by a rider on a horse, in this detail of James Newton, "A view of Boston taken on the road to Dorchester" (London: J.F.W. Des Barres, 1776). Reproduction courtesy of Norman B. Leventhal Map & Education Center at Boston Public Library.

In 1764, Gov. Shirley sold the estate to his son-in-law, prosperous merchant Eliakim Hutchinson (1711–1775). According to the Massachusetts Tax Valuation List of 1771, Hutchinson owned property including the following (emphasis added for salt marsh):

- 2 dwellings,
- 1 vessel of upwards of ten tons,
- 6 horses and mares of three years old and upwards,
- 2 oxen at four years old and upwards,
- 6 cows and heifers at three years old and upwards,
- 0 goats and sheep one year old and upwards,
- 33 acres of pasturage,
- 7 acres of tillage land,
- *17 acres of salt marsh*,
- 16 tons of salt hay produced therefrom by the year,
- 30 acres of English [hay] and upland mowing land, and
- 15 tons of English and upland hay;
- 0 acres of fresh meadow, and
- 0 tons of fresh meadow hay.[155]

The tax listing of salt marshes and salt hay shows their value in colonial farming. Oxen or cows helped gather the salt hay, although horses began to replace them in that role and in general transportation. Horses, however, were more expensive.[156]

Today, the estate remains as the historic Shirley–Eustis house and grounds. The house was built between 1746 and 1749 as a summer estate for Gov. Shirley when he was governor. It is listed in the National Register of Historic Places (1966), and was recommended in 2021 for designation as a Boston City Landmark. That included a building that was recently documented as slave quarters. A nearby stream once led about a mile to Boston Harbor. Now the house is just west of Massachusetts Avenue, South Bay Center, Rte. 93, and Carson Beach.[157]

The economic value of salt marshes and salt hay continued. Returning to the state Board of Agriculture's 1857 report, it had a survey of grass and hay. Among its 23 questions to towns and farmers were these:

> 17. If you have any experience in ditching and draining wet meadow, or ditching or diking salt marsh, will you state the result, and the comparative value of the grass before and after the operation?

> 18. What are the most valuable varieties of salt marsh grasses, and how does the hay made from them compare in value with good English hay?[158]

The 1857 survey had many responses. One farmer said, "Since the fifth of September we cut our salt hay; in this town and never found it cleaner or better, and I think it will spend [sell] well." Another farmer fed their cows a mix of English hay and salt hay, which was cheaper.[159]

We return to the economic value of salt hay later, as we discuss proposals about 1870 to improve the North River by eliminating its salt marshes.

Gathering Hay

Gathering and storing hay involved a series of procedures and implements. Much has been written about the history of salt marsh haying. For details, I recommend John Stilgoe's description in *Alongshore*, William Gould Vinal, *Salt Haying in the North River Valley (1648–1898)*, and Joseph Foster Merritt, *Old Time Anecdotes of the North River and the South Shore*, particularly chapter III, "Gundalow Days on North River." Below, we summarize the procedures and show examples of the implements which, of course, were used upland as well as in salt marshes.

Many of these implements are at the Cudworth Barn of the Scituate Historical Society. The barn, said to be from the 1700s, was moved to its current location from Norwell in the 1930s. It was donated by Dr. L. Vernon Briggs, who is discussed in more detail later in this book.[160]

First, men and boys cut the hay. Later in this book is the story of Uncle Josh, who claimed to be a master at cutting hay with a scythe. Men, boys, and animals doing the work had to contend with "green-heads." These were blood-sucking horse-flies that bit "viciously."[161]

Then, the workers gathered the hay in piles, using rakes and pitchforks (Fig. 23). The work could last days. This collective effort took place in the fall when the tides were low and the hay was fresh.[162]

Men moved the piles of hay using wooden hay poles. Two poles were slid under a pile, then two men lifted and carried the pile, like medics carrying a stretcher. Hay poles were very long. Examples at the Cudworth Barn are about 2 inches wide (diameter) and 12 feet long (Fig. 24). These have labels marked "Miss Annie F. Peirce, One pair Hay Poles."[163]

Annie Foster Peirce (c. 1860–1941) was the daughter of Elijah Foster Peirce and Sarah A. Peirce. Thus, she was the niece of Elijah's brother Silas Peirce II (1826–1898), who founded the Peirce Memorial Library, and who was the father of Silas Peirce III

(1860–1922), the first president of the Scituate Historical Society. She lived on Country Way in 1918 and 1940, presumably at her father's house. That house and its barn were next to the ancestral Peirce estate. That estate, called Meadow Crest, was home of Silas Peirce II and III. Probably the hay poles came from that barn.

Fig. 23. John Nyberg holding pitchforks about 61 inches long at Cudworth Barn, Scituate, 2023: a pitchfork with wooden handle and three sharp metal tines, labeled "Pitchfork, N944," and a wooden pitchfork with three prongs, labeled "N1156. Howard O. Frye, Old wooden pitchfork."

Fig. 24. Hay pole at back of Cudworth Barn, 2023. Perhaps donated by Annie F. Peirce.

Haystacks and Staddles

Piles of hay were collected in haystacks. It is difficult to say how tall typical haystacks were. In recent times, the tallest haystack measured, for a Guinness World Record, was 13 feet, 2 inches.[164]

Men used a tall ladder to reach the top of the haystack, build it up, and get back down. The Cudworth Barn has a wooden ladder with 13 rungs that almost reaches the ceiling, so it is about 18 feet tall. It is taller than it needs to be to reach the hayloft, the upper part of the barn. This suggests the ladder was used for haystacks, perhaps after mowing salt marsh hay. The very top rungs are angled as if to lean against a haystack (Fig. 25).[165]

Fig. 25. Wooden ladder, Cudworth Barn, 2023.
Photo courtesy of Bob Gallagher.

Haystacks were built in hayfields or meadows if inland. If on salt marshes, they were elevated from the wet tides on staddles. These were large, supporting stakes grouped in a circle.[166]

Staddles were used in the North River marshes, according to Walter Crossley. He reported finding "the remains of one of these in the big marsh below the Damons Point Pier." (See Fig. 26.)[167]

Fig. 26. Salt haying in Great Marshes, West Barnstable, with staddle. Unknown photographer and date. From the collection of Whelden Memorial Library, donated by M. Wirtenan. Thanks to Historical Society of Old Yarmouth for posting this.

Fig. 27. Martin Johnson Heade, "View of Marshfield," c. 1866–1876," Corcoran Collection, National Gallery of Art, accession number 2015.19.173, https://www.nga.gov/collection/art-object-page.101282.html. Public domain.

Staddles are visible under the central haystack in Martin Johnson Heade's painting "View of Marshfield." (Fig. 27.) Cows graze nearby on what is clearly a salt marsh, with ocean waves coming in to shore in the background. At the lower right is the rectangular form of a boat with square prow and stern. It may be a temporarily abandoned gundalow. Gundalows are discussed below.[168]

According to the Historical Society of Old Yarmouth, "Hay was usually removed from staddles in January, after the marshes had frozen." Hay could be taken from staddles or haystacks back to a farm, or the upper level (the "mow") of a barn. For this, men needed help in transportation.[169]

Transporting Hay

Salt hay was carried in carts or wagons. These were drawn by oxen, and later mostly by horses, often in teams (Fig. 28 and Fig. 29). In his book on salt haying, William Gould Vinal (1881–1973) recalled his childhood travels, in the late 1800s, in a hay cart that went down Neal Gate Street, then "jogged across the main highway [now Route 3A] to a one-horse grassy lane leading to Wills's Island, a great expanse of salt marsh."[170]

Some of the ancient cartways survived. A 1975 plan used in the town of Scituate's taking of Boston Sand & Gravel Company property shows a cart path from near Route 3A across the marshes to and across Wills' Island, and another one to Wood Island.[171]

Fig. 28. Hay wagon drawn by pair of cattle, unknown photographer, location, and date. Man at left carries large hay rake (not a ladder). Courtesy of Archives of Norwell Historical Society.

Fig. 29. Salt haying at Old Lyme, Conn., postcard (The Rotograph Co., N.Y.C., printed in Germany, 59044a), early 1900s. Team of six cattle. Author's collection.

To keep the animals from sinking in the boggy marshes, they were fitted with special shoes, called bog shoes or meadow shoes. They were handcrafted rather than mass-produced, and were bolted on to the animal's hooves. Few examples remain (Fig. 30).

Meadow shoes appear in an 1884 poem by George Lunt. He lived in what was later called the Meeting House Inn, across the road from the salt meadows at Kent Road opposite Peggotty Beach in Scituate. Here is an excerpt:

> Soon from some more inland plain
> Lumbers down the farmer's wain;
> Oft his horse's hoofs encased
> In meadow-shoes securely laced;
> Where such slumpy ground imbeds
> Slimmer feet, he safely treads;
> Drags the high-piled wagon on
> Till the solid earth be won;
> Soon within the homestead yard
> Quaint haystacks his toil reward.[172]

Fig. 30. Bog shoes at Cudworth Barn, 2023.

Hay carts had to deal with ditches dug in the marshes and occasional streams. How did they cross them? Yankee ingenuity came to the rescue, according to Newburyport historians. Temporary wooden bridges could have been loaded in the hay cart. In the winter, wooden sleds could transport hay across frozen marshes, rivers, and creeks.[173]

Gundalows

Salt marshes along the North River widened significantly downriver near Marshfield Hills and Scituate's Third Cliff. Transporting salt hay by cart or wagon from the river's edge to the upland was farther and more difficult. Instead, men used small watercraft called gundalows. They could be loaded up with hay at water's edge and carry their loads to landings along the river. Landings were at Union Bridge (site of today's Union Street Bridge), Little's Bridge (site of today's Rte. 3A bridge), and First Herring Brook (Colman's Landing, near the later wharf of the Boston Sand and Gravel Company.[174]

The term gundalow, a rare one today, seems a corruption of Venice's gondolas, which they scarcely resemble. They were flat-bottomed, low, and sturdy, propelled by oars and long poles. Their shallow drafts were appropriate for the shallow waters. They had no masts and sails until the mid-1800s, at least along the North River. They were used since the 1600s in "Down East" coastal communities of Maine, New Hampshire, and

Massachusetts, appearing as far south as Virginia. They were noted in publications as early as 1835. Or even earlier, if you accept the finding by poet and critic James Russell Lowell — "*Gundalow* is old: I find *gundelo* in Hakluyt [English writer Richard Hakluyt (1553–1616], and *gundello* in Booth's reprint of the folio Shakespeare of 1623."[175]

Gundalows were the workhorses — the work trucks, the work vans — of the eastern seaboard waterways. Gundalows transported salt hay and other items. That even included a Quaker church, moved from Scituate to Pembroke in 1706, according to tradition. Gundalows were mentioned in a Revolutionary War journal.[176]

Gundalows also appear in John Greenleaf Whittier's 1863 poem, "The Countess," part of which evidently describes the scene at a Merrimack River dock near his home:

> The river's steel-blue crescent curves
>   To meet, in ebb and flow,
> The single broken wharf that serves
>   For sloop and gundalow.
>
> With salt sea-scents along its shores
>   The heavy hayboats crawl,
> The long antennae of their oars
>   In lazy rise and fall.[177]

Old photos of gundalows are hard to find (Fig. 31).[178]

Fig. 31. Gundalow image by doctor who spent time in Ipswich: Charles Wendell Townsend, *Sand Dunes and Salt Marshes* (Boston: Dana Estes & Company, 1913), 194–195, https://babel.hathitrust.org/cgi/pt?id=hvd.32044072260185&seq=13.

Gundalow docks may still be around in Scituate's salt marshes. Plans of land in North Scituate from 1918 and 1919 provide compelling evidence (Fig. 32 and Fig. 33).

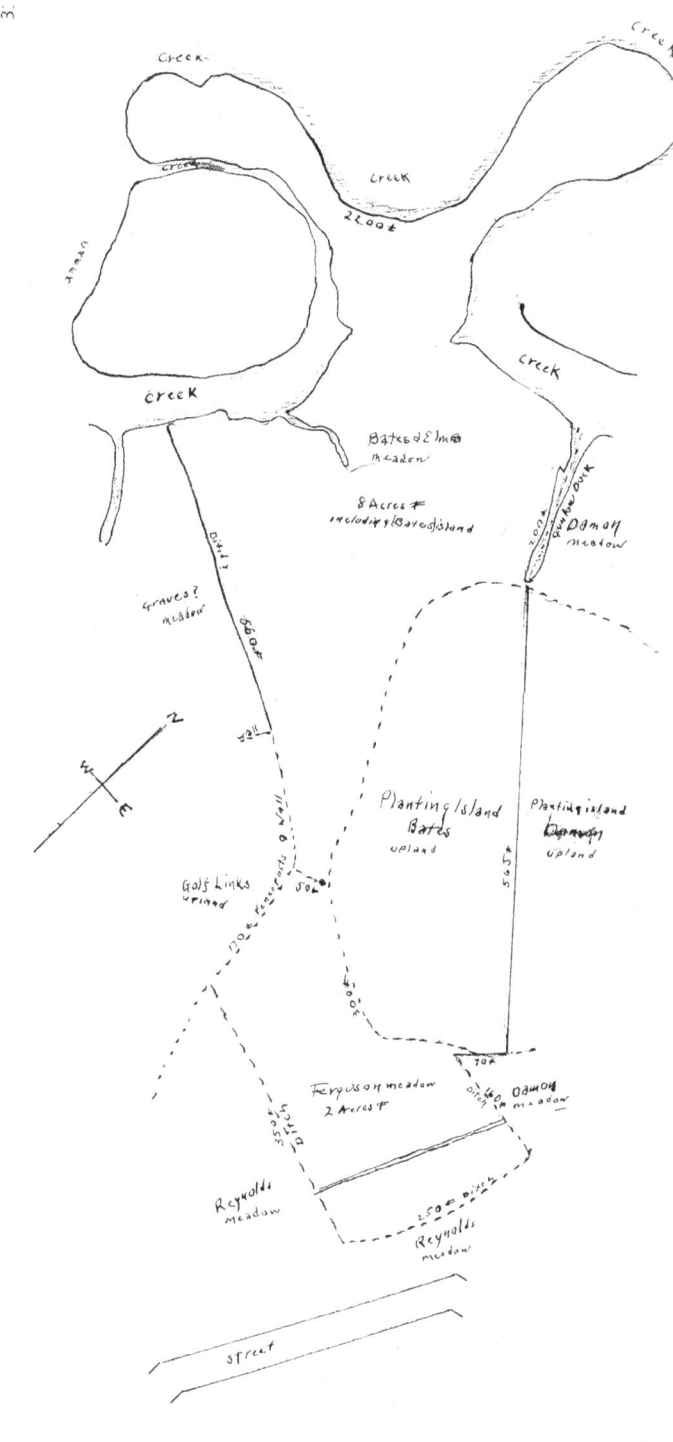

The site is near the Hatherly Country Club (established in 1899). Even at this late date, after the steep decline in salt haying, a "Gunlow Dock" appears on the 1918 plan. It is a channel about 10 to 20 feet wide. It was obviously built so a narrow gundalow could float in to collect harvested hay.

And the dock conveniently lay between (or had been cut between) two meadows. The dock connected to an upland "planting island" divided between owners Bates and Damon. With meadows on both sides, the gundalow dock minimized the distance to carry hay.[179]

A 1919 plan (detail below), was based on this 1918 plan. It shows the dock connecting with a creek that, with one "S" curve, enters Briggs Harbor. From there, the hay could move on to Cohasset Harbor and other places.

Fig. 32. Litchfield, "Plan of Lands at North Scituate Beach, Scituate, Mass., May 1918, Scale 100 ft. to an inch," PCRD plan book 3, page 83. Shows "golf links" (left, at curved line) and "Gunlow Dock" (upper right, written vertically along channel next to "Damon Meadow").

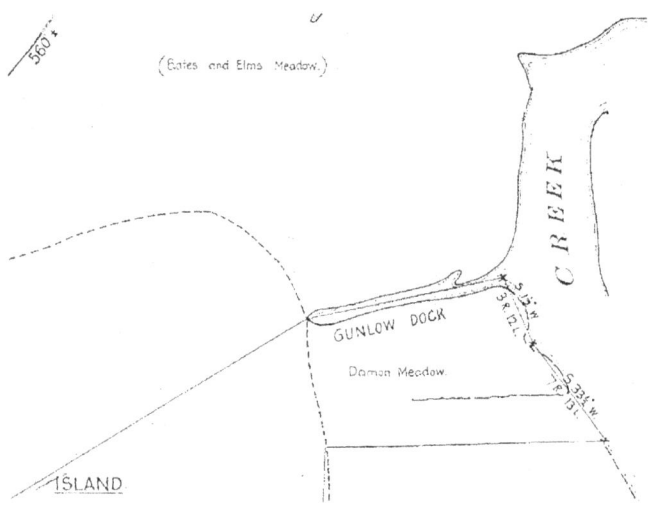

Fig. 33. Detail of Frederick E. Tupper, "Compiled Plan of the North Scituate Estate of Florence A. Reynolds, Aug. 1919," scale 100' = 1", filed May 2, 1924, PCRD plan book 3, page 725. North (not indicated) is approximately to the right. Drawn for "Ledgemer" estate at 7 Bailey's Causeway. Partially shown at left is "Planting Island (Damon Island)," probably "Plantain Island" shown on the map of Scituate, plate 31, in the Richards 1903 atlas of Plymouth County.

The planting island on these plans is now called Treasure Island (Fig. 34).[180]

Fig. 34. Treasure Island with channel (center right) leading to curve in creek. Hatherly Country Club at upper left, Bassing Beach at upper right. Aerial photo courtesy of Gary M. Banks, William E. Richardson, May 14, 2020. Also in color in *Seacoast Scituate By Air* (2022).

Eventually, haymaking and gundalows disappeared from the North River valley. Vinal said the old terms for the work grew obsolete: "Bunching, poling, tedding, raking scatters, pitching [hay], stomping the load, and wearily plodding home."[181]

3

MEN OF THE RIVER

The North River was well-known for its shipbuilding industry. In addition to shipbuilders, the industry spawned skilled river pilots, sea captains, craftsmen, ministers, doctors, storytellers, and historians. We explore some of them and their stories below.

L. Vernon Briggs, M.D., Historian

It is only right to start with the man who definitively documented the river's shipbuilding industry, L. Vernon Briggs (1863–1941) (Fig. 35 and Fig. 36). He came from a family of North River shipbuilders. His 1889 *History of Shipbuilding on North River* is a classic reference book. He based it on family source documents and interviews within the shipbuilding community. It mentions just about every shipbuilder, river pilot, and sea captain in the valley. He was a good storyteller, too, as reflected in some of the profiles below.[182]

Other rivers wish they had a Briggs to tell their shipbuilding histories.

With a focus on that book, it is easy to overlook his many other writings and accomplishments. Briggs was a polymath, a person of wide-ranging knowledge and learning. He was an accomplished psychiatrist, genealogist, historian, and photographer, even (for a short time) a newspaper correspondent. By the early 1900s, he lived and practiced medicine in Boston, specializing in mental and nervous disease. He was a nationally known psychiatrist, consulting on insanity defenses in criminal cases, and gaining fame as a reformer in the treatment of mental illness.[183]

Briggs gloried in his family's background on the North River. By 1903, he was living in his family home on Elm Street in Hanover. In 1906, he and his new wife (a Cabot) bought the historic Broad Oak Farm on Broadway in Hanover, and lived there. It was near the railroad station at Hanover Four Corners that connected to Boston. The farm traces back to early shipbuilders.[184]

Fig. 35. Maj. L. Vernon Briggs at Camp Devens, MA, 1917, detail from Briggs, *History of the Psychopathic Hospital, Boston, Massachusetts* (Boston: Wright & Potter, 1922), 156–157.

Fig. 36. Dr. L. Vernon Briggs, from "Asks for at Least 500 Beds in Bedford N. P. [Neuro Psychiatric] Hospital; American Legion Committee Foresees Growing Need of Hospital Care of War Veterans," *Boston Globe*, June 3, 1926, 16.

Uncle Josh, Salt Hay Mower

Briggs' book digressed from shipbuilding for a story about Uncle Josh, who claimed to be a champion mower of salt hay.

Elsewhere, we discuss gathering and transporting salt hay, by wagons drawn by oxen or horses and by boats called gundalows. But first the hay had to be mowed. According to Briggs, "John Tower related an anecdote in the *North River Pioneer* some years ago about 'Uncle Josh' Stetson, of Hanover":

> "Wal," said Uncle Josh. "I should raly like to see one young man more that knowed how to mow. Nobody seems to know anything about how to swing a scythe nowadays, and you can't find one man between here and Pembroke meetinghouse but what will tangle down more grass than his neck is wuth.
>
> … "We thought that you never wanted anyone to help you mow," we suggested.

"Wal, I don't; but I 'spose a man has a right to be sick once in a while, ain't he? When 1 lived down to the old place they called me the best mower on the river, and I'd beat everybody on Sitewate side, and one morning when I was down side of the river fishing for parch, who should I see coming across the medder on t'other side, but old Marmaduke McDonnellson. Says he 'Josh, I've got a boy ter hum that will mow round ye four times in half a day.' 'Fetch him down here,' says I, 'and we'll see.'… [Then] Mc. got along with his boy. Pretty soon 1 see him coming with his son Sam. 'Wal, Josh,' he said, 'where ye goin' to mow?' 'Begin right where ye stand and go down river,' says I, 'and the one that gets to White's ferry fust is the best feller.'… Wal, we struck in, and the way we made the grass fall was a caution. Grandsir went up on the hill and watched, but he told me arterwards that he couldn't see nothing but a winrow of grass flying in the air, and going at the rate of ten miles an hour."

"How did you get across Stony brook?" we inquired.

"Never noticed the brook at all, mowed right across it down past Little's bridge and Will's Island, swam across the river to the ferry, and struck in on t'other side, and in less than two hours 1 met Sam just pulling himself out of Fulling mill creek."

"That must have made about eighteen miles," we remarked.

"Wal, yes. Always mowed nine miles an hour, could mow ten if I let out a link."

We left "Uncle Josh" sharpening his scythe for a second crop.[185]

Fig. 37. Scythes and other implements hanging from rafter in Cudworth Barn, Scituate Historical Society, 2023.

This was a good tale, and a tall tale, perhaps a whale of a tale. Josh's eighteen miles would have covered almost all of the North River, from its beginning to White's Ferry, near its end. At nine miles an hour, he would have covered it in two hours. At that rate, Uncle Josh could have won the 1899 Boston Marathon. And he would not even have needed to carry a scythe (Fig. 37).[186]

In his tale, "Fulling mill creek," as best as I can tell, is also called Two Mile Creek (which had a fulling mill). It is west of Hatch Mill off Union Street in

Marshfield. It enters the North River about halfway along the river to White's Ferry. In other words, Uncle Josh claimed to be twice as fast as young Sam.[187]

Briggs left out one fact. "Uncle Josh," probably Joshua Stetson (c. 1780–1887?), resided for a time at Briggs' childhood home on Elm Street in Hanover. Briggs undoubtedly grew up listening to tales by Uncle Josh. The house is still there, across the street from Briggs' later Broad Oak Farm.[188]

Walter Crossley, Storyteller

Walter Crossley (1898–1991)[189] had many stories about the North River in the early 1900s. He knew the river well as a boy, and he lived at Damon's Point in Marshfield for a good part of his life, which included stints as a clam digger, carpenter, and shore bird whittler. In 1972–1973, he wrote a series of articles called "As I Remember" for the *Marshfield Mariner* newspaper.

His articles were engagingly written and had many personal and historical details worth exploring. There is too much to include in this book, but a few of his first-hand observations will pop up here and there.[190]

Crossley recalled the scene at Mary's Livery in the early 1900s. Now it is the site of Roht Marine next to the Rte. 3A bridge. Crossley wrote,

> Mary's Livery was also a boat rental at that time and was operated by Mary Damon. There was a stone embankment along the river that was used as a landing place, and two or three dories were kept for rent. A boat house stood near the river.
>
> … The bridge at that time was a hand-operated draw and the old toll house was still there, though no longer used. … Just below the bridge was a one-room building set on wood pilings which was occupied by Mr. William Cann.
>
> Known as Bill by all acquaintances, he fished for lobsters from spring until fall. …
>
> … The bridge was replaced in 1910 or 1911. The new one was about three feet higher and had a draw operated by manpower and a concrete counter balance. The entire track across the marshes was raised about the time the new bridge went in.[191]

Crossley reported on harvesting hay and kelp, the different kinds of marsh grasses,[192] various methods for eel fishing on the North River,[193] and clamming.[194] He also had a detailed report on rum running. Here is an excerpt with an exciting incident:

Prohibition brought a new activity to the North River. …

One incident I can vouch for happened at the Third Cliff point [the Spit].

At that time, a small marsh island lay just off the point. It made a sharp turn in the channel. The runner, who told me he was headed up Herring River for unloading, had the Coast Guard just behind him. Both boats were going at full speed. He made the turn, straightened out and the Coast Guard didn't. They hit the island so hard that the Coast Guard boat was driven into the marsh and it set upright as in a cradle when the ride left. A small buoy tender had to be sent down three days later to pull them off.[195]

William Tilden, Fisherman

Going back in time, fishing on the North River plays a role in a delightful and overlooked memoir by William Phillips Tilden (1811–1890). He was a son of a ship-carpenter. His family built a new house about 1817 at a bend in the North River, just above Union Bridge. The site, he wrote, was "known from early days as the 'Block House,' where there were a fort and garrison in Philip's War. This was the dear spot where I spent my boyhood." The site, in what became Norwell, is now about five miles from the seashore, but then about eight miles.[196]

A view of the river at the Block House is on the back cover of this book. A view of the nearby Union Bridge is below (Fig. 38).[197]

Fig. 38. Union Bridge from Bridge Street, Norwell (foreground), to Union St., Marshfield, postcard, c. 1900–1917. Hatch Tilden house (built c. 1800) behind ship at left on North River. Norwell Historical Society, *Digital Commonwealth*, https://ark.digitalcommonwealth.org/ark:/50959/sj13b083w.

The ship at left in this view, tied up on the Marshfield side, is at the location of a ship described by Walter Crossley:

> Joseph Tripp, owner and operator of the Old Howard House at Hanover's four corners, acquired a large boat and had it tied up just below the [Union] bridge on the Marshfield side. I believe he intended to operate it as a floating café. ... I do not think the project ever materialized.[198]

Among Tilden's boyhood memories are fishing in the river, described below, followed by a detailed description of a "peculiar" method of ice fishing (not copied here):

> The North River abounded in fish. Eels were caught with bobs in the spring, from the banks, with pole and line, and in winter through the ice, with spears long enough to reach the bottom and draw them out of their snug winter home. Herrings and shad were caught in abundance in seines, in the spring of the year. Perch and bass were not very plentiful, but very delicious; and the clam banks in the lower reaches of the river, near the sea, yielded an abundance of very sweet clams. These various kinds of fish, with smelts, taken by hand nets from the herring brooks, formed a large part of our food in winter-time. Taken right from the water, with mother to cook them at an open fire, they were superb.[199]

Later he was allowed to go fishing beyond the river, from a boat in the ocean. He described this first "outside" fishing in delightful detail. It happened in "certain places two or three miles from shore."

> I well remember my first experience of outside fishing – outside the beach. ... There was no land between us and Europe so that an east wind set into the bay with great force, and sometimes the breakers were so high as to make a launch through them difficult. [But the wind was inshore and the breakers moderate when he launched.] ... and with a few strokes there we are, the surf in a wreath of white foam behind us, and three thousand miles of briny deep before us.[200]

It did not end happily. He got seasick and had to be put ashore.[201]

In a bit of famous name-dropping, Tilden described his nearest neighbor, Judge Nathan Cushing, his minister, Rev. Samuel J. May, and his previous minister, Rev. Samuel Deane, who wrote a history of Scituate in 1831. "In the church we had the old-fashioned square pews of the period, with high backs to break the draught, hiding the inmates from the view of all but the minister, who could look down from his lofty pulpit, and see if all his sheep and lambs were in their pens."[202]

Tilden escaped his church pew or pen, only to become a minister. He had strong anti-slavery views. His pastorates led him to Boston, from 1862 until 1883.[203]

Jerry Gunderway, Pilot

Fig. 39. Jerry Gunderway, detail of photo, c. 1870, by Charles E. Rogers, public domain.

Jeremiah "Jerry" Gunderway (1787–1875) was a North River pilot of many boats, including the flat-bottom boats that carried salt hay, called gundalows. (His name does not seem related to "gundalows," probably derived from Italian "gondolas.") Jerry was the son of Revolutionary War veteran Richard Gunderway, a free Black. According to Briggs, he was a great smoker and quite intemperate. He gave up smoking when his cargo of salt hay caught fire from his pipe. He gave up drinking after bouts of delirium tremens, in which he had others chain him down, or confine him in the cell of the almshouse. He recovered enough to work for the town as one of more than 30 highway surveyors in 1847.[204]

Gunderway "lived at one time in a little shanty at the mouth of the Second Herring Brook, by the 'Chittenden Yard' [a boatbuilding yard]," according to Merritt's book *Old Time Anecdotes*. By the time the book was published in 1928, the shanty had long since disappeared. It would have been west of the Second Herring Brook, west of today's Norris Reservation, near the end of today's Chittenden Lane in Norwell. In the 1920s, William E. Mills acquired the property, comprising 21 acres. Deeds included any right, title, and interest in the Town Landing on the North River and the way leading thereto. According to Merritt, the Town Landing lasted until 1799, within the lifetime of Gunderway. Today it is a town landing for canoes and kayaks in what is now the town of Norwell. It has a beautiful view of the bends in the North River.[205]

Gunderway was the great grandfather of four girls shown in a school class photo of 1914. According to the Norwell Historical Society, these four were among 12 of the 33 children in the class who were Black. The school, located on River Street in Norwell, is now the home of the North River Community Theater.[206]

Tolman Family, Tool Makers (*article contributed by Thomas Whalen[207]*)

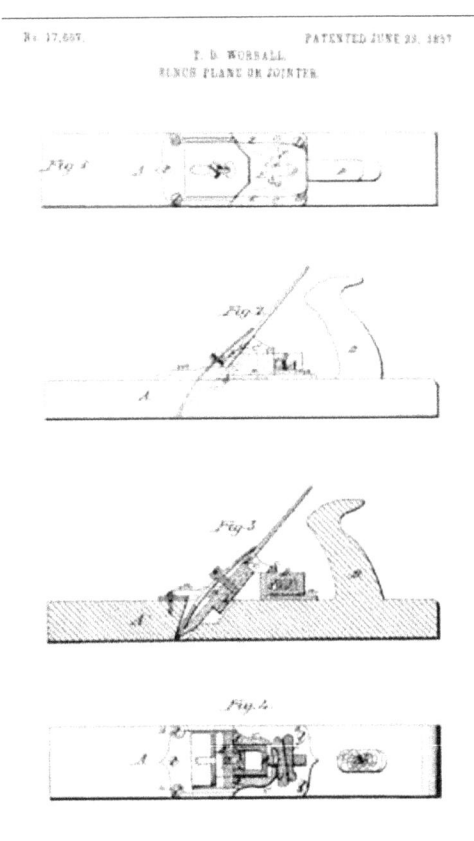

Fig. 41. Plane maker mark: J. R. Tolman Hanover Mass. (T. C. Power is probably an owner mark.) Collection of Thomas Whalen.

Fig. 40. (Above) Sample bench plane patent, by Worrall, from 1857, same year as patent by Thomas J. Tolman. http://www.handplanepatents.com/tag/1857/. Wood block holds sharp metal blade to cut wood.

Fig. 42. Typical Tolman shipwright planes. Collection of Thomas Whalen.

Shipbuilding on the North River began by the early 18th century. North River shipwrights and carpenters used tools imported from Europe or produced locally by blacksmiths and shipwrights. By 1820, many of the tools were produced commercially in America and readily available to shipyard workers. The one exception was rugged specialized wood working planes that would hold up to the rigors of shipbuilding.

Plane makers would stamp their name or mark on their planes, usually on the toe.

The Tolman family of South Scituate specialized in making wooden planes unique to shipbuilding. Joseph and his son Thomas provided high quality woodworking planes of all types to shipyard workers from the 1840s to 1880.

Joseph Robinson Tolman was born in Scituate on February 10, 1787. He learned the trade of a ship's joiner, likely in the shipyards along the North River. The *Boston Almanac* of 1818 lists Tolman as a ship's joiner. In 1820, he learned the trade of plane making. The *Boston Almanac* of 1841 lists Tolman as a plane maker working at 115 Commercial Street. Tolman's early planes are signed J. R. Tolman, with no location. In the 1840s, he returned to Scituate.

In 1849, Joseph is listed in the *New England Mercantile Union Directory* as a plane maker in Hanover. The 1860 state industrial census lists Tolman as working in Hanover, employing three hands and producing $3,000 worth of planes. The three hands working in the shop were Joseph, and likely his son Thomas and an apprentice Charles Merritt.

Although Tolman resided in South Scituate, all his planes are marked J. R. Tolman Hanover (Fig. 41 and Fig. 44). Tolman's residence and workshop were close to Hanover and the rail line. Tolman chose to use the Hanover location on his planes for shipping purposes. His planes are of high quality and are noted for producing large numbers of spar and other ship building planes. Tolman's location, near the many shipyards along the North River, drove his successful plane making business.

Joseph Tolman died in South Scituate on June 7, 1864, at age 77.

Joseph's son Thomas Jones Tolman was born in Boston on October 10, 1819. He served an apprenticeship in plane making under his father. In the 1850 census, Thomas was listed as a plane maker living with his father and Charles H. Merritt (age 23), who also apprenticed under Joseph Tolman.

On January 13, 1857, Thomas Tolman applied for and received Patent No.16412 for a method for adjusting the mouth size of a plane. (See sample patent by another plane maker, Fig. 40.) It is unknown how successful his patented plane was. Few exist in the collections of tool collectors today.

In 1860, when Thomas succeeded to his father's operation, planes were signed T. J. Tolman in Hanover. His planes with the patented mouth opening were stamped T. J. Tolman Patent Jan.1857 Hanover Mass. (see Fig. 42).

Thomas and Charles Merritt formed a plane maker partnership in 1864, Tolman & Merritt. It continued to 1874, a working period of 10 years. No planes have been reported with a Tolman & Merritt imprint stamped on the toe of planes.

Thomas Tolman died in South Scituate (now Norwell) on March 18, 1874.

Joseph and Thomas are buried in the First Parish Cemetery, Norwell.

Shipbuilders

Shipbuilding was a major industry on the North River. Many excellent books describe its history. Here is a summary by the NSRWA:

> Beginning in the mid-1600s and continuing long into the 19th century, this 12-mile waterway was home to a total of 24 shipyards. Between 1645 and 1871, more than 1,000 vessels were constructed along the river in Hanover, Pembroke, Marshfield, Norwell and Scituate.[208]

A 1734 map of the Massachusetts coastline showed the mouth of the North River, and said this about Conchasset (Cohasset) and Scituate: "Small Rivers for Wood Boats tho they build a great many Ships here & bring out at high Water."[209]

A 1795 map of Pembroke said,

> The North River which makes part of the Northern boundary is about six rods [99 feet] wide from the bridge to Marshfield. [The bridge, evidently no longer there, would have been just east of today's Rte. 3, near Lowe's home improvement store in Pembroke. See map detail below.] Vessels of between 2 & 300 tons burthen are built within 60 rods [990 feet] of said bridge, and on spring tides are moved down river.[210]

North River ships seemingly sailed everywhere. To pick one example, the brig *Oak*, built by Henry Briggs in 1820, sailed to Amsterdam, Liverpool, New Orleans, and Rio de Janeiro.[211]

Turner's shipyard was one of the earliest on the North River. As historian L. Vernon Briggs said:

> Turner's Yard was the farthest point up the river at which any vessels were built. The site is visible from the present bridge [the 1829 North River

Bridge, replaced in 1904], being but a few rods above, in a small ravine or gorge, now somewhat levelled, on the land of the late Horatio Bigelow. It was improved by Daniel Turner, previous to 1699 and later; but the names of none of his vessels have been ascertained. Daniel was a son of Humphrey Turner, of Scituate [footnote citing Deane's *History of Scituate*]. He removed from Scituate to a spot near Barstow's Bridge, which was just above North River Bridge, and in 1665 married Hannah, daughter of William Randall. He probably commenced the building of vessels soon after this date, and may have resided where Mrs. Bigelow's house now stands.[212]

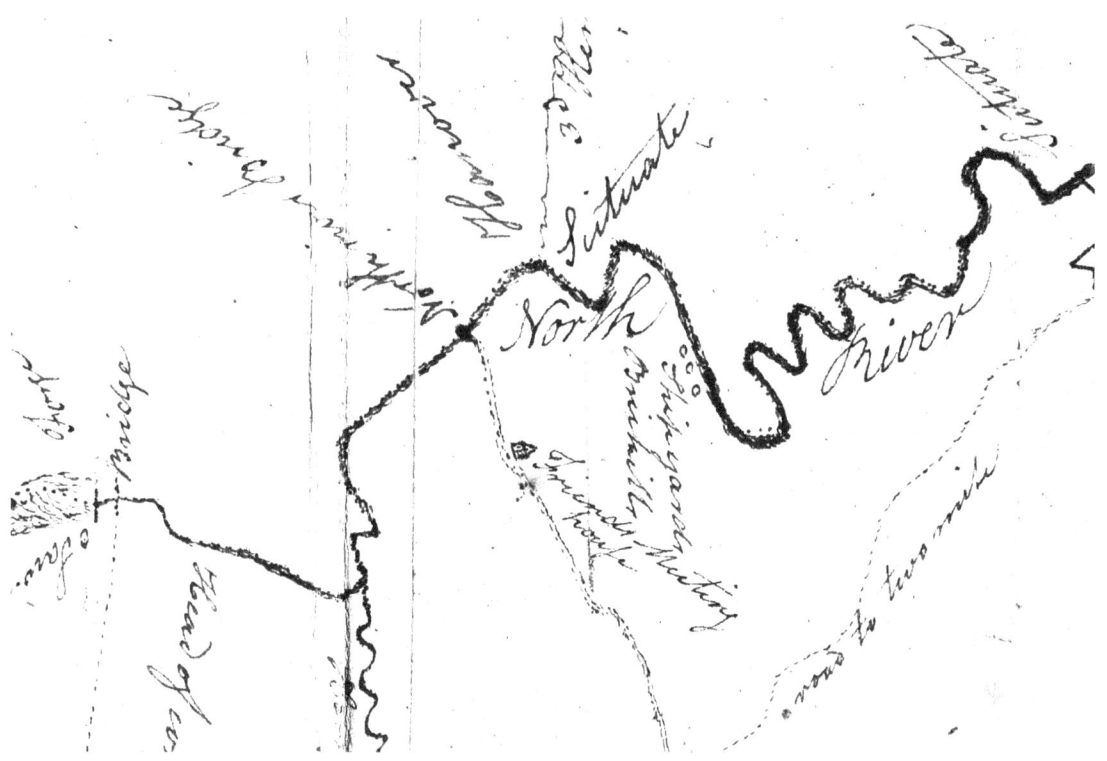

Fig. 43. "Plan of Pembroke, surveyor's name not given, dated 1794-5," Mass. Archives No. 1238, detail, *Digital Commonwealth*, https://ark.digitalcommonwealth.org/ark:/50959/2227nh04v. Three small circles in center are shipyards and brick kiln along North River. From left, Ludden's Ford pond, dam, and "Bridge;" Herring Brook (bottom, joining Indian Head River at the Crotch to start North River); old North River Bridge (black spot, with name above, almost upside down); Third Herring Brook (top, center). Hales' 1831 map is similar.

The American Geography described the river in 1795:

> Passing Fore and Back rivers in Weymouth, you come to North river, which rises in Indian Head Pond in Pembroke, and running in a serpentine course between Scituate and Marshfield passes to the sea. This river for its size is remarkable for its great depth of water, it being, in some places, not more than 40 or 50 feet wide, and yet vessels of 300 tons are built at Pembroke, 18 miles (as the river runs) from its mouth. This river is navigable for boats to the first fall, five miles from its source in Indian Head Pond; thence to

> the nearest waters which run into Taunton river is only three miles. A canal to connect the waters of these two rivers, which communicate with Narraganset and Massachusetts Bays, would be of great utility, as it would save a long and dangerous navigation round Cape Cod. [spelling modernized.][213]

At the time, shipbuilding on the North River was in its prime and could expand further if the river were connected to the Taunton River by a canal.

But shipbuilding peaked in the early 1800s, due to local limitations on growth. The river was crooked and filling with shoals. That restricted the size of vessels to be built and transported down the river to the ocean. In addition, the supply of local lumber was being exhausted. Other shipbuilding locations, such as East Boston, were able to build larger vessels, and they began to prove more prosperous.

In 1889, Briggs described the river from a perch at its origin, near the North River Bridge:

> We are now back to the Crotch, formed by the junction of the Indian Head and Namassakeeset Rivers [now Indian Head River and Herring Brook]. At this point North River begins its winding, snake-like course, through hill and vale, flowing over twenty miles to reach the ocean, ten miles distant. It is a truly beautiful stream and associated with many historical events of our country, which fame has been won for it by the ships built on its banks and which it safely bore to the ocean, from whence they gave renown to their builders and to the river on which they were built.[214]

With the river's increasing shoals in the early 1800s, shipbuilders proposed two plans for improvements. One was to build a canal from the North River to Scituate Harbor. Another was to cut through the shingle beach between Third and Fourth Cliffs, allowing direct access to the ocean there instead of the river's outlet three miles south. Either plan would avoid the shoals and shallows on the river's last three miles.

These were rival proposals. Scituate and Marshfield so vigorously pursued them because either one probably would have attracted more ship traffic and attendant business to the chosen town. Perhaps shipbuilding had already declined in Scituate compared with the Marshfield side of the river. In any event, the rivalries over time sank the proposals. The industry of building ships of any size on the North River disappeared by 1871.

These proposals to keep shipbuilding alive are discussed in a number of books, including L. Vernon Briggs' excellent *History of Shipbuilding on North River* (1889). In discussing the proposals, however, most books either summarized or overlooked some key source material in reports to the state and federal legislatures.[215]

These legislative reports are now available on the internet with diligent digital searching. They describe well the physical character of the river. They provide details that are useful even today in historical and scientific studies. In addition, diaries of John Quincy Adams reveal surprising details of rivalries between Scituate and Marshfield for improving the river. We focus on them in the next chapter.

Fig. 44. Maker J. R. Tolman mark on toe of wood plane. J. I. Tarr was likely an owner. Exhibited at North River Pop-Up Museum, March 8, 2025.

4

IMPROVING THE RIVER: EARLY YEARS

Efforts to improve the North River began very early, by 1802 if not earlier, and continued until about 1915. They show persistent pushes to change the river valley to benefit shipbuilders and then agricultural landowners along the river. Some have been well-documented, but not all. They involved John Quincy Adams and Daniel Webster.

We trace these efforts below in detail, but here is a summary:

- 1795. On Turner's 1795 map of Scituate, someone seems to have penciled in a canal from the Hanover line of the river straight southeast to meet the mouth of the river, bypassing more than 40 bends of the river.[216]

- 1802. Scituate adopts concept of connecting river to Scituate Harbor by a canal.

- Early 1800s. Area citizens petition federal and state legislatures to plan, authorize, and fund either a canal to Scituate Harbor, or a cut between Third Cliff and Fourth Cliff to create a new mouth of the river. Proponents of the cut actually dig a cut one night in 1843, but it soon filled in.

- 1852. Federal plan (preliminary) showing site of possible canal or cut.[217]

- 1854. Federal report to Congress for possible canal (favored) or cut.[218]

- 1850s. Citizens organize campaign to dredge the river and open a channel (cut) at Scituate Beach (between Third Cliff and Fourth Cliff), to benefit navigation.

- 1870. State agency has engineers study the situation and reports to the legislature supporting a dam on the North River to keep out the ocean and improve marshes.

- 1871–1873. Legislature authorizes a dam; salt marsh owners work to make it happen, without success.

- 1898. Portland Gale creates new opening for North River between Third Cliff and Fourth Cliff, at the site of the previously proposed cut.

- 1915. State agency once again considers options, focused on dredging a channel along the river. Studies and maps are generated in great detail, but agency has doubts about the project.

Attempts to "improve" the river were many, and proponents were persistent. Most efforts failed, leaving the river to become cleaner, free-running, scenic, and an environmental asset.

Early Proposals

In 1802, at the peak of shipbuilding on the North River, Scituate was already looking ahead to improving the river by building a possible canal between the river and Scituate Harbor. In 1802, the town authorized a tide dam in the harbor, but required it to reserve a place for such a canal "if it should any time hereafter be wanted."[219]

In 1806, residents of the neighboring town of Marshfield sought approval for a canal connecting the nearby Green Harbor River with Duxbury Bay, and it was built.[220]

In the early 1800s, the North River shipbuilding industry ebbed and ground to a halt during the War of 1812. Shipbuilders along the river raised petitions for federal funding to improve it. After all, Massachusetts had national political power with local figures such as John Quincy Adams and Daniel Webster.[221]

In 1822, Scituate appointed a committee "to confer with any similar committee that is or may be chosen by town of Marshfield, and after conference to report to Town on expediency or inexpediency of opening new mouth to North River lying between said Towns." It is not clear what the committee reported. However, in following years, both towns submitted petitions — also called memorials in those days — to the state legislature and to the federal government, whose support and funding were needed for these big projects.[222]

On October 4, 1826, a great number of inhabitants of Scituate, Marshfield, Pembroke, and Hanover met,

> to devise measures to remove obstructions at the mouth of said [North] river. – Samuel A. Turner, Esq. was chairman, and Capt. Wales Tilden, Secretary of the Meeting. It was then 'Voted Unanimously that the opening a new channel at the Northerly end of the Fourth Cliff, so called, would be a GREAT PUBLIC BENEFIT.' [capitalized in original.][223]

In 1828, inhabitants of those towns petitioned the US Congress for improvement of North River channels. The petition described the history of shipbuilding on the river, and said that:

> for a few years past, such has been the effect of the sea at the mouth of said river, as to heap up sand and gravel, by which the mouth, or going out of said river, is now more than a mile southerly of its former place; and the sand has washed into the river, and formed shoals for about three miles in the lower part of the river, so as to preclude the building of vessels of the largest sizes; … it costs, on an average, $125 for every hundred tons of vessels, to get them out of the last three miles of the river. This operates almost to the exclusion of ship-building on said river. … [We] contemplate opening a new channel for the river to discharge its waters through the beach, near three miles north of the present mouth of the river … .
>
> [A skilled gentleman performed a survey and he] judges it to be practicable to open such a channel; but, as it is uncertain what effect the sea might have upon the new channel, thinks it most advisable to open a channel from the northeast bend of the river, above the present obstructions, through low lands, and principally salt marsh, in a northerly direction, about one mile and a half to Scituate harbor; thus turning the river through said harbor, at the entrance of which there appears to be no danger of the seas heaving up a bar of sand or gravel, which might obstruct the ingress or egress of shipping.
>
> [The petitioners] respectfully pray your honors to direct a survey to be made of the premises, by competent Engineers, who might be directed to report the practicability, expediency, and probable expense, compared with the benefits that would accrue to the public in general.[224]

Likely, it was this petition that led to a report to Congress in December 1830 "by an engineer who made the survey under the authority of Lt. Col. Anderson." (Fig. 45.) The report found that clearing obstructions to the river at its mouth were "almost impracticable" and the same objections applied to a cut between the sand and gravel ridge (between Third Cliff and Fourth Cliff). Each would require great cost. The report recommended a three-mile channel from the river to Scituate Harbor.[225]

The 1828 petition displayed unity among the towns. In a "subsequent Congress an appropriation was made for this object, but the petitions having been (by mistake) unfortunately referred to the wrong committee, there does not appear to have been any farther action upon it."[226]

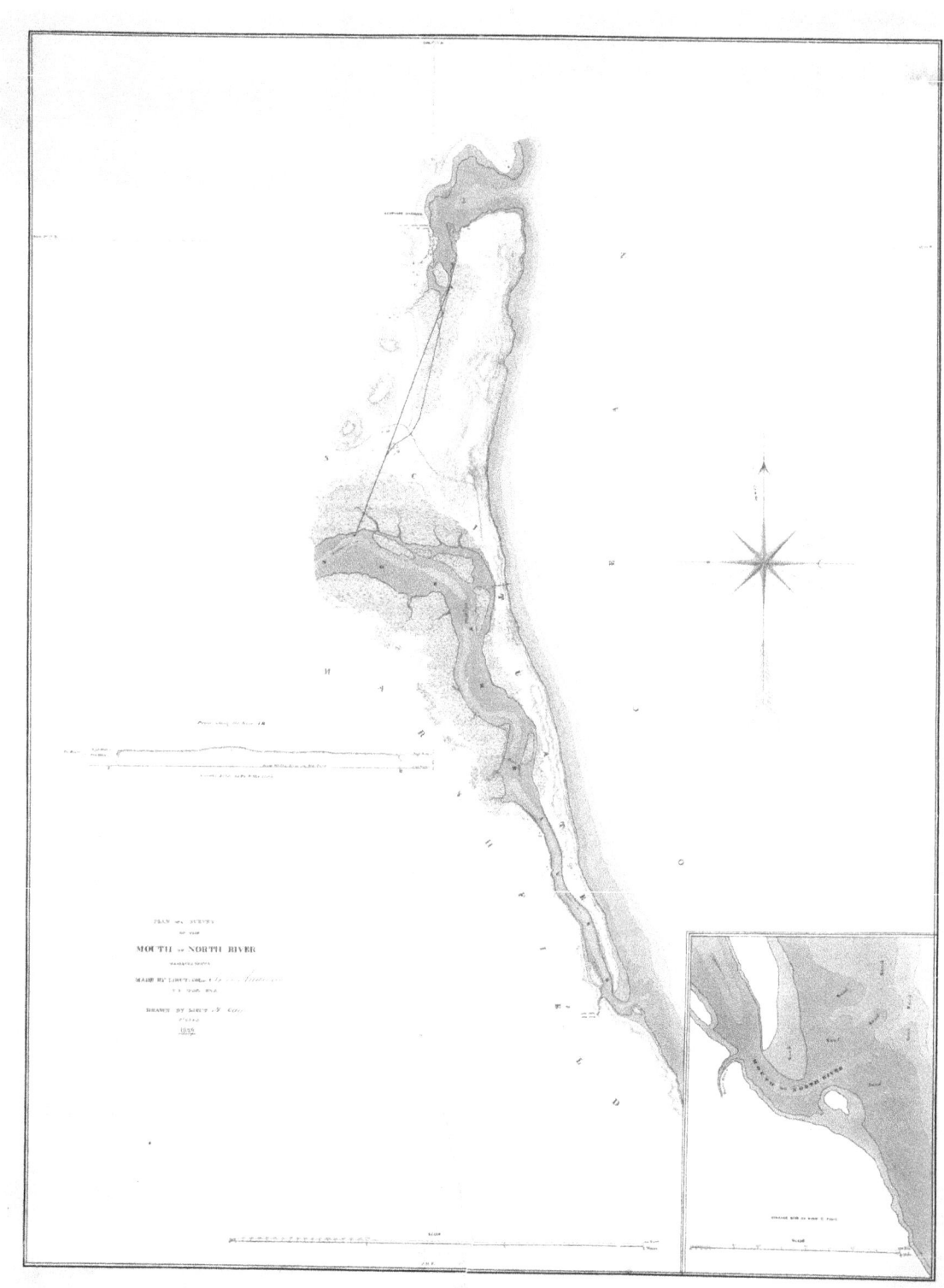

Fig. 45. Lt. Day, under direction of Lt. Col. John Anderson, "Plan of Survey of Mouth of North River," 1829, to accompany 1830 report to Congress. NARA document RG77_CWMF_B_44_01. Shows proposed canal from North River to Scituate Harbor.

Perhaps the recommendations of the 1830 report caused the towns to split. They would later turn to rival proposals – channel cut at Fourth Cliff versus canal to Scituate Harbor. That would stymie legislative action for years, until Congress authorized a survey started in 1852 by the US Army Engineers.

John Quincy Adams was US President from 1825 to 1829. He called for "internal improvements" — federally funded or subsidized infrastructure projects, such as roads, turnpikes, canals, harbors, and navigation improvements. He was defeated for re-election by Andrew Jackson. When the Whig Party emerged in the 1830s, it adopted the drive for such improvements, promising federal support to construct infrastructure and promote economic development. Adams and Webster aligned with the Whigs. Adams served as a member of the US House of Representatives from Massachusetts from 1831 to 1848 (Fig. 46).[227]

Fig. 46. John Quincy Adams, daguerreotype by Mathew Brady, c. 1843–1848. Wikipedia, public domain.

He represented towns along the North River. He appeared to have overwhelming support in Scituate. Over the years, Adams received a number of petitions for federal funding to improve navigability of the North River. (For a detail of an 1831 map showing the river, see Fig. 47.)[228]

On December 21, 1831, he wrote in his diary, "I found an opportunity to present the Petition from sundry inhabitants of Scituate and the neighbouring Towns, for the improvement of North-river; which at my motion was referred to the Committee on internal improvement."[229]

In 1832, Congress passed a bill appropriating $16,283 to improve navigation of the North River. President Jackson did not sign the bill. The *Hingham Gazette*, evidently editorializing as an anti-Jackson paper, published this:

> No one can doubt that the importance of the ship building and navigation upon North River are such as to justify a liberal appropriation .... scarce any thing had been appropriated for improvements of a "public" nature in this vicinity.
>
> Let those who support a President who disapproves of measures admitted to be of "*great public benefit*" continue to shout hosannas to him, if they can. We cannot.[230]

In 1834, a proposal was made for a canal at the mouth of the Taunton River. It would have connected the Taunton River with the Weymouth River, allowing inland navigation between Narragansett Bay and Massachusetts Bay. (The same would have resulted if the canal connected to the North River.) That was long before the navigational shortcut created by the Cape Cod Canal.[231]

Adams was approached about the 1834 proposal:

> Mr Samuel A. Turner of Scituate called upon me this Evening, about the projected Canal at the mouth of Taunton river — A fair spoken man, one year a member of the Senate of Massachusetts, chosen by the Legislature, though a Jackson man, to exclude an Anti-mason.[232]

Adams and Turner would have further meetings.

1839–1841 Federal Petitions

In 1839, Scituate shipbuilders sought Adams' help for federal funding. In his diary entry for October 9, Adams said he rode to Scituate:

> I had promised Mr Samuel Adams Turner of Scituate that I would go and take a farmer's dinner with him this day, and examine the spot where they are desirous of obtaining an appropriation from Congress for the improvement of their harbor ... I then went with Mr Turner in his Chaise about 4 miles farther to the harbour which is low and small — There I met Mr Cumings Jenkins the Inspector of the Port, Captain Ezekiel Jones, Captain of a Revenue Cutter, but upon furlough being out of health Mr John Beal, and a Mr Young inhabitants of the town — We stopped perhaps a quarter of an hour at Mr Jenkins's house and partook of a luncheon with a temperate glass of cold water — We then rode back to Mr Turner's, Mr Jenkins and Captain Jones being of the dinner party — On the way Mr Turner pointed out to me the course where they were desirous of having a Canal opened, to keep the channel of the river sufficiently deep — But there is another project petitioned for by certain inhabitants of Marshfield, which these Gentlemen, particularly Mr Turner thought would be rather

injurious than beneficial to Scituate. Mr Turner gave me a map upon which he marked the line where they wished the canal to run.[233]

Fig. 47. Robbins & Turner 1831 map, detail, showing North River with obstructions at its lower end (right side). This could be the map that Turner marked up with a canal to Scituate harbor. Courtesy of Harvard Map Collection.

The last several lines of Adams diary reveal the rivalry between Scituate and Marshfield over improving the river.

Scituate wanted a canal to Scituate Harbor. In 1802, the town had already required a harbor dam to reserve room for a canal. That was probably where Turner marked the line on the map, although we don't know for sure. That proposed canal would be studied in 1854 by the US Army Corps of Engineers.[234]

Adams continued: "I called twice to visit the Revd. Samuel J. May, a next door neighbour of Mr Turner, but he was gone to Plymouth." (See Fig. 48.)

Rev. May was a well-known abolitionist, prohibitionist, pacifist, and crusader for many causes, including women's rights. He was pastor (1836–1842) of the First Parish Church at what is now Norwell Center. (The Center is at the left side of this detail of Walling's 1857 map, Fig. 49.) He lived about 3/5 of a mile east of the church at the May Elms house (J. Stetson house on map detail).[235]

Fig. 48. "May Elms house where Rev. Samuel J. May, Pastor of First Church 1836–1842 lived." Card. Boston 16, Mass.: Bromley and Company, Inc., c. 1900–1972. Norwell Historical Society, *Digital Commonwealth,*
https://ark.digitalcommonwealth.org/ark:/50959/c534gb15p.

Fig. 49. Walling's 1857 map, detail. S. A. Turner house is in center, below main road, near road going south from main road to Union Bridge (see labels). Samuel May lived in the J. Stetson house, north of main road.

Turner gave Adams a tour of the area. They rode by the house of the late US Supreme Court justice William Cushing. "Mr Turner told me also of Judge Nathan Cushing, and of Doctor Cushing Otis, old acquaintances of mine, and both of whom lived and died at Scituate." Nathan Cushing, like his cousin William, was a justice. He served on the Massachusetts Supreme Judicial Court from 1790 to 1800.[236]

How Adams knew Turner is not clear. It could not have hurt that Turner's middle name was Adams. Turner said he was one of the many descendants of an important first settler in Scituate, Humphrey Turner. Samuel Turner had, by 1831, built a nail mill on the First Herring Brook in Greenbush, and a shingle mill on the east branch of the Second Herring Brook. Turner held a number of public positions in town and served as a state legislator. Clearly, he would have been interested in improving the town's navigable waters.[237]

Adams' diary refers to Turner multiple times. He recommended "Mr Samuel A. Turner of Scituate" for appointment as an annual Visitor at West Point, evidently on the academy's board of overseers. In 1840, not long after Adams visited Turner in Scituate, he met with War Secretary Poinsett to remind him of his recommendation.[238]

Samuel Adams Turner seems to be the S. A. Turner who surveyed the town and co-authored the 1831 map of Scituate with A. Robbins. While there were many Turners in town, he is likely the son of Charles Turner, who authored the 1795 map of Scituate.

Like father, like son? When his 1831 map came out, the town bought 500 copies. That was almost certainly the map that Adams said Turner gave him.[239]

The conflicting proposals of the North River towns had been brewing in 1839. After Adams met with Turner of Scituate, he received members of the Rogers family of Marshfield. It turned out that the Rogers, along with area residents, had earlier petitioned the US Senate (not the House) with a proposal on the North River. It was different from the one he discussed with Turner. On November 14, 1839, Adams wrote:

> Mr Luther Rogers of Marshfield came this morning with his brother Clift Rogers an inhabitant of Quincy with a copy of certain proceedings of delegates from the towns of Scituate, Marshfield, Hanover Hanson and Pembroke, last February, petitioning Congress for a new survey of the North river with a view to removing obstructions and opening a canal for the improvement of the Navigation.[240]

The Marshfield petitioners had bypassed Adams. They petitioned Daniel Webster, Senator from Massachusetts, and resident of Marshfield.

> They sent their petition to Daniel Webster to be presented to the Senate, and sent none to the House — perhaps because it was in substance a Counter petition to the one that I had presented from Scituate, which was before the Committee of Commerce of the House. Nothing was done at the last Session with either and it is apparent that if the two petitions are brought into conflict with each other at the approaching Session; nothing will then be done — Mr Luther Rogers junr left with me a copy of the proceedings of the delegates from the four towns last February; and two maps, one of Scituate of the same impression with that given me by S. A. Turner, and one of Marshfield, Scituate and the adjoining towns, which Mr Rogers said was more accurate — He said they had heard of my visit to Scituate, and viewing that harbour, and the adjoining beach and course of the North river, and they would be glad if I could again go, and view the position of Marshfield. I expressed my regret that this would be impossible before the approaching Session for which it would be necessary for me to take my departure the week after next and he said they had forborne to send me an invitation, under the expectation that I should not be able to come — I said if they proposed to petition again they would do well to forward two copies of it, one to the Senate and the other to the House of Representatives.[241]

How interesting to have two competing maps readily available to support two competing proposals. It is not clear that Marshfield's was more accurate than Scituate's, but it was newer (1838 instead of 1831) and it had compass bearings for its western boundaries.[242]

Also in 1839, in what seems to have been a separate push from those of Scituate and Marshfield, Hanover shipbuilders sought federal funding to improve the North River. John Barry, writing in 1853, and noting that by then the business of building large ships in Hanover had ceased, reported the earlier efforts:

> Several attempts have been made to obtain aid from the National Government, for the improvement of the navigation of the North River; but hitherto, with but little success. In 1839, Col. J. B. Barstow, Joseph S. Bates, and Elijah Barstow, Jr., were chosen a committee to petition for the appropriation of a small sum "for the purpose of removing sand-bars, and cutting a channel for the North River into Massachusetts Bay;" but their prayer was not favorably answered.[243]

In 1840, Marshfield and Pembroke petitioned for a new survey of the river. Adams was again involved, writing:

> Captain Parris of Boston, … came to consult with me upon the projected improvement in removing obstructions from the North river at Scituate concerning which there are before the Committee of Commerce, Counter Memorials, from Scituate, Marshfield, Hanover and Pembroke — Captain Parris appears for the Marshfield and Pembroke people who ask for a New Survey. I advised him to attend at a Meeting of the Committee of Commerce, and told him I would mention him and the subject upon which he is here, to the Chairman of that Committee Edward Curtis, which I did — and I gave to Mr Curtis the two maps of Scituate and Marshfield, which I had received from Mr S. A. Turner, and from the Marshfield and Hanover Memorialists.[244]

Later in 1840, Marshfield residents again approached Adams about improving the river. Adams wrote:

> Mr Rogers of Marshfield, with his Son Dr Rogers came to converse with me concerning the petitions from the towns of Marshfield, Hanover and Pembroke, for a new survey, preliminary to an appropriation for the clearing out of obstructions in North-river — I told him that the petitions had at the last Session of Congress been referred in the House of Representatives to the Committee of Commerce, together with the old Petitions from Scituate for an appropriation to effect the improvement recommended by the report of the former survey.[245]

Adams then made this astute analysis:

> I observed that the petitions were in conflict with each other, and asked if the parties interested could not come to some compromise among themselves, as the effect of which their petitions would not clash with each other — Mr Rogers complained that Mr S. A. Turner, and the people of

> Scituate harbour had not been quite fair, in their exertions to obtain the removal of the obstruction at the precise spot most favourable to them, who in point of numbers bore no proportion to those who wished for the new survey; but he did not encourage any expectation that the parties could come to any agreement respecting their opposite petitions — He expressed a wish that I would go and visit them at Marshfield, for which I fear I shall not be able to find time this autumn; and he requested me ask Mr Webster for perusal of the papers which they sent to him with their Petitions last winter, which I promised to do.[246]

It could not have been easy to represent towns with opposing petitions.

In 1841, Marshfield shipbuilders continued to lobby for federal funding to cut through the bar at the mouth of the river, or, in historian Briggs' words, "better still, to make a new mouth by cutting through" the shingle beach between Third Cliff and Fourth Cliff. It seems a canal through Scituate was not part of their proposal.[247]

Once again, the Marshfield shipbuilders invited Adams to visit Marshfield and see the place of their proposal. This time, he agreed. On October 11, 1841, Adams' diary reports the approach:

> One of the applications which I received last Friday was from Watterman Thomas, Bourne Thomas, Luther Rogers, Charles W. Macomber, Daniel Phillips, Edward P. Little, and John Tilden, a committee from the town of Marshfield for the improvement of North River. Their invitation is, that I would visit Marshfield and, with many of their townsmen, go to the spot where they wish to operate; and they specially desire this on account of my visit two years ago to Scituate. They further propose to me to meet their citizens in some house of public worship during my visit to Marshfield, for the interchangement of friendly feelings, and that their children may have an opportunity to look upon the man whose name is so closely connected with the honor and prosperity of their country. This is a matter of public business, interesting extensively to the inhabitants of several towns in the Twelfth Congressional District, and which of course forbids my declining the invitation to visit the spot, and, being there, I cannot decently refuse to go with them to the meeting-house. But there is competition between Marshfield and Scituate for the location of the canal. A speech in the meeting-house will be indispensable; and then what town in the district will not be entitled to a visit, a convocation in the meeting-house, and a speech?[248]

Leave it to Adams, an astute politician, to be aware of this competition between Marshfield and Scituate, and to fret about constituents' demands on his time. At the same time, he was concerned with national issues of the new country.

The Marshfield shipbuilders' proposal was a good example of the national issues at the time (and perhaps now). How much should the federal government get involved in state and local matters? Was the proposal "one that may most properly become an item of national expense"? How much power and influence should the federal government have? The North River was not clearly local — its importance crossed town lines and its ships crossed the world's seas. However, the industry itself did not cross state lines, and its proposed improvements were not necessarily of national significance. Ultimately, it would fall to Massachusetts, not the federal government, to resolve North River proposals. But not without help from the United States Engineer Department, and later, the US Army Corps of Engineers.[249]

Within weeks after the Marshfield shipbuilders' invitation, Adams visited the area. On October 28, 1841, Adams came "to visit Hanover, Scituate, Pembroke, and Marshfield, and the mouth of North River," to learn facts and data about these improvements, according to Briggs' book. Adams and others sailed from Little's Bridge to the beach between Third Cliff and Fourth Cliff, then sailed down Humarock to the mouth of the river. The book quotes a diary by the architect Luther Briggs, which he says was the only written account found of the visit.[250]

But Adams kept a diary, too. That night, Adams described his visit in his diary for October 28, 1841:

> Precisely at half past five this morning, Mr Clift Rogers was at my door with a horse and Chaise — I was ready waiting for him, step'd in and he drove me in two hours and a quarter to the house of Daniel Phillips Postmaster at North Marshfield. ... Mr Phillips is one of the Committee of the inhabitants of Marshfield, who had given me this invitation — I found at his house several gentlemen from the adjoining towns, and among them Mr Samuel J. May the minister of a Congregational Church at Situate. ... we rode about two miles farther to the house of Mr Luther Rogers who keeps an Inn — Here I met several other members of the Committee, and persons from the adjoining towns of Pembroke and Hanover — I rode with Mr Luther Rogers down to a Bridge, where we embarked in a Gondola or Scow in which we were tow'd by one sail boat and one row boat about a mile down towards the mouth of the North river. We landed on the Situate beach, part of which is a high bluff bearing upland grass and part a ridge of loose stones like those on Cohasset Beach, and over which in every North-eastern storm the surf rushes into the river — It lodges also settlements of sand in the bed of the river, and makes shoals, which stretch downwards (the channel of the river), and carry its mouth more and more Southerly. — We saw two new vessels fast bedded in the sands of shoals made by storms of the last winter, and it is apparent that ship-building must hereafter cease to be an occupation for the People of Marshfield — We returned to a temperance dinner at the house of Luther Rogers — Mr and

> Mrs Seth Sprague were there from Duxbury. Dr. Anthony Collamore from Pembroke Captain Little 87 years of age and sundry others were there.[251]

It is not clear what happened next in Congress, but it did not approve the Marshfield shipbuilders' proposal. Meanwhile, they were pursuing state help.

1842–1844 State Petitions

By 1842, shipbuilders and others pursued state approval to improve the North River by cutting a new sea channel between Third Cliff and Fourth Cliff. Their petitions to the legislature came from Pembroke, Hanover, East Bridgewater, and Marshfield, but not Scituate. The petitions were opposed by the "remonstrance of Charles W. Macomber and 140 other, legal voters of the town of Marshfield." A joint committee of the House and Senate referred the petitions in February to a committee, which completed its report after hearings and a site visit in July.[252]

The petitions said, "That owing to sand-bars and shoals, which are now found near the mouth of the river, ship-building and navigation have become nearly abandoned, and it is feared will be entirely so, unless these obstructions can be removed."[253]

The committee met in 1842 at the house of Luther Rogers. This was the same place as the meeting with John Quincy Adams the previous October, on the same subject. According to Briggs, Rogers built a few vessels, including one in 1819 near his house in East Marshfield village. "Farming was rather dull, and Mr. Rogers found that he could make more by building vessels on his farm than in raising vegetables. He took this vessel to the river at Little's Bridge, in the winter time, on sleds, and launched her on the ice." The 1838 map of Marshfield shows an "L. Rogers Wharf" across from White's Ferry, on the last few miles of the North River before it reached the sea.[254]

White's Ferry was the site of Marshfield's first shipyard, in 1705, although shipbuilding did not flourish there until later. It eventually handled the rigging of all North River shipyard production. Thus, Marshfield had a big stake in keeping the shipbuilding industry alive. Residents would have been concerned with Scituate's proposal to build a canal running north from the river without removing the shoals at the old mouth. That could hurt Marshfield's business at this stretch of the river. (Perhaps the same could be said about a channel between Third Cliff and Fourth Cliff, as was also proposed.)[255]

The 1842 meeting could have been a last gasp for the White's Ferry shipyard, as indicated by the dates (1705–1839) on this sign (Fig. 50).

Fig. 50. Sign memorializing White's Ferry Shipyard. Photo August 15, 2024.

At the 1842 meeting, the petitioners described the quantity of ships built there, and the number of people employed or associated with their construction. The remonstrants opposed, arguing, among other things, that the proposed channel could be filled up quickly by the sea, and "That the time for ship-building here had passed by; that very little timber was now to be found in this vicinity; that many of the most enterprising ship-builders formerly residing here, had recently established ship-yards along the coast, where greater facilities were afforded them ...."[256]

The remonstrants offered a proto-ecological objection, that the channel:

> would cause great destruction to, or diminution in, the value of property; that the lands near the proposed mouth would be covered with sand, gravel, &c. thrown up by the action of the sea; that the tide would rise much higher inside the beach, and thus many low lands bordering upon the marsh, now cultivated for fields, or producing valuable English grass, would become salt marsh and rendered of little value.[257]

We discuss later the effect of the 1898 storm that opened the channel. For now, it is worth noting that after the storm, the tide did rise, about 20 inches; the salt marsh seemed to survive and recover; and the cultivated fields were not flooded and not rendered "of little value." However, these were excellent questions to raise.

The 1843 report said that the beach north of Fourth Cliff, at the proposed channel, was 240 feet wide. The report had an annex from Calvin Brown, Assistant Engineer, evidently from the US Army Corps of Engineers, who had been brought in by Marshfield. He surveyed the river and beach, along with the height of their waters. At the beach, he reported:

> high water outside, which occurred some time before high tide in the river, was found to be about one foot above the level of the base, while high water in the river was about eight inches below the base, making the whole difference between high water inside and high water outside about twenty inches.[258]

This was a fateful measurement.

The committee found that the likelihood of the ocean filling in the proposed cut was improbable, and could be deterred by building a breakwater. They dismissed the 1830 report recommending a canal through a marsh to Scituate Harbor as not finding "much favor, either with petitioners or remonstrants," who did not include any representatives from Scituate. The committee added:

> A single fact may be sufficient to establish the doubtful character of this undertaking [a canal to Scituate Harbor]. It was in evidence before the committee, that the sea is regularly making encroachments upon this marsh, and that, during a late storm, a small creek, running in a line over which the proposed canal would pass, was filled up with sand and gravel, carried over the beach by the force of the sea.[259]

In other words, the committee supported the petitioners, favoring Marshfield's position. It recommended that the legislature authorize the cut, subject to "reasonable indemnification to those persons whose property may be injuriously affected by such improvement."[260]

The committee's report was in January 1843, almost a year after the legislature referred the matter to the committee. In February 1843, Peleg Ford (born 1786 in Marshfield, died 1873 in Hingham) and 91 other residents of South Scituate filed petitions with the legislature, again seeking a new channel for the river through the beach near the northerly end of Fourth Cliff.[261]

The legislature did not authorize the cut. Later in 1843, the state:

decided against the proposal, concluding that such a cut would damage the meadows upstream. Despite the state's rejection of their plea, proponents of the cut set out one night with picks, shovels, hoes, and axes, driving ox and horse teams, using only dim lanterns to light their way.

Working through the night, they managed to dig all the way across the beach, only to discover a rock-hard meadow bank beneath the sand, dense enough to prevent the completion of their mission. Water flowed through the newly-dug channel temporarily, but the beach soon filled back in.[262]

In January 1844, Isaiah Rogers petitioned the legislature, again in favor of Marshfield's proposed improvements.[263]

Isaiah Rogers (1800–1869) was born in Marshfield, son of Isaac Rogers, a farmer and shipwright. He became a nationally renowned architect. His designs in Boston included the Tremont House (1829–1895), the first hotel with indoor plumbing, and the Merchants Exchange (1842–1890) on State Street. He also designed the Astor House (1836–1926) in New York City. His 1844 petition addressed state legislators who may have been residing at the Tremont House, just steps from the Massachusetts State House.[264]

Rogers' report had a beautiful description of the river and its historical shipbuilding activities. He disputed that a shortage of trees to build ships was an obstacle, saying, "were the navigation of the river unobstructed, the facilities here appear equal to almost any other situation for the continued prosecution of this business."[265]

Rogers' report imagined improved fishing if the proposal were adopted:

> there is every reason to believe that a great increase of the fishing in the river would take place from what now exists, there evidently having been a great falling off of the elwives and shad fishing from former years, when the mouth of the river was unobstructed, depriving the inhabitants, in a great measure, of that kind of fish. In years past the aid of the Legislature has been solicited, and it has passed laws to protect the shad and elwives in the North River, all of which was very well; but protection is of little use if the river is so obstructed at its mouth as to prevent the fish coming into the river in any quantities, which now is the case. If it is of sufficient importance to legislate to preserve and protect fish in a river, it would seem to be equally so to facilitate their getting into it.[266]

Rogers' report concluded that the proposal:

> would not only re-open a port, that would contribute as it once did largely to the commercial prosperity and activity of this vicinity; but one that from its greatly increased facilities of entrance, might surpass the importance of

this river in its most prosperous days. In fact, there can be no doubt that the spacious estuary called by Deane the "New Harbor" or "Fourth Cliff Bay," would with such an entrance as may be reasonably expected from the proposed undertaking, form a harbor of no inferior convenience and capacity, and indeed vastly superior to Scituate harbor, or any other in the immediate vicinity.[267]

Eloquent, but unsuccessful.

The next significant event would not occur until 1852. By then, John Quincy Adams (1767–1848) was no longer on the scene to shepherd a solution.

1852 Plan of Harbor and Canal

We explore below an overlooked plan (map) from 1852 of the North River's eastern course, with a proposed canal connecting the river with Scituate Harbor (Fig. 51 and Fig. 52.). The plan is relevant to histories of North River fishing, salt marsh haying, and gundalow piloting, all described elsewhere in this book.

By 1852, the North River was almost no longer navigable. This was a big problem for the many shipyards along the river, which had been building ships since the 1600s. The meandering river had narrowed even more, particularly on the lower part of the river, with its many obstructions and shoals, as it headed out to the sea. This limited the size of ships that could be built and transported down the river. In addition, the nearby forests of white oak had long ago been turned into ships, and the supply depleted.[268]

Partly as a result of these changes, the centers of shipbuilding had moved from the North River, Duxbury, and Scituate Harbor to premier places like East Boston and New York. That is where larger ships, and swifter ones like the clipper ships, were being built. For example, after Sylvanus Smith built ships on the North River, in 1854 he moved with his family from Pembroke to East Boston, where he became a leading shipbuilder, rivaling the famed Donald McKay.[269]

At the same time, the fishing industry at Scituate Harbor had dwindled. Thirty years before, the harbor held 70 vessels, but now there were only a handful. The harbor was full of mud, marsh, islands, and shallow water.[270]

Shipbuilders had deplored the sorry state of these waters for years. In 1851, they clamored once more for improvements.

Tilden Ames of Marshfield, with ancient roots there, lobbied for navigational improvements to the North River. He went to Washington to present a petition from five or six towns praying for an appropriation for the improvements. Ames contacted his friend Daniel Webster, Secretary of State. Webster put in a good word in a letter to Senator Hamlin: "I am quite well acquainted with the merits of this application, as the mouth of the North River is but six or seven miles from my own residence; & I can speak with entire confidence of the utility of what is proposed."[271]

Congress authorized $1,000 for a survey, which the US Army Corps of Engineers conducted. Z. B. Tower, Brevet Major of Engineers, prepared a skilled and detailed plan that highlighted these problems.

I recently found this plan, and discuss it below. No other such detailed plan appears to exist for this time period. It is a telling and stark illustration of navigational difficulties on the North River.[272]

This plan of 1852 shows a proposed canal between the North River and Scituate Harbor, and proposed harbor improvements (Fig. 51 and Fig. 52). Features include, north to south, Scituate Harbor and First, Second, Third, and Fourth Cliffs (labeled "Bluff No. 1," etc. on the plan).

A canal or cut would shorten the trip from North River shipyards to the ocean, avoid shoals, and allow shipyards to build and transport larger ships.

In Scituate Harbor, the plan notes "1 ft. water at extreme low tide" with a channel of 5 ft. "deepest water." There is a dock at First Cliff [Stage Beach?], and two likely mill dams holding streams entering the harbor. The plan describes much of the harbor as "Mud Flats." The later 1854 report recommended dredging the harbor.

Some labels on the plan are too small to read on the copies below. They are labeled and described below next to their approximate locations on the plan.

The 1852 plan is worth a close look. The online copy provides incredible detail. The proposed canal, for example, appears narrow on the plan but scales up to somewhere between 66 and 165 feet wide in real life. That is in line with the 1854 report's proposal of a canal 130 feet wide.

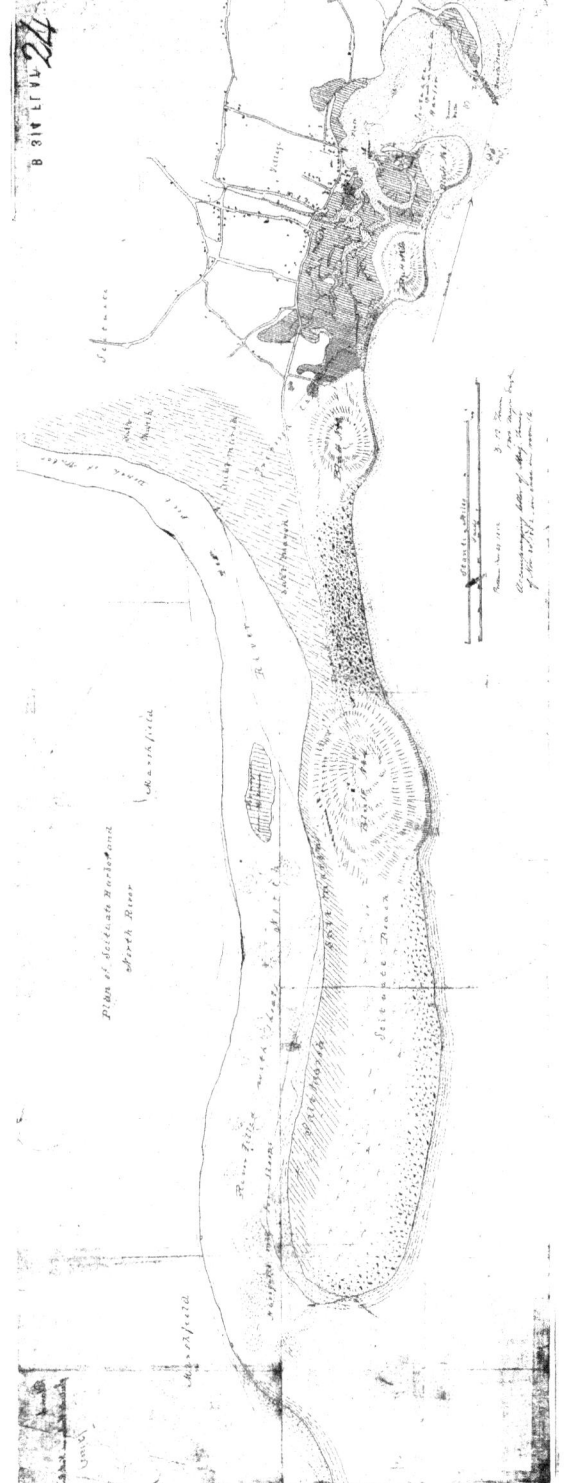

Fig. 51. [Maj.] Z. B. Tower, "Plan of Scituate Harbor and North River," (Portland [ME?]: [Army Corps of Engineers]), November 17, 1852, National Archive Catalog, NAID: 170100305, Local ID: 77-CWMF-B-314, https://catalog.archives.gov/id/170100305. Top is approximately north. On scale, top line represents 1 mile and bottom line 2,000 yards. The online version has more detail. Thanks to John Roman for editing this version.

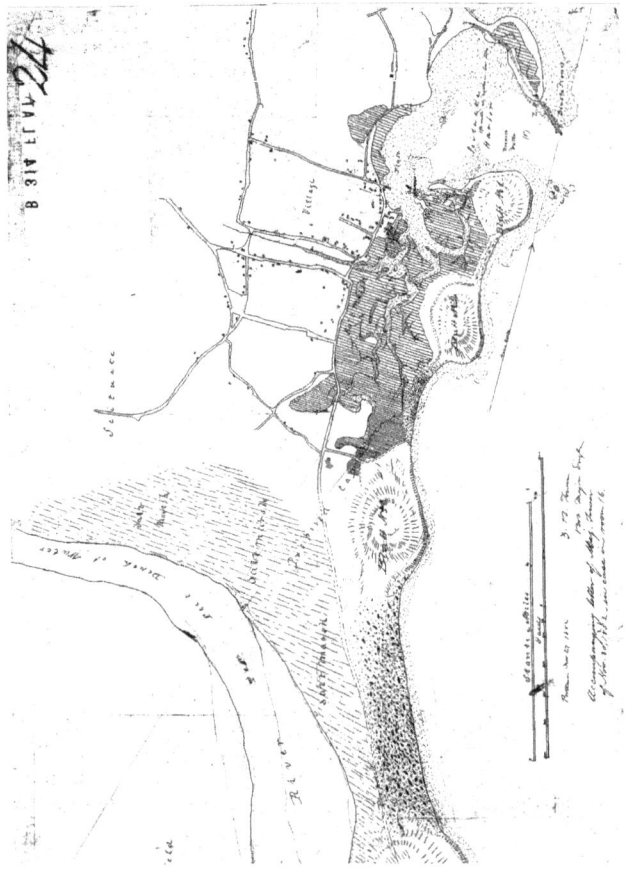

← In Scituate Harbor, the plan notes "1 ft. water at extreme low tide" with a channel of 5 ft. "deepest water" and "Mud Flats."

← Proposed canal (faint diagonal lines)

← South of Third Cliff, at North River, the plan notes, "Ten Feet Depth of Water."

← The beach between Third Cliff and Fourth Cliff (Humarock) is called "High Beach Formed of Beach Stones." The plan mentions but does not draw a "Proposed cut" here.

Fig. 52. [Maj.] Z. B. Tower, "Plan of Scituate Harbor and North River," detail of top of plan.

The 1852 plan, evidently drawn in ink, seems to use a light red pencil to sketch the proposed canal, as well as the proposed breakwater in the harbor. (Red pencil also marks true North.) The straight-line canal ends near the creek behind Peggotty Beach. Then the red pencil over-writes the very last part to steer the canal into that creek, which leads to Scituate Harbor. It appears the author was still tinkering with this plan.

As accurate and interesting as the plan is, it has flaws. First, it was just a plan or sketch for the project. It does not seem to have surveyor reference points. The later report needed to cover practical matters, such as exactly where the canal would go, how deep would it be, how much dredging was needed in the harbor, cost estimates, and the pros and cons of the overall plan. Further, the 1852 plan does not show the Driftway, established in the early 1600s, leading generally east–west, to and across Third Cliff. It shows only a road that became the north end of Gilson Road, and a possible path along the cliff's North River side. It does not show the Third Cliff farms of Michael Welch and Samuel Turner, along the path of the canal. Those farms were flooded in the great Minot's gale of April 1851.[273]

In addition, the cliffs are labeled "bluffs," accurately. But locally they were always called "cliffs" (and numbered) since the early 1630s. Evidently, the plan's author was from out of town. The plan is dated at Portland, probably in Maine, probably an office of the US Army Corps of Engineers. Under Tower's name is Bvt. [Brevet] Major Eng'r, and a note in red in different handwriting, "Accompanying letter of Maj. Tower of Nov. 30, 1852 – in case in room 16."[274]

Despite its shortcomings, Tower's plan is skilled and helpful in illustrating history. We are fortunate that it survived.

The plan has useful details of wetlands in Scituate, although it covers only part of the town. It shows salt marshes around the river about 5 ½ miles long, and about 1/5 of a mile wide, except at Third Cliff where, for about a mile, the marshes expand up to 2/5 of a mile wide. That results in about 1.2 square miles, or 768 acres of salt marsh. In addition, around Scituate Harbor, the plan shows salt marshes about 1 mile long and about 2/5 of a mile wide, resulting in about 0.2 square miles or 128 acres of salt marsh. This does not include marshland north of Scituate Harbor, such as that around Musquashcut Pond and its brook, or marshes farther upstream on the North River.[275]

The 1852 plan's roughly 768 acres was a big chunk of the North River's salt marshes. Later plans in the 1870s to improve the marshes were more expansive. They covered some 2,338 to 3,000 acres, as discussed below.

1854 Report

Tower's 1852 plan was a preliminary version of the survey for which Congress appropriated $1,000 in 1852. In late 1853, J. G. Barnard, Brevet Major of Engineers, reported that the survey was originally assigned to Major Tower and "devolved on me in June, and we executed in the months of July and August." His letter was attached to an 1854 report to the House of Representatives, "A report of a survey of Scituate harbor and North river."[276]

The 1854 report favored the proposed canal to Scituate Harbor. "There is but one method by which the navigation of this river can be restored, viz: by connecting it by a canal with the harbor of Scituate." That would speedily close up the present outlet of the river. The report also concluded that the proposed cut between Third and Fourth Cliffs would not help much for navigability and would likely be filled in by the ocean's wash over the beach. The report also said,

> A very great anxiety is felt by the citizens of Marshfield and Scituate to have something done to improve the navigation of the river and the capacity of the harbor, but unfortunately they do not agree upon any single project,

and any plan to unite the two objects does not meet with favor from a portion of the citizens of the former place. I will not say that those opposed to the plan of connecting the river and harbor by a canal are the most numerous; I have reason to believe they are not; but they have the advantage of being the most clamorous and vociferous in their objections.[277]

The proposed cut and the proposed canal never happened, although they were again considered in 1870, discussed below. The 1854 report's proposed improvements to the harbor did not happen until the 1880s.[278]

The January 20, 1854, report may have spurred proponents into further action.

1850s Pushes to Improving the River

Shipbuilders and others with interests along the North River worked collectively in the 1850s to improve the river. An example was a June 18, 1854, written agreement among subscribers to pay for hiring a dredge ("expenses of the Excavator"). In this and other simple agreements and ledgers, they covered the expenses of dredging the river, including associated costs for lumber, coal, and feeding workers. One account included 58 cents for 5 ¾ pounds of bacon and 36 cents for three dozen eggs.[279]

The surviving documents have names of subscribers and their contributions. More than 50 people contributed to various subscriptions. Among them were prominent shipbuilders.

Their work grew more serious. Here is an April 29, 1858, agreement that contemplated a cut between Third Cliff and Fourth Cliff:

> We the undersigned agree to pay the sum set against our names for the purpose of towing the Government Dredge from & to the Navy yard at Charlestown, and also the expense which may be incurred while digging a channel through Scituate Beach [the beach at Humarock.].[280]

William "Cap'n Bill" Vinal suggested that they worked at this project all summer, March to October of 1858. It does not appear that they achieved their purpose. Soon, the Navy, and the country, would be occupied with the Civil War.[281]

Fourth Cliff House

Before tourism blossomed in the North River valley, there were boarding houses to accommodate visitors. This was before the railroad came to the South Shore in 1871, and before hotels such as Eaton's Hotel in Scituate, and before the Webster House in Marshfield (discussed in the section on 1870s–1880s Developments).

Fourth Cliff had a boarding house catering to summer visitors. On top of the cliff, it was described as "a lone two-story building and an old barn [that] were for a long time the only structures to be seen. This was the Fourth Cliff House, one of the first summer boarding houses on the South Shore," according to historian Joseph Foster Merritt.[282]

> The view across the North River marshes was very beautiful and the place could be, at that time, reached by a wagon road that ran along the inside edge of the beach, on the border of the meadow. The storms of winter often carried this away and it had to be frequently renewed. Later in the season when the shore birds came, the house was filled with gunners for several weeks.
>
> An early settler on the cliff was John Tilden and several generations of the family made their home there. The last house was built by a John Tilden about 1828.
>
> The Howards of Hanover ran the place for a few years and were followed by Mr. and Mrs. William O. Merritt who came in 1879 and stayed thirteen years. The house was burned in 1902.[283]

This is worth expanding on.

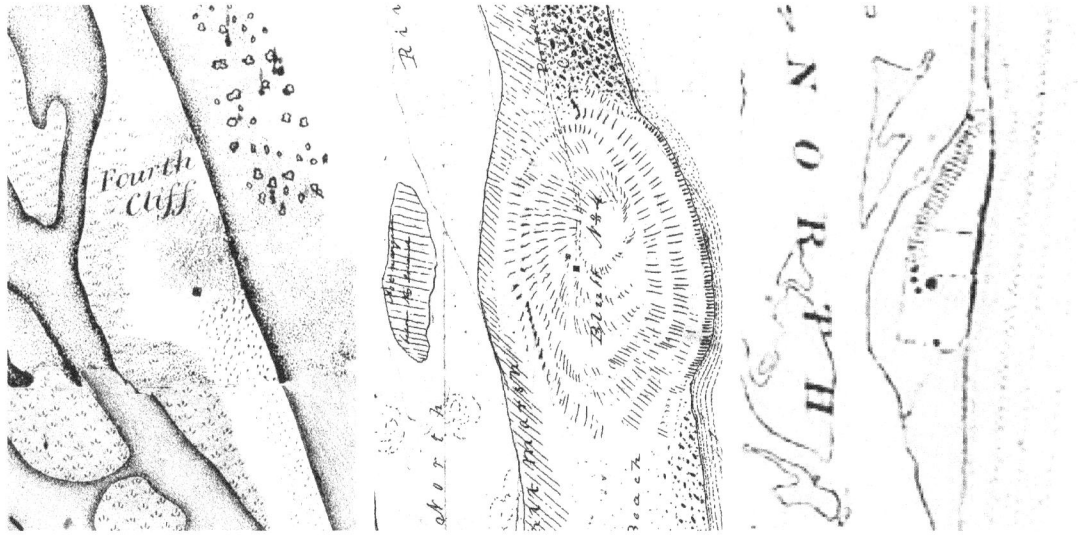

Fig. 53. 1831 Map, Robbins & Turner, detail of 4th Cliff

Fig. 54. 1852 Sketch, Z. B. Tower, detail of 4th Cliff

Fig. 55. 1877 US Coast Survey, detail of 4th Cliff

Maps in 1831, 1852, and 1877 show a lone house on Fourth Cliff, probably the eventual Fourth Cliff House. Map details are shown (Fig. 53, Fig. 54, and Fig. 55), with a small black square or dot indicating a house. Later photos show the beach between Third Cliff and Fourth Cliff, skirting the marshes of the North River. The beach had a wagon road providing access to the Fourth Cliff House.[284]

Tracing title to the property back to 1850, it appears a John Tilden acquired this Fourth Cliff property that year, and it included a "cart way over said premises to the adjoining Marshes." This was probably part of the way leading across the beach over to Third Cliff.[285]

In 1859, a newspaper correspondent rambled around the area. He wrote:

> We pursued our course beneath the Third Cliff, across a beach that seemed almost without end, and eventually arrived at the isolated residence of Capt. John Tilden. His kind lady, taking pity upon our weariness, invited us in to partake of a lunch, which invitation we thankfully accepted. The prospect from this point is not at all mean. Across the river rise the Highlands of Marshfield, covered principally with a hearty growth of timber, and far up the river you notice Little's Bridge. Capt. Tilden built this house some years ago, upon the Fourth Cliff, for the accommodation of summer boarders. Its doors are often opened to the shipwrecked mariner, affording comforts not to be found in the rudely built charity house [the hut of refuge of the Massachusetts Humane Society], situated not far to the southward.
>
> At the house of Samuel H. Turner, ... [w]e also learned that some years since, the course for a canal was surveyed, through the marsh, inside the Cliffs, from North River to the harbor, but that a number who are *bound* to oppose all schemes for the improvement of Scituate, by some means hindered the further advancement thereof.[286]

Years after this ramble, the Tilden family seemed ready to sell out. In 1872, they sold their 30 acres at Fourth Cliff for $8,000 and took back a mortgage for $4,000. The mortgage amount plus 7% annual interest was due in five years. The buyer defaulted. Tilden then foreclosed on the mortgage and sold the property in 1877 for $4,500. From there, the history of the property is described above in Merritt's book. Adding to that, an 1894 directory listed a George Hatch as operating a boarding house on Fourth Cliff.[287]

Perhaps they encountered the financial problems of the 1870s discussed below.

The *Helen M. Foster*, and Norwell History

In 1849, the town of South Scituate split off from Scituate. South Scituate was later renamed Norwell. The town borders on the North River and abounds with sites of former shipyards. They play a big part in the town's history.

As suggested in the 1854 report to Congress, by that time the shipbuilding industry on the North River had come to an end. This was only confirmed in the 1870 report, discussed below.

While that 1870 report was being prepared, however, Joseph Merritt was building one last ship of any size, though it was on the small side. "In 1871, with more than one thousand ships having been built, the last vessel, the 90-ton *Helen M. Foster*, was launched from Chittenden Landing." Or 65 tons, according to Merritt's son. Either way, she was much smaller than the largest vessel built on the river, the *Mount Vernon*, built in 1812, at nearly 500 tons.[288]

Whatever the size, in 1871, "As the vessel slid into the water she was christened Helen M. Foster after the sister of one of the owners, and the wife of Mr. Merritt, the builder." Helen came from a long line of Fosters who built ships on the North River. A year after the launch, Helen and Joseph's son was born, Joseph Foster Merritt (1872–1944). He would grow up to become a town official, first president of the Norwell Historical Society, "Norwell's Historian," and author of two books on local history: 1928's *Old Time Anecdotes of the North River*, and 1938's *A Narrative History of South Scituate–Norwell, Massachusetts*. The 1938 book (from which the above quote is taken) told the story of the *Helen M. Foster*, built by his father and named for his mother. It also had a photo of the ship's 1871 launch.[289]

The 1871 launch attracted a large crowd. It was captured by local photographer James H. Williams of River Street in Norwell (Fig. 56). His 1871 photograph appeared in Briggs' 1889 *History of Shipbuilding on North River*. A version appeared in Merritt's 1938 book. In the Briggs version, the women with parasols were close to the center (but on the right in Merritt's version), the American flag appeared more clearly than in Merritt's version, and a photo of the ship's builder Joseph Merritt was inserted. Both versions were rectangular.[290]

These photos are old and enduring. They were taken not long after Mathew Brady's famous photos of the Civil War. They were taken in the same year as photos of Yellowstone by William Henry Jackson, and other less-notable photographers, that led Congress to establish the first national park.[291]

Fig. 56. Launch of Helen M. Foster, 1871. Photo by James H. Williams. Courtesy of Archives of Norwell Historical Society.

On the back of one copy of the photo was a listing of some people at the launching. As discussed below in more detail, the names were typed up (Fig. 57), probably many years after the launch.

The list had numbered entries for 8 people on board, and at least 14 standing on the ground around the ship, including:

- #5 Abel Vinal, Captain of the ship, "large man looking at world," and
- #13 Helen M. Foster, third from left in the group of four women in the front and center of the photo, with a light colored hat.

The list is not a complete list of everyone at the launching. However, the names listed include family names that resound in the history of Norwell: Briggs, Cushing, Sparrell, Stetson, Sylvester, Torrey, and Turner.

A close examination of the photo might conclude there were at least 80 people on board, and about 119 alongside the ship, plus a horse (far right). That was a lot, for a town of 1,661.[292]

```
          Written on back of original photograph of
                Launching of the Helen M. Foster
                           On Board
   1. In stern John Turner
   2. E. A. Turner against flag staff
   3. Willard Torry, Frank and Walter half way between
   4. E. J. Fogg man amidships
   5. Lizzie Torrey directly in front of 4
   6. Mary Louisa Foster 4th right of 5
   7. Tom Pinson large
   8. Elnathan Cushing near stern, tall hat, short
         sleeves
                           On Ground
   1. Charles Merritt 1st man at extreme left
   2. Priscilla Stetson
   3. Melvin Stetson 2nd from 2
   4. Geo. Ed Jacobs with tall hat
   5. Capt. Abel Vinal large man looking at world
   6. .Chas. Sylvester below the Torreys at right
   7. Alfred Pinson with folded arms at right
   8. Frank Brooks left of 7 with light coat
   9. J.C. Nash and wife left of 8 sitting on rocks
         or lumber
  10. 2 smaller girls beside them Mary Nash and Mary
         Sparrell
  11. 2 larger girls Carrie and Sarah Briggs
  12. 2 girls near fence Lucy Nash and Jennie Burrage
  13. Mary Ann Turner (1) Martha Torrey (2) Helen M.
  14. Foster (3) Mercy Corthell (Holding Henry) 4
```

Fig. 57. List of people in 1871 photo (undated). Courtesy of Archives of Norwell Historical Society.

The Ship

The *Helen M. Foster* was a fishing schooner built of oak. After launching, moving the ship down the river from the Chittenden Yard to the ocean took five days. This "demonstrated the difficulties of building on the North River." The ship, unrigged, with a draft of 10 feet, had to be hauled by another boat, at high tides, "and at Humarock it was so shallow that it had to be keeled over on her side so she wouldn't draw as much water in the shallow current."[293]

One account said the ship was not a financial success:

> After being rigged and outfitted at East Boston, she [the ship] made several trips for her owners, part of the time under the command of Capt. William Greeley of Hingham, and partly under Capt. Abel Vinal of Scituate, but was not a financial success and in 1879 she was sold.[294]

Another account, however, said the ship was "most successful." The ship was designed by D. J. Lawlor and was built from a model, one of a number he donated to the Smithsonian Institution. The Smithsonian had a detailed description: "*Dimensions of vessel.* – Length between perpendiculars, 72 feet; beam, 20 feet; depth, 7 feet. Scale of model, one-half inch equals 1 foot." The Smithsonian later said the model was "made by Dennison J. Lawlor of Chelsea, Massachusetts. This schooner, intended for the market fishery out of Boston, was of somewhat shallower draught, than was usual in the Lawlor-designed schooners, being generally similar to the extreme clipper fishing schooners of the 1870's. Notable for her swift sailing and ability to carry sail, the *Foster* was a most successful vessel."[295]

Helen M. (Foster) Merritt (1837–1910), the ship's namesake, and her son, Joseph Foster Merritt (1872–1944), the author of the 1938 history of Norwell, are buried in the First Parish Cemetery in Norwell center.[296]

Fig. 58. Helen Foster. Courtesy of Norwell Historical Society, Foster family album.

Fig. 59. Helen Foster Merritt. Courtesy of Norwell Historical Society.

The List, Discovered

Many years later, a woman named Persis discovered (or rediscovered) a typed list of many people shown in the 1871 photo of the launching of the *Helen M. Foster*. In a note to Jeanne (probably Jeanne Garside), she said, "When I opened Merritt's [1938] book … three copies of the enclosed fell out. I'm sending you one, Emily one & keeping one. I haven't tried to match names with people yet but will later."[297]

The typed list that fell out is the one copied above.

Persis was almost certainly Persis Coons (1909–1988). She and her husband Quentin (1903–1984) were deeply involved in the history of Norwell. Persis, a student at Simmons College, and Quentin, a minister's son and a graduate of Harvard and Harvard's School of Business Administration, were married in 1928.[298] They evidently moved to Norwell in 1942.[299] They lived in a historic house on Meadow Farm Way, close to the North River and near its former shipyards.[300]

Quentin was a businessperson, and later a professor at Northeastern University. He was president of the Norwell Historical Society from 1967 to 1969. Past presidents included Joseph Foster Merritt, author of *Old Time Anecdotes of the North River* (1928) and *A Narrative History of South Scituate–Norwell*, (1938), and the son of the shipbuilder. Another past president was William Gould Vinal (1881–1976). "Cap'n Bill" Vinal was a naturalist, nature educator, professor at what became the University of Massachusetts at Amherst, and a prolific author, including the booklet *Salt Haying in the North River Valley (1648–1898)* (1953).[301]

Persis, who discovered (or rediscovered) the list of persons at the ship launching, was a trustee (1968–1971) of the Society for the Preservation of New England Antiquities (now Historic New England).[302]

Both Quentin and Persis contributed to the 1976 town report in America's bicentennial year. It "was prepared to give a feel for the history of our town," and it contained many historic photos, including those of many old milldams.[303]

The Provenance

To get a good copy of the 1871 launch photo, I sent requests to a number of people. Janet Watson, Archivist of the Norwell Historical Society, sent me a copy. Not only that, she found the list of people in the photo. And then a handwritten note, undated, which establishes the origin of the list:

> Given [to] Quentin [Coons]
>
> From Allen Lester
>
> Named on the back of what Mr. and Mrs. Joseph Foster Merritt, Jr. of Florida say is an original, faded photo of the launching of the "Helen M. Foster" recently found in a drawer.[304]

As Janet summarized,

Putting all the clues together I think this is the story. Allen Lester got the list from Joseph Foster Merritt Jr, the grandson of Joseph Merritt and Helen Foster Merritt. Joseph found it written on the back of an original photo of the launching in a desk drawer in his home in Florida.

Allen sends the list in an envelope with a note to Quentin Coons who is a local historian in Norwell. Quentin sticks it in his Joseph Merritt Sr. "History of Norwell" and forgets about it. Sometime later Quentin's wife Persis opens the book and the envelope falls out. She sends it to Jeanne Garside of the Norwell Historical Society probably some time in the 1980's. Jeanne files it in an old file cabinet. The story continues because Wendy [Bawabe] and I found it for a third time in about 2019 when we were sorting through the files in the old file cabinet that hadn't been opened for years. It's a treasure for sure![305]

Thus, the 1871 photo (1) was likely held by the shipbuilder and his wife, for whom the ship was named, and (2) included an original handwritten list of many people in the photo, probably close to the date of the photo. It is rare to have such provenance for such an old photo.

The Town Seal

These treasures reflect the importance of the North River shipbuilding industry for the history of Norwell. Shipbuilding is also reflected in the town seal.

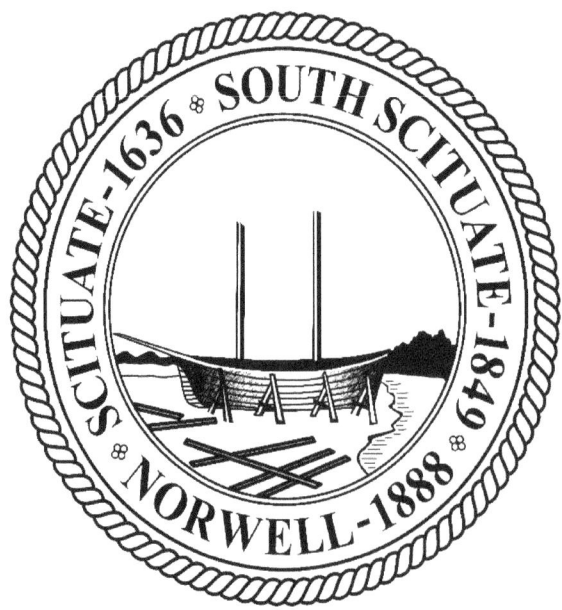

And you would probably not be surprised to learn that the name of the Norwell High School yearbook is *The Shipbuilder*.

Legacies of Shipbuilding

The Chittenden Yard, where Merritt built the *Helen M. Foster*, and other shipyards are marked on a delightful map by Anne Bonney Henderson. The map covers Norwell out to its borders with Hanover, Pembroke, Marshfield, and Scituate. The Norwell Public Library and the Scituate Historical Society have copies of the map. It depicts more than 80 buildings, including mills, tanneries, and historic houses, some dating to the 1600s. Some houses were built or owned by shipbuilders.[306]

Consider the William Delano House at 370 River Street, Norwell (Fig. 60). It has been called a "wedding cake" house for its grand appearance. It dates to 1803, the same year William married Sarah Hart of Boston. Both were from shipbuilding families. Delano was a descendant of Philippe de Lannoy, who migrated with the Pilgrims to Plymouth in the early 1600s. The same family produced such notables as U.S. President Franklin Delano Roosevelt.

Fig. 60. Delano Mansion, in DAR, *Old Scituate* (1921).

William Delano (1770 Scituate – 1815 Scituate) began constructing the 464-ton *Mount Vernon* (1815). This was the largest vessel ever built on the North River. He is buried in the First Parish Cemetery, Norwell.[307]

The North River Historical Association placed signs about shipbuilding along the North River in 1919. They refurbished the signs in 2019. The site of the Chittenden Yard has a good example (Fig. 61).[308]

Fig. 61. Chittenden Shipyard sign.

The Chittenden Yard site still offers a superb view of the North River (Fig. 62).

Fig. 62. View of North River from site of former Chittenden Shipyard, looking upriver.

5

IMPROVING THE RIVER: 1870 PLAN TO RECLAIM THE MARSHES

The end of shipbuilding on the North River, and the launch of the *Helen M. Foster* in 1871, did not stop attempts to improve the river.

The next attempts came from landowners along the river. This time, it was the agricultural interests, rather than the shipbuilders.

The push came from "the inhabitants of Marshfield in the drainage of the marshes of Green Harbor River, and of the inhabitants of South Scituate in the drainage of North River." They wanted to reclaim salt marshes, turning them into fresh water meadows. The marshes "produce nothing but the least valuable of the grasses that grow on salt marshes. Reclaimed they would produce English hay or garden vegetables."[309]

1870 Report

These attempts by the agricultural landowners led to a detailed report by the state Board of Harbor Commissioners. It was included in its report for 1870 to the state legislature. The report proposed damming the North River, converting it from one open for navigation to a closed river without tidal influence.[310]

In summary, the project called for:

- an earth dyke (dam) and sluices (gates) at Rogers' Wharf (White's Ferry), near the river's outlet to the sea
- a channel through the shoal at Slanting Spar (part of Humarock opposite Rogers' Wharf)
- raising the shingle dyke (levee) that ran from Rogers' Wharf to Third Cliff, and
- a dam at the former Waterman and Barstow shipyard in Hanover, near the river's source.[311]

The report is important for its detailed analysis of a precedent-setting project. America had few examples of damming tidal rivers to keep out seawater and turn salt marshes into fresh meadows. While the proposed dam was not grand or unique, it would be decades before a dam was built on the tidal Charles River at Boston and Cambridge. The Charles River dam was proposed in 1894, and constructed from 1905 to 1910.[312]

The 1870 proposed dam of the North River was a high-water mark for "improvement," as that word was understood by those involved. The river and its marshes were called "a section of important coast topography" by the Superintendent of the US Coast Survey.[313]

In addition, the project had the full weight of the scientific community behind it. Engineers of the Coast Survey worked in close cooperation with the state Board's professionals. They had extensive professional, academic, and geographical ties with one another.

The Team

To prepare the report, the Board asked for expert advice and measurements from a world-class cast of three professors of science and engineering:

- Prof. Benjamin Peirce, Superintendent of the US Coast Survey, Professor of Astronomy and Mathematics at Harvard
- Prof. Henry Mitchell, Chief in Physical Hydrography, US Coast Survey, and Professor of Physical Hydrography at the Massachusetts Institute of Technology (MIT), 1869–1876[314]
- Prof. Henry L. Whiting, engineer of the Board and Chief of Topography of the US Coast Survey, and Professor of Topography and Topographical Engineering at MIT[315]

MIT students also volunteered for the project.[316]

MIT was then located in Boston's Back Bay, long before its move across the Charles River to Cambridge.

MIT played a big role in the project. It had close ties with the Coast Survey. For example, in 1872, the president of MIT noted that it was "dependent upon the kindness of Prof. Peirce, Sup't. of the Coast Survey, for the use of a base-line measure, and a large altitude and azimuth instrument for triangulation, and for obtaining astronomical data for positions."[317]

Fig. 63. Benjamin Peirce, 1870s. Wikimedia Commons.

Benjamin Peirce (1809–1880) was born in Salem, graduated from Harvard, and became a distinguished professor of astronomy and mathematics at Harvard (Fig. 63). He had many other deep connections with the college and close family connections with "the full range of the learned professions of law, medicine, divinity, and higher education, as well as business, engineering, politics, and diplomacy." He was Superintendent of the US Coast Survey from 1867 to 1874.[318]

Peirce followed in the footsteps of mathematician Nathaniel Bowditch (1773–1838), considered the founder of modern maritime navigation. He, too, was born in Salem. His book *The American Practical Navigator* was first published in 1802, when Harvard awarded him an honorary degree.[319]

Henry L. Whiting (1821–1897) was a pioneer in topography. He and his wife Anna and their children lived on a farm in West Tisbury on Martha's Vineyard. Starting at age 17, he served almost 60 years in the Coast Survey. The 1870 *Boston Directory* listed him as "Prof., In Inst. Tech. office City Hall, h. at Cambridge."[320]

Henry Mitchell (1839–1902) was a native of Nantucket. Within the field of hydrography, he had won distinction in the "peculiar field" of marsh reclamation, having studied dams and dykes in England, France, and the Netherlands. The 1870 *Boston Directory* listed him as "prof., in Institute Tech. office City Hall, house at Brookline."[321]

Boston's City Hall was constructed from 1862 to 1865. It still exists on School Street where it is now called the old City Hall building. In addition to Whiting and Mitchell, City Hall held the state Harbor Commission, with a corner office on the fourth floor. The Commission was established by the legislature in 1866. Four of the five original members signed the 1870 report.[322]

Fig. 64. Boston City Hall, c. 1865, image attributed to Gridley J. Fox Bryant, Arthur D Gilman (building architects), Historic American Buildings Survey (HABS), Library of Congress, https://www.loc.gov/item/ma0445/. Possible attribution to Carl Fehmer (1838–1923), architect, per Back Bay Houses, https://backbayhouses.org/carl-r-fehmer/.

Boston had earlier engaged the scientific community in a water-related project. In 1859, the city asked the federal government for a scientific survey of Boston Harbor. The government formed a US Harbor Commission composed of Gen. Richard Delafield, US Corps of Engineers; Prof. A. D. Bache, US Coast Survey (Peirce's predecessor); and Commander Charles H. Davis, US Navy. They worked and provided surveys each year through 1866.[323]

MIT's 1869–1870 catalog had course descriptions, with Mitchell and Whiting in its list of 25 faculty members:[324]

HENRY L. WHITING,
U. S. Coast Survey . . *Professor of Topography.*

HENRY MITCHELL, A. M.,
U. S. Coast Survey . . . *Professor of Physical Hydrography.*

The 1870 team formed in the era when Boston was called the hub of the universe. If that included Cambridge (for Harvard, since MIT was then still in Boston) and the Massachusetts islands, then it was the hub of the hydrographic universe. And that hub's attention at the time was focused on the North River.[325]

The team produced an 1870 map of the North River (Fig. 68), discussed in more detail below, as part of its work. Like Whiting, many of those involved in mapping the river would have long and distinguished careers with the US Coast Survey. The lead surveyor on the 1870 map was O. H. Tittmann (1850–1938), then just 20 years old. He was an American geodesist, geographer, and astronomer. He later became the Superintendent of the Coast Survey (1900–1915), and co-founded the National Geographic Society. He was in touch with polar explorers Shackleton and Peary.[326]

But back in the mid-1800s, hydrography was just emerging as a recognized scientific field in America. For example, the word was not used in the 1854 report on the North River, even though its work by the Army Corps of Engineers was essentially hydrographic. Coast surveys were authorized by Congress in 1807, but the US Coast Survey was not firmly established, as a civilian agency, until 1832.[327]

Coast surveys were for mariners. As Mark Monmonier points out:

> Intended for maritime users, charts present a comparatively sketchy view of the land, usually only for a narrow belt along the coast. In this example [1969, 1970], topographic detail stops at a coast road a quarter mile inland — no point in cluttering the map with symbols of limited use to sailors.[328]

For a coastal sailor, the most important part of a river was its mouth. In this detail of an 1812 nautical chart (Fig. 65), the largest part of the North River is its channel up behind Humarock. The rest of its 15 or so miles was of no concern.[329]

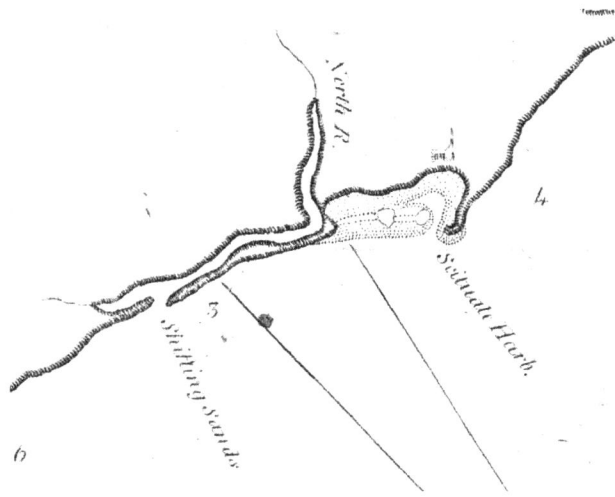

Fig. 65. Detail of S. Lambert (Salem), "Massachusetts Bay," nautical chart, 1812, NOAA #00-00-1812. North is to the right.

Today, NOAA defines hydrography as "the science that measures and describes the physical features of bodies of water and the land areas adjacent to those bodies of water." NOAA offers another, more telling definition, as "the science that measures and describes the physical features of the navigable portion of the Earth's surface and adjoining coastal areas." The words *navigable* and *coastal* reflect the field's origin in nautical charting and surveying. The field started with observing the bodies in the heavens and magnetism of the earth, and it worked itself out on the oceans.[330]

And then on land. Under superintendents Hassler, Bache, and Peirce, the Coast Survey triangulated land to cross the United States. In 1873, Peirce reported on coast surveys ranging from Maine to Florida and other coasts, and continuing work on "points in the geodetic connection between the Atlantic and Western coast."[331]

One can think of hydrographers as cartographers whose work explains land and water and their intersection. It can get technical, but the moon's gravity still pulls on the earth's waters to create tides and high water. Today, hydrography is a foundation for coastal flood mapping, flood insurance, and flood insurance premiums, which property owners pay. Some of this work extends to flooding of property near inland waterways.[332]

The 1870 North River project was significant to the Board of Harbor Commissioners. The Board itself visited the site and "met at North Marshfield several of the parties interested in this important improvement."[333]

The Board reported the work of this esteemed team, including an appendix with reports by Mitchell and Whiting. The Board mentioned their "finely executed maps." Mitchell prepared an 1871 sketch to accompany the report, and Whiting mentioned his own maps "which have been made upon a larger scale, 1:5,000, than that of our ordinary coast survey field work."[334]

Scale matters. Here are two examples of maps of the North River with different scales. On the left is an 1858 Coast Survey map at the scale of 1:10,000 (Fig. 66). It covers about three miles, from the old mouth to what would become the new mouth. The map on the right picks up the river where the map on the left leaves off. It is an 1870 Tittmann/Whiting map (sheet 1 of 2) at 1:5,000 (Fig. 67). At first glance, that map may not seem as detailed as the one on the left. However, its smaller-scale of 1:5,000 actually has more detail and it extends well inland. Sheet 1 alone covers half of the river beyond Humarock, about six miles. Sheet 2 covers the rest of the river upstream, another six miles.[335]

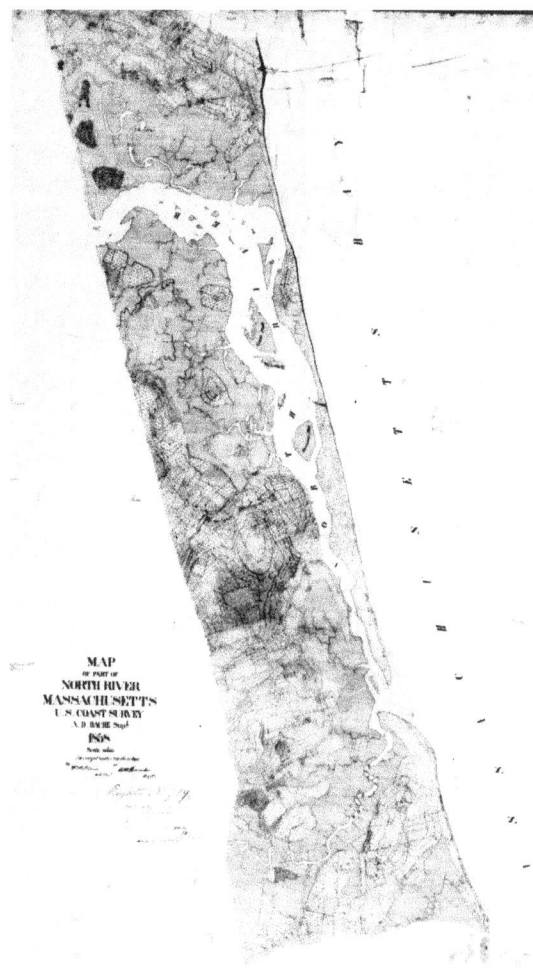
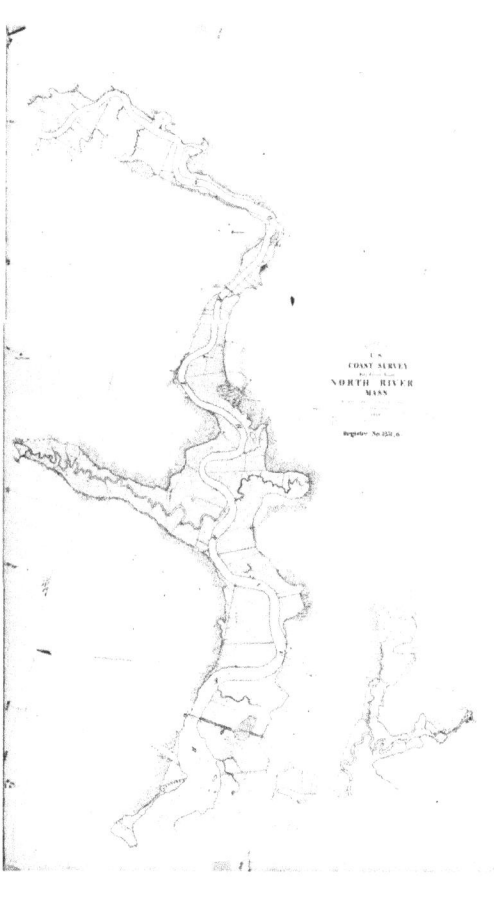

Fig. 66. Wm. H. Dennis, Sub Asst, under the direction of A. M. Harrison, Asst, "Map of Part of North River Massachusetts," 1858, scale 1:10,000, map 719a, US Coast Survey, University of Alabama. Just shows mouth and eastern reach of river. Scituate's Third Cliff at top, Humarock in middle, stretching down to the river's mouth (old mouth).

Fig. 67. O. H. Tittmann, Asst., under the direction of H. L. Whiting, Asst, "North River Mass.", 1870, scale 1:5,000, Register No. 1251,a., sheet 1 of 2, US Coast Survey, University of Alabama. Dark line at bottom is Little's Bridge (now Rte. 3A bridge) over the North River, near "Proposed Railway." To its right is First Herring Brook. At far right is the Greenbush intersection of the Driftway and what is now Chief Justice Cushing Highway, Rte. 3A. Union Bridge is left of the dark blot, upper center.

Here, we focus on the team's excellent 1870 map (sketch) of the overall North River at the scale of 1:40,000 (Fig. 68).

1870 Map

The 1870 map of the North River helps to understand the scope of the project. It was created by Whiting, Peirce, the US Coast Survey, and MIT students. Unlike the fine

1831 map of Scituate, this one covered the whole river, start to finish, both banks, all towns. And it covered it at a decent scale, 1:40,000.[336]

The map's scope is remarkable, considering that the US Coast Survey's work usually stayed near the coast. Look at Tower's 1852 plan and the Dennis map of 1858, both shown above (Fig. 51 and Fig. 66). They were typical in covering the coast and only a thin stretch of land. Here, the Coast Survey went as many as 15 miles up the river.

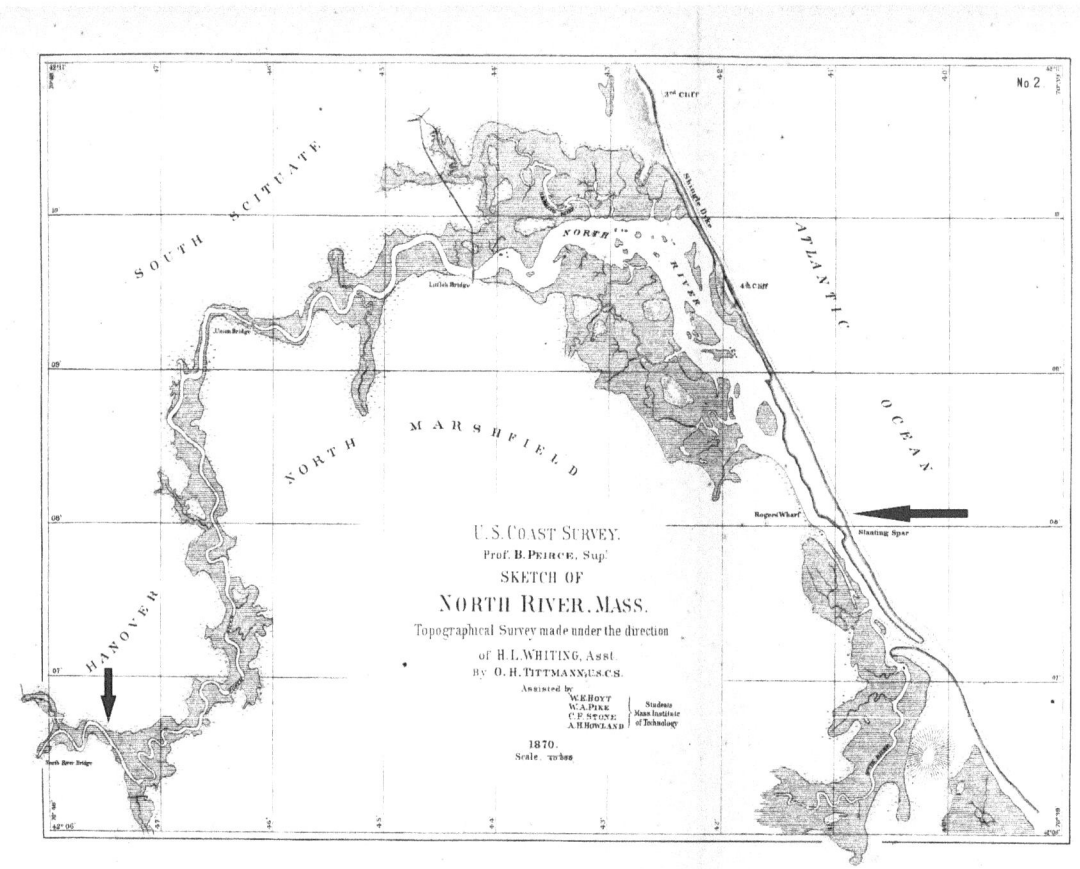

Fig. 68. O. H. Tittmann, H. L. Whiting, et al., US Coast Survey, Sketch of North River, Mass., (1870). Dark areas show extent of salt marshes. Waterman & Barstow former shipyard at far left, Rogers' Wharf at right (both with added arrows showing proposed dam sites). Rivers crawl out of frame. Source: Digital Commons at Salem State University. See details on Walling's 1857 map.

The project called for a dam on the North River at Rogers' Wharf (equivalent to White's Ferry), at the right on the 1870 map. The dam would stretch from Marshfield to Scituate's Humarock, the narrow beach opposite Rogers' Wharf. In addition, the project called for a dam at the former Waterman and Barstow shipyard in Hanover (actually in South Scituate at the Hanover border). This was at the far left on the 1870 map. Both dam locations appear below in details of Walling's 1857 map of Plymouth County (Fig. 69 and Fig. 70).[337]

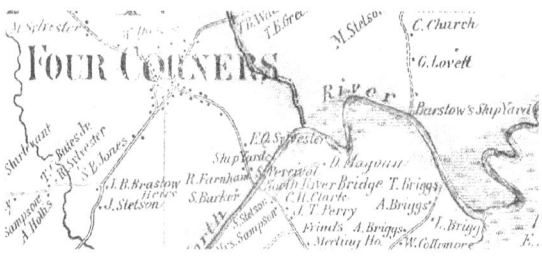

Fig. 69. Walling's 1857 map, detail showing Barstow's ShipYard on North River in South Scituate, just east of Hanover Four Corners and North River Bridge. Library of Congress.

Fig. 70. Walling's 1857 map, detail showing White's Ferry-L. Rogers' Wharf on North River, Marshfield, across from Humarock (Scituate). Library of Congress. Site of main dam in 1870 plan.

The 1870 map shows that the river's mouth, and thus the southern end of Humarock, had moved noticeably southward since Walling's 1857 map.

In addition, the 1870 map shows islands and obstructions in the lower North River as it headed to the sea. There, the navigability problems disclosed in the 1852 sketch were still present, perhaps worse. Among the islands was a jagged shape opposite the shingle beach between Third Cliff and Fourth Cliff, just as the river made a right turn to the south. This was Great Green Island, discussed later in this book. The islands and shoals there were blamed on the inroads of the sea at the narrow beach and along the Humarock shore.

1870 Report's Body

The 1870 report had a splendid description of the North River's physical form, and a discussion of past proposals for its improvement. At times, it was poetic, as when it referred to "The veins and arteries of the marshes."[338]

The report said:

> The marshes upon Green Harbor River comprise about fifteen hundred acres, and those of the North River about three thousand more. They produce nothing but the least valuable of the grasses that grow on salt marshes. Reclaimed they would produce English hay or garden vegetables. These reclamations would benefit all the towns upon these rivers, and restore to some the prosperity which was theirs when they were centres of business that has since left them for the suburbs of great seaports. A generation or more ago, North River was devoted to ship-building. … Not a vestige of [the shipyards] remains. The navigability of this river for the class of vessels that used to be built upon its banks was destroyed some

years ago by inroads of the sea … and all hope of making this river again usefully navigable has long since been abandoned.[339]

As to shipbuilding, the Board's report was correct, except for the launching of the *Helen M. Foster* in 1871. In addition, ships had been built during the 1860s. But the focus here was on reclaiming the salt marshes.[340]

The marshes comprised 3,000 acres, as noted above. Whiting's report was more precise: "The result of my survey determines an area of these marshes, including the mud flats of the water spaces, which amount to 3,074 acres."[341]

The 1870 report said:

> It was an essential part of the plan for reclaiming the marshes on North River that a sluice [gated] dam should be constructed [at White's Ferry, across from Humarock at Fourth Cliff], which would keep out the waters of the ocean during flood tide, and during the ebb drain off the waters of the river.[342]

White's Ferry, current site of the Bridgewaye Inn, was then less than two miles from the mouth of the North River. Thus, nearly the entire river would be upstream from the dam. The dam's purpose was to block the ocean tides, and control the flow of the river. It would let the river stay low and stable, and become a mighty reservoir of fresh water.

The report relied heavily on the work of Mitchell, who conducted a physical survey of the river. According to the board:

> He concludes that in spite of the large fresh-water supply afforded at certain seasons, the reclamation of these marshes can be effected by the construction of a single sluice dam. But to insure entire success, the beaches of shingle and sand that lie between the marshes and the ocean should be made secure against inroads of the sea by the construction of dikes at several weak places.[343]

Shingle Beach

One of the "weak places" was the shingle beach that connected Third Cliff and Fourth Cliff. It had a road on the river side of the beach. This is what Samuel Deane's 1831 history of Scituate described as "a beach next the sea of twenty rods width [330 feet], composed chiefly of round and polished pebbles."[344]

To define the shingle beach, Mitchell's report had tables with detailed measurements.

They showed that the beach (also called a dike or levee) had a maximum height of 17 feet above mean high water of the sea. Its width ranged from about 170 feet to 311 feet. Its length was nearly a mile.

Mitchell accompanied his report with a sheet of sketches with multiple figures (sketches) (see Fig. 71 through Fig. 74).[345]

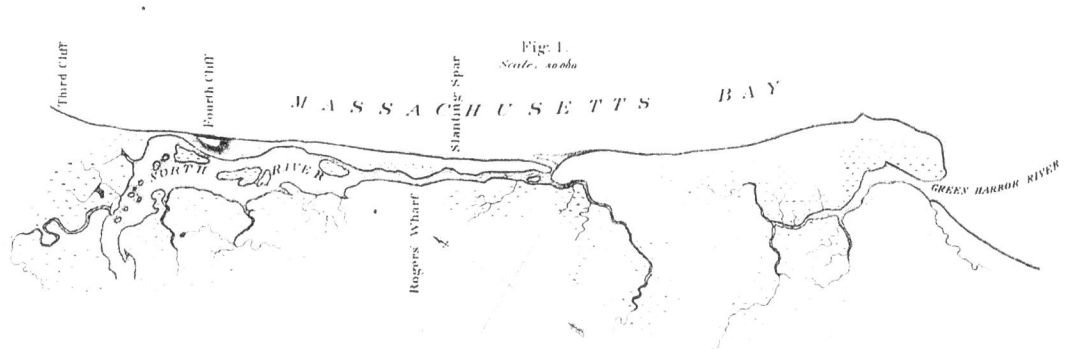

Fig. 71. 1871 Mitchell sketch, Fig. 1, showing shingle beach between Third Cliff and Fourth Cliff. State Library of MA. The Green Harbor River is shown at right and is discussed below.

Mitchell was fascinated with shingle beaches. His report discussed examples across Europe and England. His report mentions Chesil Bank, and his sketch shows a cross-section. It is an 18-mile- long beach, one of three major shingle beaches in Britain, and at that time the highest one in the world.[346]

The Mitchell sketches included cross-sections of the North River shingle beach showing its height at ten places, and then the mean dimensions of the highest eight places. The heights at the crests ranged from about 17 feet to 13 feet above mean high water of the sea. These cross-sections used different scales for height and width, which exaggerated the height of the beach.

Fig. 72. 1871 Mitchell sketch, Fig. 8, with mean section dimensions (vertical 30 ft:1 in, horiz. 100 ft: 1 in). Presumably river left, ocean right (shown as same height).

Fig. 73. 1871 Mitchell sketch, Fig. 8, adjusted by author to more realistic dimensions at same scale (vertical 17 ft max, horiz. 200 ft), same height of water.

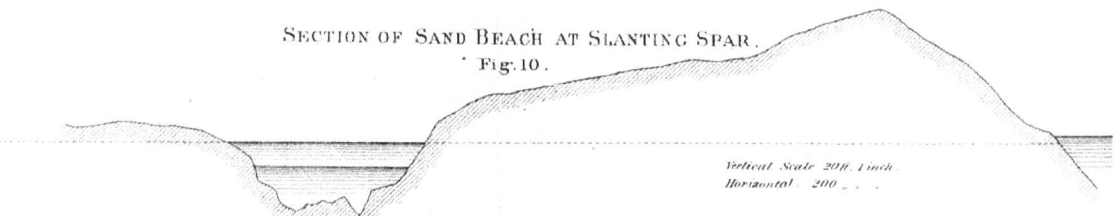

Fig. 74. 1871 Mitchell sketch, Fig. 10, showing height of river (presumably left, with high and low tide levels), and higher ocean level (right) at Slanting Spar area of Humarock opposite Rogers' Wharf — the site of the proposed dam.

The shingle beach was mostly tall enough to defend inroads of the sea. Its crest appeared almost perfectly horizontal at about 16 to 17 feet above mean high tide. However, measurements found depressions lower than this at both ends of the beach, as shown in the table, "Longitudinal Section of Shingle Levee." Some were as low as 9 feet above mean high tide. In addition, depressions farther south along the Humarock coast were even lower.[347]

These depressions, and others along the shore, needed to be raised to keep out the ocean. Mitchell considered the high water of the April 1851 Minot's gale, which destroyed the new Minot's Ledge Lighthouse off Scituate's north coast, and killed two assistant keepers at the lighthouse. An Army engineer report of that incident said,

> The height of the storm was o Wednesday, the 16th, and at that time it was a perfect hurricane. It was, in fact, unprecedented; for, notwithstanding the great gale of September, 1815, was well remembered here, it was from the S. E., and was of short duration.[348]

Destruction of property was immense, according to accounts from Plymouth, Kingston, and Marshfield. "Bridges have been carried away, and property of all kinds have been carried off." In Boston, the tide reached Broad Street with 18 inches of water. "All along the coast, great damage was done to vessels, store-houses, wharves, roads, &c., and many buildings have been washed away or blown down."[349]

In Marshfield, the 1851 gale formed a channel or "slue-way" (one might call it a "guzzle"), where afterwards seawater traversed Humarock to Rogers' Wharf at least once a year. Seawater in that channel deposited material that created shoals in the river. The 1870 report was particularly concerned about this channel.[350]

Mitchell said that dikes in Holland ranged from 10 feet "up to 21 feet above ordinary high water." Given the particular characteristics here, Mitchell recommended "that dikes are carried across the 'slue-ways' of the beach, to the height of thirteen feet above mean high water of the sea."[351]

It may give some comfort that, according to the NSRWA, "The Rexhame Dunes now stand at the site of the old mouth. The dunes rise at least 20 feet above the mean high tide level."[352]

In addition, Mitchell concluded that the dam at White's Ferry must extend "at least four and a half feet above mean high-water of the sea."[353]

To reclaim the marshes, the sea was the enemy, to be kept out.

Photos of Shingle Beach

We are fortunate to have revealing photos of the shingle beach, taken later in the 1800s (Fig. 75 and Fig. 76).[354]

Fig. 75. Stebbins, "Barrier beach with transverse scallops [and] drumlin cliffs, Scituate, Mass." View looking north of barrier beach (shingle beach) between Fourth Cliff (foreground) and Third Cliff, Scituate. Photo, 1892–1898, by Nathaniel Livermore Stebbins/Art Pub. Co., Boston, public domain. George Augustus Gardner Collection of Photographs, Harvard University, HOLLIS number olvwork419446, http://id.lib.harvard.edu/images/olvwork419446/catalog.

Above is a view of the shingle beach looking north from Fourth Cliff (foreground) (Fig. 75). The beach connects with Third Cliff, and the view may take in the other two cliffs along Scituate's shore. The North River at left appears lower than the ocean at the right. The dark hills are Coleman's Hills, before mining for sand and gravel reduced them. Houses in front of the hills were along the Driftway, which runs left–right to the top of Third Cliff.[355]

Below is another view, probably taken from the beach itself, with a close-up of the pebbles or shingles (Fig. 76). (Both terms were used to describe the beach.) In detail, both photos show the road down to the beach from the edge of Third Cliff. The large house just to the left of the road seems close to the river, perhaps due to foreshortening and high tide. The hut of the Massachusetts Humane Society, on the river side of the beach at the foot of Third Cliff, is barely visible in detail in these photos.[356]

Fig. 76. Stebbins, "Sea[shore] of beach wall [and] sea-worn pebbles, Scituate, Mass." View of barrier beach (shingle beach), looking north, photo, 1892–1898, by Nathaniel Livermore Stebbins/Art Pub. Co., Boston, public domain. George Augustus Gardner Collection of Photographs, Harvard University, HOLLIS number olvwork419445, http://id.lib.harvard.edu/images/olvwork419445/catalog.

Many of these photos were taken by Nathaniel Livermore Stebbins (1847–1922). He became a photographer about 1884 and grew famous for his maritime photos of sailing ships. The Harvard geology department acquired his photos of various geological features. The department used the photos from about 1890 to 1920 for teaching. They are now in Harvard's George Augustus Gardner Collection of Photographs.[357]

Returning to the report itself, a question arose: would the marshes sink after adding these improvements, which would build up the defenses against the sea?

Not very much, thought Mitchell. He pointed to the unsuccessful attempts in 1843 to cut through the shingle beach between Third and Fourth Cliffs. (This was called the "shingle dyke" on the 1870 map.) He concluded in his report to the Board:

> I glean one curious fact from those employed in opening this channel, viz.: the original bank of shingle was found to extend downwards only to the surface of the marsh, which was not sensibly depressed beneath its weight. I infer that as Fourth Cliff wears away the whole beach falls back and the present banks of sand and shingle are really superimposed upon ancient meadow lands or river channels. The marshes are not floating bogs like the *koogs* of Denmark or liable to slump down after enclosure, like the *polders* of Holland.[358]

Mitchell's report contained details about the elevation of the river. Upriver, at North River Bridge, the tide had been 3 to 5 feet forty years before. Now, it varied from 0.8 to 1.5 feet. (This was evidence that the shoals formed downriver were blocking the tides.) The upriver range of 0.8 to 1.5 feet continued all the way down to White's Ferry. Mitchell added, "The highest place in the river bed along the thread of the channel is 1.60 feet [19.2 inches] below the mean level of the sea." Elsewhere, he noted "Datum=High water plane of river, June 23, 1870=1.70 feet [20.4 inches] below mean high water of sea."[359]

Thus, Mitchell measured the difference between the levels of sea and river as 20 inches. That matched Calvin Brown's calculations (at high tide) contained in the 1843 report.[360]

Mitchell

Henry Mitchell (Fig. 77) was a native of Nantucket, so he must have been well acquainted with the sea. In addition, he came from an accomplished scientific family. His sister Maria Mitchell was the first woman astronomer in the US.[361]

Mitchell took a fundamentally scientific approach, connecting the tides with the moon and the heavens, including the stars in Orion's Belt. But he was not averse to borrowing rules "found among the fishermen and coasters" around Nantucket. His interest in tides extended to tidal rivers. He wrote a paper in 1868 about tides, saying, "The tides of rivers are but imperfectly understood." However, the paper offered some general rules. That paper and his 1872 paper on reclaiming tidelands were published around the time of his 1870 study of the North River.[362]

Fig. 77. Henry Mitchell in 1890s, at his house at 49 Cliff Road, Nantucket, known as Thornwell. Photo courtesy of the Nantucket Historical Association, item GPN4290.

Mitchell's 1870 report presented a bonanza of numbers and engineering calculations. Then, at one point, he said, "The marsh owners, both at Scituate and Marshfield, have wisely selected Clemens Herschel, C. E., to draw up plans of construction." That brought in even more data and calculations, which surfaced in the next few years.[363]

Herschel

Clemens Herschel (1842–1930) (Fig. 79), a Harvard graduate (class of 1860), was then on his way to become a world-renowned hydraulic engineer. An example of his calculations in a different report from 1871, may have eclipsed those of Mitchell in 1870.[364]

Oh, the calculations they made!

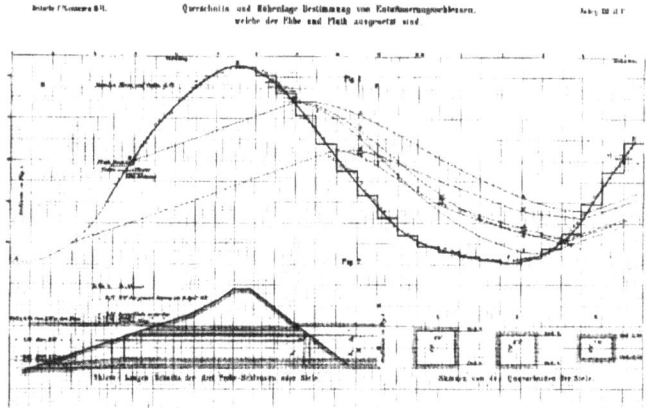

Fig. 78. Clemens Herschel, chart from 1871 paper.

Dam calculations are complicated.

Fig. 79. Clemens Herschel, 1906, published in Walter G. Kent, *An Appreciation of Two Great Works in Hydraulics, ...* (London: Blades, East & Blades, 1912). *Wikipedia*, public domain.

Clemens Herschel was famed for inventing the Venturi meter in the late 1880s. It was the first large-scale, accurate device for measuring water flow. It was based on the principles of the Venturi tube.

He developed the meter while working for the Holyoke Water Power Company in Massachusetts, where he developed the Holyoke Testing Flume, a turbine testing facility. The meter was intended to measure the amount of water used by the individual water mills in the Holyoke area, which had some 85 turbines at work. The meter gained worldwide use.

> Even Niagara itself, with its titanic forces and vast volumes of water, could be measured by this simple but efficient device.
>
> — Kent, *An Appreciation*

I wonder how many American shad passed through Herschel's devices during his time in Holyoke.

Today, Holyoke is the home of the Shad Derby, one of the region's largest fishing events, sponsored by the local utility at the Connecticut River. The Holyoke Gas & Electric website has a panoramic photo of the current dam. The Holyoke Dam, also called the Hadley Falls Dam, is recognized by the American Society of Mechanical

Engineers as a Historic Mechanical Engineering Landmark for its use by Clemens Herschel in developing the Venturi meter.[365]

Whiting

Whiting, like Mitchell, also submitted his report to the Board in 1870. He supported Mitchell's findings about the lower reach of the North River. He said they "show the capacity of the inlet and lower channel to be insufficient for the passage of a vessel suitable in size for the general purposes of freight or traffic. The inlet, as a harbor of refuge, is of no value."[366]

Whiting reported on his detailed maps, which he said would be useful "as a basis for a scheme for the drainage of the upper marshes, and of improvement by shortened reaches [stretches of the river] and corrected bends in the pathway through these marshes, of the main channel of the river." That seems odd. Towns may have wanted and lobbied for that. But the report had no recommendation to shorten the river, straighten it, or build shortcuts through the bends.[367]

Whiting analyzed soil samples from nearby Green Harbor River. He then added,

> Geographically, this territory is unlike many tracts of salt marsh bordering the main sea-board, which are generally in masses of large lateral extent. The marsh bed of North River conforms to the general pathway of the stream. … The length of river, following its windings through the marsh from its mouth to the head of its tide-water at North River Bridge in the town of Hanover, is about fifteen miles.

As to the marshes, Whiting said:

> The plane of these marshes is below the range of spring and high storm tides which continue to overflow the entire valley, … These occasional excessive floods of salt water are injurious, in their effect upon the grasses of the marsh. It is a natural condition to all extensive tracts of salt marsh, that the margin of the main streams and tributaries, from their more ready drainage, become firmer and even higher ground than the rearward portions, which cannot cast off their surface waters quickly. The result is, that stronger grasses and firmer roots take hold of the best drained sections, which tends still more to keep back the ebbing water, so that in portions of marsh remote from the main streams, the grasses are sometimes entirely killed out by the long standing and stagnant water.[368]

Whether Whiting was correct or not (and later research would challenge it), it seemed a good argument at the time in favor of draining the marshes.[369]

Whiting's report continued, "Any large expenditure of money for the purpose of establishing maritime commerce only, could scarcely be made to pay, and would probably never become of material value to the community settled upon the shores of this small river." So he agreed with Mitchell's conclusion that it was feasible "to shut out the tide-water, and to drain the river and the marshes successfully." He agreed that the value "of the improved marshes as an agricultural district … must far exceed any other use to which they can be put."[370]

Of course, this depended on one's view of value. Here, the plan focused on economic value, specifically for growing crops on meadows. The plan would have turned most of the North River into a freshwater pond, practically eliminating herring and other anadromous fish like shad (discussed earlier in this book). It would have removed salt marshes as a buffer against sea level rise and greenhouse gas emissions (discussed later in this book). But the report did not consider these ecological impacts, nor were they valued at the time. In fact, the word *ecology* had only recently been coined, by the German scientist Ernst Haeckel, in 1866.[371]

Conclusion

The Board of Harbor Commissioners wholeheartedly supported this work of the three professors and engineers. Its 1870 report said:

> the Board do not hesitate to recommend the passage of a law authorizing the construction of the sluice-dam on North River, …
>
> The Board is not aware that any reclamations of salt marshes have been made in this Commonwealth upon the large scale proposed in these plans for Green Harbor and North Rivers.
>
> In Europe such reclamations are common. In Nova Scotia they have been undertaken with complete success. Very recently in New Jersey the drainage of the Newark meadows has been attempted, and the results thus far are full of promise and encouragement. There must be many thousands of acres of salt marshes in this Commonwealth that could be made to yield the most abundant and profitable harvests. These soils are of the richest character and worked with the greatest ease. They only need drainage and protection from inundation from the sea. In many cases these can be secured without too large an outlay for a handsome profit. Such reclamations are positive additions to the wealth of the State, and the Board is glad to be able to promote them.[372]

The Board's report was mainly from an engineering point of view. It noted no local opposition, unlike the 1840s petitions to the legislature. The general idea was to build dams and dikes like those in the Netherlands, to keep out the sea. That would have left little or no future for the state's salt marshes.

The 1870 report was detailed and scientific. It would later be relied on heavily by the Board of Harbor and Land Commissioners in an equally detailed 1915 report, discussed below.[373]

In his report to the Board, Whiting said: "The course of the river and valley is also of much favor to the community through which it passes, as it winds its way by almost every farmer's door and grounds, giving to the man of few as well as many acres the benefit of its improvement."[374]

How could anyone object, with such an anodyne description? Yet some did, and they were men of many acres.

In the process, nobody pointed out that the plan would add the first two significant dams in the history of the North River.

1871 Objections

The 1870 report in favor of draining the North River marshes was dated January 1871. Word spread. In April, landowners along the river filed objections with the state legislature. These were reported in an article in the *Hingham Journal* for April 14, 1871.[375]

Using quotes from that article, here are the main contentions between the petitioners (proponents of the plan) and the objectors (called "remonstrants" in those days).

The objectors questioned who the real interested parties were. "The persons who own land on North river, do not, as a general thing, own land on South river." Those interested in a plan for one river should not be pooled with those interested in a plan for the other river.

The objectors said they owned some 2,560 acres of meadow land in Scituate along the North River "which we wish to retain as it now is rather than run the risk of damming out the salt water, thinking to improve it." They seemed to represent a large part of the 3,000 acres of marshes that the petitioners wanted to improve.

The petitioners wanted to drain the salt marshes to allow growing more valuable crops such as English hay. The objectors said that salt hay was almost as valuable as English hay, and cost less to grow, as no fertilizers were needed. They said draining would curtail other current crops, like cranberries being grown near the North River bridge, and "there would consequently be a clashing between the cranberry and the grass producers, should there be any alteration in that locality."

The petitioners said the river had lost its value for shipbuilding and was no longer navigable. The objectors said "The North river is navigable. … There is now in progress of construction, on said river, a vessel of one hundred tons [the *Helen M. Foster*]. All the shoals in said river remain the same as they were when the Mayflower dropped anchor in Plymouth harbor, except a new shoal near the mouth of the river, [which shoal could be removed]."

The petitioners, and the 1870 report, did not address the plan's impact on fishes and fishing. The objectors said the proposed dams would limit or destroy the fishery, which had been improving in the last forty years. "Large quantities of herring, shad, bass, eels, &c., were formerly taken from the river. The facilities for propagating fish are as good now as at any former period; all that is needed to give them a good chance to run up into the Indian ponds in Pembroke, there to spawn, where there are several large sandy bottom ponds, the best we have seen in the State."

The damming and drainage plan was practicable, according to the petitioners. They backed this up with expert opinions of leading hydraulic engineers and hydrographers, included in the 1870 report. They said that such reclamations were common in Europe and recently attempted with promise in New Jersey's Newark meadowlands. They concluded the plan was feasible, given that the height of the proposed protective barriers against the sea took into account past extreme storms.[376]

The objectors, on the other hand, said storms would wash away the protective barriers. "We have no faith in trying to stop the water out of said river" at the proposed site of the dam. They said the State Geologist of New Jersey mentioned meadow reclamation problems in its report for 1869. While the objectors did not furnish expert reports, the Massachusetts Board of Harbor Commissioners' 1870 report said, "The Board is not aware that any reclamations of salt marshes have been made in this Commonwealth upon the large scale proposed in these plans for Green Harbor and North Rivers."[377]

The plans were, in a word, experimental. That word was not used in the 1870 report to describe the plans. It would appear later, as discussed below, in the flawed implementation of the Green Harbor River plan.

Then we come to cost. The 1870 report concluded, "Such reclamations are positive additions to the wealth of the State, and the Board is glad to be able to promote them."[378]

The objectors advised the legislature that:

> The towns of Scituate and Marshfield have recently voted to take stock in the Cohasset and Duxbury railroad, to the amount of $150,000, and it is now in progress of construction; each town having a war debt, which will increase their indebtedness to nearly $200,000. We, the farmers, owners of marsh lands, do severally pray that your Honors may not do anything to increase our burdens, as we fear we now have more than we can bear.[379]

Taxpayers had a point.

Scituate's town report for 1871, said that the railroad debt as of February 1, 1872, had *increased* (italics in original) by $30,000 to a total of $75,000, compared with ordinary debt (including interest on railroad debt) of $12,651.98. In other words, railroad debt increased from three times ordinary debt to six times ordinary debt. And that was just Scituate. Marshfield and Duxbury also had railroad debt.[380]

1871 Legislature Authorizes Dam

State lawmakers were persuaded by the 1870 report of the Harbor Commissioners, despite the objections filed in April. On May 12, 1871, they passed "An Act to Authorize the Construction of Dams Across North River in Plymouth County." The act authorized the marsh proprietors to build dams to drain the marshes "as if the same [North River] had never been navigable," subject to certain conditions. That authorized the proposed dams at White's Ferry and at Waterman and Barstow's former shipyard. The act did not give funding to the proprietors. As Herschel would advise them in 1872, the benefited landowners would have to fund the project.[381]

The act authorized the commissioners to build the dikes (dams) on the shore "as a protection for said marshes from the sea." The harbor commissioners had the duty to "construct fish-ways in said dams in the manner approved by the fish commissioners of the Commonwealth." It is not clear why this duty was not specifically imposed on the proprietors who would build the dams or who would be responsible for their maintenance.

The act did not cover the Green Harbor project, which was also included in the 1870 report. That project is discussed separately below.

1872 Further Objections

The 1871 act did not stop objections.

Records of Scituate's town meeting of March 4, 1872, say:

"Voted To accept and adopt the following Resolutions offered by Israel H. Sherman.

Resolved That the Town instruct the Selectmen to remonstrate against any Petition for a Bridge [perhaps meaning dam?] across North River at any point near 4th Cliff.

Also against any movement to drain North River for agricultural purposes at the expense of the Town.

Also To instruct our Representative to oppose the above measures."[382]

Despite that, the town of Scituate did not seem to have enough clout in the legislature to stop these measures. Plymouth County had 15 representatives, one each for the following districts along the North River:

I. Cohasset and Scituate – Moses R. Colman, Scituate

III. South Scituate, Hanover and Hanson – Thomas B. Waterman, South Scituate

IV. Marshfield, Pembroke and Halifax – John T. Z. Thompson, Halifax[383]

Later that year, the 1870 plan moved forward.

6

IMPROVING THE RIVER: IMPLEMENTING 1870'S PLAN

1872 Reclamation and Development Plan

In 1872, the 1870 proposal to reclaim the North River marshes was further developed by civil engineer Clemens Herschel.

An August 1872 newspaper article outlined his plan to reclaim and drain the marshes. According to the article, he was "acting under the instructions of the town of South Scituate [now Norwell] and other owners of the North river marshes."[384]

The news account was detailed, but the plan itself was lost in obscurity for years. It was contained in a handwritten letter from Herschel to "the Town of South Scituate, Thomas J. Tolman, and others, owners of North River Marshes," dated June 15, 1872. Tolman was the lead on the petition that led to the 1870 report. In 1961, the letter was discovered by William "Cap'n Bill" Vinal. As he described it,

> These papers [the 1872 Herschel plan and 1850s efforts to improve the river] were found in the attic of a local house. They were about "to be shoveled out" for the dump heap. Fortunately the writer was invited to "see if there was anything he wanted." … It is believed that this material has never been published before.[385]

That is how history is preserved. Vinal filed the letter with the Scituate Historical Society, with a copy for the Norwell Historical Society.[386]

It was a big plan. It covered 2,338 acres of marsh and 815 acres of rivers and creeks.[387]

Herschel had work to do, and he was detail-oriented. For example, his plan said:

> The amount of fresh water to be emptied through the sluices [at the proposed dam at White's Ferry] was ascertained by measuring the outflow at North River Bridge and of every stream emptying into the North River below this point, April 3d, 4th, & 5th, 1872, at a time when the snow was

melting, at what may be called ordinary spring high water. Their sum total was found to be 256 cubic feet per second.

In the calculations, provision was also made for discharging this quantity and besides and effective rainfall of 2 inches per 24 hours on about 3500 acres, which amounted to 291.5 cubic feet per second more, making a total capacity of discharge of 547 cubic feet per second, without raising the water level higher than about 2 feet 2 inches below the present marsh level. These duties are evidently all that need be required of the proposed sluices.[388]

Here are key elements of the plan.

Dam

The plan's centerpiece was a dam (dyke and sluices) at White's Ferry (Rogers' Wharf), as proposed in 1870. The dam would be "formed of gravel from the adjoining hill." It is not clear whether the hill was at Scituate's Humarock or Marshfield's Ferry Hill, but probably the latter.[389]

In the 1870 report, Mitchell had advised that the dam must extend "at least four and a half feet above mean high-water of the sea." We discuss and attempt to show this height in more detail below.[390]

Dyke/Levee Along the Coast

Herschel's plan called for raising the "natural dyke or shingle levee" between Third Cliff and Fourth Cliff, and on down to White's Ferry (where the dam would be located). In the 1870 report, Mitchell had recommended raising them to a height of 13 feet above mean high tide. Herschel's plan raised that to 14 feet.[391]

> Altogether about 5000 feet in length or one mile, will have to be raised about 2 feet on the average, to make this natural dyke nowhere less than 14 feet above mean high water of the sea.
>
> There is this in favor of this part [?] of the enterprize and of important advantage, that the natural tendency expressed for a great length of time, is to build up and lengthen this natural barrier.
>
> Nature will favor any attempt at raising the same and work against any attempt to cut through or lower it.[392]

(This is the part of the plan where the 1871 objectors said they had no faith. And Nature had other plans, as it broke through the natural barrier in the storm of 1898.)

To protect the river against another flood from the north, the 1870 report called for raising the Driftway leading to Third Cliff by "two or three feet for a length of about 100 feet."[393]

Herschel's report described how the past flood arose from the Minot's Light Storm of 1851. He advised:

> The road leading by Coleman's Hill to 3rd Cliff [the Driftway] should be the same level as the dyke at Rogers Wharf, which would prevent the recurrence of an event as just described.
>
> I have not had opportunity to take levels on this road, but judge that the amount of work required at this point is quite small and inexpensive, consisting probably of raising the road some 2 or 3 feet over a length of say 100 feet.[394]

This low point on the Driftway is still there, a place for historical musings, errant golf balls, and occasional puddles.[395]

Cost/Finances

Herschel's plan gave detailed cost estimates, with a total cost for the project of:

> $27,665, or about $11.83 per acre of marsh benefited. The fact that this cost equals, or more than equals, the present value of the land, is not, in the opinion of Mr. Herschel, to be regarded. The question is whether, if drained, the lands would be worth $22 per acre. If so, and enough of the owners are ready to advance the necessary funds, the improvement need wait no longer.[396]

Herschel noted that by law the funds advanced would need to be secured by "a tax assessed and in default of payment of said tax, a tax title, on all the land benefitted."[397]

All this work by the landowners, their consultant Herschel, and the state's 1870 report, ripened into a public proposal to reclaim the North River marshes.

1873 Proposal to Reclaim the Marshes

Landowners along the river called a public meeting for January 20, 1873, to promote improving the marshes. Their poster called this "reclaiming" the marshes for agricultural purposes (Fig. 80).[398] (Note that "improving" was subjective, and "reclaiming" was a stretch, since the marshes had been there for centuries and needed no reclaiming.) They said the rich and fertile soil of the marshes was "a mine of plant food deposited in the ages that are past, and awaiting conversion to the use of man."[399]

RECLAMATION
—OF—
NORTH RIVER
MARSHES

The owners of Marshes bordering upon, and adjacent to North River and its tributaries, lying between White's Ferry and Waterman & Barstow's Ship Yard, are requested to meet at the

TOWN HALL,
SOUTH SCITUATE,
On MONDAY, JAN. 20, 1873,
AT 1 O'CLOCK, P. M.

The undersigned, take the liberty to thus call together said owners, having in view the important matter of reclaiming the said Marshes for agricultural purposes by drainage, by damming out the tide water, according to the provisions of Chap.——of Acts of 1871 and Chap. 148, of General Statutes.

The object of the meeting, is to discuss the subject of improving the Marshes, and take any steps that may be thought best to initiate and carry forward the work.

ISRAEL NASH.	H. A. OAKMAN	PARKER WELCH.
THOS. J. TOLMAN.	ELISHA W. HALL.	GEO. H. WEATHERBEE.
DAVID P. HATCH.	WM. C. TOLMAN.	WALES R. CLIFT.
NATH'L PHILLIPS, 2d.	CUMMINGS LITCHFIELD.	

JANUARY 9, 1873

J. FRANK. FARMER, Printer, 18 Exchange Street, Boston.

Fig. 80. "Reclamation of North River Marshes," poster, 1873. Courtesy of North River Commission.

Names of eleven men appeared on the poster.

One name was E. Parker Welch (1833–1917). This gave the plan powerful backing. He was an entrepreneur who arose from his father's farm on Third Cliff in Scituate. He would become a major landowner, town official, large public figure, and co-founder with his son George of the well-known Welch Company. At the time, the Welch family owned much of the marshland at Third Cliff next to the North River. On the 1870 map, it is the big blotchy area north of the river (Fig. 68). It was perhaps the largest single stake in the North River marshes.[400]

Fig. 81. E. Parker Welch, in *Biographical Review, Vol. XVIII* (1897), after 398, public domain.

Another prominent signer was Thomas J. Tolman (1819–1874). He was a moderator of the town meeting of South Scituate (Norwell). He and his father Joseph made planes used in smoothing and joining boards for North River ships, as discussed above. Thomas owned a house, land, and mills along River Street near Hanover Four Corners.[401]

Besides Welch of Scituate, and Thomas Tolman of South Scituate, about six were from Marshfield and three from South Scituate. Three were, or had been, prominent shipbuilders: Litchfield (Norwell), Oakman (Marshfield), and Weatherbee (Marshfield). They and most of the others were from old shipbuilder families, whose names appeared on the 1850s subscriptions to improve the river. In addition, many of their homes appeared near the North River on Walling's 1857 map.[402]

These men wanted to reclaim the marshes, as the poster said, to improve them "for agricultural purposes by drainage, by damming out the tide water." That would turn the marshes into upland meadows to be farmed once salt water was evicted. The crops planted there would be more profitable than whatever salt marsh hay was being harvested. There is a long history of draining salt marshes to improve them, explored in more detail in my book, *Ditching the Marshes*. This project would both drain the marshes and dam the river.[403]

The scope of the proposed reclamation was vast. It would extend from White's Ferry to Waterman & Barstow's shipyard, as the poster suggested and as the 1870 report stated. White's Ferry was at the eastern end of the North River, just a few miles above its mouth. The Waterman & Barstow shipyard was at the western end, near the start of the river. The project covered most of the North River, from end to start.[404]

The big meeting was set for Town Hall in South Scituate. It was in the center of South Scituate village. This would have been convenient for many of those whose names appeared on the poster. The Tolmans lived nearby, probably within walking distance. The Town Hall appears on the 1879 Walker atlas (Fig. 82). The Town Hall was not replaced until 1885.[405]

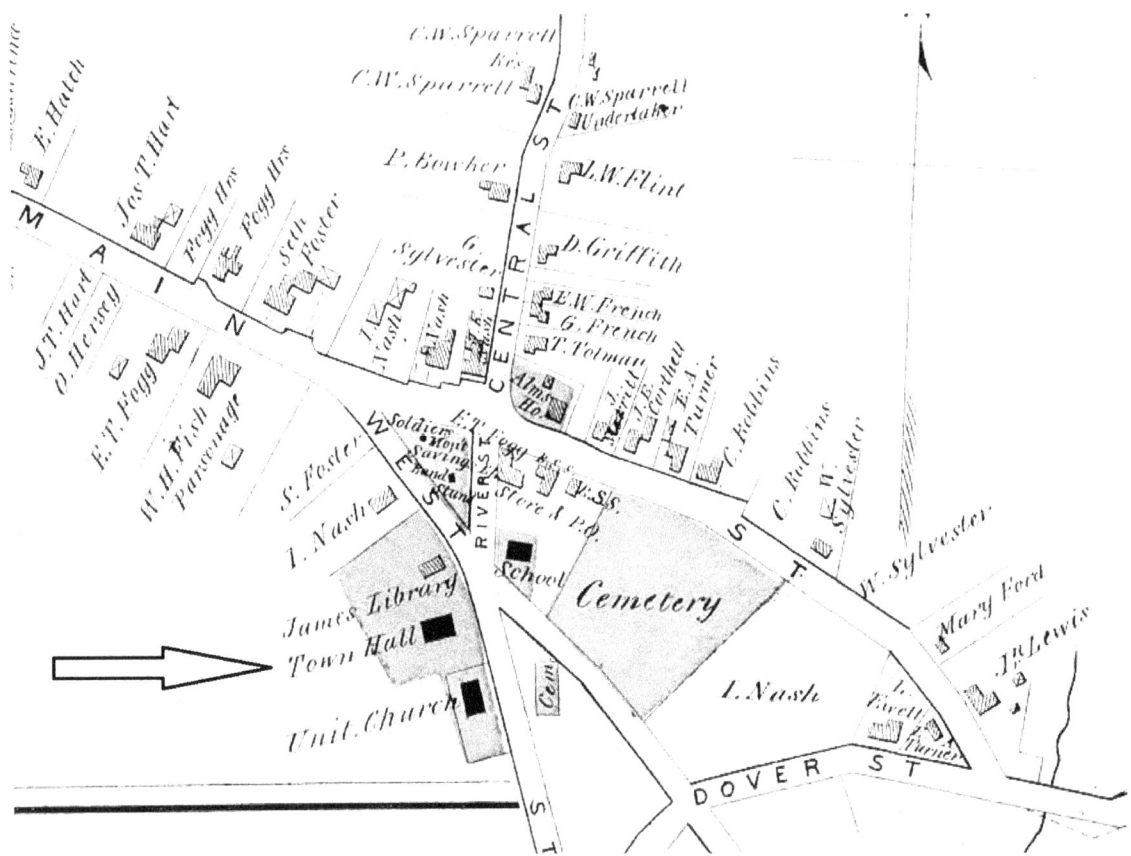

Fig. 82. 1879 Walker atlas, detail from Village of South Scituate, page 32. Arrow added to point to location of town hall. Source: State Library of Massachusetts.

What happened at the big meeting at Town Hall in January 1873 is not known. The plan did not go forward.

Perhaps opposition to the plan, as expressed in the 1870 Scituate town meeting vote, played a role. Probably the plan did not make financial sense. The timing was bad, because the Great Boston Fire of November 1872 cast a pall over investments in property development.

Significant proposals to improve the North River would not surface again until 1915, as discussed below. In the meantime, there were regional and national economic disasters. And there was churn in the real estate market, promising economic value in developing property in the river valley besides reclaiming marshes. We discuss these after considering how this proposed dam compared with others.

Dams Compared

How did the proposed dam compare with others, particularly those of its time?

Its height and capacity were difficult for me to determine from the 1870 report. I am not a hydrographer or a mariner. But here is my analysis.

Mitchell's 1870 report recommended that the dam be 4 ½ feet above mean high tide. Page 58 of the report has a table of measured elevations. Here is his note, "Datum=High water plane of river, June 23, 1870=1.70 feet below mean high water of sea." This measurement was on a specific date and did not state the river's *mean* high water level.

The table shows an elevation at the sea (on the other side of Humarock from the dam site) of *minus 4 feet*. This generally accords with an 1898 Coast Survey chart showing ocean depths of about 5 feet (presumably at low tide), and with Mitchell's associated 1871 sketch, Fig. 10 (right side) (see Fig. 74).

The table lists depths ranging from 4.5 to 4.9 feet at the center of the river channel. Then add a tide range of 8.90 feet at nearby Green Harbor River on June 30, 1870, according to page 42 of the report. Or only 0.8 feet at White's Ferry (Rogers' Wharf), per page 65. And then add Mitchell's recommended 4.5 feet. You get a dam about *10* to *18* feet tall, base to top.

I was curious how this might look in today's scene.

The proposed 1870 dam is close to the Sea Street Bridge (built in 2010) between Marshfield and Humarock, dedicated as the Captain Frederick Stanley Memorial Bridge. A mariner had reported that the bridge had a clearance of more like 11 feet at *mean* high tide, but clearance depends on the actual high tide, which could be higher. That compares to the 1870 proposed dam of 4.5 feet above the then-mean high tide.

So, it seems the dam's top would have been about 11 feet minus 4.5 feet equals 6.5 feet below the bottom of today's bridge.[406]

You can see these numbers reflected in the photos below (Fig. 83 and Fig. 84), from my visit to the Sea Street Bridge on August 15, 2024. Numbers are in feet. The scale is the measured bridge railing height of 3.5 feet (42 inches), and tide charts on that day for *Humarock Beach* (on the other side from the river). Tides vary by time and place. The ones for August 15, 1.3 and 6.9 feet, are a sample only. Later in the week, they ranged from minus 1.31 feet to plus 10.17 feet.[407]

Based on this, the top of the dam would be about level with the top of today's embankment – in other words, about one foot below Ferry Street. You could see the dam's top at about eye-level from the site of today's Bridgewaye Inn.

Fig. 83. Sea Street Bridge over South River, August 15, 2024, 2:30 p.m., low tide, looking south. Humarock (Scituate) on left, Marshfield on right.

Fig. 84. Sea Street Bridge, same view, numbers in feet. At left, low and high tides 8/15/24. At right, 1870 dam's possible height.

The dam could even have been another three feet higher, almost reaching the bottom of the current bridge. But maybe not, since mean high water of the sea was lower in 1870. A recent dig into historical data about tides showed that "sea-level in Boston (MA) rose by nearly a foot (0.28m) over the past 200 years, with most occurring since 1920."[408] Herschel's calculations did not seem to anticipate this sea level rise.

By the way, during my visit I tried to find the boulder that Mitchell used as a surveying benchmark for his 1870 report. I was unsuccessful. The embankment here was extensively altered in building the succession of bridges. The likely site is now the home of a shipbuilder, Crawford Boatbuilding. Yes, there are still boat builders in Marshfield.[409]

Whether 10 or 18 feet tall, the dam was not tall compared with those in Europe at the time, particularly in the Netherlands (Holland). Those were, as Mitchell says in his 1870 report, "up to 21 feet above ordinary high water."[410]

The proposed dam's capacity or volume would have been about 3,780 acre-feet by my calculations.[411]

It may help to peruse the National Inventory of Dams (NID). Yes, there is such a thing. It is authorized by Congress and maintained by the US Army Corps of Engineers. It includes more than 91,000 dams. Half are less than 25 feet in height, and only two percent are more than 100 feet tall. The average age is 63 years.[412]

Those dams built in the 1880s number 2,508. This period included dams of large American rivers, such as the Schuylkill (1822), the Susquehanna (1830), and the Concord (1839). That would have been big company for the proposed North River dam. Perhaps more pertinent is, say, the Birch Pond Dam (1873) in Lynn, MA, NID ID MA00237. It is an earth dam later raised to 25 feet high. It has 1,300 acre-feet of storage, about one-third that of the proposed North River dam. It is evidently not affected by the tides, even though they are only three miles away, because it is an inland reservoir.[413]

Thus, by any measure, the proposed North River dam was unexceptional in height and capacity for its time.

What about older dams? A search of the NID for dams built between 1630 and 1700 yields 12 results. They include the Wampatuck Pond Dam in Hanson, MA. The oldest dam is the Old Oaken Bucket Pond Dam in Scituate, MA, built in 1640. Both are still around, both are on tributaries of the North River, and both appear toward the end of this book, in describing a nice drive in the country.[414]

An Idaho dam's history serves as a caution:

> In his travel guide *Idaho for the Curious*, Cort Conley writes, "There have always been more politicians than suitable damsites. Building the highest straight axis gravity dam in the Western Hemisphere, on a river with a mean flow of 5,000 cubic feet per second [18,000,000 cf/hr], at a cost of $312 million, in the name of flood-control, is the second-funniest joke in Idaho. The funniest joke is inside the visitor center: a government sign entreats, '…help protect this delicate environment for future generations.' The North Fork of the Clearwater was an exceptional river with a preeminent run of steelhead trout, and the drainage contained thousands of elk and white-tail deer. The Army Corps of Engineers proceeded to destroy the river, habitat, and fish; then acquired 5,000 acres for elk management and spent $21 million to build the largest steelhead hatchery in the world, maintaining at a cost of $1 million dollars a year what nature had provided for nothing."[415]

Green Harbor River

The 1870 report covered two projects to reclaim salt marshes by damming their rivers. The North River ran within a mile of the Green Harbor River in Marshfield, and that was the companion project.

Both projects germinated in the early 1800s, when the idea arose of making salt marshes "pay," an idea promoted in earnest after the Civil War. In 1870, both projects were favorably received by the Board of Harbor Commissioners. Unlike the North River project, however, the Green Harbor River project went ahead (Fig. 85).[416] There, according to Stilgoe,

> In July 1872, a private company began building a dike eighteen hundred feet in length and nearly seven feet high, enclosing 1,412 acres of marsh, some 200 of which lay so far inland that everyone considered them essentially fresh. [The legislature authorized this, with a tax on] every landowner who benefited from the diking.[417]

The Green Harbor River's dike was built. Its marshes were productive for a while. The project had mixed results, as described in more detail in John Stilgoe's book *Alongshore*.[418]

The farmers' dike was vigorously opposed by local fishermen. They blew up the dike with dynamite several times, among other defiant acts.[419]

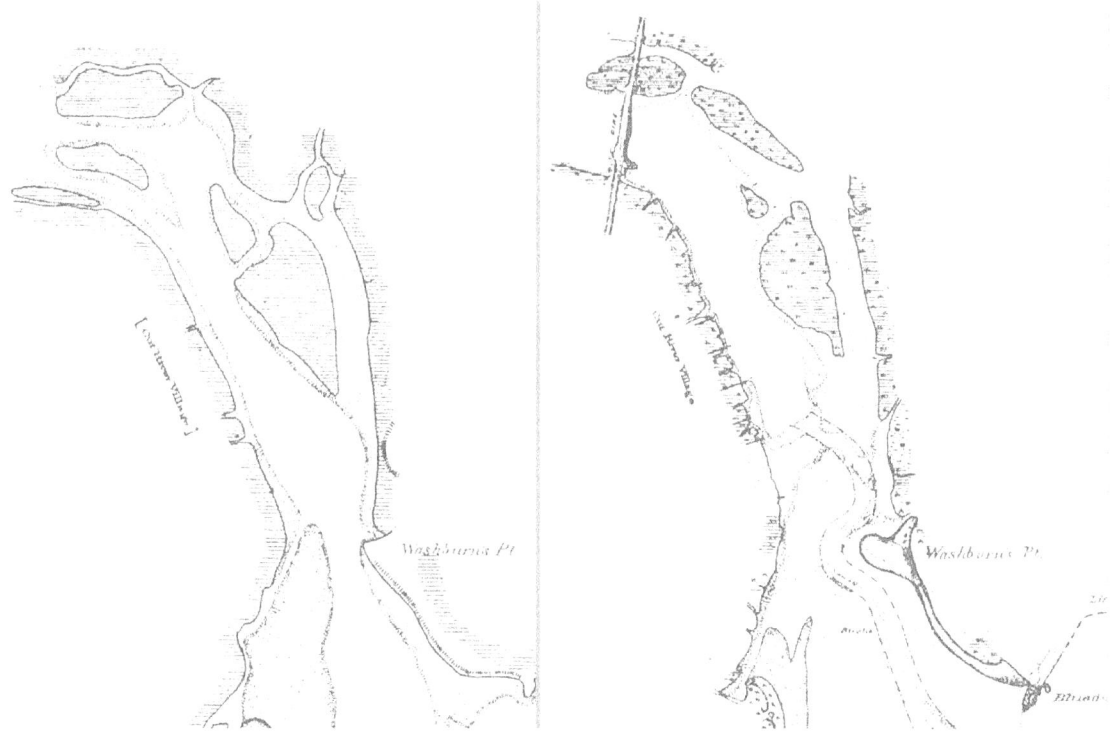

Fig. 85. Change in Green Harbor River from 1857 (Coast Survey map, left) to 1876 (right), after dike added (top). Detail, edited, from "Mouth of Green Harbor River, Massachusetts, Scale 1:10,000" (1876), Harbor Commissioners, State Library of Massachusetts, *Digital Commonwealth*, https://www.digitalcommonwealth.org/search/commonwealth-oai:ww72bf402.

In 1875, the Board of Agriculture reported Prof. Goessmann's detailed chemical and other analyses of the area. He found "inefficient drainage" from the ditches that had been built in the marshes, "leaving the saline constituents behind" to injure new growth. He said:

> These spots appear, in the latter part of the season, as if the torch had passed over them, for nothing but a few genuine salt-plants are usually left.

Goessmann's highly technical report seemed to show that the Green Harbor River diking project was a work in progress.[420]

It was more promising two years later, when the Board's 1877 report included praise for the "new soil on Green Harbor." They were reporting on county exhibitions of produce. Edward White of Marshfield competed for a premium (prize) for a crop of rye "grown upon one acre of the central portion of the dyked marsh-land on Green Harbor River." White said, "The experiments on the Green Harbor marsh have been very successful, and are worthy the serious consideration of all persons owning lands of similar character on the coast."[421]

The state reports of that time are full of anecdotes and experiments like this. They lack statewide scientific analysis of, for example, the value of salt hay versus English hay.

Besides, hay was being produced in abundance in other places, such as the Midwest. The Homestead Act of 1862 opened up federal lands for cultivation. By 1870, the Massachusetts total production of hay (not split out into types) was 597,455 tons. Plymouth County (home to the North River) accounted for only 17,595, far behind Worcester County's 130,185. Compare Massachusetts total production of 597,455 to Michigan's 1,290,923, for example. Although the hay market would have been local, it seemed the North River valley was not a big producer. And it did not seem to make sense spending more to change the land to produce English hay instead of salt hay.[422]

Reclaiming the marshes came down to economics for the agricultural interests of the state. As Prof. Shaler's essay in the Board of Agriculture's 1891 report said:

> The reason for the relative neglect of the excessively watered lands in this country is doubtless to be found in the fact that hitherto frontier land might be had almost for the asking, and consequently it was not economical to undertake the considerable outlay which is always necessary in order to subjugate these excessively humid fields of the marine marshes and fresh-water swamps.[423]

Yet Shaler found that the marine marshes could be made productive if one were "to exclude the salt water and to permit the egress of that which comes from the land by means of a sufficient dike or dam, provided with flood gates which close at the time of the incoming tide and open during the later stages of the reflux." His analysis went on to describe how this could happen, over a matter of three years. This process could apply to 90,000 acres in Massachusetts, including 10,000 acres in Plum Island. Shaler's 1891 essay ended by saying:

> So far the only considerable effort to win these marshes to tillage has been in the town of Marshfield, where, a number of years ago, an area of about fifteen hundred acres was diked off from the sea. Unfortunately, litigation and even violence has delayed the work of bringing the greater part of this area under tillage, yet the results show the admirable fertility of the soil. Fields which of old gave only scanty crops of marsh grass now yield very large returns of hay and root crops. Imperfect as this experiment has been, it serves to assure us as to the great possibilities which are open to drainage processes of this description.[424]

Perhaps the key word here was "experiment." It became costly to repair and maintain the dike and the harbor. By the late 1890s, the state had become responsible for repairing Green Harbor and was committed "to an eternity of dredging."[425]

The Portland Gale of 1898 washed away 50 or 60 feet of the Green Harbor River dike, according to a *Boston Globe* article, and it halted construction of an anchorage basin,

> which was the result of the agitation of many years, commencing in 1871, for the removal of the dyke in the harbor. ...
>
> A county road crowns the dyke, and it is assumed in some quarters that the selectmen of Marshfield will be compelled to go ahead and rebuild the road, as it leads to the richest farming land in Massachusetts, which has been made through the construction of the dyke.
>
> There are about 1500 acres of this land, very little of which has been cultivated, but that which has been has shown its value.[426]

That seems like a small return in value for diking all that acreage, after almost 30 years. In any event, the dike was rebuilt. The state government continued to pay. In 1902, for example, the *Hingham Journal* reported:

> Green Harbor River in Marshfield, which was dredged about three years ago by the government at a cost of $80,000, has so filled with sand as to be unnavigable at low tide. A 50 foot channel, with eight feet of water at ebb tide, was dug, together with an anchorage basin. The channel has filled up, while the basin is about half its original depth. This, with the previous expenditures in building a dyke across the river in 1870, makes a waste of $130,000 in attempted improvements here. The fishermen hope for the taking away of the dyke by the government. It is believed this will scour out the sand in the river and restore the excellent harbor of the olden days.[427]

In 1978, a century after the dike was built, a historical marker was placed on the dike, now part of Dike Road (Rte. 139). The marker says:

> The Dike: Built 1872. Widened 1879 to carry road between Green Harbor and Brant Rock. Originally a toll road. Cause of a feud between dikers (farmers) and anti-dikers (fishermen).

The town documented the marker in the state's cultural resource database, MACRIS. The document concluded:

> Except for a few cranberry bogs, no great amount of farming was done on the land the farmers wanted drained for that purpose. The dikers lost invested money and the anti-dikers their tempers. The harbor remains and so does the fishing industry.[428]

Today, Green Harbor is home to recreational boating and fishing. The Green Harbor River area is mostly open space and includes the Marshfield Municipal Airport. The area has patches of prime farmland, as well as 660 acres of wooded swamp out of 1,045 acres of total wetlands.[429]

Despite damming the Green Harbor River, and the many attempts to dam the North River, there are still marshes in Marshfield![430]

So the Green Harbor River project was an experiment. That word would have applied even more strongly to the North River project. These were experiments in the sense that America began emulating projects tried in Europe, including dikes in the Netherlands. At least the Green Harbor River project moved ahead. It had its struggles but with some successes at the time. In contrast, The North River project did not move ahead.

In hindsight, these projects were ahead of their time. Projects to reclaim salt marshes would continue to crop up in other states into the 1900s. Where once they were challenging, unique engineering projects that attracted leading hydrographers, like those in the 1870s, they now were commercial business prospects by promoters. They showed little respect for the marshes and their grasses. For example, see this article of October 7, 1906, about reclaiming salt marshes in Connecticut and Long Island, NY:

> Between Bridgeport and Stratford, on the Sound shore, is a tract of 1,000 acres crossed by small creeks and covered with a rank growth of salt grass. In the past this grass has been gathered and has found a market of indifferent character, being used for packing and bedding. It brought only $8 a ton and on that basis barely paid for the work of gathering it. About a year ago the work of reclaiming an area of ten acres was undertaken under the direction of E. J. Hollister who was the organizer and is now the general

adviser of the Winona Agricultural Institute, at Winona Lake, Indiana and who has supervised reclamation projects at many places in the United States and Canada. One of his more recent undertakings in this part of the country resulted in converting a large tract of lowland and bogs at Locust Valley, L.I. …

Mr. Hollister feels justified in predicting that this practically worthless tract can be made to yield annually hay or tame grass as he calls it, worth at least $45 an acre with a certain increase of this amount to $100 an acre after the soil has been more thoroughly treated and made suitable for planting other crops such as "sweet corn["], celery, and asparagus.[431]

It seems this site of 1,000 acres became almost fully developed. It left fewer than 700 acres of salt marsh, of which 421 acres are now protected by the Great Meadows unit of the Stewart B. McKinney National Wildlife Refuge.[432]

Scientific interest would later move on from dikes and dams and reclamation, to focus more on our environment, our landscape, and our salt marshes.

In the meantime, economic interests moved on, from agricultural reclamation to seacoast housing developments on land, not on marshes.

7

DEVELOPING THE VALLEY

1870s–1880s Developments

Economic conditions were difficult in the early 1870s. True, the railroad came and gave a boost to Scituate, Marshfield, and Duxbury. But the Great Boston Fire in late 1872 destroyed buildings in Boston, and destroyed investments there and on the South Shore. Bostonians stopped investing in the new Eaton's Hotel at the new Greenbush rail station in Scituate, and the hotel's associated real estate development plans fell flat. The Financial Panic of 1873 and the subsequent "Great Depression" pressured banks, railroads, and investors in various parts of the country. In short, it was a time of economic distress.[433]

During this time, E. Parker Welch bought property in Scituate, including roughly 12 acres of swamp or salt marsh. Arguably, a few of the parcels were close enough for their value to increase if the North River reclamation proposals were adopted. Some of these purchases were not recorded in the Plymouth County Registry of Deeds until later, on February 18, 1873. This was the month after the big meeting announced in the poster for January 1873. Perhaps the timing was a coincidence, or irrelevant.[434]

After all, Parker Welch and his father Michael already owned much real estate, including house lots, pastures, swampland, and other valuable properties as of early 1875. That included 58 acres of salt marsh. The salt marsh was valued for tax purposes at an average of $19 per acre. That meant, if the Welches so calculated, the dam would have brought only a marginal increase in the value of their salt marsh, maybe close to the $22 per acre that consultant Herschel had suggested. In addition, that $22 per acre was somewhat speculative, and the project could have caused damages to property not otherwise calculated, such as construction disruption to farming.[435]

Parker Welch would go on to found the iconic Welch Company, with his 20-year-old son George, in 1879.[436]

But his dealings raise the question of what else was going on in the real estate market around the North River. Plans were afoot to develop coastal and agricultural land into housing and accommodations for summer visitors. It turns out there was at least one big deal, in Marshfield.

A Hill of Dreams

The *Boston Globe* for August 22, 1873, ran this article, almost a promotional advertisement, "Important Land Sale in Marshfield Highlands — A Large Crowd and a Partially Successful Sale." The article called the place "Hatch farm" at "Sea View." The owner was Mr. H. P. Flint. The sale, or auction, was held August 21.[437]

On that day, about 500 people visited the property, attracted partly by free transport on a special train from Boston (typically as much as $1.25) and by free lunch. The property, according to the article, "is situated on the brow of a hill overlooking the North River and directly opposite what is known as Fourth Cliff." There was an "extensive line of beach which stretches out in the plain below."[438]

Not a word mentioned the proposal, months earlier, to build a dam there "formed of gravel from the adjoining hill." Sea View would have overlooked this proposed construction site. (Perhaps the proposal had perished by then.) Instead, the article promised a new hotel on the crest of the hill, new avenues including one along the beach, and a new bridge across the North River.[439]

The article said the lots sold in this proposed colony were the most desirable, and "the average price was about 1 ¼ cents per foot, about $550 per acre. The same land a year ago was purchased for $100 per acre." The article said about forty-five lots were sold, and, "Nearly all the land in the vicinity has been bought up in large parcels by land companies and others." The article concluded, "although the competition was not lively, there was enough to indicate that in a few years Sea View will rank prominently amongst the popular Summer resorts of Massachusetts."[440]

I sent the article to my friend Ray Freden, formerly of Sea View, an expert on its history.

His response: "Wow, I have never seen this. I'm pretty sure that is the now Holly Hill, once called Hatch Hill & Governor's Hill. 1873 was the year Littletown was changed to Sea View, two years after the first RR Station was built in Littletown."[441]

Ray and I tried to sort out this little mystery.

Below is the plan of the new development (Fig. 86). Presumably, auctioneer N. A. Thompson handed out copies to the 500 people who visited the property on August 21. The plan had about 363 lots, most about 15,000 to 18,000 square feet, located on about 170 acres. It did not show a hotel.[442]

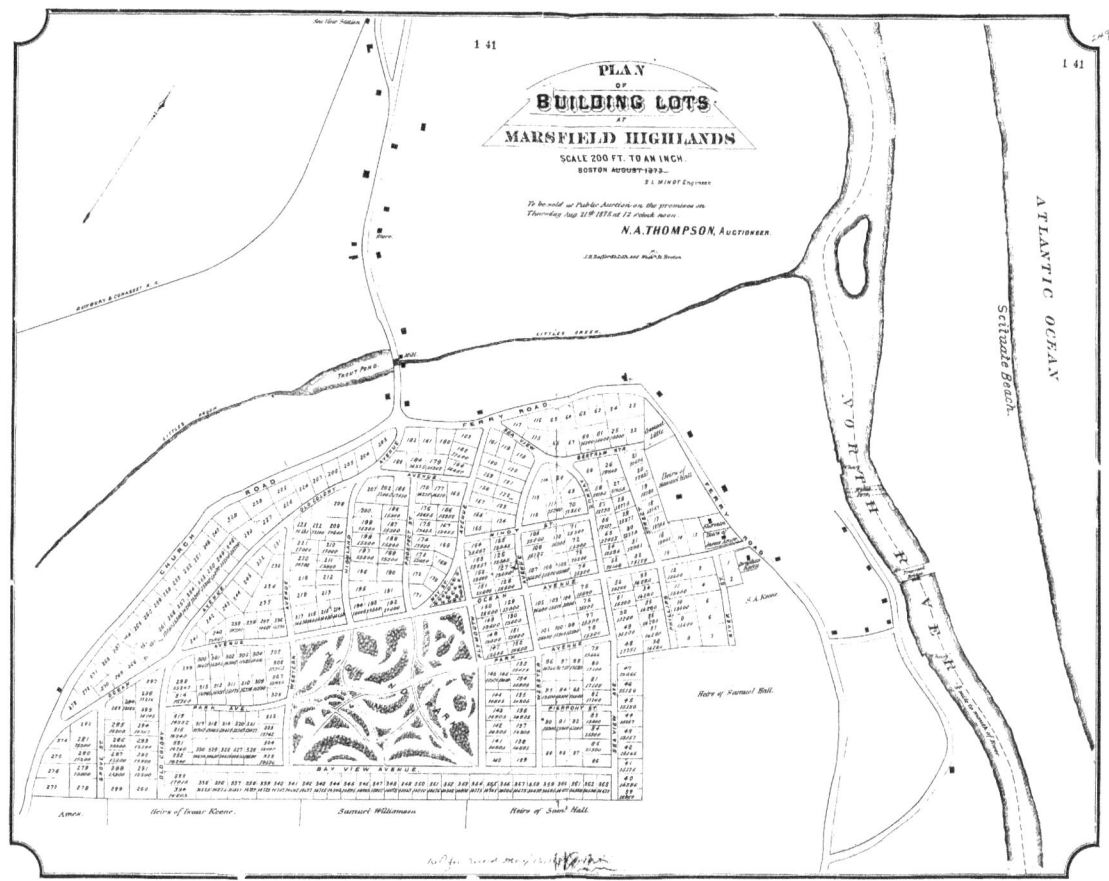

Fig. 86. S. L. Minot, "Plan of Building Lots at Marsfield [sic] Highlands, Scale 200 ft. to an inch," August 1873. White's Ferry shown, along with "Proposed Bridge" crossing North River.

Parts of the plan were accurate, but the plan was mostly speculative. The news article contained some questionable statements. As Ray remarked,

> A large hotel to be built, yes, so rumored, never happened, and yes the Sea View Station was in view back then.
>
> The clincher as to the exact location, to me, is the fact an Avenue was to be built along the Peninsula connecting the east side of the hill over a new bridge. The bridge was built in 1881&2 along with the Humarock Hotel. And the new Sea St. ran to the hill's base.
>
> … In 1873 there were no named roads on Hatch's Hill.[443]

Yet the plan had plenty of named streets, probably speculative, including a Minot St., probably in honor of the plan's drafter.

So what really happened after the plan? We need to trace the history of the property's recorded deeds.

In early 1872, Stephen M. Allen of Duxbury, later Boston, acquired 170 acres called Hatch's Hill from several Hatch family members and others. Allen was evidently a short-term land speculator. In late 1872, many Boston investors, maybe including Allen, lost money in the Great Boston Fire.[444]

On February 8, 1873, Allen sold the land to Horace P. Flint of Boston, perhaps another short-term land speculator. The price was $17,000. That is $100 per acre, matching the statement in the later news article. Allen took back a mortgage in that amount from Flint. The mortgage mentioned two notes that Flint gave Allen (amounts not specified), and contained a nebulous, optional down payment of $1,200. In case of default, Allen or his executors had the right to sell the granted premises with all improvements thereon. The mortgage contemplated partial releases as lots were sold, at a minimum of $500 per release. On October 13, 1873, Allen gave a small partial release of the mortgage to Flint as to lot 78, with 15,300 square feet, in exchange for $114.75.[445]

Meanwhile, the auction on August 21, 1873, produced a few sales. However, according to recorded deeds, they fell far short of the 45 sales claimed in the article on the day after the auction. On October 25, 1873, Flint made a $2,600 sale to Martha D. Luce, of Edgartown, for three lots (lots 361–363) comprising almost an acre. He made a similar $2,772 sale (lots 10–12) to Luce, who soon resold them. These were aberrations for their high prices (and of questionable legitimacy). Leaving those aside, Flint made eight recorded sales of nine lots from September 26 through roughly the end of the year, for about $4,908 total. That was about $545 per lot, with an average 13,403 square feet per lot. That was much more than the $550 per acre claimed in the August news article (another questionable amount). Taking at face value those sales, plus the sales to Luce, meant that Flint was more than halfway to paying off the $17,000 mortgage.[446]

The following year 1874 brought in about 13 sales of 18 lots through July 24. (Seven sales were to one man who soon resold some of his lots.) The proceeds could have been more than enough to pay off the mortgage, and for Flint to make a profit. But that overlooks the cost of building a hotel, and a break in Flint's relationship with the mortgage holder.[447]

It turns out that Allen had assigned the mortgage to James Deshon, perhaps yet another speculator, on June 23, 1873, even before the August 21 auction (and even before Allen's partial release of Flint). The stated consideration was $17,000. On August 20, 1874, Deshon, presumably having lost patience, foreclosed on the mortgage for breach of condition, thereby becoming owner of the property. (It is not clear what effect this might have had on those who purchased lots over the previous year.) Years later, in 1881, Deshon sold the property for $1,500 (compared to his purchase price of $17,000) to George G. Currall of Marshfield, who sold it on the same date for the same amount to George Emery of Marshfield. Emery's estate there is discussed below.[448]

Meanwhile, in October 1874, Flint sold his remaining interests (if any) to Thomas Flint (formerly of Peabody) (a son?), in return for $8,000.[449]

The 1873 plan to build a large hotel on the hill seems to have been more than an idle promise.

William B. Stinson had a contract to build a hotel to be called the Webster House in Sea View. The price was $25,000. He had nearly completed it, but, failing to get his payments from the owner, he stopped work and got a mechanic's lien on the building. He also got a fire insurance policy from the Royal Insurance Company in July 1875. On September 10, 1875, the *Hingham Journal* reported, "The large four-story wooden structure known as the 'Webster House,' recently erected at Sea View, East Marshfield, was destroyed by fire on Wednesday night last." It was unoccupied at the time.[450]

The only surviving image of the hotel is likely to be this small sketch made by a surveyor of North River Flats in June 1875 (Fig. 87).[451]

Fig. 87. Detail of H. G. Reed, "Survey of North River Flats, Made June 1875, Scale 100 ft. to an inch, Hummock Flat," PCRD plan book 1/52, sheet 3/7, recorded January 7, 1876. With notation "South Chimney of Hotel in Marshfield."

Stinson, the builder, probably doubted he could recover his loss from the owner, whoever that was at the time. Also, it is not clear that either Flint or Allen had insured the project. So Stinson sued the insurance company, was awarded $5,344, and the case went to the US Supreme Court. The court affirmed the judgment in an 1881 opinion.[452]

About the 1875 fire, Ray said, "Not a single town historian has ever published any information of this event."[453]

You might say that the Allen-Flint-Deshon venture was a grand failure. However, the 1873 news article was right to predict that Sea View's rank as a summer destination would rise. It just took longer than the "few years" mentioned in the article.

In 1888, "George Ireland bought all the available land on Ferry Hill and began developing it into small lots, geared for tents and hunting camps," according to an

NSRWA article. The story of Ferry Hill's early years and development are told and illustrated well in a 2023 blog post by Ray.[454]

Meanwhile, in 1881, George Emery picked up where Flint trailed off. His property acquisitions went beyond those of Allen-Flint-Deshon, and the speculations of the early 1870s on what had been called "Hatch's Hill."

It was called "Governor's Hill" for George Emery (1835–1909), the former governor of Utah Territory (1875–1880) (Fig. 88). He grew up in Medford, MA, graduated from Dartmouth College in 1858, became a lawyer, and in 1866 married Marcia Hall, from the famed North River shipbuilding family. He bought about 500 acres in Marshfield, much of "Hatch's Hill," starting in 1881.[455]

Fig. 88. George W. Emery, unknown photographer and date, *Biographical Review, Vol. XVIII* (1897), 486, public domain.

Fig. 89. Emery mansion, unknown photographer and date, courtesy of Ray Freden.

Emery's estate was grand (Fig. 89), as described in an 1897 biographical sketch:

> Governor Emery settled in that part of Marshfield called Sea View, where he has a beautiful country seat. The commodious dwelling, built by himself in 1885–86, is picturesquely situated on a sightly elevation near the shore, surrounded by extensive grounds, embracing several hundred acres diversified with trees and shrubbery, which form a part of his estate.[456]

Emery was a director of the New England Agricultural Society for many years, and was a president of the Marshfield Fair.[457]

Fig. 90. Unknown photographer, late 1800s, showing two barns of ex-Gov. George Emery on opposite sides of Ferry Street. Courtesy of Ray Freden.

This photo, probably from the late 1800s, shows two of Emery's barns, on opposite sides of Ferry Street (Fig. 90).

At right is the "Phillips - Hall, Sam – Emery House" at 1000 Ferry Street. It still exists and is well documented in MACRIS. In the background are extensive salt marshes and a dark peninsula, likely Snake Hill. Ray and I believe the light-colored peninsula in the far background, is Rexhame. At far left would be the southern tip of Humarock, then separated from Rexhame by the old mouth of the North River, up until the storm of 1898.[458]

This interpretation of the photo is based on some educated guesswork.

Assuming the photo was taken from the Emery mansion, or in a field between the mansion and the two barns, then the camera would have pointed south-southeast. Key points are circled on the detail of the Richards 1903 map, plate 27, below left (Fig. 91). This plate covers Marshfield. It has a subplan of Ferry Hill, below right (Fig. 92). The subplan displays "Holly Grove," Gov. Emery's estate.

In the Richards 1903 map, this plate 27, and the equivalent plate for Scituate, both show the old mouth of the river closed. This plate labels the river as both "South River" and "North River."[459]

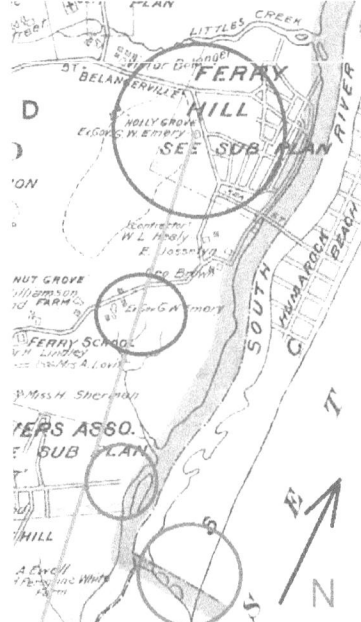

Fig. 91. Detail of Richards 1903 map, plate 27, marked (from top): likely camera position, two Emery barns, Snake Hill, and old river mouth.

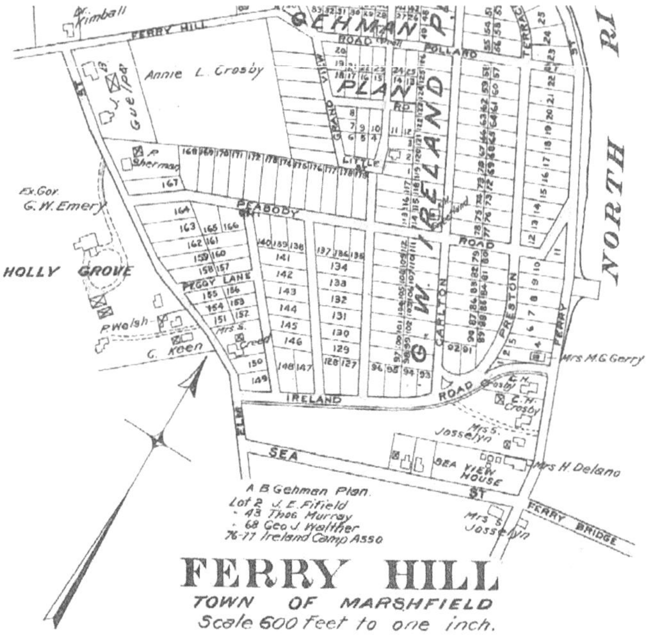

Fig. 92. Detail of Richards 1903 map, plate 27, subplan of Ferry Hill, with its planned streets and lots, and Emery mansion at left on Holly Hill, here labeled Holly Grove.

From his estate, Gov. Emery had a wide view of the ocean, the river, salt marshes, and the shore. That included the Marshfield home of the late Daniel Webster, then and perhaps still, the most famous graduate of Dartmouth College.

Emery's estate on Holly Hill was not the end of development schemes there. For more on that, you need to read Ray Freden's blog on Hatch's Hill, Part 2, and follow the Dwight and Parker sagas. This was truly a hill of dreams.

Today, some people, even Marshfield residents, are unsure where these places are.

Holly Hill is just west of Ferry Hill, across Elm Street. A good image is the Ferry Hill subplan from the Richards 1903 map, shown above (Fig. 92). As shown below, the USGS series of topographic maps from about 1900 typically show those hills but do not label them, and they sometimes do not label Sea View (see Fig. 93 and Fig. 94). That place name, now somewhat neglected, appears on a few maps, including a recent USGS map (Fig. 95). "Governor's Hill" does not.[460]

Fig. 93. 1885 USGS topographic map, Duxbury quad, 1893 ed., detail. Typically for this map series, no labels appear for Sea View, Holly Hill, Ferry Hill, or Sea Street bridge to Humarock.

Fig. 94. 1917 partial revision of 1885 USGS topo map. It labels Sea View (center), but not Holly Hill, Ferry Hill (center right, with planned streets), or Sea Street bridge to Humarock (here, with planned streets).

Fig. 95. 2021 USGS topographic map, Scituate quad, detail, mostly Marshfield. At lower center, Sea View makes a triangle with names of Ferry Hill and Holly Hill. Also, this shows extent of salt marshes. At upper center is Trouant Island, discussed in text below.

Great Green Island, Flats, and Other Islands

Once there was a big island in the middle of the North River, in the North River Flats. It was next to the beach between Third Cliff and Fourth Cliff. It was called the Great Green Island. It was probably built up by sand washed over the beach by storms. The storm of 1898 destroyed the beach. Afterward, that island seems to have disappeared, along with others in the flats.[461]

The island is probably the jagged one at the angle where the North River turned south, shown on the 1831 Robbins & Turner map (Fig. 96). Note that the line down the river probably denoted the main channel of the river, and thus the boundary between Scituate and Marshfield.

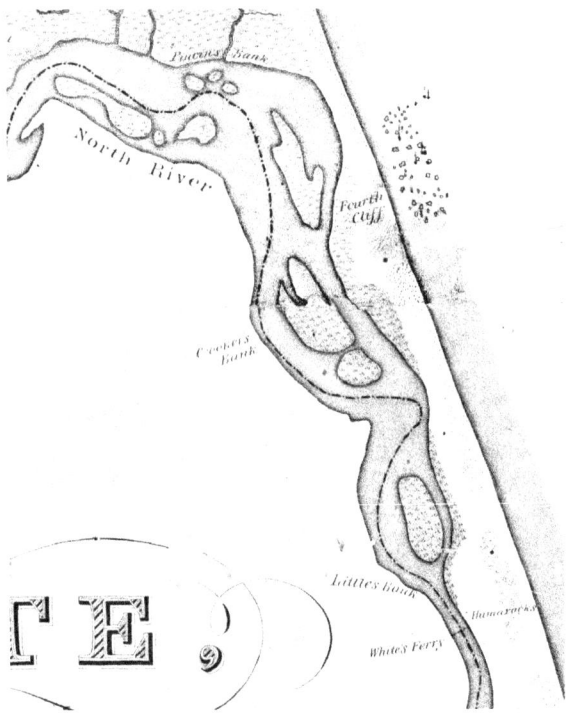

Fig. 96. Detail, highly edited, showing North River islands on 1831 Robbins & Turner map of Scituate. Courtesy of Harvard College Library.

Perhaps the island was the shoal mentioned in the 1843 legislative report recommending a cut between Third Cliff and Fourth Cliff:

> It is true, a small shoal is found at the angle of the river, where the proposed new channel would be opened; but this shoal, your committee believe, would soon disappear, from the action of the sea and the ebbing and flowing of the tide, in which case, all serious obstacles to navigation would be removed.[462]

The records do not specify the size of Great Green Island. It could have been anywhere from three to nine acres by my rough calculations. The three acres came from the 1870 map (see Fig. 68), where the island appears about the same size as the three-acre Wood Island. The nine acres came from the 1875 plan, copied below (Fig. 97), using one of the surveyor's measures of 285 feet, producing an island about 285 feet wide and 285 feet times 5 ½ long. Your calculations may vary. Town real estate tax valuation lists in 1848 and 1849 do not include town property, so do not specify its size.[463]

People used the North River Flats from colonial times. They harvested thatch for roofs of their dwellings. Towns regulated that. For example, at a town meeting of June 26, 1668, "The Town did agree and Conclude that if any man did cut any Thatch on the North river flats before the 15 day of agust annial hee shold forfit ten shillings a day or part of a day to the Townes use."[464]

The Great Green Island appeared in town records as early as 1733, when the island was to be "let out" (leased). This was evidently for cutting thatch, harvesting salt hay, and shellfishing.[465]

Centuries later, people harvested clams from the flats. That, too, was regulated.

A 1909 state report said, "There is no clam industry at Scituate. The selectmen of the town have forbidden all exportation of clams for market, and consequently the few clams dug are utilized for home consumption. … Affairs at Marshfield are in practically the same state of inactivity as at Scituate." The biggest production for the market came from Newburyport ($61,000), Ipswich ($18, 750), and Salisbury ($16,500). Production had declined since 1879, and the report blamed overfishing.[466]

At times, such as in 1907, officers of Scituate and Marshfield waged "A vigorous war on illegal clammers who are digging clams for market [not for their own use]." They made arrests.[467]

In 1908, Scituate prosecuted John P. Gaffney of Marshfield, who dug six bushels of clams. A news report said,

> Mr Gaffney pleaded not guilty, and, conducting his own case, contended that the spot where the clams were dug, Hummock flats, belonged to the towns of Pembroke and Marshfield, and that the selectmen of Scituate had no jurisdiction in the matter. … Selectman [E. Parker] Welch testified as to the action of the board in the matter, and claimed that the town of Scituate controlled the North river flats which bordered on the town of Scituate. Deputy Sheriff Turner, who prosecuted the case, told of posting the warning signs in regard to digging clams [and these were dug in the closed season].[468]

The court found Gaffney guilty and fined him $50. Perhaps he should have argued that the flats were owned by Norwell, as discussed below, but the court did not seem sympathetic to his cause. He appealed, presumably again acting as his own counsel, but we do not know the outcome.

It seems enforcement loosened up a few years later. Walter Crossley saw no need for permits and said, "We dug on any flat that had clams, Marshfield or Scituate, it made no difference." And this was digging for market.[469]

***

Although the 1908 case against Gaffney was prosecuted by Scituate, in fact the town had already conveyed North River flats, including the Great Green Island, to South Scituate (later Norwell), as they split apart in 1849.[470]

The 1849 deed to South Scituate included:

> the Salt Meadows or Flats on the North River known by the following names, To Wit — The Gulph Island, The Middle Green Island and Sunken Flat, The Jacob Flat, The Northey Flat, the Great Green Island, The Great Flat, and The Hummock Flats, they being all the flats that have been annually let at auction.[471]

Why would South Scituate want these flats? They were outliers, closer to Marshfield than the new town of South Scituate. My guess is the new town held hopes of reviving its shipbuilding industry. The industry was in decline, almost terminal by then. But, as we have seen above, in the mid-1800s ships were being built and proposals were made to improve the river. Owning the flats could make it easier for South Scituate to construct ways around the obstructions to navigability.

Later, in 1875, eminent local engineer H. G. Reed drew a detailed plan of Great Green Island (Fig. 97). This was one of his five plans of North River Flats. It was recorded by William S. Danforth of Plymouth, evidently the Register of Deeds. Danforth ran for that office (presumably successfully) every three years from 1864 to 1900. Reed's plans offer no clues why the plans were needed and who paid for their creation.[472]

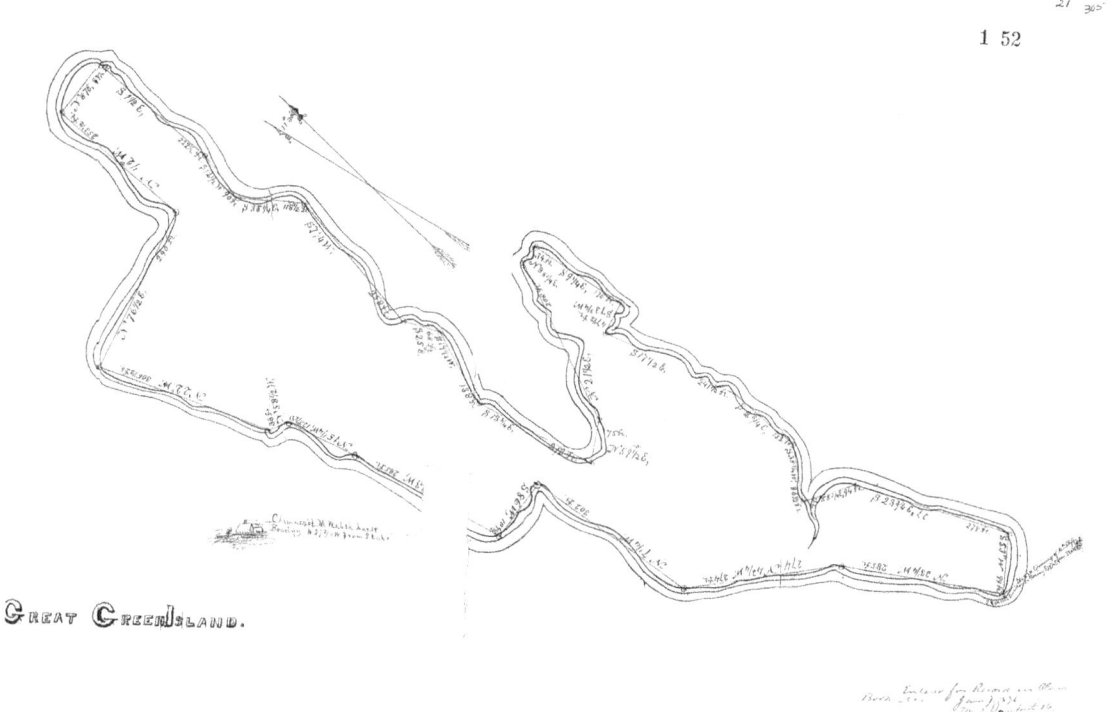

Fig. 97. H. G. Reed, "Great Green Island," probably June 1, 1875, PCRD plan book 1/52, sheet 4 of 7, recorded January 7, 1876. Part of series on North River flats. Reference point, lower left, has sketch of M. Welch house on Third Cliff.

Reed's plan of the Great Green Island is notable because it:

- shows a distinctive double-barbed shape formed by two triangles or peninsulas, a narrow waist in its center, and evidently a stream that almost bisects the very southern end of the island, otherwise featureless
- has North arrows pointing to upper left, no scale given, except metes and bounds notes (references to local features)
- uses a house on Fourth Cliff as a reference point, with a tiny sketch (looks like an ordinary farmhouse, smaller than Welch's, not a hotel), and a note "North Chimney of 4th Cliff house Bearing S18 [?] E from Stake" — almost certainly the Fourth Cliff House, a two-story building, "one of the first summer boarding houses on the South Shore," discussed above[473]
- uses the Welch farmhouse on Third Cliff as a key reference point, noting "Chimney of M. Welsh house Bearing N37 ¾ W from Stake"
- includes a tiny sketch of the Welch farmhouse, built before 1821, one of the earliest depictions of the house. It looks like a typical farmhouse, five bays in front, gable roof, another structure behind, maybe a wing or separate barn, all set on a hill with a tree[474]

The Great Green Island's distinctive jagged shape shows up on many maps and plans: Scituate in the 17th Century (Bangs, 1997), 1831 (Robbins & Turner, Fig. 47 and Fig. 96), 1838 (Ford, Marshfield), 1870 (Fig. 68), 1887 (Boston Bay), 1888 (Fig. 98), 1898 (pre-storm), and even the 1902 post-storm atlas of town boundaries (Fig. 3). It does not appear on the Richards 1903 map.[475]

Great Green Island's distinctive jagged shape shows up on an 1888 USGS topographic map (Fig. 98). Here it is mistakenly labeled Trouant Island. Trouant Island, also called Trouants or Trouant's Island was a bit southwest, with a different shape and size, and its own history, which is discussed below.

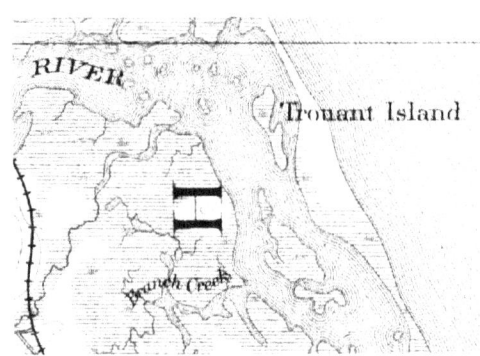

Fig. 98. 1888 USGS topo map, Duxbury, detail showing possible Great Green Island next to Fourth Cliff, mislabeled as Trouant Island, which is across the river at the sideways "H."

The island was around for a long time, at least 165 years from its mention in 1733 town records to its evident demise after the Portland Gale of 1898. It was a part of Scituate's history. Or, rather, Norwell's history, since Scituate deeded it to South Scituate, which later became Norwell. Or, better said, it is a part of the North River's history.

Perhaps Great Green Island just washed away in the 1898 storm, as predicted in 1843. Or maybe after the 1898 storm, Great Green Island (or parts of it) migrated to another town, attaching itself to Scituate's Fourth Cliff, or Marshfield's Trouant Island. Only a good geomorphology study might say what happened to Great Green Island.

Farther upstream, two marsh islands survived the storm, and were known as Onion Island and Potato Island. In the early 1900s, according to Walter Crossley,

> These were favorite picnic and blueberry stops. Onion was the larger and usually had cattle pastured on it.
>
> I well remember one picnic lunch that was interrupted by a bull. Naturally, everyone ran for the boat. But upon looking back, we saw my father on all fours bellowing at the intruder. This was a new experience to the animal and after a spirited exchange of pawing the ground and roaring, he backed down and grumbled off on his way.[476]

If you are looking for islands with drama, Great Green Island is not the best. Read Briggs' book, *Shipbuilding on North River*, to find adventures waiting for ships built on the North River as they sailed around the world, often with Scituate captains.[477]

For example, the *Globe* left Nantucket in December 1822 on a whaling voyage to the Sandwich Islands, Hawaii, Japan, back to Sandwich Islands, and then Fanning Island, which is about 1,000 miles south of Hawaii. There, crewmembers committed a murderous mutiny. The ship made it back to Nantucket. Not all the original crewmembers did.[478]

Trouant Island

Trouant Island seems to go back to a colonial settler named Truant. A 1664 record mentions "a parcel of meadow on the southerly side of the North River near Steven Tilden's Island, bought from Morris Truant." The island lies on the west side of the river, opposite the tip of Fourth Cliff. It is in Marshfield, not Scituate or Norwell. It appears in the center of this detail of a 1935 map, circled within a circle (Fig. 99).[479]

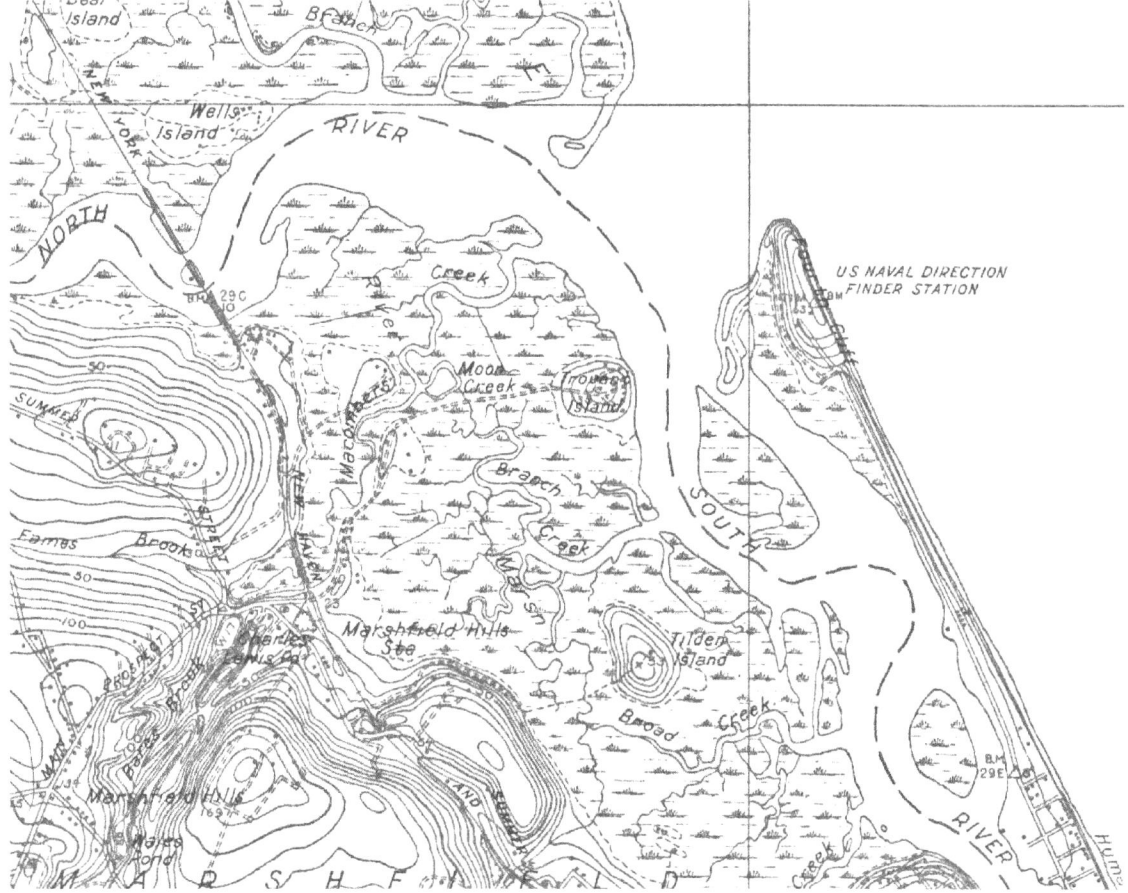

Fig. 99. 1935 USGS topo map, Scituate, detail (1:24:000).

This 1935 USGS map (Fig. 99) has no island that looks like Great Green Island. The map shows a large amount of wetlands on both sides of the river. By the time of this map, the river had broken through between Third Cliff and Fourth Cliff, as discussed in more detail in the next chapter (see also Fig. 100).[480]

Fig. 100. Panoramic view at river mouth looking south, 3/26/25, high tide. From left: Fourth Cliff, spit running across middle half of photo, opening to South River, Trouant Island with houses.

Trouant Island became a place for summer camps (cottages). They offered nearby hunting, fishing, clamming, or canoeing. There was even haunting by a lady ghost in the early 1900s, described by prolific local author and storyteller Edward Rowe Snow.[481]

Walter Crossley (1898–1991) also had stories about Trouant Island:

> The first [memory] was my being in the area about '07-'08 when my father and the late Charles Turner of Pembroke bought a power boat and rented a place on Trouants Island. They did this for a couple of summers. At that time the sand bar at the north end of the cliff [Fourth Cliff] ran almost due west and from the island one looked across the bar to see the bay outside the beach.[482]

The place name is and has been pronounced "Trowants."[483]

The Howard family had a long history here. Jack Howard (1875–1971) was an outdoorsman and photographer. His photos document hunting trips in Maine as well as summer shore life in the early 1900s at Trouant Island (Fig. 101, Fig. 102, and Fig. 103).[484]

Jack Howard's grandson said, "My father had endless stories about the Island, about rowing to Humarock to buy cold soft drinks, digging clams, and working on Rob Tilden's farm as a teenager. My grandfather's correspondence shows that he was very distressed when it became clear that the island would be sold." He closed up the family cottage in 1956 or 1957.[485]

Jack Howard's grandson provided some photos of those long-ago days at Trouant Island.

Fig. 101. Clamming on Trouant Island, 1914 by these boys, John Brooks Howard (1908–1929) and Frank Howard (1910-1962). Photo by John Brooks (Jack) Howard (1875-1971). Courtesy of John Brooks Howard 3rd, nephew of the boys.

Fig. 102. Rowing near Trouant Island, 1914. Building(s) in background may be the old life-saving station on Humarock (Fourth Cliff), destroyed by fire in 1919. The woman rowing is Helen (Pellerin) Howard (1885-1978). By John Brooks (Jack) Howard, 1875-1971. Courtesy John Brooks Howard 3rd, her grandson.

Fig. 103. Hunting shore birds near Trouant Island, 1914 (?). By John Brooks (Jack) Howard (1875-1971). Courtesy of John Brooks Howard 3rd.

Fig. 104. Aerial view of river mouth showing Trouant Island (center) and part of Fourth Cliff, 12/11/1934, Fairchild Aerial Surveys, Inc., N.Y.C., scale 1:36,000. The photo shows about a dozen cottages on the island. Courtesy of MassDOT (A-2-D_473).

In 1934 and in 1965, there were a dozen cottages on Trouant Island. More recently, Trouant Island was described as "accessible over a narrow causeway that is otherwise submerged at high tide."[486]

Today, Trouant Island has been transformed from a "unique and wild place" with "tiny seasonal cottages and secluded tranquility," to a private 26-acre island offering houses for sale at close to $4 million.[487]

8

1898 Portland Gale and Aftermath

Nature Had Other Plans

Plans to improve the North River and develop the valley were upended by the 1898 Portland Gale. It dramatically changed Scituate's shore and the course and character of the North River. The storm has been extensively discussed in news reports and books. It was and still is something to marvel at, talk about, and learn from.[488]

NSRWA's website summarizes the storm: "Named after one of over 100 ships that were wrecked during the course of the storm, the Portland Gale claimed more than 400 lives in under 24 hours. It is considered to be New England's worst maritime disaster, with widespread destruction of homes, railroad tracks, and bridges."[489]

The storm also took lives. Shortly after the storm, a local cottager called "Auntie Ria" made a diary entry:

> But the sad part of the storm to us was what happened on the Marsh. Every fall our boys go on the marsh a gunning. The have lots of sport. They start about 2 o'clock in the morning, and generally arrive home about 8 in the evening. In the latter part of the fall they take their Duck and Goose Decoys and stay until the flight is over. There was quite a number down on the island of different Shant[ies?] for this purpose. It commenced to storm of a Saturday evening but these poor souls thought they were sa[fe?]. But the wind kept increasing and the blinding [snow?] and a High course of tide was too much for the poor souls. And when the tidal wave came it swept them in different directions. Two Clapp Brothers escaped in another Shanty. Fred and Joe Henderson, Albert Tilden and Joe Ford the[y] were all lost of a Sunday morning. The bodies were found during the week.[490]

The storm smashed through the beach between Third Cliff and Fourth Cliff, creating a new mouth of the North River. Coast charts called it "New Inlet." This is just where a cut or opening had been proposed in the mid-1800s.[491]

Below are "before" and "after" views (Fig. 105 and Fig. 106; see also Fig. 100). Note the former beach from Fourth Cliff continued around the foot of Third Cliff.

Fig. 105. Stebbins, 1892–1898, "Barrier beach with transverse scallops," detail, Gardner Collection, Harvard University.

Fig. 106. Same view of Third Cliff from Fourth Cliff, 2017. No beach connects the cliffs.

The new mouth was about three miles north of the old mouth. Water still flowed between the two mouths, old and new. Which way or how often the flow went was not clear for a while. It may have been a stagnant backwater, a slough, a tidal lagoon.

Mapmakers were confused. For a while, they labeled the river between the two mouths as "North River." Scituate's Fourth Cliff (Humarock) was on one side and landward Marshfield on the other. The South River continued to exit for a while at the old mouth in Rexhame. Thus, the two mouths made Humarock an island (see Fig. 107).[492]

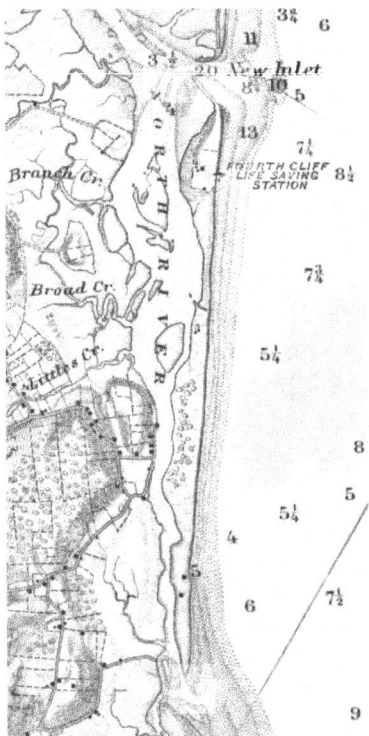

Fig. 107. Coast Chart 109 (1872, 1898, corrected to 1902), detail, edited. New Inlet at top, old river mouth at bottom, river between labeled as North River. Humarock as island down center.

A few years later, the old mouth silted up. The South River, which once met the North River at the old mouth, then ran farther north to meet the North River at the new mouth.

160

Humarock was no longer an island. It was connected by land at Rexhame to Marshfield, not Scituate.

When did this happen? Two sources can help answer the question. One is a map and one is a first-hand recollection.

The state's Harbor and Land Commission was churning out atlases of town boundaries between various towns. It published one for Marshfield, Pembroke, and Scituate in 1902 (no specific date given). This one was earlier to recognize the changes here than the Coast Chart above (Fig. 107). It, again, labeled the river between the old and new mouths as "North River." But it showed the "Old Outlet" as closed (Fig. 108).

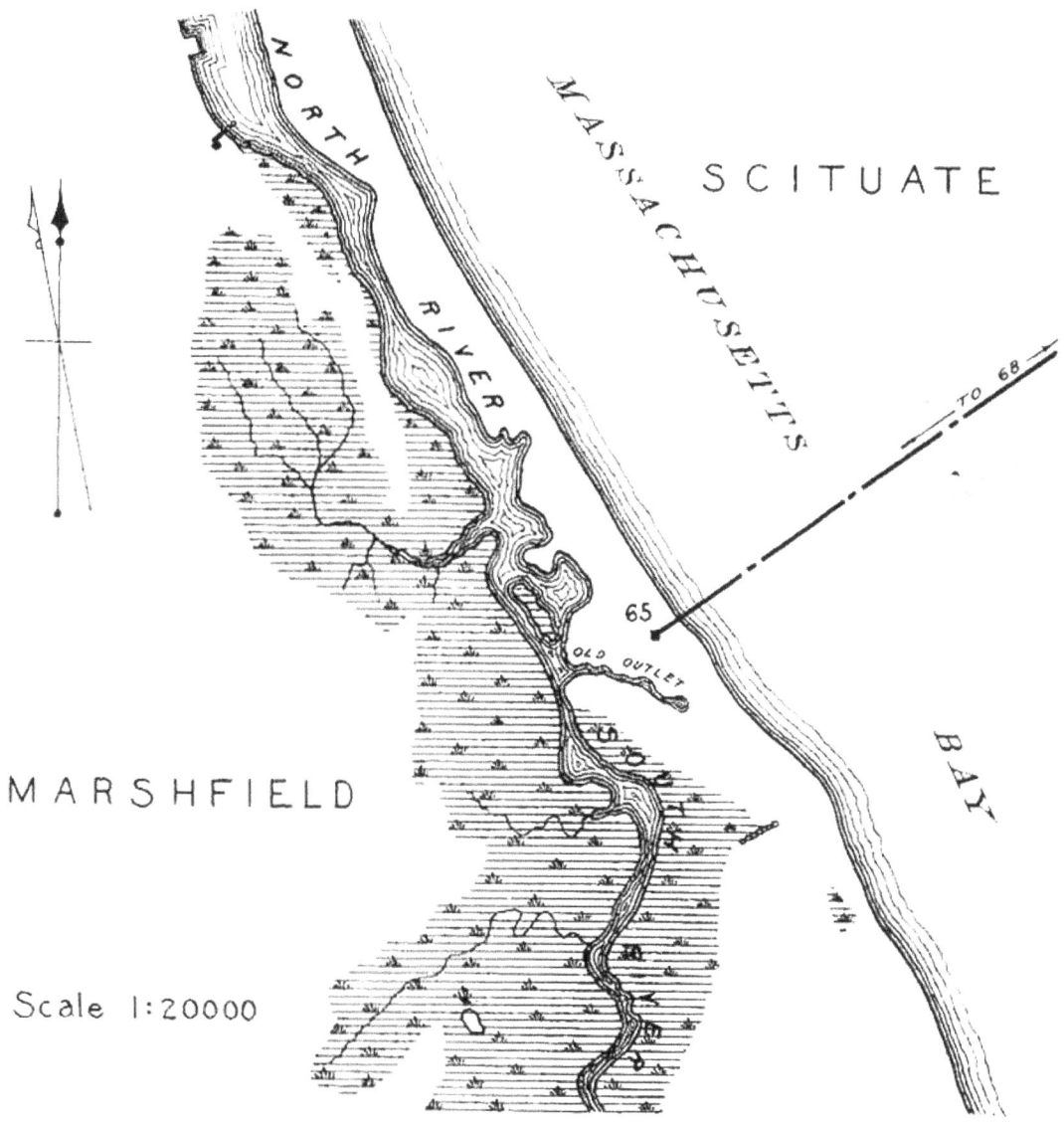

Fig. 108. 1902 atlas, still naming it North River down to the old mouth, sheet 22, corner 65, State Library of Massachusetts, http://hdl.handle.net/2452/47879.

John F. Smith of Marshfield was there at the time. He reported in a 1954 letter that he took guests at the Hotel Humarock on a motor boat through the old mouth in the summer of 1900, and he was ready to do so in 1901, except the hotel had burned June 16, 1901. He added, "The old mouth of the river closed some years after that in a heavy northeast storm in the winter." This could have been early in 1902, since the 1902 atlas shows the old mouth closed. It certainly closed before the end of 1903, according to news reports and the Richards 1903 map. Coast charts took a while to catch up with the dramatic changes, and USGS topographic maps took even longer.[493]

What was the environmental aftermath of the storm?

The storm suddenly and enduringly raised the water levels of the river and its marshes. It exposed them more directly to the actions of the ocean.

The storm erased the pronounced difference in height between the river and the ocean. That is why Calvin Brown's measurement in the 1843 report was fateful: "making the whole difference between high water inside and high water outside about twenty inches." This was affirmed by Mitchell's measurements and sketches for the 1870 report.[494]

As a result of the 1898 storm, tides in the North River were higher, more frequent, and saltier.

The new opening, as historian Jim Glinski noted, "changed the nature of the salt marshes of the region. Now, instead of flooding a few times a month, the marshes flooded twice a day." The increased salinity "killed off the cedar trees and others and led to an increased number of what are known as Ghost Trees on the edges of the marshes." Another writer blamed the death of the trees on increased water height, saying, "These trees were killed by the water reaching a higher level upon their bases."[495]

In 1911, photographers returned to the area. Their photos in Harvard's Gardner collection show the impact of the 1898 storm on some of the river valley's vegetation (Fig. 109, with top cropped).

Whether it was salinity or higher water levels, the storm's aftermath left ghost trees. They stand in the marshes now (Fig. 110). They may date to the 1898 storm. Or they may have grown later. In 1972, Crossley said "I was pleased to see, on my most recent trip up river, that new cedars and other vegetation are growing again in the marshes."[496]

Fig. 109. Photo by D. W. J., 1911, "Trees killed by breaking of barrier at North River, [between] Marshfield [and] Scituate, Mass." Harvard University, Gardner Collection. Seems a view of west end of Bear Island. Trees are white at base. Marsh stream runs across photo, with side ditches in foreground. In distance at left, probably new houses in Rivermoor, Third Cliff, and ocean beyond.

Fig. 110. Ghost trees in marsh, south side of Bear Island, November 2022.

Blaming the 1898 storm, a 1921 book about Scituate said, "The tidal flats of the river, where once the farmers cut their 'salt hay,' are now mud flats yielding clams."[497]

That was a little misleading. There were already clam banks here in the early 1800s, according to William Tilden, quoted above. Starting in the late 1800s, in addition to clammers, the area attracted geologists, photographers, and perhaps a few hydrologists. The scenery attracted summer visitors, and led to the development of the Rivermoor summer colony on Third Cliff overlooking the North River.[498]

By 1903, the remaining but separated tips of Third and Fourth Cliff swung inland, showing the force of ocean waters against the North River. Maps call this the "New Inlet" (see Fig. 107). That seems a better name than "outlet" or "mouth," or at least it indicates the relative power of the ocean. Today, the Spit at Third Cliff and its counterpart at Fourth Cliff curve up the North River (Fig. 95). They are like double gates swung open by ocean tides surging into the mouth of the river.[499]

Scenic Images

The "geology" photos by Stebbins of the 1890s are reminiscent of Impressionist watercolors by Thomas Buford Meteyard (1865–1928), who painted here in the 1890s. They serve as a model for what the area looked like before the 1898 Portland Gale. Here is Meteyard's watercolor view, looking south (Fig. 111, here in black and white).[500]

Fig. 111. Meteyard, "Scituate – Fourth Cliff from Second Cliff [Third?]" 1884–1900. North River at right. Courtesy of Meteyard family and Mark Murray Fine Paintings.

Compare this watercolor with the same view looking south, *after* the storm (Fig. 112) (photo cropped at top).

Fig. 112. Photo by D. W. J., 1911, "Cliffs in till (top) and Sand (below) at Third Cliff, Scituate, Mass. Fourth Cliff in Distance and 1897 [1898] Break in Beach Between," Harvard University, Gardner Collection (above crops original at top), http://id.lib.harvard.edu/images/olvwork420875/catalog,

Clearly, geologists continued to be attracted to this area even after the shingle beach was destroyed in the storm of 1898. And there were commercial opportunities. A nearly identical photo of the scene was used for postcards (Fig. 113). The photo showed Welch's *Marguerite* house and farmer John Donahue's cows.

Fig. 113. "View from Third Cliff, looking South, SCITUATE, Mass." postcard, after 1898 storm. *Marguerite* house (3 Driftway, built 1908) and farm (probably John Donahue's) at top of cliff. Courtesy of Scituate Historical Society.

The 1898 storm may also have marked the end of hunting shore birds in this area. Previously, hunters flocked to the Fourth Cliff House and other hotels for "gunning." One of them, who spent some of his youth on Bear Island and Trouant Island, wrote:

> In the Fall duck hunters took over. In those days shore-bird shooting for plover, yellow legs and other birds was legal both Spring and Fall. Those were the days of the market hunter who made good money selling his take of shore-birds, ducks and geese. …
>
> The Curtis family from Jamaica Plain were there before our crowd. Old man [Charles H.] Curtis, the grandfather of my friend Herman, had a camp there many years before the break through in the North River, and a wonderful family they were. The grandfather was a real old timer and a real sportsman and I can remember when he sat on his camp porch and really cried when it came impossible for him to get out and sit in his blind on the marsh in the duck and goose shooting season.[501]

Whatever impact the 1898 storm had on the North River itself, the scenic views there survived. So did scientific and commercial interest in the North River. How nice to live in an area that is of interest to scientists.

9

NORTH RIVER IN THE 1900S

1915 Report — Overview

Another North River project came before the Board of Harbor and Land Commissioners. The Board addressed the project in its 1915 report to the Massachusetts legislature. The report included a splendid description of the physical character of the North River and a discussion of past proposals for its improvement. The report relied heavily on the 1870 report with its expert analyses. It also added its own expert analyses and measurements.[502]

Not much seemed to have been done at the river since the 1870 report. Its recommendations had not been implemented. The Board had done a further study, the Corps of Engineers had done a partial survey in 1910, and the Board had boulders removed from certain sections of the river in 1911. In 1914, perhaps with local pressure, the legislature had authorized funds for "examination, survey, map and estimates of the cost of improvement" of the North River, and other projects.[503]

It was not clear who was behind the 1915 proposal. Newspapers did not cover it. The report itself mentioned only that the newly formed Boston Sand and Gravel Company, which was mining Colman Hills in Scituate, "would like an increased depth of channel to permit full loading of their large barges on a low run of tides."[504]

The 1915 proposal focused on dredging a channel along the North River. No dam was involved because the Portland Gale of 1898 had created the new mouth of the river. The report says, with a touch of irony, "It was just as well that the dike [dam] was not built at White's Ferry, as the present entrance to the river is 2 miles above it."[505]

We discuss the report itself further below.

1915 Map

Associated with the 1915 report was a superb map (plan) prepared for the Harbor and Land Commission (Fig. 114). It had seven sheets.[506]

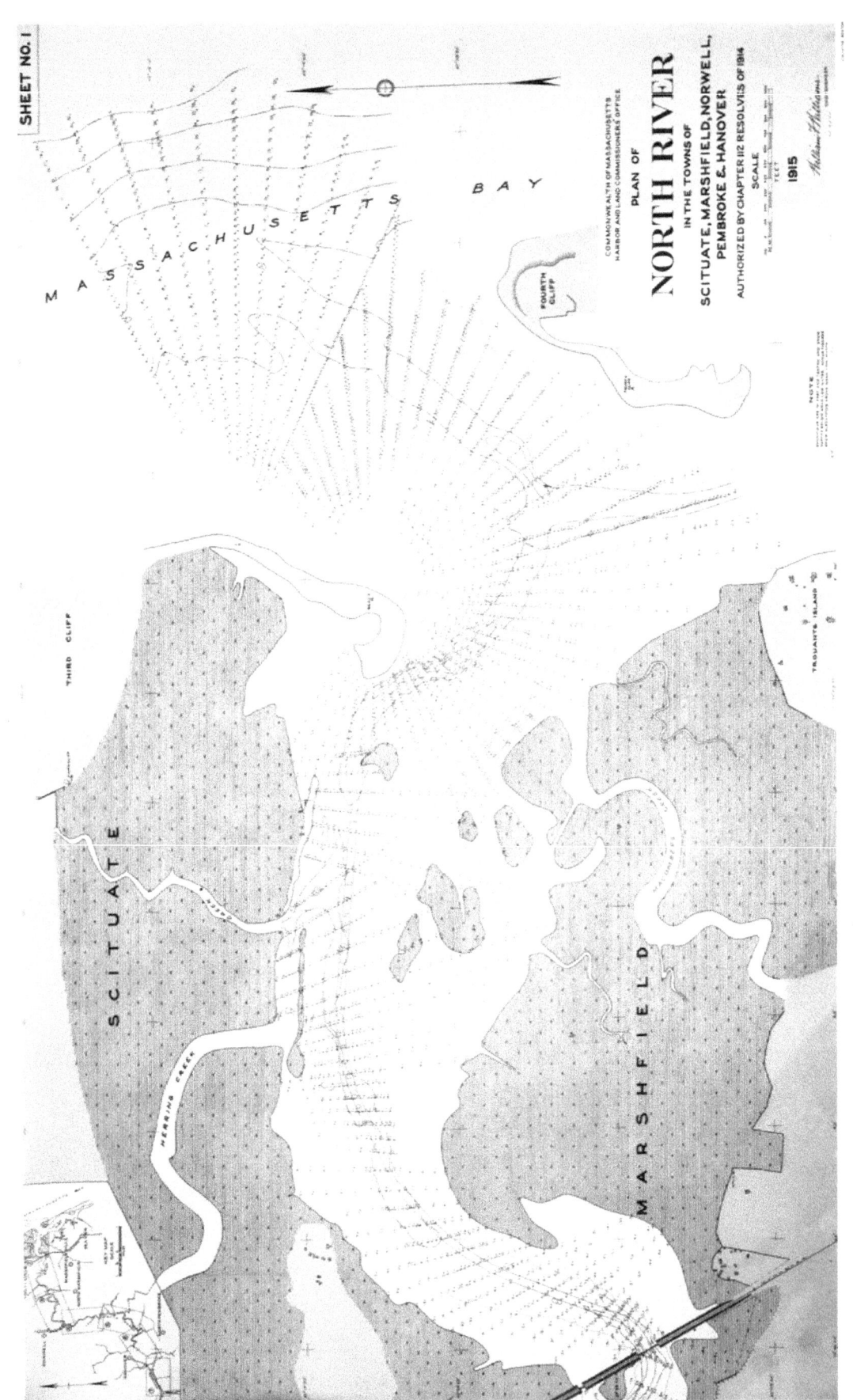

Fig. 114. (opposite) "Plan of North River in the Towns of Scituate, Marshfield, Norwell, Pembroke & Hanover" (MA Harbor and Land Commission, 1915), sheet 1 of 7. In the center, off Third Cliff, is the Spit (here, "Beach"). At lower right is Fourth Cliff and Trouants Island. Railroad bridge at lower left. Courtesy of Massachusetts Archives and Bill Keegan, edited by John Roman.

The 1915 map covers the length of the North River, and its mouth at Massachusetts Bay, in fine detail. That includes measurements of the water's depth (soundings) made along the length of the river about every 150 feet. (Previous surveys had not done such soundings.) The soundings appear as a great number of lines perpendicular to the North River. (Almost like a hairy caterpillar crawling up the river.) Along the proposed channel between the railroad bridge and the river's mouth, the soundings were about 4 to 8 feet.

In addition, the map shows the extent of marshes along the river. The report itself was more specific,

> There are 1,160 acres of salt marsh on both sides of the river below the Hanover bridge, and between the present outlet and the old outlet there are 830 acres of salt marsh on the west side of the old river. There are also 820 acres of fresh marsh above Hanover bridge.[507]

Map copies that are readily available are not in high resolution. A hunt for better copies led to the Massachusetts State Archives. They have original copies of sheets 1, 3, 5, and 7 of the seven sheets. (Please let me know if there are others.) Higher resolution copies are now available from my website.[508]

1915 Report

The survey's scope was vast:

> Our survey extended from the 30-foot contour, about 2,600 feet outside of a line drawn across the entrance to the river in an extension of the shore line at high water, to a point on the Indian Head River, about 2,000 feet above the dam of R. C. Waterman & Son's tack factory, in the town of Hanover [see Fig. 15].[509]

The survey's length was one thing, but the river's length was another: "The distance between the 30-foot contour and the dam measured on the center line of the channel is 78,570 feet, but in a generally straight line it is 44,240 feet, which shows the extremely crooked character of the waterway."[510]

The survey's expansive scope covered parts of the Indian Head River, so the report qualified its findings:

There seems to be some question as to just where the North River ends. The map of Indian Head River, made from a. survey by the Topographical Commission in 1898, shows that river joining the North River at Herring Brook about 4,900 feet above the Hanover bridge. According to this map our survey covered about 9,000 feet of the Indian Head River. Some older authorities evidently considered the North River as extending to South Hanover. However, accepting the map of 1898 as correct, the chief sources of the North River are the Indian Head River and Herring Brook. The tributaries are three brooks on the Scituate side and two brooks on the Marshfield side; but our survey did not include any of these streams except the lower part of the Indian Head River in the town of Hanover, as noted above.[511]

In other words, the North River then was 66,970 feet long, after taking the survey's 78,570 feet and subtracting the survey's (a) 2,600 feet outside the mouth of the river, and (b) 9,000 feet of the Indian Head River. The length thus calculated was 12.7 miles. This did not include the three or four miles lost (to the South River) by the Portland gale of 1898.

NORTH RIVER BRIDGE.
(SHOWING THE LOCATION OF THE BRIDGE SHIPYARDS, HANOVER, ON THE RIGHT.)

Fig. 115. "North River Bridge," third one, built in 1829 (replaced in 1904), from Briggs, *Shipbuilding on North River* (1889), frontispiece.

The 1915 report made a somewhat different calculation of the river's length, about a mile shorter. This used the Hanover Bridge as the basis, which was the 1904 replacement of the old North River Bridge (Fig. 115).[512]

> The river is navigable from the sea to the bridge at Hanover, a distance of 11.76 miles. At this bridge the tide rises about 3.2 feet. Beyond the bridge the river becomes a narrow stream between steep banks, with many boulders in its bed. There is a perceptible tide to a point about 1.5 miles above the bridge.
>
> About 1 ½ miles above Hanover bridge the river is crossed by a stone dam 12 feet in height, and about ¾ of a mile further up the river is a second dam 10 feet in height.[513]

These are the dams at Ludden's Ford, that stop herring runs and shad runs, as discussed elsewhere in this book. Compare the tide rise here of 3.2 feet with previous measures of 3 feet to 5 feet (Deane, 1831), and 0.8 to 1.5 (1870 report).[514]

Evidently, the shorter river caused by the 1898 storm allowed for higher tides. Walter Crossley (1898–1991), an old river man from Pembroke with a summer camp at Damon's Point in Marshfield since 1906, remarked:

> Before the November storm of 1898, the river was approximately three miles longer, entering the bay near the present parking lot at Rexhame. The mouth at that time was partially choked with sand bars and prevented a large portion of the present rise and fall of the tide. This condition resulted in a fresher, quieter stream [before the storm].[515]

The 1915 report continued, with some detailed observations about the North River marshes.

> From Hanover bridge to the sea the river winds its way through marshes of various widths, whose surface is about 1 foot below high water. Before the present outlet was created [in 1898] the ordinary tides rose to about the level of the marshes. The area of the marshes is so extensive that their reclamation was the basis of the report of Professors Mitchell and Whiting in 1870.[516]

The report found that "the mean range of tide as determined is 9.4 feet at the entrance, 7.3 feet at Little's bridge and 3.2 feet at Hanover bridge. High water at Hanover bridge is about four hours later than at the entrance to the river."[517]

The report noted there were few houses, due to the wide marshes. It did not mention the burgeoning Rivermoor summer colony on Third Cliff, or herring or shad, or draining the marshes to deter mosquitoes.[518]

The 1915 report first listed all the bridges on the river. It found that navigability was limited by the railroad bridge and Little's Bridge. Above there, navigability was acceptable for small vessels, except for a ledge across the river above Union Bridge that reduced the water's depth from 5 feet to 1.5 feet.[519]

The report then described the bridges crossing the North River – the railroad bridge (now gone), Little's Bridge (Fig. 116) (now the site of the Rte. 3A bridge), Union Bridge, and Hanover Bridge (the 1904 version of the North River Bridge on Washington Street connecting Hanover and Pembroke).[520]

> The bridges below the Hanover bridge are low structures with inadequate appliances for rapid opening of the draws, and none of them maintain attendants, so that arrangements must be made with the railroad and town officials for the passage of vessels well in advance of their arrival. As a matter of fact, there is very little use of the river above the railroad bridge by craft that cannot pass, under the superstructure of the various bridges.[521]

Fig. 116. Old North River Bridge ("Little's bridge," now site of Rte. 3A bridge), from 1922 George F. Welch Company calendar. Courtesy of Scituate Historical Society (North River file). At left was a toll booth; just left of center is the Rogers homestead (extant), now site of Roht Marine.

By this time, smaller craft plied the North River. The 1915 report called this "pleasure boating." As John Galluzzo noted:

> Not long after the last ship was built on the river [1871], and while gundalows still pushed quietly up and down its course with mounds of salt marsh hay, new, smaller types of boats became prevalent on the North River. Local boys who could afford them and summer visitors who had more money than they had ideas for spending it purchased small pleasure boats of all kinds – rowboats, canoes and small sailboats — and turned the river from an exclusive place of work to one of seasonal leisure time enjoyment.[522]

The Commission priced out two possible projects, each for dredging a channel in the river. The more costly project was estimated at $521,431.50. That would be more than $15,000,000 in 2024 dollars. They recommended against both projects for the North River. They saw it as adding little value. However, they viewed it as a possible adjunct if a separate proposal were approved for a canal from Taunton to Brockton, and perhaps then on by the North River to Massachusetts Bay and Boston. That did not happen. Grand schemes, no results.[523]

1934 and Later Aerial Photos

Aerial photos of the North River go back to 1934, if not earlier. Below are two examples of the river's eastern end in 1934 (Fig. 117 and Fig. 118). In both photos, Peggotty Beach in Scituate is in the upper right. Route 3A runs diagonally top to bottom, crossing the river.[524]

An extensive set of aerial photos was made in 1952. An example below is Fig. 139, an aerial photo of Hanover Four Corners area. This comes from the William P. MacConnell Aerial Photograph Collection (FS 190), Robert S. Cox Special Collections and University Archives, University of Massachusetts Amherst Libraries. Many are marked up to indicate land uses. The photos are part of a larger collection of aerial photos commissioned by the US Department of Agriculture and flown by Robinson Aerial Surveys, Inc., out of Newark, NJ.

In 1968, the town of Scituate had aerial photos taken of the whole town. The Town Archives has a set of copies, in the form of interpositives (like negatives). They have additional aerial photos in a printed volume.[525]

Private pilots-photographers also took aerial photos of the North River.[526]

Fig. 117. Aerial view of North River (Norwell, Scituate, Marshfield), 7/9/1934, Fairchild Aerial Surveys, Inc., N.Y.C., scale 1:36,000. Courtesy of MassDOT (A-2-A_176).

Fig. 118. Aerial view of North River mouth (with Third Cliff & Fourth Cliff), 12/11/1934, Fairchild Aerial Surveys, Inc., N.Y.C., scale 1:36,000. Courtesy of MassDOT (A-2-D_473).

1966 Report

In 1966, the Massachusetts Division of Marine Fisheries issued *A Study of the Marine Resources of the North River*. As the title indicated, it inventoried the river's fish species: (winter flounder, white hake, alewife, shad, etc.), and shellfish (clams, quahogs, lobsters, etc.) (see Fig. 119). In addition, it described the river's physical conditions (size, flow, salinity, etc.), tidemarshes, and historical background.[527]

Originally, the state's estuarine research plans did not include the North River. That changed in early 1964, when the river "became the subject of considerable controversy. With proposals by the towns of Scituate and Rockland to construct sewage treatment plants on tributaries of the river, many area citizens became fearful that the river would be subject to contamination." Rockland's effluent was already a problem. Those concerns resulted in this study.[528]

Researchers measured the river's depth (5.6 – 10.1 feet mean depth, by soundings), length (11.7 miles), and salinity. They determined the salt marsh area was 1,540 acres (2.41 square miles), with 150 acres of intertidal flats. The tide speed could be 1.5 feet per second (about 1 mph) *in*, and 2.4 (1.5 mph) *out*. The tide rise and fall near its start at the Indian Head River was less than four feet. Astoundingly, the tides more than doubled the river's volume, from 93 million cu. feet to 247 cu. feet. Try that in your bathtub or swimming pool![529]

Based on historical records, researchers concluded the river was cleaner than a century before, largely because industries and mills in the area disappeared. "This is an anomaly when contrasted with most other rivers on the east coast of our country."[530]

The study's discussion of salt marshes ("tidemarshes") was revealing. These coastal wetlands constituted an "irreplaceable habitat." They held various kinds of grasses (*spartina*) important to life there. They needed the recent laws that regulated their dredging and filling. As the study concluded, "The North River marshes constitute one of the largest entire and unspoiled tidemarsh units on the coast of Massachusetts."[531]

The study examined ownership of these marshes. At the time, "Of the 2300 acres of marsh bordering the North River, relatively little is publicly owned." In Marshfield, all (about 635 acres) was privately owned. In Scituate, most (about 560 acres) was privately owned. In Norwell, of about 475 acres, the town owned 70 acres, the Norwell Conservation Commission had acquired 49 acres, and most of the rest was privately owned.[532]

The report is notable for using early environmental language, for being concerned about sustainability of the fish and marine stock, and mentioning value in terms much different from those of the 1870 report.

Dense set of seed clams occurring in river during spring of 1964

Fig. 119. Clam rake and clam bed, North River, from Fiske 1966 report, 36.

Environmental Awareness

Values have changed since the 1870 report, which focused on economic value, specifically for growing crops on meadows instead of salt marshes.

The attempts to improve the river in the 1800s focused on quick increases in the area's economic value for individuals, rather than ecological value over time for society. You could view this as a battle between progress and conservation.

The late 1800s brought environmental awareness. The Audubon Society, started in 1886, got a push from Bostonian socialite Mrs. Augustus Hemenway in 1896, and the National Audubon Society launched in 1905. Wildlife refuges (often covering salt marshes) were an idea from Theodore Roosevelt, who created the first national one in 1903.[533]

Environmental awareness built in the 1960s. For example, to strengthen the federal government's role in improving water quality of US waters, Congress passed the Federal Water Pollution Control Act Amendments of 1961. In 1962, Norwell's town meeting adopted a Salt Marsh Conservation District as part of its code. In 1963, Massachusetts passed the Jones Act to protect the state's marshlands.[534]

One hundred years after the 1870 report, environmentalism had become a movement, producing significant changes. In 1970, America designated April 22 as Earth Day (earth as in planet, not land). Congress passed the Clean Air Acts of 1963 and 1970, the Clean Water Act of 1972, the Safe Drinking Water Act of 1974, and the Magnuson–Stevens Fishery Conservation and Management Act of 1976. In addition, Congress passed the Anadromous Fish Conservation Act in 1965, helping shad, among other fish. The US Environmental Protection Agency was founded in 1970. That same year, the North and South Rivers Watershed Association (NSRWA) was created.[535]

These laws and their regulations grew, and they were joined by the Comprehensive Environmental Response, Compensation, and Liability Act of 1980 (CERCLA), commonly known as Superfund. It deals with polluted sites.

Environmentalism moved from a technical/engineering approach, as reflected in the 1966 report, to approval by the general public. It appeared in popular music, as well, including the classic hit song "Mercy Mercy Me (The Ecology)" by Marvin Gaye on his 1971 masterpiece album "What's Going On."[536]

Here on the South Shore, William "Cap'n Bill" Vinal was a prominent voice for improving the North River. He wrote newspaper articles. He provided a paper for a 1968 conference in Boston on protecting tidal waters of Massachusetts.[537]

In a 1970 paper, Vinal raised awareness and alarm:

> We do not have to travel very far north to find the natural environment suffering from fumes, noise, sewerage, overcrowding, crime, polluted water and unclean air. A 'Creeping paralysis' is headed this way. The price could be the death of the South Shore. Whether we work with or against nature may make the difference.[538]

Vinal led "The Battle for the North River," as described in the summer 2023 newsletter of the Norwell Historical Society. The battle began in the early 1960s when the towns of Rockland and Scituate proposed sewage treatment plants that discharged to the river. US Supreme Court Justice William O. Douglas, a noted conservationist, toured the river in 1964, and dined on North River clams and local lobsters. In a speech at

Scituate High School auditorium to an audience of 600, he stressed the growing need for improved sewage disposal. WGBH-FM recorded his speech and re-broadcast it.[539]

In spite of environmental objections, however, construction of Rockland's sewage plant started in 1964 or 1966, and Scituate's plant began operating in 1967. Both discharge into the North River or a tributary.[540]

Massachusetts environmental laws took the arc of federal legislation. The Jones Act of 1963 and the Hatch Act in 1965 were combined in the Massachusetts Wetlands Protection Act of 1972. Since then, environmental organizations such as the North and South Rivers Watershed Association have been active in preserving wetlands.[541]

In 1979, the environmental and geological history of the mouth of the North River was analyzed in an article by Marshfield's Reed F. Stewart (1926–2023), geology professor at Bridgewater State College. His article also assessed the possible future of Fourth Cliff, including the possibility of "Massive earth moving operations" to replenish Humarock beach. In an adjacent article, Walter Crossley with his years of experience there suggested the beach would replenish itself.[542]

The North River has not been free of environmental problems. In the 1980s, it was polluted so much that clamming was closed. Clam beds reopened by the early 2000s but occasionally have had to be closed due to overflows from sewage treatment plants.[543]

Today, we recognize the ecology. Dams like those proposed in 1870 are being demolished, along with their inadequate or abandoned fishways. Shad, herring, and other fishes may now swim as far up the North River as they can.

We recognize the ecological value of wetlands such as the extensive salt marshes of the North River. They capture and store carbon. They buffer us from the effects of climate change and sea level rise. Now we aspire to preserve and restore them rather than improve or reclaim them.[544]

Frontiers of Environmentalism

It was noteworthy that US Supreme Court Justice William O. Douglas visited the North River in 1964. Perhaps it was not surprising. He was a lifelong advocate for the environment, writing books and articles, and taking protest hikes in threatened areas. He opposed dams, particularly big dams, and he criticized the Army Corps of Engineers as just digging and constructing with no environmental or conservation standards. His Supreme Court opinions were some of the first to use the words "ecology" (in 1967) and "environmental" (in 1970).[545]

Douglas became famous for his 1972 dissenting opinion in *Sierra Club v. Morton*. He wrote that natural features should have "standing" (the right to sue):

> Inanimate objects [such as corporations] are sometimes parties in litigation. … So it should be as respects valleys, alpine meadows, rivers, lakes, estuaries, beaches, ridges, groves of trees, swampland, or even air that feels the destructive pressures of modern technology and modern life. The river, for example, is the living symbol of all the life it sustains or nourishes — fish, aquatic insects, water ouzels, otter, fisher, deer, elk, bear, and all other animals, including man, who are dependent on it or who enjoy it for its sight, its sound, or its life. The river as plaintiff speaks for the ecological unit of life that is part of it. Those people who have a meaningful relation to that body of water — whether it be a fisherman, a canoeist, a zoologist, or a logger — must be able to speak for the values which the river represents and which are threatened with destruction.[546]

"He was writing for the future," Douglas's biographer said, "and it's had some resonance in international law in various countries in their constitutions, and even in America for various municipalities who have put that into their regulations."[547]

This resonance refers to an emerging environmental concept, the Rights of Nature. According to one article, "This innovative perspective challenges the traditional notion of nature as a mere resource for human consumption and instead recognizes it as a living entity with inherent rights." So far, there are more than 150 laws that give nature rights, in countries that include Bolivia, Ecuador, New Zealand, India, and Mexico.[548]

For example, on March 20, 2017, the Whanganui, the third longest river in New Zealand, officially became a person. And then this, in 2024: "The Brazilian city of Linhares [a world-renowned surf destination] has legally recognized its waves as living beings, marking the first known time part of the ocean has been granted legal personhood." The city is located at the mouth of the Doce River ("Sweet River" in English). It acted after a dam broke upriver, killing people and discharging toxic mining waste. It was reported, "The new law requires the city to protect the physical shape of the river, the ecological cycles that make the waves unique, and the water's finely balanced chemical makeup through public policies and funding."[549]

New Zealand in January 2025 went further and granted personhood to Mount Taranaki, now known as Taranaki Maunga, its Māori name.[550]

Let us not forget that requirements for "standing" (the right to sue) are concepts of the judiciary. People can still speak for nature and represent its rights and interests, whether enforcing laws and regulations or causing new ones. They can do this individually, through governments and legislative representatives, and through associations like the North and South Rivers Association.

Fig. 120. North River and marshes, August 28, 2023. Courtesy of Lori Wolfe.

10

CHANGING VALUES

To see the growth of environmentalism, look at this chart (Fig. 121), from Google Books NGram Viewer that shows the frequency of words. The use of the word "pollution" peaks strongly in 1973:

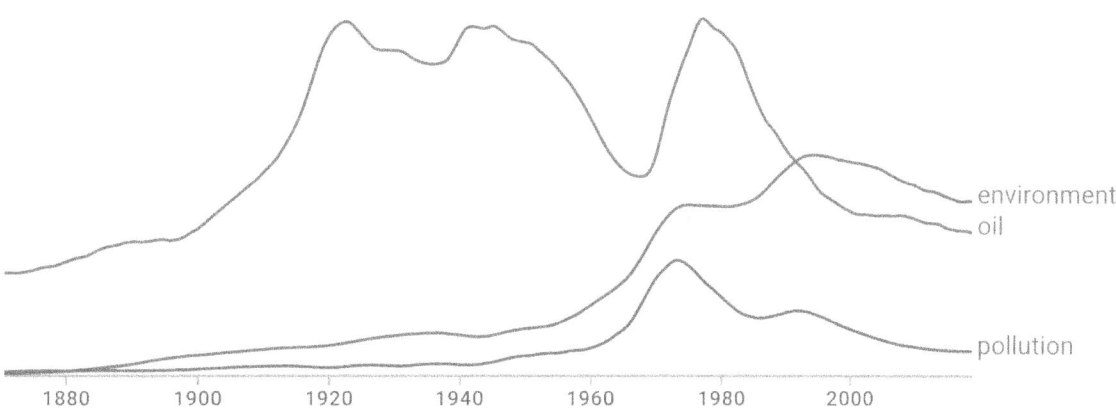

Fig. 121. Google Books NGram Viewer, 1870–2019, "oil,environment,pollution" accessed 2024.

Clearly, values have changed since 1870.[551]

Terminology has changed as well. The 1870 report and plans for reclaiming the North River talked about value, but in different ways than how we talk about rivers and marshes today.

The word "reclamation" back then meant draining wetlands for agriculture, developing land previously submerged, and adding economic value. Now, "reclamation" could describe turning land, such as the cranberry bogs mentioned above, back into coastal wetlands. That is undoing the dikes and channels created by the old reclamation projects. Today we might use a word similar to "reclaim," such as to "restore" to describe environmental restoration of areas back to natural conditions. Sometimes the word "rewilding" is used. Some places are "rebuilding" former marshes. Likewise, salt marshes were once called breeding grounds for mosquitoes. Now they are nurseries for vegetation, endangered birds, and aquatic life such as fish, crabs, and clams. It seems to be a return to Nature.[552]

US Fish & Wildlife Service biologist Susan Adamowicz, Ph.D., explained: "Just as we, as a nation, are turning to the restoration of our built infrastructure (roads and bridges), we also need to be mindful of the natural infrastructure — coastal wetlands and barrier islands — that protect our shores and coastal communities."[553]

Historian Paul McCarthy of Marshfield probably said it best:

> The proposals [in 1870] by Mitchell and Whiting to drain the North River and reclaim the marshland was particularly riveting. 109 years later [after the 1915 proposal to dredge the river] we have an active Watershed "watchdog" [NSRWA] protecting our fragile river valley for posterity. Added to that the various conservation organizations such as the Wildlands Trust; the Trustees of the Reservations et al have preserved significant parcels for the public to enjoy. I am chilled to the bone to think what our little Valley would look like today if the White's Ferry sluice Dam had ever become a reality.[554]

11

CLIMATE CHANGE AND RECENT STUDIES

Climate Science

Climate change and sea level rise have attracted a multitude of recent scientific studies. They focus on coastal impacts and extend to inland waterways, including estuaries such as the North River and its marshes.

For example, a 2013 study by Kleinfelder Associates assessed the impact of sea level rise on South Shore towns. Its title is "Sea Level Rise Study. The Towns of Marshfield, Duxbury, Scituate, MA." Its maps show anticipated areas inundated, with and without tidal surges, for 25 years and 50 years after the study. That includes potential negative impacts to tidal salt marshes.[555]

Since that study, data sources and amounts of data on sea level rise have multiplied. There is a seemingly unending quest for more data, better data, and finer data about our world. Perhaps even researchers could use artificial intelligence to keep track of what is happening in tidal wetlands research.[556]

A recent study demonstrated that all wetlands in mainland France can be mapped with fine detail. It used remote-sensing data, field data, and artificial intelligence. The resulting binary map ("wetland" vs. "not wetland") is significantly more accurate than existing maps. As the study noted, "Wetland mapping is an ongoing process that is updated as technological advances and new data become available." It concluded, "Using satellite variables that combine soil moisture and new deep-learning models is a promising avenue to further improve identification of these threatened ecosystems."[557]

Still, hand measurements and surveys (as in the 1870 report) are essential. Still, photogrammetry using aerial photos (from the 1930s on) are useful. Interpretation of these and other images is a basis of the National Wetlands Inventory (NWI).[558]

Satellites sense our world. They send data, producing maps such as the ones early in this book that display global tides and global marshes. For example, the new global map of tidal marshes is based largely on radar and optical sensing data from satellites, machine training and learning, and the processing power of Google Earth Engine App.[559]

And now there are drones with LiDAR (Light Detection and Ranging) technology that collect fine-scale data on wetlands.[560]

This earth-looking data is collected in Geographic Information Systems (GIS), computer systems that store, analyze, and display data related to earth locations. The data is often displayed on maps with multiple layers of information from multiple sources. Use of GIS data is common in federal, state, and local governments. Analysis of this data can produce visualizations and insights about our world.[561]

Massachusetts has abundant and accessible GIS data based on digital orthophotos.[562]

Yet these measurements are being challenged. Even a basic term like elevation – how high the land or water is – is subject to inaccuracy, at least for tidal marshes, and can vary from place to place. One study constructed a US-scale map of relative tidal elevation, noting:

> Airborne light detection and ranging (LiDAR) data have the potential to generate high-resolution digital elevation models (DEMs) for mapping flood potential and are an important part of coastal wetland monitoring (Chmura 2013). However, they are often built to accuracy specifications relevant to assessing potential property damages (ASPRS 2004; Coveney 2013); coastal wetland processes are sensitive to centimeter-scale gradients and usually covered by thick vegetation and litter (Schmid et al. 2013) through which LiDAR cannot fully penetrate to the ground. As a result, LiDAR can overestimate elevations in vegetated settings as much as 1 m (Chassereau et al. 2011).[563]

Being off by 1 meter (about 3.3 feet), could mean the difference between comfort and a flooded basement, for those living near wetlands.

For another example, see the discussion below of recent research by NERRS using elevation-mapping and historical mapping to improve the National Wetlands Inventory. It found tidal marshes were more extensive than shown in the NWI.

Floods

Sea level rise caused by climate change may increase coastal flooding. Not only that, but climate change also involves extreme weather episodes that cause inland flooding. The year 2024 had many examples.

Heavy rainstorms and Hurricane Beryl caused extensive flooding in Vermont, particularly in river valleys. About the same time, southwestern Connecticut was hit with a "historic" 1,000-year flood.[564]

Heavy rains followed by Hurricane Helene devastated parts of western North Carolina and other states. A few weeks later, Hurricane Milton hammered Florida. Some places near Tampa got 1,000-year floods.[565]

As climatologists would say, a 1,000-year flood is not one that happens every 1,000 years and then goes away. It is one that has a one-in-1,000 chance of happening in any particular year. And the same chance in the following year. Ellicott City, MD, for example, got two 1,000-year floods in two years, 2016 and 2018.[566]

In addition, chances and predictions are educated guesses. A *Washington Post* analysis of Helene's damage in the North Carolina mountains said that FEMA's flood maps, "which rely only on floods observed in the past and don't take into account flooding from heavy rain, small streams and tributaries, or climate change's future impact – can fall short when assessing current risks in a wetter, hotter world."[567]

Such risks are reflected in higher home insurance costs.[568] A recent article describes and shows their impacts on homeowners.[569] In addition, such risks call for further research into flooding and the role of coastal wetlands.

Flooding Research

Whether it was the result of the floods of 2024, or work already in process, that year brought new or expanded data modeling and visualization tools to forecast flooding.[570]

Federal agencies provide National Water Prediction Services (NWPS), and Flood Inundation Mapping (FIM) services. In 2024, the government said it had:

> developed and demonstrated high-resolution inundation modeling capabilities which complement and expand upon existing static FIM libraries providing geo-referenced visualizations of forecast flooding extent at the continental scale. … New inundation mapping capabilities translate analysis and forecasts of streamflow into operational maps that communicate impact by showing where flooding may occur.[571]

The new inundation mapping services were available in 2024 for 30% of the US population, with more coverage to follow.[572]

Coverage now includes areas of coastal Massachusetts, particularly (in Plymouth County) the South River, the Green Harbor River, and the lower half of the North

River). The NWPS map of the US has layers of data that include stream reach (length), soil moisture analysis (good for showing how much rainfall the ground can absorb), and snow depth (good for showing how snow melt can cause water inundation).[573]

Whether it is snow, rain, or groundwater, or whether it is NOAA or USGS, planetary science brings us data from all directions: the heavens down, the ocean out, and the ground up. This informs not just the North River, but also our oceanic, riverine, estuarine, marshy, and solid earth worlds. Our salty and fresh water worlds.

This deluge of water data and its visualizations may signal peak hydrography. The 1870 team of Peirce, Mitchell, and Whiting, along with MIT students, would be thrilled. The Global Coastal Wetlands Lab says, "We are in a golden age of access to remote sensing data and technological advancement."[574]

With this data, the scientific community and others are responding to flooding risks, whether coastal or inland. It is not clear how much this matters along the North River as a whole. My historical research, for example, mentions no major flooding there after the Minot's gale of 1851. In addition, reports of flooding in Scituate seem to be along the actual coast, not so much on inland or tidal waterways.[575]

But the North River needs to be considered, along with other tidal rivers, in the climate change equation, including flooding. The North River and its marshes face the risks of sea level rise; at the same time, they buffer us from sea level rise, ocean storms, and their consequent flooding of our inland communities.

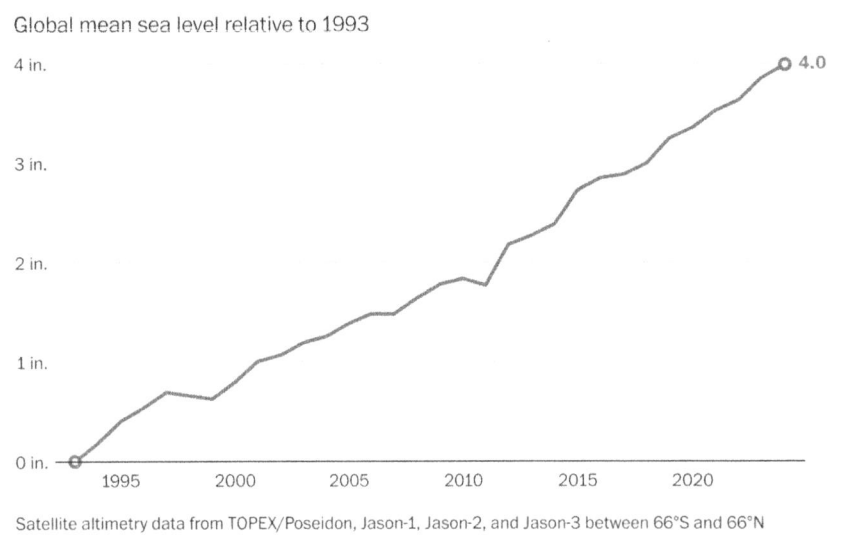

The sea level rose four inches since 1993.

Kasha Patel, "Global sea level rose higher than expected last year. Here's why." *Washington Post*, March 14, 2025.

12

COASTAL WETLANDS RESEARCH

Threats to Coastal Wetlands

Daniel Wolff and Dorothy Peteet wrote a wonderfully informative essay, "Why a Marsh." That recent essay gives a succinct view of the threats to salt marshes:

> Before Europeans arrived, what is now the continental United States had more than 200 million acres of wetlands — an area twice as big as California — distributed along rivers, in prairies, by oceans. More than half that has been lost to agriculture, housing, environmental change. From the early 1950s to the early '80s, during the postwar suburban build-out, the country lost over half its remaining marshland. [citation omitted] More recently, sea level rise has taken 20,000 acres of marsh along the Atlantic, 140,000 on the Gulf Coast.[576]

Scientists are mapping wetlands loss globally. A 2022 study, for example, was called "the first consistent global accounting of salt marsh locations and changes" creating "a new global map of wetland losses and gains." The study showed that the world lost 561 square miles of salt marshes over the previous 20 years. The overall loss was equivalent to two soccer fields every hour. About two-thirds of that loss was in Russia and the US.[577]

In addition to using numbers, the "Why a Marsh" essay describes the loss in metaphysical terms: "Many areas were dredged or filled, as if the uneasiness of a marsh — neither land nor water, therefore "unproductive" — had to be resolved one way or the other." Excess nitrogen from fertilizer runoff and inadequate sewage treatment were other causes.[578]

Whatever the causes, these threats are reported for a number of places and in many news articles.

Consider Galveston, Texas, built on a barrier island. An article in 2024 said, "the ocean wants this barrier island back." Galveston's slogan is "It's Island Time." With sea level rise, its time may be short.[579]

The Outer Banks are a string of barrier islands and spits off the coast of North Carolina and southeastern Virginia. Recently, shorefront homes have been collapsing into the ocean.[580]

At the North River, the 1870 report proposed building a sea wall along a shingle beach, which Nature demolished in a single storm in 1898. Now, we would call that a barrier beach. We would look for a managed retreat in the face of coastal erosion and rising sea levels, rather than trying to hold back the sea. Many people resist, and are not sure or not happy with what "managed retreat" means. The threats and the uncertainties for barrier islands are the same for salt marshes, dunes, coastlines, harbors, beach houses, and town centers near the sea.[581]

Sea level rise can erode or drown remaining salt marshes. It is a race against time and tides.[582]

Even as they face threats to their existence, coastal and tidal wetlands provide many benefits. Chief among them is buffering populated inlands from the same chief threat, sea level rise.

Benefits of Coastal Wetlands

Environmental scientists have responded to coastal wetlands threats with many recent studies. They focus on salt marshes, like those along the North River. One calls them, "the ecological guardians of the coast."[583] To summarize, studies find the following key benefits of salt marshes. They:

- buffer land against sudden or gradual rising water
- buffer land against sea level rise
- provide critical habitats for many forms of life
- filter runoff from human habitats and industries
- act as carbon sinks to capture and store carbon dioxide, reducing emissions that contribute to global warming
- archive data about climate change, and
- provide beautiful landscapes and recreational opportunities.

Studies suggest that marshes that remain, like those along the North River, should be preserved and restored. They buffer us from ocean waves, tides, storm surges, flooding, and associated property damage.

Marshes provide essential habitats for migrating birds, juvenile fish stocks, and other forms of life. That includes shrimp, crabs, snails, many fin fish, minnows, mummichogs, microbes, and plants such as salt hay.[584]

After clam beds on the North River were closed in the past because of pollution, they have been reopened for clamming. A license is required from local authorities. Only certain areas are designated for harvesting soft-shell clams (steamers, *Mya arenaria*), and other shellfish.[585]

Marshes archive data about climate change. This is useful for historical environmental research. For example, paleoecologist Dorothy Peteet's project dug core samples in a marsh at the edge of Jamaica Bay in southern Queens, New York. The samples contained material that goes back to about 1624, the year Dutch colonists first settled in Manhattan. As she noted, once such marshes are gone, so is the data they hold.[586]

Dorothy Peteet was also involved in samples dug at a Hudson River marsh (Piermont Marsh), down about 45 feet. The samples had macrofossils more than 2,000 years old, and tree information between 653 and 1292.[587]

Marshes are a well-known carbon sink, capturing and storing carbon dioxide from the air that otherwise would contribute to global warming. Some call them "nature's best carbon sink." Others point out that "Despite taking up just four to six percent of the Earth's land area, wetlands such as marshes, bogs and mangrove forests hold a quarter of all the carbon stored in the Earth's soil."[588]

Peatlands, a form of wetlands that include marshes, store twice as much carbon as all the world's forests.[589]

However, marshes should not be overestimated as carbon sinks. Research continues, and questions arise as to their help in mitigating climate change. Oceans are the largest carbon sinks, absorbing 25% of all carbon dioxide emissions, although with the undesirable side effect of making the ocean more acidic. Further, rising sea levels can decrease carbon storage in salt marshes.[590]

Restoring marshes can be cost-effective compared to building or raising seawalls, according to October 2024 reports of an MIT study. Researchers tested their model in Salem, Massachusetts, where the town:

> planted two species of native seagrass, *Spartina alterniflora*, locally known as cordgrass, and *Spartina patens*, or salt hay, to restore the marshes. Armed with information about species, density of plantings and coastal topography, the study's modeling estimated the seawall could be up to 1.7 meters (5.5 feet) shorter if it is behind a healthy marsh.[591]

Some marshes can expand horizontally as sea levels rise. Others have limited room to do so. For example, a study at Elkhorn Slough in California (at Monterey Bay) said,

> Our results suggest that potential for salt marsh migration to track sea level rise is very limited, due to the steep topography adjacent to most current marshes. The greatest extent of marsh migration is theoretically possible in the southern estuary, along the old Salinas channel and Tembladero floodplains. However, since these are highly productive and valuable farmlands, and since they are beyond the current focus area of the land trusts active in the Elkhorn Slough area, enabling marsh migration to the south may be very challenging.[592]

"Challenging" is the right word for other places where marshes might migrate. For example, "Scarborough Marsh, the largest contiguous salt marsh in Maine, is getting boxed in at higher elevations by housing developments and roads. These are places where the marsh would ideally migrate upland as seas rise rapidly on the other side." Towns can use their zoning and taking powers to help the marshes, but these can be controversial and expensive approaches.[593]

In addition, some marshes are subsiding, even as sea levels rise. The 1870 report on the North River discussed this issue and determined there would be limited sinking of the marshes if the river were dammed.

Of all the tidal marshes in America, those in the Northeast (particularly New York and Massachusetts) seem least able to migrate to avoid sea level rise.[594]

Some of this marsh loss can be prevented, reversed, restored, or mitigated. It seems quaint now, but President Bush once proclaimed "no net wetlands loss."[595]

Below we explore a sample of marsh research and restoration projects. Some of these are from a recent study of estuaries surrounding the 30 National Estuarine Research Reserves (NERRs) in the NERR System (NERRS). This 2024 NERRS study is discussed later.[596]

Sample Projects

CA — Protecting Elkhorn Slough

This complex estuarine system near Monterey, California, contains salt marshes. They occupied 709 acres in the past and 252 acres now. As noted above, they have limited room to migrate to avoid sea level rise.[597]

NY — Protecting Piermont Marsh

Piermont Marsh is the largest of four tidal marshes in the Hudson River estuary. It is the scene of the previously mentioned essay, "Why a Marsh." The marsh encompasses 278 acres within a 1,000-acre site of the Hudson River NERR, managed in collaboration with the NY State Department of Environmental Conservation. It lies on the west side of the Hudson River, about two miles south of the Tappan Zee Bridge (now the Governor Mario M. Cuomo Bridge). In the latter half of the 1900s, the marsh was quietly invaded by *phragmites* (tall reeds), brought about by building, development, fertilizer runoff, and chronic and severe sewage infiltration.[598]

Authorities are trying to save what remains. A recent project at Piermont Marsh attempts to stabilize a part of the shoreline to protect it against erosion from waves, boat wakes, and ice scour.[599]

WA — Preserving Padilla Bay Marshes

Surrounding Padilla Bay in Washington State were more than 7,000 acres of tidal marshes and tidal swamps in the mid-1800s. Those have shrunk to fewer than 200 acres. In 2023, NOAA awarded funds that allow "the Padilla Bay NERR to permanently protect and restore these acres of former and current tidal marsh, and is part of a broader effort to restore up to 105 acres of tidal marsh to Padilla Bay." Funds came from the Bipartisan Infrastructure Law.[600]

MA — Restoring Cranberry Bogs

In 1870, there were cranberry bogs near the upper North River and Green Harbor River. It reminds us that southeastern Massachusetts has farmed cranberries for more than 200 years.

In recent years, scientists and government officials have been working to transform abandoned cranberry bogs into coastal wetlands, in part to defend against sea level rise. The Mattapoisett Bog is a good example. Restoration ecologists like Sara Quintal have worked since 2011 to carefully map historical water flow and rebuild natural waterways at the bog. It lies next to the Mattapoisett River about two miles from Buzzards Bay. A recent project restored a 55-acre site.[601]

MA — Waquoit Bay (Falmouth–Mashpee)

Waquoit Bay National Estuarine Research Reserve (WBNERR) is on the south side of Cape Cod. Its website calls the reserve:

a living laboratory and regional resource at one of the northeast's most studied estuaries. Slated for development, most of the Reserve lands were bought by the Commonwealth of Massachusetts at the urging of the Citizens for the Protection of Waquoit Bay (CPWB) in the early 1980's. In 1988, the Reserve was designated a National Estuarine Research Reserve for the purpose of studying this area in order to improve the understanding of coastal ecosystems and human influences on them, then translating that information to promote more informed decision making regarding coastal resources. Waquoit Bay is a representative example of shallow bays throughout the northeastern U.S."[602]

The Waquoit Bay NERR protects some 2,804 acres, of which 300 acres are salt marsh.[603]

English Salt Marsh, Marshfield

Maps from 1870 and recent years show substantial salt marshes along the North River. Large salt marshes lie along the shores of Marshfield, including those between the old mouth and the new mouth of the North River.

Many of these marshes are scattered throughout Marshfield. They appear on an excellent conservation map from 2002, and a later GIS version on the town's Conservation Commission website.[604]

The largest of these salt marshes is in the English Salt Marsh Wildlife Management Area. It is owned by the Commonwealth of Massachusetts, and managed by its Division of Fisheries and Wildlife. It now encompasses 289 acres, mostly salt marsh. It surrounds Trouant's Island. It is the third largest parcel of conservation land in Marshfield.[605]

How did the state come to own this, and why "English"? The simple answer is that it came from a family named English, whose title went back to 1954.

William Sturtevant English donated most if not all this property to the state in 1994. He had acquired the property from his father, Clayton F. English in 1974. And his father acquired it from the Trouant's Island Club, Inc., in 1954. And the club acquired it in multiple parcels mostly in the early 1920s.[606]

Clayton English and his son William were leaders of the Sturtevant Mill Company (founded in 1883). Now William Sturtevant English, Jr., manages the company.[607]

The English family was from Quincy, and had Scituate connections. Clayton English married Laura Sturtevant in 1935 in Quincy. Both seemed to have spent summers in

Scituate. In 1931, they attended a party in Scituate featuring a treasure hunt that ended with dancing at the Scituate Country Club on Third Cliff. It overlooks the North River. In the 1940s, the couple became members of the Scituate Yacht Club.[608]

2024 NERRS Study

An interesting study completed in 2024 covered tidal estuaries surrounding the 30 National Estuarine Research Reserves (NERRs). The study sought to enhance our ability to visualize the full extent of an estuary.

The study found that estuaries often extend beyond the areas currently mapped by the US Fish & Wildlife Service's National Wetland Inventory. The NWI is typically based on interpretation of aerial photographs. The study added elevation-based maps and historical maps. That included detailed topographic maps, called T-sheets, prepared by the US Coast Survey between 1834 and 1980. The maps were digitized and georeferenced. Researchers said, "Historical mapping, conducted consistently across diverse regions, provided a valuable window into past ecological conditions."[609]

The study addressed the basic questions of where estuaries *are*, *were*, and *could be*. Estuaries may be the most altered ecosystems on earth. In sum, historical mapping, along with elevation-based mapping, can increase our understanding of the extent of tidal estuaries and their changes over time. In turn, that can inform future mapping, management, and restoration of the estuaries.[610]

North River Marsh Size

The 2024 NERRS study's use of historical maps inspired me. Could the historical maps discussed in this book, along with current marsh data, tell us how the North River marshes are doing now?

Start with the map at the beginning of this book, a Global Tidal Marsh Distribution map using satellite data and the Google Earth Engine App.

I thought of overlaying that 2020 view onto the excellent 1870 map of the North River, which displays marshes. I used layers in Photoshop. The resulting image is below (Fig. 122). It shows, I think, that the extent of these marshes remains nearly intact after more than 150 years.[611]

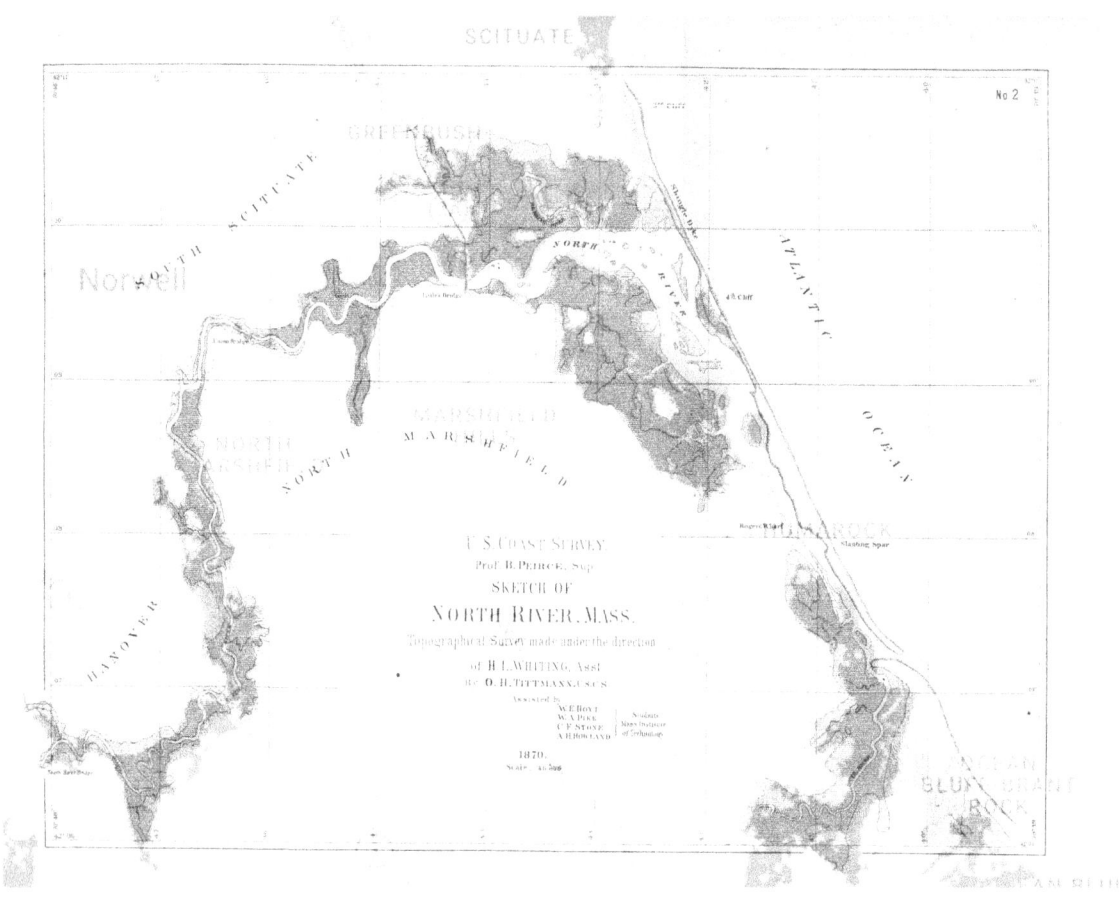

Fig. 122. South Shore marshes, 1870 to 2020. Extent of marshes on 1870 map shown in light gray (horizontal stripes), and on 2020 map in darker gray (from Global Tidal Marsh Distribution data). Image by author.

Besides this visualization, there are other measures of salt marsh extent.

In 2023, geologist Tom Bell analyzed North River marsh loss for the NSRWA. He compared channel widths in 1952 aerial photographs with 2014 digital coast elevation measurements from NOAA. As river banks slump into the river, marsh is lost. Bell found that the North River alone lost more than 220 acres of salt marsh in that time, resulting in 2,025 acres now.[612]

In addition, Bell found that of the 220 acres, about 128 acres were lost near the mouth of the river. Marshes facing Massachusetts Bay have retreated about 600 feet, with about 40 acres lost. Half a dozen islands in the main channel have been lost.[613]

Even with the losses, the extent of these South Shore marshes may be unusual, considering the country's loss of tidal wetlands over the years. We take a deeper look at this, next.[614]

Marshes Compared

Among salt marshes, how do those along the North River rank?

For size, there are many ways to calculate the extent of salt marshes. Parks like the Weir River Estuary Park and reserves like the NERRs have many acres, and they protect more estuarine resources than salt marshes. Many reported acres include salt marsh, salt meadow, and tidal flats. Some also include ponds and fresh marshes.

We first look at sites reviewed above, then turn to the larger context.

Considering just salt marshes in the places reviewed above, it seems the North River marshes rank high. Using sources referenced above results in the following data:

Table 1. Salt marsh examples, sorted by recent size in acres

Site	Map Year	<1900	1900-1915	2024	
MA, North River to old mouth	1870	3,000	1,990	*2,370*	1
MA, North River to new mouth			1,160	2,025	2
MA, South River to new mouth				*650*	3
NY, Jamaica Bay, Queens			16,000	700	4
NH, Great Bay NERR	1908		571	504	5
MA, Waquoit Bay NERR (Falmouth-Mashpee)	1891	650		455	5
CT, Great Meadows, Stratford			1,000	421	6
NY, Piermont Marsh, Hudson River NERR	1860	497		324	5
MA, Marshfield, English Salt Marsh				289	7
CA, Elkhorn Slough NERR	1854	709		252	5
WA, Padilla Bay NERR	1886	1,243		203	5
MA, Weir River Estuary Park (Hingham-Hull)				129	8

Sources:

1. 1870 report, 74 (3,074), is excessive since it included "the mud flats of the water spaces;" 1915 report (1,160 + 830 to old mouth); 1964 report (1,540 + 1915's 830); 2024 same.
2. 1915 report; Tom Bell analysis, 2023
3. Author analysis of "Town of Marshfield Conservation Map 2002" (360 plus 290 [all of English Salt Marsh])
4. Maag, "Armed with Saran Wrap," *NY Times* and *Boston Globe* (2024)
5. 2024 NERR study and individual reserve reports
6. 1906 news report; "Great Meadows Unit," Stewart B. McKinney National Wildlife Refuge
7. "English Salt Marsh WMA," Mass.gov; more marshes nearby, see Herb Heldt MapWorks, "Town of Marshfield Conservation Map 2002"
8. UMass Boston, "Weir River ACEC," 14 (129 acres of salt marsh of 950 total)

There is data before the years in this table. Online summaries show Marshfield tax records for 1771, with 1,647 acres of salt marshes, producing 1,227 tons of salt hay. The top ten single parcels ranged from 20 to 70 acres each. Similar records for towns such as Scituate have not survived and are not counted in the online summaries.[615]

In addition, in 1865, South Scituate (Norwell) had crop land of 8,898 acres; English mowing [hay] 1,169; wet meadow 425; salt marsh 121; and Indian Corn 160. Most of the 121 salt marsh acres must have been along the North River.[616]

Other ways to calculate the current acreage of the North River salt marshes include: (1) following the protocols in the 2024 NERR study, or (2) using the NWI.

Based on these numbers, both the North River and the South River have significant amounts of salt marshes. However, consider the great marshes of the past and present.

Before Europeans arrived, continental America had "more than 200 million acres of wetlands — an area twice as big as California." More than half has been lost.[617]

South of Boston, the Neponset River estuary has 600 acres of salt marsh that serve as a nursery for fish and shellfish. Like the North River, it has twice-daily 10-foot changes in the water level as tides ebb and flow.[618]

On the South Coast of Massachusetts, reports say, "Of the more than 250 miles of shoreline along Buzzards Bay and Narragansett Bay, approximately one third has salt marsh, totaling 4,900 acres."[619]

The largest marsh in New England is the Great Marsh. It extends across the Massachusetts North Shore, from Gloucester to Salisbury. The Great Marsh Area of Critical Environmental Concern (ACEC) includes 25,500 acres of barrier beach, dunes, salt marsh, and water bodies. Of that, more than 10,000 acres are salt marsh. That is the largest salt marsh system north of Long Island, NY. It includes Plum Island, Castle Neck, Crane Reservation, and the 2,900-acre Parker River National Wildlife Refuge.[620]

At the Parker River NWR, wildlife biologist Nancy Pau recalled:

> "I just remember this one meeting we had, probably in 2015. We were all individually in the marsh and we were seeing really alarming signs: plants dying, pools forming, banks collapsing," said Pau. "In that meeting when we realized the scale of the problem – that it wasn't just on our land, it was everywhere in the Great Marsh – that meeting brought the urgency of having to do something."[621]

The Parker River NWR has an ambitious project to restore 1,450 acres from 2024 to 2027, "forming New England's largest marsh restoration effort to date."[622]

13

2022 Report

In recent years, a team of scientists visited the salt marshes along the North River and the South River. They collected one-meter sediment cores during 2018. They came to study how the marshes responded when the 1898 storm opened the new ocean inlet and raised the water level significantly. The investigation was geology, hydrography, ecology, and history. It was a natural case study of how marshes might respond to sea level rise.

The team, led by Brian Yellen and Jon Woodruff, wrote a paper published in a professional journal in 2022. It described their study, and it is quite readable. The team concluded that these marshes recovered from the 1898 storm nicely (my words, not theirs). A key finding: "Increased mineral sediment deposition after the inlet switch played a dominant role in allowing marshes along the North River channel to adjust to greater inundation."[623]

In other words, the ocean nourished these marshes. Here, sediment accreted at 2 to 5 times the rate of sea level rise. That helped them recover from the 1898 storm's abrupt increase in inundation depth.[624]

This view contrasts with the mid-1800s views that blamed the ocean for inundating the North River, creating shoals, and potentially damaging the marshes.

The study also noted, "Based on these observations [1870, 1960, 2019], channel widening of the North River has been somewhat continual and has averaged about 1.5% per decade." (This matches Tom Bell's 2023 analysis of channel widening.) The channel widens as it heads to the sea. It seems to have widened to accommodate the 1898 storm's increase in tidal prism.[625]

The team's core samples of *foraminifera*, an ancient single-celled organism, revealed a change from high marsh to low marsh species around the time of the 1898 storm. In addition, samples near the new inlet showed a high rate of depositing sediments, along with a high rate of sinking, suggesting that the "dense channel network" (ditching) in the marshes was efficiently draining marsh peat.[626]

Brian Yellen gave a talk about this study for the NSRWA and Mass Audubon on February 28, 2024. It is available on YouTube.[627]

The study offers hope that marshes are capable of withstanding or recovering from significant sea level rise. Sea levels are expected to continue rising rapidly, affecting shores around the world. Not all marshes will survive, but the North River valley seems resilient and well-positioned to do so.[628]

14

VALUES OF NORTH RIVER

In addition to its other values, the North River watershed is a critical source of fresh water for people who live in the valley. For example, the First Herring Brook watershed supplies 80% of the water supply for Scituate. The brook collects water from other inland areas of Scituate and feeds it into Old Oaken Bucket Pond. There, the town's Water Department uses an adaptive system of streamflow management, including notched boards in the fish ladder to allow herring migration.[629]

The North River has always had scenic value. Samuel Deane's history of Scituate said it well in 1831:

> The scenery here is on a sublime scale, when viewed from Colman's hills, or from the fourth cliff. The broad marshes are surrounded by a distant theatre of hills, and the River expands and embraces many islands in its bosom.[630]

In 1978, Massachusetts passed legislation designating this as the first state Scenic Protected River, to be managed under a protective order administered by the North River Commission. The commission was established, with representatives from Pembroke, Hanover, Norwell, Marshfield, Hanson, and Scituate. They oversee a corridor that extends 300 feet from the banks of the river, with rules for activity that might alter the landscape. They administer the Scenic and Recreational River Protective Order for the North River, issued by the state Department of Environmental Management (now the Massachusetts Department of Conservation and Recreation).[631]

An NSRWA-related presentation raised the question of whether the Protective Order has worked, with some aerial photos showing housing built near the river after 1978. It is worth supporting the North River Commission's work.[632]

Drinking water, environmental values, and scenic values are not the only values. The river and its valley have historical value. It was home to an expanding Plymouth Colony and an important shipbuilding industry since the 1600s. The history is told through many books and is also documented by historical commissions. Among other things, the Massachusetts Historical Commission maintains the Massachusetts Cultural Resource Information System (MACRIS).

MACRIS Maps lets you zoom in on these historical resources and then go to more detailed descriptions and photos of the many properties and areas in the North River valley. These are highlighted in the map below (Fig. 123). This is a good resource for armchair travel, or historical research, or places to see. They may enhance your paddle on the river, or a nice drive in the country.

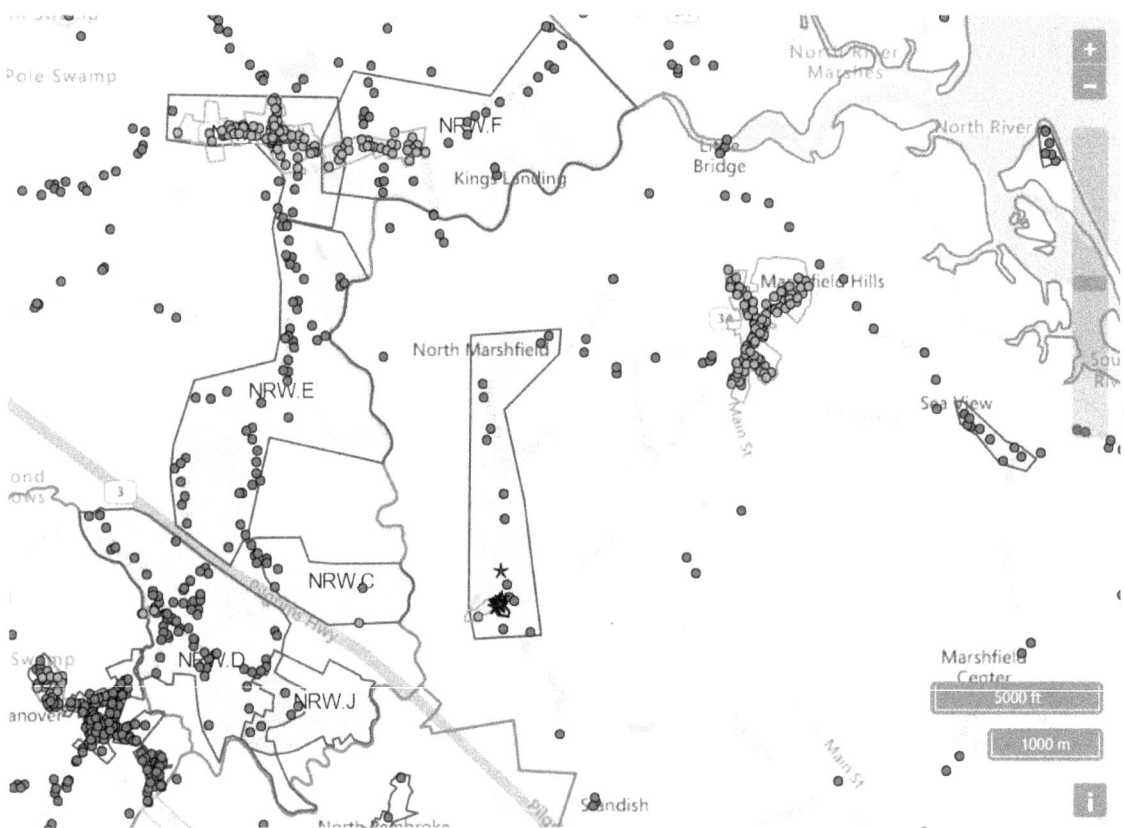

Fig. 123. Cultural and historical properties (dots) and areas (shaded) cluster along the North River (squiggly line), and roads along the river, in this detail of MACRIS Maps, accessed 2024. Mouth of river is at upper right, and Columbia Road (Rte. 53) and Hanover Bridge in Hanover/Pembroke are at lower left.

15

Streams, and A Nice Drive in the Country

In a book about water, you may find it strange to read about the country. But this is where streams start to flow to the North River and ultimately the sea. And fishes from the sea swim up many of these streams, notably the herring runs in the spring.[633]

Most weeks I drive west from Scituate, along River Street in Norwell and Broadway in Hanover, to East Bridgewater, and then back. The road crosses three main tributaries of the North River – from the west, Third Herring Brook, Second Herring Brook, and First Herring Brook. Only Third Herring Brook has a sign by the road I travel.

Sometimes, I use an alternate route along Route 14 through Pembroke that goes past a historical mill in Hanson, and then across the Herring Brook, at Herring Run Historical Park, where the brook runs north to join the North River. Once I took a short detour over to Ludden's Ford (formerly known as Luddam's Ford).

Below we sample some of the sights along these roads, looking for historical sites. This is a nice drive in the country.[634] Let's start, driving east from Hanson (Fig. 124). You can follow along using the locator map at the start of this book (Fig. 2).

Fig. 124. A country road east of Hanson, MA.

Driving this route, you may not notice the river's tributaries. The bridges are inconspicuous. But if you look closely, you can see a pair of railings (guardrails) on opposite sides of the road, often made of cast concrete. That indicates a bridge or overpass. The railings are there to prevent driving or falling off the road into the water below.

The concern is ancient. In 1826, Scituate's town meeting directed the Selectmen "to cause Mill Dam near Wid. Elenor Stockbridges to be properly railed." Evidently, this was a passageway on top of the Stockbridge Mill at today's Old Oaken Bucket Pond. The rail issue festered. In 1830, the town established a Dam Railing Committee to study railing the Stockbridge mill dam, "to do what they shall think proper, and most for the interest of the Town."[635]

Again, in 1916, as automobiles were becoming popular, Scituate's town meeting approved funding "to repair the guard rails along its highways, and to put in two rails on all fences that cross a bridge or culvert."[636]

Hanson

The town of Hanson has an attractive Italianate town hall overlooking Wampatuck Pond.

With the town hall and pond on your right, follow the road south a short distance. Here the road goes over a bridge, a dam underneath. On the left, opposite the pond, is a parking area with a replica of an old mill. This is where Indian Head Brook begins.[637]

In the 1600s, Col. Nathaniel Thomas built a dam here on the site of a beaver dam. According to NSRWA's website:

> Col. Thomas completed the work the beavers had begun and constructed a dam here in 1694–1695 — the first dam in Plymouth Colony to power a water wheel. Shortly thereafter Nathaniel's son Isaac built a sawmill there. By 1712, the mill was known as Colonel's Old Mill.[638]

The mill had several uses as a gristmill and factory before burning down in the 1830s. A rebuilt mill produced nails, tacks (Fig. 125), and trunks, and later became a sawmill, until about 1900.

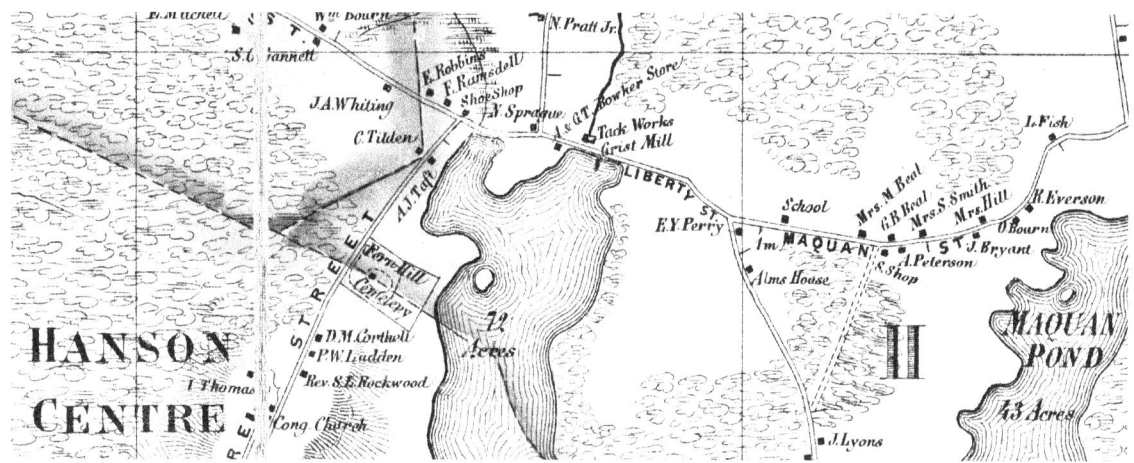

Fig. 125. Henry Francis Walling, "Map of the town of Hanson, Plymouth County, Mass.: surveyed by order of the town," S.l: s.n., [1856], detail with dam and mill at upper center, above unlabeled Wampatuck Pond (72 acres). *Digital Commonwealth*, https://ark.digitalcommonwealth.org/ark:/50959/1257bd15g.

It is the fourth mill on the site, the previous one having burned in the 1920s. "The current mill building (Fig. 126) was constructed by volunteers in 1976, as part of the town's Bicentennial celebration." "The flume leading water to the wheel was installed and the wheel began turning on Dec. 6, 1986." The town now owns the site. It is a good example of the type of mills that flourished in early America.[639]

Fig. 126. Nathaniel Thomas Mill, 583 Liberty St, Hanson.

Let's examine the claim that the 1694–1695 dam here was the first in Plymouth Colony to power a water wheel. Note that, according to Benno Forman,

- water mills had been used for centuries in England to drive labor-saving devices
- a sawmill, like any mill, could be powered by water, wind, tides, or humans; early sawmills were pit mills where two men sawed lumber vertically
- mills could be used for lumber, shingles, grain (grist), fulling (a process to finish wool cloth), manufacturing, etc.
- there is no claim that a mill was built here before the dam was built in 1694–1695
- mill technology spread fast in the colony: by 1700, and "virtually every township in Massachusetts had at least one sawmill"
- there is uncertainty about where in Plymouth Colony this "first" dam or mill was built[640]

Sources say the claim was "according to tradition."[641]

So where did the tradition come from?

- An 1841 gazetteer said, "For more than 40 years after the settlement at Plymouth, this town contained the only sawmill in the colony." The statement is in a capsule history of Pembroke, with no sources cited. It does not mention that Pembroke was not established until 1712, and Hanson (the former West Precinct of Pembroke) in 1820.[642]
- Bishop's 1861 *History of American Manufactures* said: "The King's Commissioners, who visited New England in 1664, reported the old Colony of Plymouth to contain 'about twelve small towns, one Saw-mill for boards, etc.' The Saw-mill is believed to have been in Pembroke, then a part of Duxborough."[643]
- The King's Commissioners did not visit New England to survey sawmills. They were sent for much broader, political purposes, to assert the king's sovereignty in New England and to subdue New Netherland (New York) for Britain.[644]
- On the same page mentioning the sawmill believed to be in Pembroke, Bishop's history said: "It is mentioned in 'The Description of Scituate' [citations omitted] that Robert Studson [Stetson], Mr. Hatherly, the founder of the town, and Joseph Tilden, built a Saw-mill at that place in 1656, which the writer observes 'may be the first in the Colony.'"[645]

The sawmill noted by the King's Commissioners in 1664 must have been the mill built in 1656 on Third Herring Brook in Scituate by Cornet Robert Stetson. (Cornet is an obsolete military title.) He acquired a large tract of land at Third Herring Brook in 1656.

On November 10, 1656, the town of Scituate granted liberty to set up a sawmill on Third Herring Brook on various conditions. Stetson soon began building the mill.[646]

By 1673, Stetson had sold "Cornet's Mill," and by 1676 it was in a state of decay. In addition, in 1673, Stetson sold his interest in land on the west side of Third Herring Brook, one half mile below Cornet's Mill "on account of his building a corn mill [citation omitted]." If the new mill was for corn, it would seem that the nearby Cornet's Mill was a sawmill. It is gone now, but its site is at Hanover Four Corners, not Hanson.[647]

Another possible site for the 1664 dam with waterwheel is on the Drinkwater River. This flows into Forge Pond and Factory Pond about two miles north of the Nathaniel Thomas Mill site in Hanson. It is near the Hanson/Hanover border, about three miles west of Third Herring Brook. A historian admits, "The building of this sawmill at Drinkwater (Nan-u-mack-e-uitt) has been shrouded in mystery," but then, "with absolute proof," he dates it to 1656. Again, whether this was powered by water is not clear, and he may have conflated this with Robert Stetson's 1656 sawmill on Third Herring Brook.[648]

Scituate's Stockbridge Mill and dam were built about 1640. That included a gristmill and a sawmill. It seems, however, that the sawmill was powered by humans, not water, as discussed below in more detail. So that sawmill was probably not the one noted in 1664.

From the mill at Hanson, you can take an alternate route south on Rte. 14 (Mattakeeset Street) and over to Pembroke Center. This takes you past Herring Brook (not First, Second, or Third) in Pembroke. The NSRWA has a good description of the brook:

> In earlier times, Herring Brook was known as Barker's River, and also the Namassakeeset River [or Namattakeese]. Namassakeeset means "place of much fish." Long before Pembroke was incorporated in 1711, there was a large Native American settlement on the north side of Herring Brook — the Mattakeeset band of the Massachuseuk (or Massachusett) Native American tribe, who lived for thousands of years in the North River watershed. Their village included most of today's Pembroke and Hanson.
>
> ... Herring Brook rises from Furnace Pond in Pembroke, and flows through the town for a few miles before it merges with the Indian Head River, to form the North River, at a place called The Crotch.[649]

My travels sometimes take me this way, but I usually go north on Winter Street, then east on Broadway.

Hanson/Hanover

Myette's Corner Store with its red siding is at 1143 Broadway at the corner of Cross Street in Hanover. It has been family-owned for three generations and celebrated its 50th anniversary in 2021. It is just steps away from a North River tributary.[650]

From the east on Broadway, take a right and the road quickly becomes State Street in Hanson. Just on the left is a parking area at 249 Cross Street. Across the road is a pond of the Indian Head River (Fig. 127). Its waters run under the road. Here were mills and industries such as an iron forge, anchor forge, gristmill, and factories that produced bar iron and tacks. You can still see remains of an old building (Fig. 128).[651]

The dam here is one of those proposed for removal to restore the river and fish passage.[652]

Fig. 128. Indian Head River outlet at Cross Street dam, with foundation of old building.

Fig. 127. Indian Head River pond at Cross Street dam.

Hanover/Pembroke, Ludden's Ford

Hanover and Pembroke both have parks on opposite sides of the Indian Head River. The towns are connected by the Elm Street/West Elm Street bridge over the river. After this, the river soon flows into the North River, where other bridges connect the towns. Here at Ludden's Ford are scenic and pleasant places for a picnic.[653]

The site is also historic. It was named for a man named James Ludden, formerly and incorrectly called Luddam. He was the guide who carried Governor John Winthrop of the Massachusetts Bay Colony across the river here to visit Governor William Bradford of Plymouth Colony in 1632. In addition, "Early on it [the river] served as a pathway for Indian canoes and provided the Native Americans with fish such as shad, alewives, trout, perch, and pickerel among others."[654]

Settlers built a dam here by 1693. Industries then developed, using the river's waterpower. Two dams now cross the river at Ludden's Ford. They no longer supply waterpower to industries, which have departed. The dams are technically weirs, since they allow water to pass over them (Fig. 129, Fig. 130, Fig. 132, and Fig. 133). The upper (upstream) dam has a central, long fishway (Fig. 131). I understand it is a kind of fish ladder, and is not useful or maintainable. So this is where fish runs end. Fish such as herring and shad must stop and congregate below here to spawn, instead of running farther upriver. See separate chapter in this book about shad.[655]

In 1973, Ernst Halberstadt took a series of photos (not shown here) of the "new" dam and fish ladder.[656]

NSRWA recently presented proposals to remove the dam(s) and restore the site and the river.[657]

Fig. 129. View of Ludden's Ford dam under arch of Elm St. Bridge, at Indian Head Reservoir, Hanover/Pembroke.

Fig. 130. Ludden's Ford, upper dam.

Fig. 131. Ludden's Ford, upper dam, with central fishway.

Fig. 132. Ludden's Ford, lower dam.

Fig. 133. Ludden's Ford, lower dam, from Pembroke side.

Hanover

A short mile from Ludden's Ford is Previte's Marketplace in Hanover. It is on Route 53 (Columbia Road), at the Broadway intersection with traffic lights. Previte's new building occupies the site of the former Sylvester Company's large hardware store. It is in the historic Hanover Four Corners area. It is a good place to stop for a sandwich, groceries, Italian pastry, and other treats.

In addition, Previte's makes a good reference point for tributaries of the North River. A mile south is where the Indian Head River and Herring Brook join the North River. A half mile down Columbia Road is the North River, and another mile and a half brings you to Pudding Brook. A half mile northeast of Previte's is Third Herring Brook.

To stop and view Third Herring Brook here is a challenge, compared with the ample parking at Ludden's Ford. At least the brook is marked by a road sign. Upstream of the bridge is a tangled marshland. It seems much like the photo in a book from about 1923, captioned as an "almost impenetrable thicket." Downstream is an idyllic woodland, private property. A stone wall lines the east bank of the brook (Fig. 134).[658]

Fig. 134. Third Herring Brook, just downstream of bridge on River Street in Norwell.

Hanover Four Corners has other old treasures. A few miles east were mills owned in 1832 by Samuel Salmond (1788–1859) of Hanover. They were on Third Herring Brook in Scituate. Salmond soon had a tack factory there built in 1834 by his brother-in-law, Captain Zephaniah Talbot, and his brothers John and William Salmond. The site was historical, tracing back to a mill or mills built by Charles Stockbridge in the 1670s, different from Stockbridge's mill in Greenbush, Scituate. Salmond's mills and factory were south of Tiffany Pond, at what became 49 Tiffany Road, Norwell. This was just off River Street, close to Church Hill. Family descendants and others operated the historic factory until the mid-1900s. It burned down in 1983.[659]

According to a history of Hanover, "In 1838, Samuel Salmond, who had spent his life up to that time in Maine, in the South and in Cuba, settled permanently in Hanover." A later historian said he "was a good business man. He was engaged in the tack business and accumulated a considerable fortune. The Salmond family was generous to the town of Hanover, giving money towards Sylvester School, and financing Hanover Academy and the Salmond School." He and his family lived in a fine colonial house near Hanover Four Corners, a mile or two from the tack factory.[660]

Across Washington Street from the Salmond house is Sylvester Field (Fig. 135). This ten-acre parcel is one of the area's oldest remaining landscapes. The Hanover Historical Society, in promoting a history and nature walk there, said that it "was in use for centuries from the 17th into the 20th for farming and haying. … [It] has never been developed, and looks much as it has for the past few hundred years. It was purchased by the Wildlands Trust with help from Hanover's Community Preservation Act funds and many individual donors in 2021." It extends down to Third Herring Brook.[661]

Fig. 135. Sylvester Field, Hanover.

From the Salmond House and Sylvester Field, a short excursion takes you farther down Washington Street to the "River House" in Pembroke. It dates to about 1715, and was at times a headquarters for the ancient Turner's Shipyard. It is set back from the road. The house is well-documented by its owners, the Sullivan family. It is next to the North River in Pembroke.[662]

The Hanover Bridge here connects Hanover and Pembroke. It was built in 1904. Its predecessors were built in 1829, 1682, and 1656 (Barstow). Many histories, and the 1870 report, referred to the "North River Bridge" here. This 1904 version has two bronze tablets describing the history of shipbuilding here. Do not confuse this bridge with the nearby bridge upriver on Columbia Road (Route 53). That was built in 1930, and carries much traffic. You can see it, just to the west, from this old bridge (Fig. 136).[663]

Fig. 136. North River, view of Columbia Road (Rte. 53) bridge from Washington Street bridge.

Kayakers paddle here (Fig. 137 and Fig. 138). Going with the tide is fun, but you must be sturdy to paddle against the tide. A newspaper columnist once cautioned, "That 6 m.p.h. current, plus wind, is nothing to fool with, whether you are just upstream of the Route 3A bridge at the Norwell–Scituate line or breasting the rapids under the Washington Street Bridge at Hanover–Pembroke."[664]

Fig. 137. Down the river go these three kayakers, with tricky, rocky approach to the 1904 Hanover Bridge on Washington Street.

Fig. 138. And the kayakers made it safely under the bridge.

Below is an aerial view from 1952 of the area around the old Hanover Bridge (Fig. 139). It shows the North River's curvy nature. Maybe "squiggly" is a better description. The river's darkness stands out from its surrounding marshes.[665]

Here are a few notes on this 1952 photo. At lower left, Indian Head River joins Herring Brook to create the North River. At left is Hanover Four Corners. Columbia Road (Rte. 53) runs diagonally from the left down to the bottom. Intersecting it is Schoosett Street (Rte. 139) in Pembroke, running left to right, below (south) of the river. River Street runs from Hanover Four Corners diagonally up to the top. Sylvester Field is part of the large light-colored area just left of center, skirted by Third Herring Brook, which runs into the North River. Nearby are the two bridges crossing the river. This was the upper extent of shipyards along the river. What else do you see in this photo?

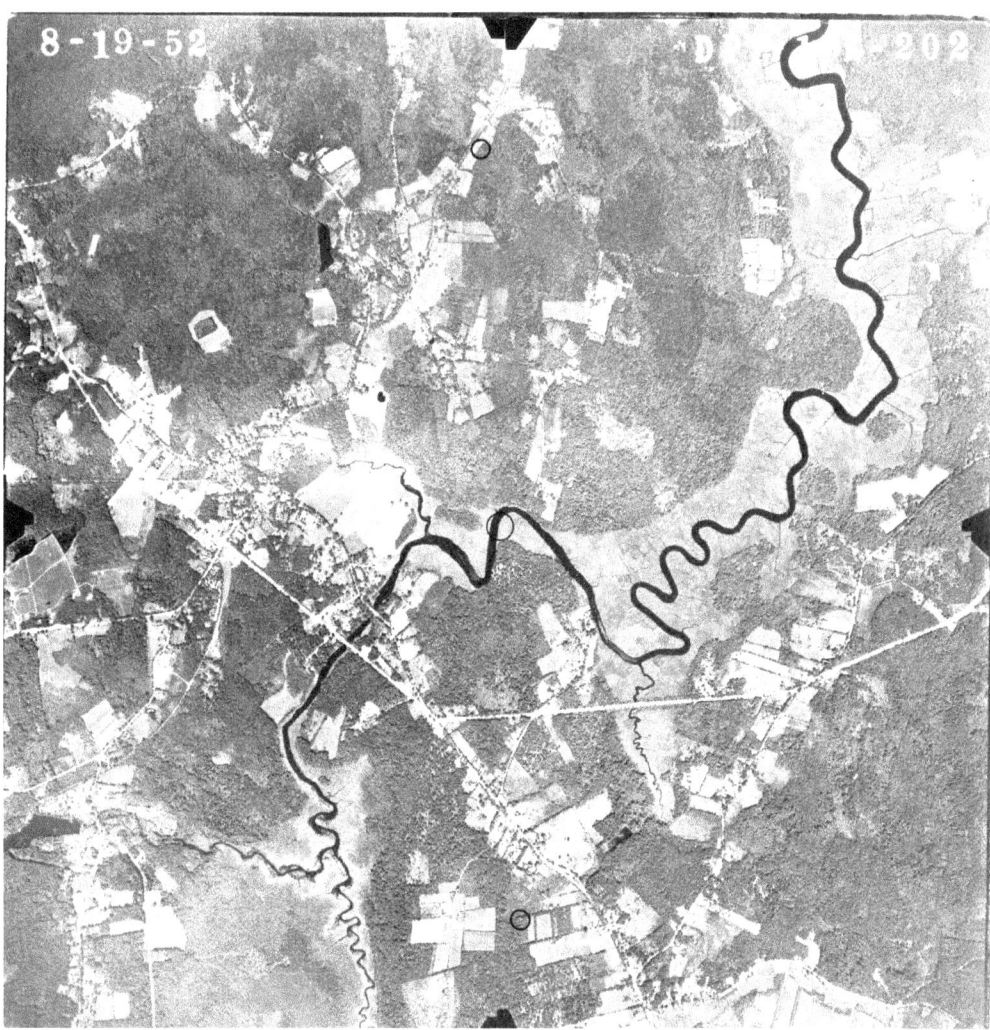

Fig. 139. Aerial photo of Hanover Four Corners area (dpt-10k-202), 1952. Long diagonal road starting upper left is Columbia Road (Rte. 53). North River runs lower left to top right. William P. MacConnell Aerial Photograph Collection, Robert S. Cox Special Collections and University Archives, UMass Amherst Libraries. By permission.

Sylvanus Smith (1817–1901) worked at the shipyards and lived a short distance down Washington Street in Pembroke with his wife Judith and family. About 1854, the family moved to East Boston, where Sylvanus became a top shipbuilder. Judith Smith (1821–1921) was an early woman's suffragist who worked and lived long enough to see America give women the right to vote in 1920. In 2023, the state named the Schoosett Street bridge on Rte. 139 the Judith Winsor Smith Memorial Bridge. The stories of Sylvanus and Judith open windows on old times along the North River.[666]

Norwell

Leaving Hanover and entering Norwell, Broadway becomes the aptly-named River Street. It runs along the north side of the North River. It is an old road. In 1653, River Street was laid out along an old Native American path by Cornet Stetson of Scituate, a road surveyor and leading figure of the town.[667]

Down Norwell's River Street and Main Street (Route 123), side streets memorialize old shipyards. The street names include Wanton Shipyard, Chittenden Lane, and Blockhouse Lane. Blockhouse Lane is named for the Block House Shipyard, which was "named for the building that was used as a garrison house, or 'block house' during King Philip's War [1675–1678]." Not, as I often imagined, a place where they constructed wooden "blocks" used with "tackle" (ropes) to raise heavy sails on ships. These street names are almost all that is left of the shipyards.[668]

Another side street off Main Street is Old Meeting House Lane. It is near the Scituate border. At the corner is reportedly a cemetery, established in 1644. The meeting house of the Second Parish Church was located nearby from 1645 to 1680.[669]

Meanwhile, back where River Street nears Norwell Center is the Norris Reservation. Ample parking is on Dover Street, across from the Post Office. This is a popular place to walk through woods, streams, and ponds, reaching open views of the North River. It is a gem.[670]

Nearby, Second Herring Brook crosses under the road exactly at the split between Route 123 and Dover Street (Fig. 140).

The upstream side is carefully sculpted to highlight dams (weirs) that remain from previous industrial activity (Fig. 141). This was the site of the Bryant-Turner Mill, burned in 1927. Downstream are pleasant woodlands (Fig. 142).[671]

Fig. 140. Second Herring Brook, upstream of Dover St./Rte. 123 fork, upper left.

Fig. 141. Second Herring Brook, upstream, with two dams.

Fig. 142. Second Herring Brook, downstream.

Culverts channel the brook under the road (Fig. 143). Here we pause to consider a potential risk from climate change. Roads are often built over drainage pipes or culverts rather than bridges. Some culverts can be six feet tall and wide, and they generally date to the 1950s and 1960s. Such culverts, according to a recent *Boston Globe* article, may be beyond their useful life, in bad shape, and undersized for today's increasingly intense weather. Water from heavy rainstorms can flood the streams and, with inadequate drainage, wash out roads and bridges. Mitigating the risk can be costly.[672]

It is unknown if the stream crossings described above in the North River valley have been evaluated for flood risk. The *Washington Post* news article in 2024 said, "According to state regulations, storm water infrastructure ought to be 1.2 times the natural width of the stream it crosses."[673]

Fig. 143. Second Herring Brook, downstream, showing culverts.

Scituate

English colonists soon harnessed the power of Herring Brook in Scituate. It would later be called First Herring Brook, since other herring brooks emptied into the North River. In a way, our drive east through the North River watershed is a trip into the past. Consider the history of mills.

Between 1637 and 1640, Isaac Stedman dammed the First Herring Brook to create a sawmill at what is now called Old Oaken Bucket Pond. It is considered the oldest recorded dam in America. About 1650, alongside the sawmill, John Stockbridge built a water-driven gristmill to grind corn. It remains, on Old Country Way, across from Old Oaken Bucket Pond (Fig. 146). It is the oldest grist mill in America.[674]

The gristmill stands alone now. The sawmill and other neighboring buildings are no longer there. It seems the first sawmill was inside a building with a pit that required two men to move the saw up and down by hand, based on Charles Lincoln's notes at the Scituate Historical Society. This was a pit saw or "whip saw" with a six-foot blade.

As Lincoln said:

> The Pit man or helper stood in the pit and pulled the saw down, doing all the work and getting all the sawdust as the saw cut on the down stroke only.

The sawmill was later converted to an "Up & Down" saw, taking power from the water wheel shaft in the gristmill.[675]

A postcard posted in 1906 (Fig. 144) shows, from left, an ice house (said to have been used as a shingle mill), the low grist mill, and a two-story sawmill (maybe not the first). The sawmill, according to Charles Lincoln, was converted to an ice house in 1909 (Fig. 145). There was also a blacksmith shop next door. There was much activity in this, the Greenbush section of Scituate.[676]

Fig. 144. Stockbridge Mill (center) in Greenbush, postcard published by F. N. Damon Curio Co., similar to one postmarked 1906. Author's collection.

Fig. 145. Stockbridge Mill (center), postcard published by H. A. Dickerman & Son, postmarked 1911. Author's collection. Building on right is gone. Dwelling on left in back still exists, SCI.47, MACRIS.

Fig. 146. Stockbridge Mill, Old Country Way, Greenbush, Scituate, across from Old Oaken Bucket Pond. Oldest gristmill in America. Photo by Lyle Nyberg 2024.

First Herring Brook runs through Old Oaken Bucket Pond, over the dam, and under the road. Part of the water goes to the Stockbridge Mill, then re-joins the remaining part from the dam. A short run later, the brook goes under the Driftway next to a Dunkin' Donuts shop (Fig. 147). The only sign mentioning the brook is one for a commercial development, "Herring Brook Place" at 29 New Driftway. Here the brook runs free to the North River (Fig. 148).

Fig. 147. Outlet of First Herring Brook at New Driftway, heading to the North River. Building of Sanctuary at Herring Brook (along Rte. 3A) is in distance, right of center.

Fig. 148. First Herring Brook, Scituate, with North River and Marshfield hills in far distance, Bear Island in far middle distance. The brook meanders like the river. View from Peak Physical Therapy, Jacob Hatch Building, November 2024.

This concludes our drive through the North River watershed and its streams.

If you want to explore more, see the excellent NSRWA map of the river and these tributaries. It has symbols of fishes swimming up them. It also describes points of interest and has a handy tide chart. Or get paddling![677]

Concluding Reflections

We are fortunate to have this "faire river" and its marshes after centuries of use and various plans to improve them.

Some of the plans now seem unfortunate, even abusive to the environment. Plans in the 1800s to dam the river and "reclaim" the marshes would have removed salt marshes and excluded shad and other anadromous fish from the river. But it is worth understanding those involved in the plans. They were not so different from us.

They had:

- close connections to the river and its existing and possible uses
- forward-thinking ideas
- stout support from the scientific community, with world-class engineers and hydrographers, open to experimenting based on European experience
- public input and review of their plans
- strong local support and legislative approval for their plans.

They did not anticipate, and could not reasonably have anticipated the:

- Portland Gale of 1898 and its dramatic impact on the North River
- migration of hay farming to the Great Plains
- worldwide destruction of salt marshes
- rise of environmentalism
- global warming and the role salt marshes can play to buffer sea level rise.

It is only human to want to build, grow, expand, make money, and make good use of the land and the water — and, in this case, the land that sometimes lies under water ... tidelands. That is why the English settled here, built towns, and built a shipbuilding industry that, for centuries, was recognized around the world. That is why landowners wanted to improve marshes to produce better and more profitable crops.

We always want the "highest and best" use of our places. The term originated from economists around the turn of the twentieth century and it is used in connection with zoning laws and regulations. It is a concept in real estate appraisal. According to The Appraisal Institute, it means "The reasonably probable and legal use of vacant land or an improved property that is physically possible, appropriately supported, financially feasible, and that results in the highest value."[678]

People evidently abhor vacant land just as Nature abhors a vacuum. And people want value for the land, whether financial or otherwise.

The concept of "highest and best use" is mainly financial. Finances were the focus for those who proposed to dam the North River and reclaim the marshes in the 1870s. The world-class hydrographers of the 1870s were oriented to the "how" rather than the "why" of those proposals, and to their economic feasibility. As Clemens Herschel put it, "The question is whether, if drained, the lands would be worth $22 per acre."

As we have seen in this book, this concept of value did not include environmental value or certain social values. Some of those values may not translate into financial terms. In addition, the future matters. Drained marshes are costly or impossible to recover.

Values change. We now value the environment, including tidal rivers like the North River. The public largely accepts such value. It is recognized in state laws protecting coastal wetlands, state ownership of places like the English Salt Marsh in Marshfield, town zoning bylaws, town ownership of conservation land, private ownership of land with conservation restrictions, land trusts like the Trustees of Reservations and the Wildlands Trust, and nonprofits like the North and South Rivers Association.

Will values change? Plans for the North River that sounded reasonable and confident in the 1870s came to seem disastrous later. Perhaps the lesson is to be cautious in changing the environment. While scientific inquiry has advanced since the 1870s, and needs to continue addressing issues such as global warming, we should be careful about responses like geoengineering the oceans or the atmosphere. Will today's plans for the environment, including tidal rivers, later seem quaint and risky, with future generations asking: *what were they thinking?*

For now, we are fortunate to live near the river and its marshes, or be able to visit them, or to paddle on the river, or to learn from their history. We are fortunate they survived the industries and mills established upstream since Colonial days and the plans of the 1870s. We are fortunate to have an abundance of history and natural beauty, places to explore. Not every place has such a fascinating mix of fresh water, salt water, land, tidelands, and marshlands, as does the North River.

We should cherish what we have and preserve it to the best of our values, including environmental. We should support scientific studies of marshlands and estuaries. We should ask what we have learned and are learning that helps us chart a good future, while being cautious about adopting far-ranging experiments like the 1870 plans.

All this leaves still more to say about the North River, its salt marshes, and the area's shores. I hope to keep writing … another book awaits.

Notes on Sources

General. Below are key sources of information, and some abbreviations, used in this book. The many histories of this area are mentioned in the start of the book. This supplements the extensive endnotes and mostly attempt to follow the Chicago Manual of Style.

The endnotes hyperlink to many websites. This may be particularly helpful if you use the electronic version of this book. The links were good when consulted for this book and most were still good at time of publication. Unfortunately, some special-interest websites last less than five years, less than it took to write this book. So some of these websites no longer work ("former" websites or "dead links"). To find or recover these websites, try a Google search, or the Internet Archive's Wayback Machine.

***

Assessor's Databases, various towns, online, including Town of Scituate, http://www.assessedvalues2.com/index.aspx?jurcode=264.

Bangs. Jeremy Dupertuis Bangs (1946–2023), *The Seventeenth-Century Town Records of Scituate, Massachusetts*, three volumes (Boston: New England Historic Genealogical Society, 1997, 1999, 2001), https://catalog.hathitrust.org/Record/010029242. Astonishingly detailed and authoritative. Documents include digests of some land divisions and property deeds. Bangs also transcribed and edited the town records of Sandwich, Eastham, Marshfield, Duxbury, and previously unpublished records and deeds of Plymouth Colony.

Biographical Review, *Vol. XVIII: Containing Life Sketches of Leading Citizens of Plymouth County, Massachusetts* (Boston: Biographical Review Publishing Co., 1897), ("*Biographical Review*"), https://archive.org/details/biographicalrevi1897biog and https://books.google.com/books?id=7qd5EML7tYYC&source=gbs_navlinks_s.

Boston Globe. Most citations are from www.bostonglobe.com online archives, powered by Newspapers.com. The word "Daily" is omitted. For other newspapers, see Scituate Town Library below, and Hingham Public Library, https://hingham.advantage-preservation.com/.

Maps. See Figure captions and endnotes that provide sources. See also Sanborn Maps (below) at State Library, and Leventhal Map & Education Center at the Boston Public Library. A key map is the Richards 1903 map, J. E. Judson, *Topographical Atlas of Surveys: Plymouth County together with the town of Cohasset, Norfolk County, Massachusetts* (Springfield, MA: L. J. Richards & Co., 1903), State Library of Massachusetts, Massachusetts Real Estate Atlas Digitization Project, https://www.mass.gov/info-details/massachusetts-real-estate-atlas-digitization-project-by-the-state-library.

Massachusetts Cultural Resource Information System ("MACRIS"). It documents old buildings and other resources, and is a database of the Massachusetts Historical Commission, online at http://mhc-macris.net/.

NOAA, US Coast Survey Historical Map and Chart Collection. The Office of the Coast Survey's historical digital library allows users to search for and download maps and charts of the lands and waters of the United States dating to the early 1800s. https://historicalcharts.noaa.gov/.

North and South Rivers Watershed Association ("NSRWA"), https://www.nsrwa.org/.

Photos. For landscape photos (Stebbins and others), see George Augustus Gardner Collection of Photographs, Harvard University, HOLLIS number olvwork419446, https://id.lib.harvard.edu/alma/990114204590203941/catalog. For aerial photos, see Maps above.

Plymouth County Registry of Deeds ("PCRD"). Deeds and plans back to colonial times are online at http://www.plymouthdeeds.org/.

Sanborn Maps. They covered parts of towns along the North River, including Scituate (1909, 1918, 1926, and 1939). On file on microfilm at State Library of Massachusetts, Special Collections. Outstanding collection by Library of Congress, with introduction at https://www.loc.gov/collections/sanborn-maps/about-this-collection/, and search start, https://www.loc.gov/collections/sanborn-maps/

Scituate Historical Society ("SHS"), http://scituatehistoricalsociety.org/.

Scituate Town Archives ("Town Archives"). A great resource, located at Town Hall. WPA card index is useful, online at https://www.scituatema.gov/archives (click on "Scituate Public Records Indices 1636–1936," and "Scituate Town & Selectmen Meetings Indices 1659–1939").

Scituate Town Library. Local history books. Website has digitized local newspapers and town reports, https://www.scituatema.gov/town-library (tab for Research/Local History & Genealogy).

Scituate Town Reports. Published annually by the Town of Scituate, they are on file in the Town Archives and the Scituate Historical Society. They are available online from Scituate Town Library and Scituate Historical Society websites. They list printers, including The Memorial Press of Plymouth, Boundbrook Press of North Scituate, and Sanderson Brothers of North Abington, MA. Notes in this book omit the place of publishing and printing, and the year (normally the year after the one in the title). Other towns have town reports online to some extent.

State Library of Massachusetts. A key source for historical maps, including Sanborn maps. The library's Real Estate Atlas Digitization Project put many atlases online.

Valuation Lists. ("*Valuation List*," or "*VL*" in notes). Tax valuation lists for Scituate (and presumably for other towns) were prepared each year by hand in bound ledgers, on file in the Town Archives. In addition, they were printed and published occasionally, with partial information, as part of town reports, including those for 1876, 1886, 1896, 1906 and 1927. Some or all are available online from the Scituate Town Library website. The one for 1896 is in the set of 1892–1898 reports, and the one for 1906 is in the set of 1906–1908 reports. Note that taxpayers are listed alphabetically only by first letter of last name, and nonresidents appear in a separate section at the end.

    1896: https://archive.org/details/annualreportofto1892scit/page/n311/mode/2up

    1906: https://archive.org/details/annualreportofto1906scit/page/n137/mode/2up

NOTES

[1] Stilgoe email, April 15, 2022.

[2] L. Vernon Briggs, *History of Shipbuilding on North River, Plymouth County, Massachusetts* (Boston: Coburn Brothers, Printers, 1889), 364–365, https://archive.org/details/historyofshipbui00brigg; Samuel Deane, *History of Scituate, Massachusetts, From its First Settlement to 1831* (Boston: James Loring, 1831), https://archive.org/details/historyscituate01deangoog/page/n4/mode/2up; Joseph Foster Merritt, *Old Time Anecdotes of the North River and the South Shore* (Rockland, MA: Rockland Standard Publishing Company, 1928), https://catalog.hathitrust.org/Record/010027973; Joseph Joseph Foster Merritt, *A Narrative History of South Scituate-Norwell, Massachusetts* (Rockland, MA: Frank S. Alger [publisher of Rockland Standard Publishing Co.] and Joseph F. Merritt, 1938) [a version of Merritt's *Old Time Anecdotes*], 151, https://archive.org/details/narrativehistory00merr; William Gould Vinal, *Salt Haying in the North River Valley (1648–1898)* (Cohasset, MA: Vinehall, 1953); John Galluzzo, *The North River: Scenic Waterway of the South Shore* (Charleston, SC: The History Press, 2008); John R. Stilgoe, *Alongshore* (New Haven: Yale University Press, 1994), and other books.

A particularly helpful history of the North River is a student submission, *The Tidal North River: Issues and Recommendations, 1976–77* (Cambridge: Harvard University, 1977), Department of Landscape Architecture, Harvard Graduate School of Design, permalink https://id.lib.harvard.edu/alma/990030492850203941/catalog. A copy is in the Norwell Historical Society.

[3] *Historic & Archaeological Resources of Southeast Massachusetts* (Boston: Massachusetts Historical Commission, 1982, 2007 PDF version), 36 (Map 3), 40, https://www.sec.state.ma.us/divisions/mhc/preservation/survey/regional-reports/SoutheasternMA.pdf;

[4] Prof. Lawrence B. Mish, ed., William Vinal, author, "The New North River Almanac" (Norwell: South Shore Nature Center, 1965, 54 pages) (hereafter "Mish, *Almanac*"), 10 (quoted), copy courtesy of John Stilgoe. A copy is also on file at the Norwell Historical Society, 800.VI(1).

[5] "North River Wildlife Sanctuary," NSRWA website, https://www.nsrwa.org/listing/north-river-wildlife-sanctuary/; see discussion in text below.

[6] *Explore South Shore Recreation Guide Map* (Norwell, MA: North and South Rivers Watershed Association, 5th ed, 2019) ("NSRWA *Guide Map*"), site 56 (Hanover Canoe Launch).

[7] See maps, above, including Board of Harbor and Land Commissioners of Massachusetts, *Atlas of the boundaries of the towns of Marshfield, Pembroke and Scituate, Plymouth County* (Boston: Commonwealth of Massachusetts, Harbor and Land Commission, 1902) ("1902 atlas", sheet B (quoted), sheet 1 (map), http://hdl.handle.net/2452/47879. See also MassDOT interactive GIS map displaying the approximate locations of city and town corners, which relies in part on the 1902 atlas (MassDOT "book 46"), https://geo-massdot.opendata.arcgis.com/datasets/MassDOT::town-corners/explore; and "MassGIS Data: Municipalities," https://www.mass.gov/info-details/massgis-data-municipalities. For more, see John R. Stilgoe, *Landscape and Images* (Charlottesville, VA: University of Virginia Press, 2005), chapter "Jack-o'-lanterns to Surveyors: The Secularization of Landscape Boundaries."

[8] Jeremy Dupertuis Bangs, *The Seventeenth-Century Town Records of Scituate, Massachusetts*, three volumes (Boston: New England Historic Genealogical Society, 1997, 1999, 2001), 3:45, https://catalog.hathitrust.org/Record/010029242. Astonishingly detailed and authoritative. Documents include digests of some land divisions and property deeds.

[9] *Fifth Annual Report of the Board of the Harbor Commissioners* (1870) (Boston: Board of Harbor Commissioners, 1871) ("1870 report"), State Library of Massachusetts, https://archives.lib.state.ma.us/items/39376f05-1bb4-4239-b05e-bb9cee156c23, URI http://archives.lib.state.ma.us/handle/2452/756651, or go to https://archives.lib.state.ma.us and search the repository entering title of document.

[10] "1915 House Bill 1850. Report Relative To The Improvement Of Salem Harbor, North River, Wellfleet Harbor, Edgartown Harbor And Wareham River, And To Building A Breakwater In Provincetown Harbor." (Boston: Board of Harbor and Land Commissioners, 1915) ("1915 report"), 7–15, https://archives.lib.state.ma.us/bitstream/handle/2452/396171/ocm39986872-1915-HB-

1850.pdf?sequence=1&isAllowed=y; in collection with permanent URI, https://hdl.handle.net/2452/393354, or go to https://archives.lib.state.ma.us and search the repository entering title of document.

[11] "Timing the Tides," NSRWA presentation, slide 48, https://nsrwa.s3.us-east-2.amazonaws.com/wp-content/uploads/2024/10/07165040/Timing-the-Tides-10-3-24.pdf; H. E. Baranes, J. D. Woodruff, W. R. Geyer, B. C. Yellen, J. B. Richardson, & F. Griswold (2022), "Sources, mechanisms, and timescales of sediment delivery to a New England salt marsh," *Journal of Geophysical Research: Earth Surface*, 127, e2021JF006478, Figure 1, https://doi.org/10.1029/2021JF006478. For excellent overviews of rivers, see "Rivers, Estuaries, & Deltas," Woods Hole Oceanographic Institution, https://www.whoi.edu/know-your-ocean/ocean-topics/how-the-ocean-works/coastal-science/rivers-estuaries-deltas/; "Understanding Rivers," *National Geographic*, updated October 19, 2023 (see credits at end), https://education.nationalgeographic.org/resource/understanding-rivers/.

[12] See text below about memorials to the state in 1828 (by locals) and 1844 (by Isaiah Rogers). The 1915 report is "1915 House Bill 1850. Report Relative To The Improvement Of Salem Harbor, North River, Wellfleet Harbor, Edgartown Harbor And Wareham River, And To Building A Breakwater In Provincetown Harbor." (Boston: Board of Harbor and Land Commissioners, 1915) ("1915 report"), 7–15, https://archives.lib.state.ma.us/bitstream/handle/2452/396171/ocm39986872-1915-HB-1850.pdf?sequence=1&isAllowed=y; in collection with permanent URI, https://hdl.handle.net/2452/393354, or go to https://archives.lib.state.ma.us and search the repository entering title of document.

[13] "Rio de Janeiro Travel Guide: Rio de Janeiro History," https://www.latinamericaforless.com/brazil/travel-guides/rio-janeiro-guide-history.php; "Rio de Janeiro History," https://www.riodejaneiro.com/v/history/.

[14] "Jamestown, Virginia," https://en.wikipedia.org/wiki/Jamestown,_Virginia.

[15] "Plymouth Colony," https://en.wikipedia.org/wiki/Plymouth_Colony.

[16] Patrick Browne, "A Tale of Two Plymouths…and Pilgrims," January 21, 2014, https://historicaldigression.com/2014/01/21/a-tale-of-two-plymouths-and-pilgrims/. See also J. B. Harley, "New England Cartography and the Native Americans," in Emerson W. Baker et al. *American Beginnings: Exploration, Culture, and Cartography in the Land of Norumbega* (Lincoln: University of Nebraska Press, 1994), 312: "Such maps are more than an image of the landscapes of English colonization in New England. They are a discourse of the acquisition and dispossession that lie at the heart of colonialism." My research indicates it was Squanto, one of the first Native Americans to meet with the *Mayflower* colonists, who told them that the English had already named that place Plymouth. Squanto was originally from that place (Patuxet). He had lived in London, might have been familiar with Smith's map, and was a guide in New England for explorer Thomas Dermer. Dermer wrote about Squanto, and said the place had been named Plymouth on Smith's map, in a letter dated June 30, 1620. That was months *before* the Pilgrims left England. For months after their arrival, they seemed unaware of the Plymouth name until meeting Squanto. See William Bradford, *Of Plimoth Plantation* (Boston: Mass. Sec. of Commonwealth, 1898, original written 1630–1650), 117 (transcript of Dermer letter), https://archive.org/details/bradfordshistory00brawi/page/n7/mode/2up; Darrett B. Rutman, "The Pilgrims and Their Harbor," *The William and Mary Quarterly* 17, no. 2 (1960), 166, 171, https://doi.org/10.2307/1943350.

[17] "New York City," Wikipedia article, https://en.wikipedia.org/wiki/New_York_City.

[18] As to shipbuilding, see Briggs, *Shipbuilding*; Galluzzo, *North River*; Bangs, *Town Records*, 3:118.

[19] 1915 report, 11.

[20] William Vassall to Rev. John Wilson of Boston, letter, June 7, 1643, as quoted in Deane, *History of Scituate*, 47 (more fully at 66), and Bangs, *Town Records*, 1:38–39. The "ten miles" would go along several present-day towns north of the North River. The "meeting house" was the First Parish Church in Scituate, built in 1634, documented in "Meeting House Lane Area," SCI.I, MACRIS.

[21] "William Vassall," Wikipedia article, https://en.wikipedia.org/wiki/William_Vassall; Mary L. F. Power, "The Vassalls at Belle House Neck," a chapter in Daughters of the American Revolution (DAR), Chief Justice Cushing chapter, *Old Scituate* (Scituate: DAR, 1921), 30 (quoted), https://archive.org/details/oldscituate00mass_0/page/n5/mode/2up; Bangs, *Town Records*, 1:22, 1:39, 1:43, 3:12.

[22] Bangs, *Town Records*, 1:39; Stephen R. Valdespino, *Timothy Hatherly and the Plymouth Colony Pilgrims* (Scituate: Scituate Historical Society, 1987), 67–69, at 68. The group, who broke away from the First Church congregation in 1645, and "who preferred baptism by sprinkling, rather than immersion, built their meetinghouse upriver near the present site of Union Bridge." Cynthia Hagar Krusell, *Plymouth County, 1685* (Plymouth: Pilgrim Society and Plymouth County Development Council), 1985), 27. The site of the meetinghouse and associated cemetery was mentioned in records of 1658 and 1680 ("then new"). Deane, *History of Scituate*, 13, 116, 191. "This cemetery on Main Street at the corner of Old Meetinghouse Lane was

established in 1644. The meeting house of the Second Parish Church was located nearby from 1645 to 1680." "Second Church Graveyard at Wilson Hill," Norwell Cemetery Dept, https://norwelldpw.com/historical-cemeteries-in-norwell/second-church-graveyard-at-wilson-hill.

[23] For example, see Douglas Lind, "Doctrines of Discovery," 13 *Wash. U. Jur. Rev.* 001 (2020), 1 (tracing the doctrine to 16th century Spanish philosopher Francisco de Vitoria), https://openscholarship.wustl.edu/law_jurisprudence/vol13/iss1/5; Robert Miller, and others, "The Doctrine of Discovery," *Discovering Indigenous Lands: The Doctrine of Discovery in the English Colonies* (Oxford, 2010; online edn, Oxford Academic, 1 Sept. 2010), https://doi.org/10.1093/acprof:oso/9780199579815.003.0001.

[24] Bangs, *Town Records*, 1:11.

[25] Brian Donahue, *The Great Meadow: Farmers and the Land in Colonial Concord* (New Haven: Yale University Press, 2004), 59, 86–88, 88 (English hay), 168 (three generations).

[26] For examples, see Nathaniel B. Shurtleff, ed., *Records of the Colony of New Plymouth in New England: Printed by Order of the Legislature of the Commonwealth of Massachusetts*, Vol. 1 & 2 (Boston, 1855), https://archive.org/details/recordsofcolony0102newp/page/n7/mode/2up; https://www.sec.state.ma.us/arc/arcdigitalrecords/pcolony.htm; for examples of recorded deeds, see Bangs, *Town Records*, 1:76.

[27] See Lyle Nyberg, *Ditching the Marshes* (Scituate: Lyle Nyberg, 2022), 7; Mish, *Almanac*, 12 (oysters).

[28] "The Royal Parks," https://en.wikipedia.org/wiki/The_Royal_Parks; "Deer park (England)," https://en.wikipedia.org/wiki/Deer_park_(England); "History" in "A Former Royal Deer Hunting Park – Hyde Park," London Through the Eyes of a Londoner, April 21, 2024, https://tabbylondon.com/blog/f/a-former-royal-deer-hunting-park---hyde-park.

[29] Bangs, *Town Records*, 3:186 (1679); "Municipal Regulations," in Deane, *History of Scituate*, 110–112.

[30] Massachusetts Office of Coastal Zone Management (CZM), "Public Rights Along the Shoreline" (2005), Mass.gov website, https://www.mass.gov/service-details/public-rights-along-the-shoreline; Heather J. Wilson, "The Public Trust Doctrine in Massachusetts Land Law," 11 *B.C. Envtl. Aff. L. Rev.* 839 (1984), quotation from 840, https://lira.bc.edu/work/sc/f0385a41-45b1-47e0-8171-e7e6a69b6ba7.

[31] Bangs, *Town Records*, 1:24–26, lists 171 people living in Scituate between 1633 and 1639, of which about 47 were women.

[32] J. Hammond Trumbull, *The Composition of Indian Geographical Names* (Hartford, CT: Press of Case, Lockwood & Brainard, 1870, ebook 2006), 32, n. 72, https://www.gutenberg.org/files/18279/18279-h/18279-h.htm; R. A. Douglas-Lithgow, *Dictionary of American-Indian Place and Proper Names in New England: With Many Interpretations, Etc* (Salem, MA: Salem Press, 1909), 119, 124, 222 ("great outlet of a tidal river"), https://books.google.com/books?id=FyYtAAAAYAAJ; Elroy S. Thompson, "Indian Names in Plymouth County" in *History of Plymouth, Norfolk and Barnstable Counties Massachusetts*, vol. I (NY: Lewis Historical Publishing Co., 1928), 47, https://archive.org/details/historyofplymout01thom/page/48/mode/2up; memo from R. D. Sayrs, Norwell Historical Commission, to J. Carty, Chair, April 4, 2005, in North River file, SHS.

[33] "Packet Landing," NSRWA, https://www.nsrwa.org/listing/packet-landing/; Cynthia Hagar Krusell and Betty Magoun Bates, *Marshfield: A Town of Villages 1640-1990* (Marshfield Hills: Historical Research Associates, 1990), 140-141 (quoted).

[34] Nyberg, *On a Cliff*, 1, and sources cited.

[35] Arthur L. Shaw, Claude T. Wilson, "The Project of a Concrete Sea Wall at Humarock Beach, Sea View, in the Town of Scituate, Massachusetts," thesis, Massachusetts Institute of Technology, Department of Civil Engineering, 1909, WorldCat https://search.worldcat.org/title/38525911, https://hdl.handle.net/1721.1/156243.

[36] Geographic Names Information System (GNIS), USGS, https://www.usgs.gov/us-board-on-geographic-names/domestic-names; "North River (Hudson River)," Wikipedia article, https://en.wikipedia.org/wiki/North_River_(Hudson_River). The GNIS entry for the North River links to an excellent aerial map, on which you can see my house, and maybe yours.

[37] The river's length is 10 miles, according to "North River Wildlife Sanctuary," NSRWA website, https://www.nsrwa.org/listing/north-river-wildlife-sanctuary/. Other NSRWA sources say 12 miles. Another source says the river is 23 miles long (10 as the crow flies), and it drains 79,000 acres including the South River (Galluzzo, *North River*, 9). For other figures, see the discussion in the text. The NSRWA's figure of 59,000 acres covers wetlands, salt marshes (which we attempt to measure separately in this book), fresh marshes, meadows, mudflats, and other natural features of the river's watershed. A good overview of the NSRWA and its mission, with excellent photos, is at https://www.reba.net/UserFiles/files/docs/river/PP_Woods_compressed.pdf.

[38] 1915 report, 12. The 1852 plan, discussed in text below, includes only part of Scituate. Just on this plan, salt marshes run about 5 ½ miles long, and about 1/5 of a mile wide, except at Third Cliff where, for about a mile,

the marshes range up to 2/5 of a mile wide. That results in about 1.2 square miles, or 768 acres of salt marsh. In addition, around Scituate Harbor, the plan shows salt marshes about 1 mile long and about 2/5 of a mile wide, resulting in about 0.2 square miles or 128 acres of salt marsh. This does not include marshland north of Scituate Harbor, such as around Musquashcut Pond and its brook, or in North Scituate near Briggs Harbor.

[39] "The World's Tidal Marshes Are Finally on the Map: The Nature Conservancy and the University of Cambridge publish first-ever comprehensive map of Earth's tidal marshes, call for increased restoration," The Nature Conservancy, June 7, 2023, https://www.nature.org/en-us/newsroom/tidal-marshes-on-the-map/?vu=marshes, and its linked reports. Massachusetts offers similar views, based on photointerpretation of 2005 aerial photography. "MassGIS Data: MassDEP Wetlands (2005)," December 2017, https://www.mass.gov/info-details/massgis-data-massdep-wetlands-2005.

[40] The image is based on the recent Global Tidal Marsh Distribution map, which uses satellite data from 2020 and is in color. Part of that map was modified using Photoshop to highlight the marshes in this area, so the image may not be an entirely accurate representation. Mostly, color hues were significantly adjusted and then converted to grayscale. The image is comparable to the National Wetland Inventory map, which is typically based on aerial photographs. For this area, the NWI notes, "The wetlands and deepwater habitats in this area were photo interpreted using 1:40,000 scale, color infrared imagery from 1995." https://fwsprimary.wim.usgs.gov/wetlands/apps/wetlands-mapper/.

[41] Jesslyn Shields, "The 9 Longest Rivers in the World: From the Nile to the Congo," HowStuffWorks, updated February 27, 2024, https://science.howstuffworks.com/environmental/earth/geophysics/9-longest-rivers-in-world.htm; Jamie Dwelley, "The Deepest and Most Dangerous Rivers in the World," Sky History, https://www.history.co.uk/articles/the-deepest-and-most-dangerous-rivers-in-the-world; Amanda Onion, "What Is the World's Shortest River?" HowStuffWorks, https://science.howstuffworks.com/environmental/earth/oceanography/worlds-shortest-river.htm.

[42] "Stream gradient," Wikipedia article (emphasis added), https://en.wikipedia.org/wiki/Stream_gradient.

[43] "Boston Marathon Course Analysis," *Run* website, updated January 24, 2024, https://run.outsideonline.com/road/road-racing/boston-marathon-course-analysis/.

[44] "Indian Head River," Wikipedia article (3 feet), https://en.wikipedia.org/wiki/Indian_Head_River; Metropolitan Area Planning Council for Town of Hanover, "Hanover Open Space and Recreation Plan 2017–2018 Update with Public Comments," 34 (10 feet), available from https://www.hanover-ma.gov/open-space-committee/pages/open-space-plan. By comparison, the Americans with Disabilities Act (ADA) standard for a ramp slope ratio (the rise divided by the run) is 1:12 (8.333%).

[45] "Tides and Water Levels," National Ocean Service, NOAA, https://oceanservice.noaa.gov/education/tutorial_tides/tides08_othereffects.html; "Tides & Currents Products," NOAA, https://tidesandcurrents.noaa.gov/products.html; "King tide," https://en.wikipedia.org/wiki/King_tide.; Erin Douglas and Ken Mahan, "Another 'wicked high tide,'" *Boston Globe*, October 19, 2024, B1.

[46] US Harborside website, accessed November 30, 2024, with predictions for December 2024 at Scituate and Boston, https://www.usharbors.com/harbor/massachusetts/scituate-harbor-ma/tides/, and https://www.usharbors.com/harbor/massachusetts/boston-harbor-ma/tides/.; "Timing the Tides," NSRWA presentation, slide 57, https://nsrwa.s3.us-east-2.amazonaws.com/wp-content/uploads/2024/10/07165040/Timing-the-Tides-10-3-24.pdf; NSRWA *Guide Map*, "Tide Offsets." See also "Scituate Harbor, MA Tide Gauge," https://catalog.data.gov/dataset/scituate-harbor-ma-tide-gauge.

[47] "Datums for 8445138, Scituate, Scituate Harbor, MA," NOAA Tides & Currents, https://tidesandcurrents.noaa.gov/datums.html?id=8445138.

[48] US Harborside website. Commercial data on upriver tides seem to default to Damon's Point data, and NOAA does not have upriver stations.

[49] Email from Brian Taylor, NSRWA, December 2, 2024; Water Data For the Nation (WDFN), USGS website, https://waterdata.usgs.gov/monitoring-location/01105730/#parameterCode=00065&period=P7D&showMedian=false.

[50] Email from Alex Mansfield, NSRWA, December 12, 2024; "Plan of Pembroke, surveyors name not given, dated 1794-5," Massachusetts Archives (#1238) (note "Head of common tides"), *Digital Commonwealth*, https://ark.digitalcommonwealth.org/ark:/50959/2227nh04v. Home page for USGS water data is https://waterdata.usgs.gov/nwis. See also "About Hydrograph," NOAA National Water Prediction Service, https://water.noaa.gov/about/hydrograph.

[51] "Timing the Tides," NSRWA presentation, slides 46–47, 66, https://nsrwa.s3.us-east-2.amazonaws.com/wp-content/uploads/2024/10/07165040/Timing-the-Tides-10-3-24.pdf.

[52] Robbi Bishop-Taylor, November 14, 2024, https://bsky.app/profile/satellitesci.bsky.social, and https://bsky.app/profile/satellitesci.bsky.social/post/3lav77sc5e22o?utm=, with post by Ted Dunning linking to NASA data: Greg Shirah, "Barotropic Global Ocean Tides," NASA Scientific Visualization Studio, November 5, 2020, updated October 10, 2024 (with further credits, and a note, "Ocean tides are not simple"), https://svs.gsfc.nasa.gov/4821. Thanks to Philip Bump for finding this and mentioning it in "How to Read This Chart," *Washington Post* newsletter, December 7, 2024, see https://bsky.app/profile/pbump.com?utm=.

[53] *North River Packet*, Norwell Historical Society, December 2024, 2, online edition, https://norwellhistoricalsociety.org/.

[54] Donald G. Scothorne in "An Archaeological Salvage Along the North River," *Bulletin of the Massachusetts Archaeological Society* 31:3&4, 26 (April-July 1970), https://vc.bridgew.edu/bmas/115/.

[55] Donald G. Scothorne in "Oak Island Site: The Archaic Defined," *Bulletin of the Massachusetts Archaeological Society* 29:3&4, 37 (April-July 1968), https://vc.bridgew.edu/bmas/120/; "Masthead Drive Trail," NSRWA, https://www.nsrwa.org/listing/masthead-drive-trail/.

[56] "Fishing weir," Wikipedia article, https://en.wikipedia.org/wiki/Fishing_weir; Jessica Hill, "Wampanoag members fight to keep winter fishing traditions alive," *Cape Cod Times*, March 4, 2021, copied at https://www.herringpondtribe.org/2021/03/04/wampanaog-members-fight-to-keep-winter-fishing-traditions-alive/; Van Wagner, "Eel dam / weir archeological site Danville PA, Susquehanna River," YouTube post and video, June 30, 2020, https://www.youtube.com/watch?v=RcbbKJ17_No.; "Boylston Street Fishweir," Wikipedia article, https://en.wikipedia.org/wiki/Boylston_Street_Fishweir; Gary Sanderson, "New Weir Information," Tavern Fare blog, April 25, 2024 (Connecticut River valley), https://tavernfare.com/?p=2921. See discussion in text below, particularly about seines; Native Americans had a number of names for weirs or fishing places with weirs. (P) For examples, see J. Hammond Trumbull, *Indian Names of Places etc., in and on the Borders of Connecticut: With Interpretations of Some of Them* (Hartford: Press of the Case, Lockwood & Brainard Co., 1881), 10, 90, Wikimedia.org.

[57] *Historic & Archaeological Resources of Southeast Massachusetts* (Boston: Massachusetts Historical Commission, 1982, 2007 PDF version), 36 (Map 3), 40, https://www.sec.state.ma.us/divisions/mhc/preservation/survey/regional-reports/SouthesternMA.pdf; Ray Freden, "The North River, over 100 years ago, Part 1," blog post, March 26, 2021, https://wrayfreden.com/2021/03/26/the-north-river-over-100-years-ago/. See also "Documentary Research and Archaeological Investigations at the Turner House, Pembroke, Massachusetts" (Pembroke: Pembroke Historical Commission, 2021), 7 (referring to PEM.HA.1 about native fish weir at Herring Brook and Historic Drinking Fountain), https://www.pembroke-ma.gov/sites/g/files/vyhlif3666/f/uploads/umass_turner_hs_report_final_w_cats.pdf.

[58] Kathleen L. Bragdon, *The Columbia Guide to American Indians of the Northeast* (New York: Columbia University Press, 2001), incl. *xvi* (Maps), 154 (Squanto); "Duxbury in Brief: A Historical Sketch," Duxbury Rural & Historical Society, https://duxburyhistory.org/local-history/. See also sign "The Mattakeeset Massachuseuk" at dam at 249 Cross Street, Hanover.

[59] Skip DeBrusk later published this, with the title *Driving South to the North Pole*, available at Buttonwood Books in Cohasset, MA.

[60] John McPhee, *The Founding Fish* (New York: Farrar, Straus and Giroux, 2002), 60–61.

[61] James Garner and John Sheppard, "Shad: America's 'Founding Fish'" NSRWA, WaterWatch Lecture Series 2024, January 31, 2024, https://www.nsrwa.org/event/waterwatch-lecture-series-2024/; "American shad," Wikipedia article, https://en.wikipedia.org/wiki/American_shad; Brad Chase, "Creature Feature: American Shad (Alosa sapidissima)," Massachusetts Division of Marine Fisheries, July 16, 2021, https://www.mass.gov/news/creature-feature-american-shad-alosa-sapidissima; McPhee, *Founding Fish* ("savory" on page 86); "American Shad," brochure, Delaware River Basin Commission (with map of spawning cycle and migration routes), https://www.nj.gov/drbc/library/documents/Shad-flyer.pdf.
Shad fisheries are included in a comprehensive 1887 survey, George Brown Goode, *The Fisheries and Fishery Industries of the United States* (Washington, DC: US Commission of Fish and Fisheries, 1887), https://www.google.com/books/edition/The_Fisheries_and_Fishery_Industries_of/zk85AQAAIAAJ?hl=en.
A good survey of alewife history on the North River also mentions shad: Orlando N. Cavallo, Jr., in cooperation with the Pembroke Herring Fisheries Commission, "The Pembroke Herring Run: A History of the Valley and Fishery, and The Alewife: A Biological Examination," Town of Pembroke MA website, https://www.pembroke-ma.gov/sites/g/files/vyhlif3666/f/uploads/pembroke_herring_run_history_booklet.pdf.

[62] Alex Mansfield email, January 30, 2025, referring to Ron Powers, "Massachusetts Fishing Report- November 21, 2024," On The Water, https://onthewater.com/fishing-reports/2024/11/massachusetts-fishing-report-

november-21-2024; "Hickory shad," https://en.wikipedia.org/wiki/Hickory_shad. There are or have been several species of "alewives" (alewife and blueback herring) in the North River, and in its region, according to Prof. Emeritus Charlie Hall, SUNY ESF, email, February 1, 2025. Commentary in text added by author.

[63] "Tipping the Scales: Restoring American Shad in the Delaware River Basin," June 13, 2023, StoryMap produced by The Nature Conservancy in Pennsylvania and Delaware in partnership with the National Park Service, https://storymaps.arcgis.com/stories/bb5be5620202488d82c80496cb774eaa. See also Walt Dietz, "PA's Most Mighty Migratory Fish," Pennsylvania League of Angling Youth, https://www.envirothonpa.org/wp-content/uploads/2014/04/MightyMigratoryFish.pdf.

[64] G. Brown Goode, with illustrations by Sherman F. Denton, *American Fishes: A Popular Treatise upon the Game and Food Fishes of North America* (New York: W. A. Houghton, 1888), 140–141, https://catalog.hathitrust.org/Record/100526914. The book has 44 chapters. None are devoted to the shad, but they are covered in "The Herring and Its Allies."

[65] McPhee, *Founding Fish*.

[66] *Mourt's Relation: A Journal of the Pilgrims at Plymouth, 1622, Part VI*, as transcribed and digitized by The Plymouth Colony Archive Project, http://www.histarch.illinois.edu/plymouth/mourt6.html. Thanks to Squanto (Tisquantum) for helping the English plant and grow corn.

[67] Nathaniel B. Shurtleff and David Pulsifer, eds., *Records of the Colony of New Plymouth, in New England*, Vol. 1: 1633–1640 (Boston: Commonwealth of Massachusetts, 1855), 1:17, https://archive.org/details/recordsofcolonyo0102newp/page/n37/mode/2up.

[68] Google nGram Viewer, "shad,herring" for 1600–2019.

[69] "Native people hunted in the meadows along the Schuylkill River," philahistory.org, August 8, 2023, https://philahistory.org/2023/08/08/native-people-hunted-in-the-meadows-along-the-schuylkill-river/.

[70] See "The Geographic Names Information System (GNIS) Domestic Names Search Application, https://www.usgs.gov/us-board-on-geographic-names/download-gnis-data. Note all the straight lines leading into the creeks in this area of Salisbury, probably drainage ditches in the Great Marsh. See Nyberg, *Ditching the Marshes*. The GNIS lists no Shad Brooks, few Shad Creeks, many Herring Brooks (mostly in Massachusetts) and Herring Creeks.

[71] Adams, Digital Diary, 2 August 1839, at https://www.masshist.org/publications/jqadiaries/index.php/document/jqadiaries-v42-1839-08-02-p158#sn=193. Adams' diary for August 28, 1840, says the shed was in Cohasset.

[72] Bangs, *Town Records*, vol. 1, multiple pages.

[73] "Stockbridge Grist Mill," NSRWA website, https://www.nsrwa.org/listing/stockbridge-grist-mill/; "The Stockbridge Grist Mill, 1650," Scituate Historical Society website, https://scituatehistoricalsociety.org/historic_property/grist-mill/; "Old Stockbridge Grist Mill," Wikipedia article, https://en.wikipedia.org/wiki/Old_Stockbridge_Grist_Mill.

[74] Prof. Quentin L. Coons, in "Stetson, Cornet Robert and Honor Tucker House," 8 Meadow Farms Way, NRW.7, MACRIS. See also Bangs, *Town Records*, 1:88 (Stockbridge, 1673) and 1:336 (Stockbridge, 1674).

[75] Merritt, *Narrative History*, 151.

[76] "Nathanial Thomas Mill," NSRWA website (quoted), https://www.nsrwa.org/listing/nathaniel-thomas-mill/.

[77] Kezia Bacon, "The Power of Water: Milling and Manufacturing in the North River Valley," Nature blog post, April 22, 2008 (a nice survey of those dams), http://keziabaconbernstein.blogspot.com/2008/04/power-of-water-milling-and.html.

[78] McPhee, *Founding Fish*, 218–219; Sean McDermott, "stripers past the troy dam," March 29, 2013, https://www.stripers247.com/threads/stripers-past-the-troy-dam.27431/; Suzanne Spellen, "Where the Tides End – The Troy Federal Lock and Dam," March 2, 2022, https://suzannespellen.substack.com/p/where-the-tides-end-the-troy-federal. See also John Roche, "All About Dams!" including discussion of Conowingo Dam (1928) across the Susquehanna River, https://mde.maryland.gov/programs/Water/StormwaterManagementProgram/Documents/All%20About%20Dams.pdf.

[79] "MHC Reconnaissance Survey Town Report: Marshfield" (Boston: Massachusetts Historical Commission, 1981), 8, https://www.sec.state.ma.us/mhc/mhcpdf/townreports/SE-Mass/mrs.pdf; John Ford, Jr., "Map of Marshfield, Mass." (Boston: Thomas Moore's Lithography, 1838), Boston Public Library, Norman B. Leventhal Map Center, *Digital Commonwealth*, https://ark.digitalcommonwealth.org/ark:/50959/cj82ks27p. A short summary of mills, including their ownership by the wealthy Charles Stockbridge and his heirs, is in Krusell, *Plymouth County, 1685*, 27.

[80] Henry D. Thoreau, *A Week on the Concord and Merrimack Rivers* (Boston: James Munroe and Co., 1849), 39, https://archive.org/details/weekonconcordmer1849thor/page/38/mode/2up, quoted in McPhee, *Founding Fish*, 75.

[81] Charles Turner, "Plan of Scituate, made by Charles Turner, dated 1794-5," Massachusetts Archives #1242, *Digital Commonwealth*, https://www.digitalcommonwealth.org/search/commonwealth:2227nn79r ("Turner's 1795 map").

[82] Turner's 1795 map; First Parish of Norwell website, https://www.firstparishnorwell.org/; Norwell First Parish Church, NRW.19 (built 1830), MACRIS; Deane, Rev. Samuel - Hartt, Samuel Windmill, 625 Main Street, NRW.915 (built c. 1810), MACRIS, or perhaps the May Elm water tower on the postcard shown here: https://norwellhistoricalsociety.org/gallery; Briggs, *Shipbuilding*, 220 (Church Hill). As to the water tower, in 1794 the town of Scituate voted to grant "permission to erect and maintain a Windmill at or near the South Meeting House on the Common land, near the site of the old Windmill." "Town Meeting" entry in WPA card index, online at Scituate Archives website, citing town meeting of May 12, 1794, vol. C-8, pages 142 ½ – 143. Later in 1794, the town voted to look into hiring a surveyor for the map, required by an order of the Massachusetts General Court. "Town Meeting" entry in WPA card index, online at Scituate Archives website, citing town meetings of October 6, 1794, vol. C-8, p. 144, and November 3, 1794, vol. C-8, p. 145 ½. In 1794, the town voted to pay Charles Turner for surveying the town. "Town Meeting" entry in WPA card index, for May 6, 1795, vol. C-8B, p. 2 ½.

Turner's 1795 map is discussed in more detail in John R. Stilgoe, *Landscape and Images* (Charlottesville, VA: University of Virginia Press, 2005), 60–61, at end of chapter "Jack-o'-lanterns to Surveyors: The Secularization of Landscape Boundaries," https://books.google.com/books?id=OFFQBgAAQBAJ&source=gbs_navlinks_s. The equivalent 1794–1795 map for Pembroke shows a number of mills on what is probably the Indian Head River, west of where it joins Herring Brook and the North River; this includes, at one pond, probably at Ludden's Ford, a forge and anchor shop, saw mill, and bridge, with a note "Head of common tides." "Plan of Pembroke, surveyors name not given, dated 1794-5," Massachusetts Archives (#1238), *Digital Commonwealth*, https://ark.digitalcommonwealth.org/ark:/50959/2227nh04v.

The equivalent map for Marshfield is not helpful in showing North River tributaries. "Plan of Marshfield, surveyor's name not given, dated 1794-5," Massachusetts Archives (#1236), *Digital Commonwealth*, https://ark.digitalcommonwealth.org/ark:/50959/2227nm460.

[83] Turner's 1795 map.

[84] "Plan of Hanover, surveyors name not given, dated 1794-5," Massachusetts Archives, *Digital Commonwealth*, https://www.digitalcommonwealth.org/search/commonwealth:2227ng643.

[85] "Plan of Scituate and North River, in reference to Bridge … from Papers of Act June 19, 1801." [Bridge over North River, Plymouth Co.], surveyor's name not given, 200 rods to an inch, Massachusetts State Archives (#1586), "Maps and Plans," SC1/series 50, Third Series Maps, v. 25, p. 21.

[86] "Plan of North River through Pembroke, Scituate and Hanover," surveyor's name not given, dated 1812, Third Series maps, v. 41 p. 9. SC1/series 50, Massachusetts Archives, Boston; Deane, *History of Scituate*, 21. Thanks to Caitlin Ramos, Head of Reference at the Archives for this 1812 plan. Seines were used in North Carolina to catch both river herring and shad. Kip Tabb, "Salmon Creek seines: Shad, herring fisheries were once big," North Carolina Coastal Federation, https://coastalreview.org/2023/02/salmon-creek-seines-shad-herring-fisheries-were-once-big/.

[87] A. Robbins and S. A. Turner, "Plan of Scituate made by A. Robbins and S. A. Turner, dated 1831," Massachusetts Archives (#2095), *Digital Commonwealth*, https://ark.digitalcommonwealth.org/ark:/50959/25152m521.

Equivalent plans were required by Massachusetts Resolves of 1829, ch. 50. See "Town Plans, 1830," *Digital Commonwealth*, https://www.digitalcommonwealth.org/collections/commonwealth:25152f91p.

The equivalent 1831 map for Hanover shows many mills along "Herring Brook" at its border with Scituate, and dams, foundries, forges, and a tack factory along the Indian Head River before it joins the North River. Nice map. John Groves Hales, "Plan of Hanover made by John G Hales, dated 1831," *Digital Commonwealth*, https://ark.digitalcommonwealth.org/ark:/50959/25152m18q, also at Digital Archives (#2082), Secretary of State, http://digitalarchives.sec.state.ma.us/uncategorised/IO_e287b0fe-84da-4b31-a627-3180a501fb25/.

[88] "Charter of the Province of the Massachusetts-Bay," October 17, 1692, in *The Acts and Resolves, Public and Private, of the Province of the Massachusetts Bay … Volume I* (Boston: Commonwealth of Massachusetts, 1869), 1, at 19–20, https://archive.org/details/actsresolvespass9214mass/page/n5/mode/2up. This ended the separate political entity of Plymouth Colony. Krusell, *Plymouth County, 1685*, 6.

[89] Massachusetts Lobstermen's Association website, https://lobstermen.com/.

[90] "Chapter 127. An Act in addition to the several acts to prevent the destruction of alewives and other fish in Ipswich river," 1813, State Library of Massachusetts, http://hdl.handle.net/2452/109079.

[91] "Weir," Wikipedia article, https://en.wikipedia.org/wiki/Weir; "Fishing weir," Wikipedia article, https://en.wikipedia.org/wiki/Fishing_weir; "The Fish Weir Project," Plimoth Patuxet Museums, https://www.youtube.com/watch?v=GGRII5TeySo/; Edward Winslow, with William Bradford, *A Relation or Journal of the Beginning and Proceedings of the English Plantation Settled at Plimoth in New England* [*Mourt's Relation*] (London: John Bellamie, 1622; Boston: J. K. Wiggin, 1865, annotated edition), 102, 110 ("wire") https://archive.org/details/mourtsrelation00dextgoog/ [not word-searchable], and *Mourt's Relation: A Journal of the Pilgrims at Plymouth, 1622, Part II*, The Plymouth Colony Archive Project, http://www.histarch.illinois.edu/plymouth/mourt2.html.

[92] "Chapter 7. An Act to Prevent Nusances by Hedges, Wears and Other Incumbrances Obstructing the Passage of Fish in Rivers," in *Acts and Resolves of Province, Vol. I*, 644–645, at *The Acts and Resolves, Public and Private, of the Province of the Massachusetts Bay* (Boston: Commonwealth of Massachusetts), State Library of Massachusetts, https://www.mass.gov/lists/acts-and-resolves-volumes-1692-to-1959#acts-and-resolves:-1692-to-1779/1780-, linking to https://archive.org/details/actsresolvespass5768mass/page/n3/mode/2up.

[93] "Weir River (Massachusetts)," Wikipedia article, https://en.wikipedia.org/wiki/Weir_River_(Massachusetts); "Weir River Estuary Park," NSRWA website (saying the Park is 950 acres), https://www.nsrwa.org/listing/weir-river-estuary-park/, with link to "Weir River Estuary Park: A Paddling Guide" brochure, https://nsrwa.s3.us-east-2.amazonaws.com/wp-content/uploads/2022/01/11155141/WeirRiverEstuaryParkBrochure.pdf. The extensive salt marsh system is mentioned at "Weir River ACEC," Mass. Dept. of Conservation & Recreation, https://www.mass.gov/info-details/weir-river-acec. This area is detailed in a thorough and informative document by Urban Harbors Institute, University of Massachusetts Boston, "Weir River Area of Critical Environmental Concern, Natural Resources Inventory," Massachusetts Department of Environmental Management (June 2002), https://www.weirriver.org/resources/Weir_NRI_report.pdf. Salt marshes (129 acres) are discussed at page 14.

[94] "Chap. 0011. An Act To Prevent The Unnecessary Destruction Of The Fish Called Alewives, In The Town Of Hingham, In The County Of Suffolk, And To Enable The Said Town To Regulate And Order The Taking And Disposing The Same," State Library of Massachusetts, at 467 [Province Laws.—1761–62], http://hdl.handle.net/2452/116585.

[95] "Plan of Hingham, surveyor's name not given, dated May, 1795," Massachusetts State Archives #1245, *Digital Commonwealth*, https://ark.digitalcommonwealth.org/ark:/50959/2227nn555.

[96] "Chapter 34. An Act for Preventing the Unnecessary Destruction of Alewives, and Other Fish, Within This Province," *Acts and Resolves of Province, Vol. IV*, 774 [Province Laws. — 1764–65].

[97] Chapter 34, Province Laws, *Vol. IV*, 774.

[98] Chapter 34, Province Laws, *Vol. IV*, 775–776.

[99] "Chapter 37," *Acts and Resolves of Province, Vol. IV*, 91–92. For a photograph of dip nets used in Pembroke's herring runs, see discussion below about herring, and Fig. 19.

[100] Deane, *History of Scituate*, 21 (an act that I was unable to find); examples include this from 1758: "Chapter 37. An Act in Addition to an Act Intitled 'An Act for Preventing the Unnecessary Destruction of Alewives and Other Fish Within This Province," in *Acts and Resolves of Province, Vol. IV*, 91 [Province Laws. -- 1757–58].

[101] Entry in WPA card index, online at Scituate Archives website. Entry for "Peakes, William, Capt. (Representative)" citing town records Vol. C-9, Page 2, Dec. 31, 1821, says: "Appointed agent to appear before Committee of General Court on the Interior fisheries and oppose their granting prayer of Pembroke's Agent respecting Alewife fishery and defend rights of Scituate to Shad & Alewife fishery by Seines in North River in Town."

[102] "North River" entry (1) in WPA card index, online at Scituate Archives website. The 1829 entry calls for a petition to allow another day for seining in North River.

[103] "North River" entries (1848 and 1855) in WPA card index, online at Scituate Archives website.

[104] John D. Fiske, Clinton E. Watson, and Philip G. Coates, *A Study of the Marine Resources of the North River*, Monograph Series No. 3 (Division of Marine Fisheries, Department of Natural Resources, The Commonwealth of Massachusetts, 1966), 52 pages, 16 (quoted, citing Merritt), 29 (shad), on file at State Library of Massachusetts, Scituate Historical Society ("North River" file), and other places.

[105] Susquehanna River Anadromous Fish Restoration Cooperative (SRAFRC), "Migratory Fish Management and Restoration Plan for the Susquehanna River Basin" (2010), 7–8, quoted, citing C. H. Stevenson 1897 bulletin, and containing excellent Appendix 1. Life History of Migratory Fishes, https://www.nrc.gov/docs/ML1327/ML13274A047.pdf.

[106] *Pocono Living Magazine* (Aug/Sept 2023), 26–27, https://issuu.com/poconolivingmagazine/docs/plm_augsept_2023; "Delaware Water Gap," Wikipedia article, https://en.wikipedia.org/wiki/Delaware_Water_Gap; "Worthington State Forest Overview," NJDEP | Worthington State Forest | New Jersey State Park Service, https://nj.gov/dep/parksandforests/parks/worthingtonstateforest.html; "Delaware Water Gap National Recreation Area," National Park Foundation (200 miles), https://www.nationalparks.org/explore/parks/delaware-water-gap-national-recreation-area.

[107] McPhee, *Founding Fish*, 313–317 (pain and stress), 99 (quoted).

[108] Daniel Wolff & Dorothy Peteet, "Why a Marsh," *Places Journal*, May 2022, https://placesjournal.org/article/the-deep-history-and-uncertain-future-of-a-marsh-on-the-hudson/.

[109] M. Amelia Raines, "How Geology Shapes History: The Atlantic Seaboard Fall Line," under "Rivers" and "Cities," Library of Congress, https://www.loc.gov/ghe/cascade/index.html?appid=8caec0ea0f45442396e539c227ee192c; see also discussion of a dam at Augusta, Maine, in McPhee, *Founding Fish*.

[110] Deane, *History of Scituate*, 21 and 24 (distinguishing among herring, shad, and alewives).

[111] Briggs, *Shipbuilding*, 7.

[112] Jedediah Dwelley and John F. Simmons, *History of the Town of Hanover, Massachusetts, with Family Genealogies* (Hanover: Town of Hanover, 1911), 206, 208 (history of Clapp mill), https://archive.org/details/historyoftownofh00dwel/page/n241/mode/2up.

[113] (1) 1902 atlas, sheet 14 (page 26 of 36), corners 14, 15, & 22, and corners 24, 25, & 26, http://hdl.handle.net/2452/47879; (2) 1917 *Sanborn Fire Insurance Map from Hanover, Plymouth County, Massachusetts* (Nov. 1917) (1917 Sanborn map), image 3, Library of Congress, Geography and Map Division, Sanborn Maps Collection, http://hdl.loc.gov/loc.gmd/g3764hm.g037421917, and https://www.loc.gov/item/sanborn03742_001/.

[114] Dwelley and Simmons, *History of Hanover*, 208; *Biographical Review, Vol. XVIII: Containing Life Sketches of Leading Citizens of Plymouth County, Massachusetts* (Boston: Biographical Review Publishing Co., 1897), 572, https://archive.org/details/biographicalrevi1897biog. "Ludden's Ford Park," NSRWA, https://www.nsrwa.org/listing/luddens-ford-hanover/. For a historical tour of the area, see "Ancient Landmarks: Pioneer Settlers Along the Old North River," *Boston Globe*, February 19, 1886, 4.

[115] Briggs, *Shipbuilding*, 10–11.

[116] Dwelley and Simmons, *History of Hanover*, 204–205, 208.

[117] E. H. Clapp Rubber Company, by Receivers, to Abraham Starr, deed, January 10, 1935, PCRD 1686/76.

[118] Barbara Barker, "Project Dale," June 1996, *Focus on History*, https://www.hanover-ma.gov/sites/g/files/vyhlif12081/f/file/file/focus_on_history.pdf; Kezia Bacon, "Project Dale and Pembroke's Tucker Preserve," NSRWA, March 20, 2019, https://www.nsrwa.org/project-dale-and-pembrokes-tucker-preserve/; "Tucker Preserve - Pembroke, MA," Wildlands Trust (with trail maps), https://wildlandstrust.org/tucker-preserve, and https://www.pembroke-ma.gov/sites/g/files/vyhlif3666/f/uploads/tucker_preserve_trail_map_and_summary.pdf; "Tack Factory Dam Removal & Third Herring Brook Restoration," Division of Ecological Restoration, https://www.mass.gov/info-details/tack-factory-dam-removal-third-herring-brook-restoration. The site of the former Waterman factory seems to be at 360 Water Street, Hanover. Photos of Lemuel C. Waterman and his son Rudolphus [Rodolphus] C. Waterman are on file in the Massachusetts Historical Society, Ms. N-2161, St. Andrew's Church, OS Scrapbook #1, p. 11–20, fol. 3. Rodolphus was a selectman in Hanover and served on the town history committee. Dwelley and Simmons, *History of Hanover*, 3, 28, 249 (home on Water St.), 439.

[119] Bacon, "Project Dale." See also Skip Stuck and Rob MacDonald, "Human History of Wildlands: Tucker Preserve and the Indian Head River Trail," Wildlands Trust, July 9, 2024, https://wildlandstrust.org/news-blog/2024/7/9/human-history-of-wildlands-tucker-preserve-and-the-indian-hear-river-trail.

[120] Briggs, *Shipbuilding*, 41, following Deane, *History of Scituate*, 23–24.

[121] Goode, *American Fishes*, 348 (quoting Prof. Baird on dams).

[122] McPhee, *Founding Fish*, 71.

[123] McPhee, *Founding Fish*, 71.

[124] Garner and Sheppard, NSRWA WaterWatch Lecture Series 2024; Warren Winders, "Shad Fishing in the North and South Rivers," NSRWA article, May 18, 2020, https://www.nsrwa.org/shad-fishing-in-the-north-and-south-rivers/ (excellent); Joe Danubio, "Fly Fishing for the American Shad at the Indian Head River," NSRWA website, March 2017, https://www.nsrwa.org/wp-content/uploads/2017/03/Fly-Fishing-for-the-American-Shad-and-River-Conservation-at-the-Indian-Head-River.pdf (detailed; 10–15 miles). Winders' article

disputes the premise of John McPhee's book, *The Founding Fish*, that it was shad and not alewife herring that the Pilgrims found in Plymouth's Town Brook.

[125] Bradford C. Chase, John J. Sheppard, Benjamin Gahagan and Sara Turner, "American Shad Habitat Plan for Massachusetts Coastal Rivers," Massachusetts Division of Marine Fisheries, submitted to Atlantic States Marine Fisheries Commission (Boston: Massachusetts Division of Marine Fisheries, 2021, updated 2022) (a comprehensive report), 10, 11, http://www.asmfc.org/files/ShadHabitatPlans/MA_ShadHabitatPlan_revisedNov2022.pdf. DMF technical reports and other publications are available at https://www.mass.gov/marine-fisheries-publications. See also "Fish ladder," Wikipedia article, https://en.wikipedia.org/wiki/Fish_ladder. Photos of Ludden's Ford Dam are included later in this book in "Streams, and A Nice Drive in the Country." And see Ernst Halberstadt, "Dam showing fish ladder," photograph, April 23, 1973, *Digital Commonwealth*, https://ark.digitalcommonwealth.org/ark:/50959/8336kj80s.

[126] Kezia Bacon, "A History of the Indian Head River," 2025 WaterWatch lecture series, January 29, 2025, NSRWA, https://www.youtube.com/watch?v=u_ghOPfCXpE.

[127] McPhee, *Founding Fish*, 34 (quoting Boyd Kynard).

[128] McPhee, *Founding Fish*, 67 (quoted).

[129] J. B. MacKinnon, "The Other Side of the World's Largest Dam Removal," *Hakai Magazine*, November 12, 2024, https://hakaimagazine.com/features/the-other-side-of-the-worlds-largest-dam-removal/.; Cassandra Profita, "Watch: Klamath River reemerges after the removal of four dams," Oregon Public Broadcasting, October 22, 2024, https://www.opb.org/article/2024/10/22/klamath-dam-removal-river-southern-oregon-northern-california-salmon/; Reis Thebault, Alice Li, Melina Mara, "Nature, Undammed," *Washington Post*, December 14, 2023, https://www.washingtonpost.com/climate-solutions/interactive/2023/klamath-river-dam-removal/; Hallie Golden (AP), "Salmon return to lay eggs in historic habitat after largest dam removal project in US history," *Boston Globe*, November 17, 2024, C1 (quoted), and Associated Press News, https://apnews.com/article/klamath-dam-removal-salmon-spawning-4240169b4bfa327a6a67383ab536e971.

[130] Karin Limburg, "Dams in the Hudson," https://sites.google.com/esf.edu/k-limburg-site/research/dams-in-the-hudson; "Hudson Undammed," https://hudsonundammed-esf.weebly.com/.

[131] Chase, "American Shad Habitat Plan," 12–13; NSRWA project, https://www.nsrwa.org/protect-our-waters/healthy-rivers/dam-removals/indian-head-river-restoration/.

[132] More details on the proposed dam removal are in Town of Pembroke, Minutes of the Select Board Meeting, December 16, 2020, 2–3, recording a presentation by Samantha Woods, NSRWA, https://www.pembroke-ma.gov/sites/g/files/vyhlif3666/f/minutes/mins_12_16_2020.pdf. See Will Parson, "Photo Essay: American shad make their incredible journey; Restoration efforts help the migratory species recover in Chesapeake Bay tributaries," April 26, 2016, https://www.chesapeakebay.net/news/blog/photo-essay-american-shad-make-their-incredible-journey.

[133] McPhee, *Founding Fish*, various, see 38; "American Shad Release at Conte Lab," USGS website, October 13, 2023, https://www.usgs.gov/media/images/american-shad-release-conte-lab; USGS profile of Theodore Castro-Santos, at Conte Center, https://www.usgs.gov/staff-profiles/theodore-castro-santos; UMass profile of Theodore Castro-Santos, https://www.umass.edu/natural-sciences/about/directory/theodore-castro-santos; University of Massachusetts, Amherst, McCormick Laboratory, Environmental Physiology of Fish, http://www.bio.umass.edu/biology/mccormick/Location.html; "Kynard, Boyd," https://eco.umass.edu/people/faculty/kynard-boyd/; "Boyd Kynard," https://www.umass.edu/natural-sciences/about/directory/boyd-kynard; "Boyd Kynard," http://www.kynard.com/wp/?page_id=468.

[134] "Massachusetts Facts," Massachusetts Secretary of State, 13 of 52, https://www.sec.state.ma.us/divisions/cis/download/Mass_Facts.pdf; "Official State Fish of Massachusetts," State Symbols USA website, https://statesymbolsusa.org/symbol-official-item/massachusetts/state-fish-aquatic-life/cod.

[135] "Sacred Cod," Wikipedia article, https://en.wikipedia.org/wiki/Sacred_Cod.

[136] Christine Woodside, "A Tale of Shad, the State Fish," CT History, April 4, 2021, https://connecticuthistory.org/a-tale-of-shad-the-state-fish/ (excellent); Stephen Wood, "110. Haddam Shad Museum," Connecticut Museum Quest, May 31, 2009, https://ctmuseumquest.com/?page_id=8148 (detailed); "American Shad (Alosa sapidissima) – Native," Connecticut Department of Energy & Environmental Protection website, https://portal.ct.gov/DEEP/Fishing/Freshwater/Freshwater-Fishes-of-Connecticut/American-Shad.

[137] Briggs, *Shipbuilding*, 7; Wesley H. Osborne, Jr., "Stocking Atlantic salmon in the North River," photograph, April 1973, *Digital Commonwealth*, and University of Massachusetts Boston, Joseph P. Healey Library, http://openarchives.umb.edu/cdm/ref/collection/p15774coll6/id/8795; three photos from EPA's

Documerica Program 1972–1977, NAIC: 550047, https://catalog.archives.gov/id/550047; Robert Cooke, "Coho salmon my reunite ecologists, N-plant," *Boston Globe*, October 23, 1974, 64.

[138] Walter Crossley, "On The Cod And Clam," *Marshfield Mariner*, early summer, 1974 (?).

[139] "Town Meeting" entries in WPA card index (quoted), online at Scituate Archives website, citing town meetings of May 5, 1794, vol. C-8, page 142 ½, and November 3, 1794, vol. C-8, page 146.

[140] Image of postcard in text and similar views are in *Pembroke 1712–2012: Ancient Trails to the 21st Century* (Pembroke: Pembroke 300th Anniversary Committee, 2012), in chapter by Orlando Cavallo Jr., "Pembroke Herring Run: A History of the Valley and the Fishery," 140–141 (source of additional caption for postcard in text). See also Orlando Cavallo Jr., and Pembroke Herring Fisheries Commission (PHFC), "Herring Run Brochure: A History of the Valley and Fishery," and "The Alewife: A Biological Examination," https://www.pembroke-ma.gov/herring-fisheries-commission/pages/herring-run-brochure-and-migration-route-map.

[141] "Along Old Trails," *Scituate Herald*, April 22, 1938, 6.

[142] Patricia Nealon, "Husbanding alewives: Southeast Mass. Herring runs woven into fabric of town life," *Boston Globe*, May 2, 1996, 27. See also "Born to Run," *Boston Globe*, May 17, 2020, B1.

[143] "[22] Herring Habitats Overwhelmed: Exploring the Wonders of Collective Nouns for Herrings!" https://www.collectivenounslist.com/herrings.

[144] "Cran (unit)," Wikipedia article, https://en.wikipedia.org/wiki/Cran_(unit).

[145] Lori Wolfe, "See the Herring Runs on the South Shore," NSRWA website, April 16, 2024, https://www.nsrwa.org/see-herring-runs-south-shore/.

[146] Lori Wolfe, "See the Herring Runs"; Lori Wolfe, "Herring Counters Needed – Be a Citizen Scientist!" NSRWA website, February 22, 2024, https://www.nsrwa.org/herring-counters-needed-be-a-citizen-scientist/. You can zoom in on a map of herring habitat at "Diadromous Fish," MassGIS, https://www.arcgis.com/home/item.html?id=055c9aee46bc428abcc51ae6ea047383. See also "Essential Fish Habitat Mapper," NOAA Fisheries (maps in all kinds of digital complexity), https://www.fisheries.noaa.gov/resource/map/essential-fish-habitat-mapper.

[147] Thanks to Alden R. Ludlow, Project Archivist, Wellesley Historical Society, for the information about Denton following this introductory paragraph.

[148] See also "Sherman Denton, Artist, Dies at 80," *Boston Globe*, June 18, 1937, 19.

[149] William Bradford, *Of Plimoth Plantation* (Boston: Mass. Sec. of Commonwealth, 1898, original written 1630–1650), https://archive.org/details/bradfordshistory00brawi/page/n7/mode/2up; Browne, "A Tale of Two Plymouths;" Nathaniel Philbrick, *Mayflower: A Story of Courage, Community, and War* (New York: Viking/Penguin, 2006).

[150] Deane, *History of Scituate*, 111 (thatch, 1668); Nyberg, *Ditching the Marshes*, 8, 9; William Cronon, *Changes in the Land: Indians, Colonists, and the Ecology of New England* (New York: Hill and Wang, 1983, first revised ed. 2003), 31; Bobby Bascomb, "Marshes are cost-effective for protecting coasts: Study," Mongabay, October 31, 2024 (quoted), https://news.mongabay.com/short-article/marshes-are-cost-effective-for-protecting-coasts-study/; "Spartina," https://en.wikipedia.org/wiki/Spartina.

[151] *Fourth Annual Report of the Secretary of the Massachusetts Board of Agriculture* (Boston: Commonwealth of Massachusetts, 1857("1857 report"), 101, https://catalog.hathitrust.org/Record/007905215.

[152] "Haying," National Park Service – Boston Harbor Islands, updated February 26, 2015, https://www.nps.gov/boha/learn/historyculture/haying.htm.

[153] See Wolff & Peteet, "Why a Marsh."

[154] James Newton, engraver, drawn by W. Pierre, "A view of Boston taken on the road to Dorchester," (London: J.F.W. Des Barres, 1776), Norman B. Leventhal Map & Education Center, https://collections.leventhalmap.org/search/commonwealth:7h149z76m; "William Shirley," https://en.wikipedia.org/wiki/William_Shirley.

[155] Shirley - Eustis House, 31–37 Shirley St, BOS.12785 (mentions salt marshes), MACRIS; Shirley-Eustis Outbuilding, 42–44 Shirley St, BOS.17262, MACRIS; Boston Landmarks Commission, Public Archaeology Lab, "Shirley-Eustis Place, Boston Landmarks Commission Study Report," July 6, amended July 30, 2021, 24 (Eliakim) and addendum by Aabid Allibha, "Working Report on Slavery at the Shirley-Eustis House," May 20, 2021, 32 incl. notes 59 & 60 (link to copy of Hutchinson tax valuation), https://content.boston.gov/sites/default/files/file/2021/07/272.21%20Shirley-Eustis%20Place%20Study%20Report_Final%20Amended.pdf; Henry Pelham and Francis Jukes, "A Plan of Boston in New England with its environs…1775 and 1776" (London: H. Pelham, 1777), Norman B. Leventhal Map & Education Center, https://collections.leventhalmap.org/search/commonwealth:3f462w840 ("Gov. Shirley" estate just west of "Salt Meadows" in center left).

[156] See Lyle Nyberg, *Counting Cows*, draft paper, 2024, on file with author.
[157] Shirley - Eustis House, 31–37 Shirley St, BOS.12785, and other sources listed in note above.
[158] 1857 report, 136–138.
[159] 1857 report, 144 (quoted), 339, 397.
[160] Lyle Nyberg, "Cudworth House Barn and Cattle Pound," memo, 2023, on file, Scituate Historical Society.
[161] "Old Time Town Meeting At Scituate," *Scituate Herald*, September 15, 1933, 1, at 5.
[162] Betsy H. Woodman, "Gathering The Salt Hay: A Measure of Man and Marsh," 5th Annual Newburyport, MA, Maritime Society Antique Show Catalogue, 34 (October 14–16, 1983); and see Douglas MacLeod and Betsy H. Woodman, "Collected Scatterings: Reminiscences of Salt Hay Farming," 5th Annual Maritime Society Catalogue, 42. Thanks to John Stilgoe for providing copies of these excellent articles.
[163] Author's measurements, September 17, 2023. Other information, including sidebar on Annie Foster Peirce, based on 1880 and 1940 US Federal Census reports, HeritageQuest; *Scituate Herald*, May 30, 1941, 4, col. 5, and May 15, 1942, 2, col. 5; Harold Howard, compiler, *Towns of Scituate and Marshfield Massachusetts Directory 1918: Containing an Alphabetical List of the Inhabitants, a Summer Resident Directory, Street Directory and Classified Business Directory; a List of Town Officials and Churches, Diagrams of Boston Theatres and Census of Massachusetts* (Boston: Harold Howard, 1918), 49, on file, Scituate Historical Society; Lyle Nyberg, "Sunnycroft: A Scituate Summer Estate," *New England Journal of History*, Vol. 79, No. 1 (Fall 2022), 85–116; Nyberg, "Cudworth House Barn and Cattle Pound." See "E. F. Peirce" on Richards 1903 map: J. E. Judson, *Topographical Atlas of Surveys: Plymouth County together with the town of Cohasset, Norfolk County, Massachusetts* (Springfield, MA: L. J. Richards & Co., 1903), plate 27, State Library of Massachusetts, Massachusetts Real Estate Atlas Digitization Project (hereinafter Richards 1903 map), https://www.mass.gov/info-details/massachusetts-real-estate-atlas-digitization-project-by-the-state-library.
[164] "Hay," https://en.wikipedia.org/wiki/Hay; "Largest haystack," Guinness World Records, https://www.guinnessworldrecords.com/world-records/largest-haystack.
[165] Gallagher photo and author visit from 2023. This is probably the same ladder mentioned in the article cited above, *Scituate Herald*, September 15, 1933.
[166] Bruce Thurlow, "Scarborough Marsh: 'Land of Much Grass'" at "Scarborough: They Called It Owascoag" site, http://scarborough.mainememory.net/page/1396/display%3Fpage=1.html, with a good description of salt marsh haying; "What are staddle stones?" Shire Oak (UK) website, November 29, 2021, https://www.shireoak.net/blog/staddle-stones-what-are-they-why-are-they-useful. Staddles are shown and described at "Marsh Staddle, Scarborough [ME], ca. 1900," Maine Memory website, https://www.mainememory.net/record/29358.
[167] Walter Crossley, "Using Nature For Its Assets," *Marshfield Mariner*, July 27, 1972, 2.
[168] Martin Johnson Heade, "View of Marshfield," c. 1866–1876," Corcoran Collection, National Gallery of Art, accession number 2015.19.173, https://www.nga.gov/collection/art-object-page.101282.html. See Sarah Cash, on Heade's "View of Marshfield," in *American Paintings to 1945* (2012), 129–130, https://www.nga.gov/content/dam/ngaweb/research/publications/pdfs/corcoran-american-art.pdf. In Vinal, *Salt Haying*, page 26 says staddles for haystacks were never used in the Scituate marshes, unlike those in Barnstable and Medford (and, he might have added, in Newburyport). Perhaps he was not aware of those in the North River town of Marshfield, as shown in Heade's painting.
[169] "Cape Cod Salt Marshes – Asset or Swamp?" Historical Society of Old Yarmouth, December 18, 2022 (excerpted from an article by Duncan Oliver) (with great photo of staddle and salt hay harvesting, copied above in text), https://www.hsoy.org/blog/2022/12/13/the-cape-cod-salt-marsh.
[170] Vinal, *Salt Haying*, 3, and see 7, 22.
[171] Loring H. Jacobs Co., surveyor, "Compiled Plan of Land in the Town of Scituate, Massachusetts/Driftway and Chief Justice Cushing Highway Route 3A," scale 1"=200', November 12, 1975, Parcel 6A, PCRD, plan book 18/722, sheet 1 of 3; see also Boston Sand & Gravel Company to Town of Scituate, deed confirmatory of taking, August 14, 1975, PCRD 4091/733.
[172] George Lunt, "Seashore Idyl" in *Poems* (Boston: Cupples, Upham and Company, 1884), 266 at 268, https://books.google.com/books?id=tmATAAAAYAAJ&source=gbs_navlinks_s. Lunt was a native of Newburyport, on the Merrimack River, also the home of salt marsh haying and gundalows. More about Lunt is on my archived website listed at https://www.lylenyberg.com/copy-of-links-suffrage. Which of today's toils will be memorialized in such poetry?
[173] Woodman, "Gathering The Salt Hay;" MacLeod and Woodman, "Collected Scatterings."
[174] Vinal, *Salt Haying*, 16.
[175] "Gathering Salt Marsh Hay," Historic Ipswich, https://historicipswich.net/2021/02/12/salt-marsh-hay/; William E. Trout, III, "The Gundalow," in "Let's Roll a Hogshead!" Scottsville (VA) Museum,

https://scottsvillemuseum.com/transportation/homehogshead.html; Harriet Prescott Spofford, "Newburyport and its Neighborhood," 161 at 174, *Harper's New Monthly Magazine*, Volume 51 (July 1875), https://books.google.com/books?id=tnI_5-A3phAC&newbks=1&newbks_redir=0&source=gbs_navlinks_s; Erik Ronnberg, "Gundalow/Scow," Fitz Henry Lane project, Cape Ann Museum, http://fitzhenrylaneonline.org/historical_material/?type=Vessel+Types&section=Gundalow+%2F+Scow; "What is a gundalow?" Gundalow Company, https://www.gundalow.org/about-us/what-is-a-gundalow/; Joseph Holt Ingraham, *The South-West, Volume 1* (New York, Harper & Brothers, 1835), 105 ("the 'Down East' gundalow"), https://books.google.com/books?id=T5ZKAAAAMAAJ&newbks=1&newbks_redir=0&source=gbs_navlinks_s; Seth C. Bruggeman, "The Shenandoah River Gundalow: Reusable Boats in Virginia's Nineteenth-Century River Trade," *Virginia Magazine of History and Biography* 118, no.4 (2010), 314–349, as cited in National Archives Library Information Center (ALIC) > Journals and Periodical Literature > Record Group Clusters > Compilation of Periodical Literature: 2010; Nancy Coffey Heffernan & Ann Page Stecker, *New Hampshire: Crosscurrents in Its Development* (Hanover, NH: University Press of New England, 3d ed., 2004), 70–72, preview at https://books.google.com/books?id=IainON4omb8C&source=gbs_navlinks_s; Merritt, *Old Time Anecdotes*, 21–27 (chapter III, "Gundalow Days on North River"); "Last Gundalow on the Piscataqua," *Boston Globe*, July 3, 1910, 55 (or 3); "The Gundalow," *Scientific American* (New York: Munn & Co.), September 10, 1898, 171, at 172 (sails), https://books.google.com/books?id=CBU4AQAAMAAJ&newbks=1&newbks_redir=0&source=gbs_navlinks_s; James Russell Lowell, *The Writings of James Russell Lowell: Poems* (Boston: Houghton, Mifflin, 2d ed., 1890), 195 (The Biglow Papers), https://books.google.com/books?id=F2URAAAAYAAJ&newbks=1&newbks_redir=0&source=gbs_navlinks_s. An excellent history of gundalows is set forth in Rich Clyborne, "Sail Freight: The Piscataqua Gundalow," Hudson River Maritime Museum, History Blog, August 11, 2023, https://www.hrmm.org/history-blog/category/sail_freight.

[176] Merritt, *Narrative History*, 3; Jonathan Baldwin, *The Revolutionary Journal of Col. Jeduthan Baldwin, 1775–1778* (Bangor, ME: printed for The De Burians, 1906), 63–64, 80 (Crown Point, probably British fortress along the western bank of Lake Champlain), https://books.google.com/books?id=7-HUFSwyqzcC&newbks=1&newbks_redir=0&source=gbs_navlinks_s.

[177] John G. Whittier, "The Countess," in Eliakim Littell, Robert S. Littell, eds., *Littell's Living Age, Volume 77* (Boston: Littell, Son, and Company, 1863), 335 (quoted), https://books.google.com/books?id=DyLVAAAAMAAJ&newbks=1&newbks_redir=0&source=gbs_navlinks_s.

[178] The Portsmouth (NH) Athenaeum has several of them, https://portsmouthathenaeum.org/. So does the Smithsonian National Museum of American History, listed in "Guide to the Historic American Merchant Marine Survey Records," https://sirismm.si.edu/EADpdfs/NMAH.AC.0240.pdf, with a nice example being "[Gundalow loaded with salt hay on the Parker River, Newbury, Massachusetts, b&w photoprint.]," https://sova.si.edu/search/ark:/65665/ep867e1b96d062f4e60a9c8f42c403a9275. In addition, photo comments reveal that gundalows were used around Harpers Ferry, WV, per "Masonic Hall, Shenandoah Street, Harpers Ferry, Jefferson County, WV; Photos from Survey HABS WV-279," Library of Congress, https://www.loc.gov/resource/hhh.wv0374.photos?st=gallery. Thanks to Google Ngram for locating the early publications.

[179] Henry A. Litchfield, C. E., "Plan of Lands at North Scituate Beach, Scituate, Mass., May 1918, Scale 100 ft. to an inch," PCRD plan book 3/83 (showing "golf links"); Frederick E. Tupper, "Compiled Plan of the North Scituate Estate of Florence A. Reynolds, Aug. 1919," scale 100' = 1", filed May 2, 1924, PCRD plan book 3/725 (based on 1918 Litchfield plan).

[180] This was probably the "Dammans Island" described in 1700 as the fourth parcel in a deed or allotment of land to James Briggs dated July 6, 1700, bounded "Every way to the medow" of Rodulphus Elmes, per Bangs, *Town Records*, 2:378–379. It was possibly the eight-acre planting island laid out to John Baily by surveyor Steven Otis, March 29, 1695 (although the current Treasure Island measures under four acres), per Bangs, *Town Records*, 2:380–383. "Bailyes" or "Baily's" planting island was the subject of, or mentioned in, other land transfers, for example, documents of March 10, 1709, Bangs, *Town Records*, 2:504, and May 8, 1710, Bangs, *Town Records*, 2:571, #581, Vol. C-2.

"Plantain Island" was listed as two acres owned by George H. Damon in the 1886 *Town Annual Report*, *Valuation List*, 30. Treasure Island may include or be near the meadowland parcel of three acres in John B. Damon to Abner S. Dalby, deed, September 27, 1902, recorded December 5, *1917*, PCRD 1292/394. In recent years, houses on Treasure Island were offered for rent. See "The Salt Marshes at Treasure Island," https://www.thesaltmarshes.com/.

[181] Vinal, *Salt Haying*, 24.

[182] Briggs, *Shipbuilding*, v (family, hospital), x-xii (photos), 295 (Briggs genealogy); "Dr. Lloyd Vernon Briggs," FindaGrave memorial, https://www.findagrave.com/memorial/145001543/lloyd-vernon-briggs;

[183] Hanna Clutterbuck-Cook, finding aid, "L. Vernon Briggs papers, undated, 1774–1940 (inclusive), 1911–1938 (bulk). H MS c162," Harvard Medical Library, Francis A. Countway Library of Medicine, Boston, Mass., https://id.lib.harvard.edu/ead/med00204/catalog and
https://hollisarchives.lib.harvard.edu/repositories/14/resources/6622; Gina C. Giang, finding aid, "Lloyd Vernon Briggs' collection of Massachusetts family records [1650–1933]," The Huntington Library, San Marino, California, http://www.huntington.org, and https://oac.cdlib.org/findaid/ark:/13030/c8zk5nxx/entire_text/; Kim Frontz, finding guide, Briggs papers, Arizona Historical Society, https://arizonahistoricalsociety.org/wp-content/uploads/2019/02/library_Briggs-Lloyd.pdf; Headsman, "1912: Bertram Spencer," September 17, 2011, Executed Today website, http://www.executedtoday.com/tag/lloyd-vernon-briggs/; Winfred Overholser, "The History and Operation of the Briggs Law of Massachusetts," 2 *Law and Contemporary Problems* (1935), 436–447, https://scholarship.law.duke.edu/cgi/viewcontent.cgi?article=1770&context=lcp. WorldCat lists dozens of his books, https://search.worldcat.org/search?q=au=%22Briggs%2C%20L.%20Vernon%22.

[184] 8 Elm Street, HNV.349, MACRIS; "Broad Oak Farm," 336 Broadway, HNV.173, MACRIS.

[185] Briggs, *Shipbuilding*, 354–355.

[186] "Champions of the Boston Marathon, Men's Open Division," Boston Athletic Association website (Lawrence Brignolia, US, 2:54:38 for the then-24.8 mile course), https://www.baa.org/races/boston-marathon/results/champions.

[187] Kezia Bacon, "The Chesapeake, The Shannon, and the North River Boys Who Got Between Them," NSRWA website, December 14, 2018, https://www.nsrwa.org/chesapeake-shannon-north-river-boys-got/; Kezia Bacon, "The Power of Water: Milling and Manufacturing in the North River Valley," Nature blog post, April 22, 2008, http://keziabaconbernstein.blogspot.com/2008/04/power-of-water-milling-and.html.

[188] Briggs lived less than one mile west of the North River and near its origin from the Indian Head River. Dwelley and Simmons, *History of Hanover*, 246. The same page of the book said the house was "now owned by L. Vernon Briggs, M. D." and "quaint Joshua Stetson resided here for many years preceding his death." It is the house marked "L. Briggs" at the split between Broadway and Elm Street on Walker's 1879 atlas, *Atlas of Plymouth County, Massachusetts* (Boston: Geo. H. Walker & Co., 1879) (hereinafter "1879 Walker atlas"), page 46, inset for Village of Hanover 4 Corners, State Library of Massachusetts, URI http://hdl.handle.net/2452/205573. It was built c. 1869 in the Greek Revival or Italianate style. 8 Elm Street, HNV.349, MACRIS.

[189] "Walter Edmund Crossley," FindaGrave memorial,
https://www.findagrave.com/memorial/205928427/walter-edmund-crossley.

[190] Thanks to Jim Glinski for loaning me a collection of copies of his articles.

[191] Walter Crossley, "On The North River Banks," *Marshfield Mariner*, June 29, 1972, 2. The scene is shown in Fig. 114.

[192] Walter Crossley, "Using Nature For Its Assets," *Marshfield Mariner*, July 27, 1972, 2.

[193] Walter Crossley, "Eel Fishing On The North River," *Marshfield Mariner*, August 3, 1972, 1.

[194] Walter Crossley, "Mudslinging For Profit Years Ago," *Marshfield Mariner*, July 26, 1973, 2; Walter Crossley, "On The Cod And Clam," *Marshfield Mariner*, early summer, 1974 (?).

[195] Walter Crossley, "Rum Running in Marshfield," *Marshfield Mariner*, August 10, 1972, 2 (at 6).

[196] William Phillips Tilden, *Autobiography and Personal Tributes* (Boston: Press of Geo. H. Ellis, "printed, not published," 1891), 19 (quoted),
https://books.google.com/books?id=YzcbAAAAYAAJ&source=gbs_navlinks_s. The second Union Bridge (pictured) also appeared on a postcard, "Union Bridge, Norwell Mass." with a note "went out in 1917," Norwell Historical Society, *Digital Commonwealth*, https://ark.digitalcommonwealth.org/ark:/50959/sj13b074x; and see later postcard, "Union Bridge, Norwell, Mass." Norwell Historical Society, *Digital Commonwealth*, https://ark.digitalcommonwealth.org/ark:/50959/sj13b0802. The Hatch Tilden house in the pictured postcard was built about 1800; Hatch Tilden was the toll keeper at the first Union Bridge from 1801 to 1850, when it was made a free bridge. "Hatch Tilden House," 1354 Union Street, Marshfield, MRS.212, MACRIS. See also MRS.924/NRW.900 about the 1961 bridge, and update at NRW.F about the 2009 bridge. The boat that appears in the pictured postcard is probably the one discussed by Walter Crossley, in W. Ray Freden, "The North River over 100 years ago, Part 4," November 9, 2021, https://wrayfreden.com/2021/11/09/the-north-

river-over-100-years-ago-part-4/. See also "Union Street Bridge," NSRWA, https://www.nsrwa.org/listing/union-street-bridge/.

[197] Another view is "Union Bridge, Norwell, Mass." Norwell Historical Society Postcard Collection, *Digital Commonwealth*, https://www.digitalcommonwealth.org/search/commonwealth:sj13b074x?view=commonwealth%3Asj13b076g.

[198] Walter Crossley, "Boating On The North River," *Marshfield Mariner*, June 22, 1972, 2 (at 16).

[199] Tilden, *Autobiography*, 11–24. Tilden said his nearest neighbor was Judge Nathan Cushing (1742–1812), who lived at Main Street and Lincoln Street in what is now Norwell. "Nathan Cushing," Wikipedia article and sources cited, https://en.wikipedia.org/wiki/Nathan_Cushing. See "Note on Justice Nathan Cushing (1742–1812) and Justice William Cushing (1732–1810)," Town of Norwell, https://www.townofnorwell.net/sites/g/files/vyhlif1011/f/uploads/note_on_nathan_cushing_1742-1812_william_cushing_1732-1810.pdf, and Alan Prouty, "Justice Nathan Cushing," *North River Packet*, Winter 2020, Norwell Historical Society, https://img1.wsimg.com/blobby/go/3564ec8d-06a8-4768-8bd3-7a892ae6e046/downloads/Winter%202020%20newsletter--web.pdf?ver=1615047229469. Judge Nathan's more famous relative, Chief Justice William Cushing (1732–1810), lived about three miles east, at Belle Neck. Tilden's book makes a nice companion to Briggs, *Shipbuilding*.

[200] Tilden, *Autobiography*, 26–27.

[201] Tilden, *Autobiography*, 27–29.

[202] Tilden, *Autobiography*, 34 (quoted), 140–149, 156 (quoted), 211–212. Frederick Douglass spoke in Tilden's church and spent the night at his home (page 99). Tilden described his mother's father, Capt. William Brooks (page 40). The Brooks house was farther upstream along the North River, and it is still there at 315 River Street, Norwell, NRW.131, MACRIS. The current owner is a part owner of Wood Island in the North River salt marshes of Scituate.

[203] Tilden, *Autobiography*. Church Green in Boston was the site of several churches until the fire of 1872. "The Church Green Buildings" (Boston Landmarks Commission, 1979), section 5.1, https://www.cityofboston.gov/images_documents/church%20green%20bldgs%20portrait_tcm3-19814.pdf. See Sidney Lawton Smith, "The New South, Church Green, Boston, 1850," print, 1900, *Digital Commonwealth*, https://ark.digitalcommonwealth.org/ark:/50959/37720q46j.

[204] Briggs, *Shipbuilding*, 58–59; "Chittenden Yard and Canoe Launch," NSRWA website, https://www.nsrwa.org/listing/chittenden-yard-and-canoe-launch/; "Gundaway, Richard," and "Gundiway, Richard," *Massachusetts Soldiers and Sailors of the Revolutionary War: A Compilation from the Archives* (Boston: Secretary of the Commonwealth, 1899), vol. 6, 950, https://archives.lib.state.ma.us/handle/2452/122025?show=full; Pattie Hainer, *Slaves, Servants, and Free People of Color in Scituate-Norwell, Massachusetts: 1635–1875* (Norwell [?] by author [?], 2014), https://archive.org/details/slavesservantsfr00hain; 1848 town annual report, 53 ("Jeremiah Gundaway"), https://archive.org/details/annualreportofto1848scit/page/n51/mode/2up?q=gundaway. See also, Wayne Tucker, "North River Early Black Heritage Trail," https://uploads.knightlab.com/storymapjs/789cdfa48fd72c9ea6f6c668885d8273/north-river-black-history-trail/index.html. Gunderway ancestors were said to have come from Jamaica or Barbados, according to Hainer, *Slaves*, 152 (unnumbered). One wonders if they were enslaved by the family of William Vassall (1592–1656), who settled in Scituate in 1635 with large landholdings, and who moved to Barbados by 1648, establishing a slave-labor sugar plantation that would enslave 3,865 people. "MEprof," "William Vassall," Wikipedia article, https://en.wikipedia.org/wiki/William_Vassall; see Bangs, *Town Records*, 1:154, 3:102. Briggs, *Shipbuilding*, has a photo of Gunderway before page 59. The photo, by Charles E. Rogers, is from a carte de visite, c. 1870; see similar version offered by Swann Galleries. The knees of his waders or overalls are ripped.

[205] Merritt, *Old Time Anecdotes*, 23; Horace T. Fogg, Admin., to William E. Mills, deed, June 27, 1923, PCRD 1499/185; Horace T. Fogg to William E. Mills, deed, December 10, 1925, PCRD 1444/126; "Norris Reservation," Trustees website, https://thetrustees.org/place/norris-reservation/; "Norris Reservation," NSRWA website, https://www.nsrwa.org/listing/norris-reservation/; Briggs, *Shipbuilding*, 243; *Explore South Shore Recreation Guide Map* (Norwell, MA: NSRWA, 5th ed., 2019), site 37; Norwell Assessor Parcel ID 2920, Map ID/mblu 71-037; author visit to landing October 23, 2023. The 1831 map shows what appears to be the way to the Town Landing, about where Chittenden Lane now is, but the path of the Second Herring Brook appears different, flowing from the pond south of Dover Street directly into the North River without any intermediate pond or meander; this also seems to be the case on a 1915 plan, "Plan of North River in the Towns of Scituate, Marshfield, Norwell, Pembroke & Hanover" (Harbor and Land Commissioners, 1915)

("1915 plan"), sheet 3 of 7, left side, copy available from North River Commission, http://www.northrivercommission.net/, copied and discussed later in text.

[206] *North River Packet*, Norwell Historical Society, Winter 2024, 2, https://norwellhistoricalsociety.org/newsletters%3A-2020-2024.

[207] Courtesy of Thomas Whalen, Marshfield, author of "Patented American Wood Planes," *Early American Planes* website, https://www.earlyamericanplanes.com/copy-8-of-items-1-1-4-2, and co-author (with Dale Butterworth) of *From Logs to Lumber* (2007).

[208] Kezia Bacon, "Noteworthy North River Ships," NSRWA website, August 24, 2018, https://www.nsrwa.org/noteworthy-north-river-ships/. For a short article on the river's history of shipbuilding, see Feliks Banel, "All Over The Map: Vanished shipyards connect Pacific Northwest and Boston," MYNorthwest History website, February 19, 2021, including a classic photo of the launching of the *Helen M. Foster* in 1871 (discussed below in text), and quoting Caleb Estabrooks and Norwell resident Scott Babcock, https://mynorthwest.com/2611456/all-over-the-map-vanished-shipyards-connect-pacific-northwest-boston/.

[209] Unknown author, "The Sea of New England," nautical chart, NOAA #807, https://historicalcharts.noaa.gov/, or direct, https://www.historicalcharts.noaa.gov/image.php?filename=807-00-1734.

[210] "Plan of Pembroke, surveyors name not given, dated 1794-5," Massachusetts Archives (#1238), *Digital Commonwealth*, https://ark.digitalcommonwealth.org/ark:/50959/2227nh04v.

[211] Briggs, *Shipbuilding*, 315 (*Oak*). Shipbuilders had a global eye and would later draw from Irish immigrants such as James Fields, who "came from Ireland during the famine and settled in Scituate (1850 census). He worked for the Briggs family (shipbuilders). His earring was for crossing the equator as a mariner in Ireland." James Field, photo and description, DPLA and UMass Boston, https://openarchives.umb.edu/digital/collection/p15774coll6/id/3576.

[212] Briggs, *Shipbuilding*, 64, 80–82. A house here was built in 1715, owned at times by a Turner, and used at times as an office for the Turner yards. See later discussion of the River House, and in PEM.9, MACRIS.

[213] Jedidiah Morse, *The American Geography; or, a View of the Present Situation of the United States of America* (London: John Stockdale, new ed., 1794), 314, https://www.google.com/books/edition/The_American_Geography/yJNcAAAAcAAJ?hl. The earliest reference to Indian Head Pond or River that I found was from 1650. Bangs, *Town Records*, 1:22–23. In 1653, Native American chief Josias Wampatuck sold land to English settlers bounded from the mouth of the North River along the river to Indian Head River to the pond at the head of it. Bangs, *Town Records*, 1:150. The Indian Head River is shown but not named on the 1794–1795 plans of Pembroke and Hanover. "Plan of Pembroke, surveyors name not given, dated 1794-5," Massachusetts Archives (#1238), *Digital Commonwealth*, https://ark.digitalcommonwealth.org/ark:/50959/2227nh04v; "Plan of Hanover, surveyors name not given, dated 1794-5," Massachusetts Archives (#1234), *Norman B. Leventhal Map & Education Center*, https://collections.leventhalmap.org/search/commonwealth:2227ng643.

[214] Briggs, *Shipbuilding*, 6. Namassakeeset (Namatakeeset) River is now called Herring Brook.

[215] Briggs, *Shipbuilding*; Galluzzo, *North River*; DAR, *Old Scituate*, in "North River, and Shipbuilding on Its Banks" chapter at 147.

[216] Turner's 1795 map.

[217] [Maj.] Z. B. Tower, "Plan of Scituate Harbor and North River," (Portland [ME?]: [Army Corps of Engineers]), November 17, 1852, National Archive Catalog, NAID: 170100305, Local ID: 77-CWMF-B-314, https://catalog.archives.gov/id/170100305.

[218] Letter from Secretary of War Jefferson Davis, January 20, 1854, "A report of a survey of Scituate harbor and North river," H.R. Doc. 31, 33d Cong., 1st Sess. ("1854 report"), https://archive.org/details/unitedstatescon338offigoog (starting at page 583 of 624), and https://books.google.com/books?id=DXZHAQAAIAAJ&source=gbs_navlinks_s.

[219] "Canal-Scituate Harbour to North River" entry in WPA card index (quoted), online at Scituate Archives website, citing town meeting direction of Nov. 1, 1802; Nyberg, *On a Cliff*, 22–23.

[220] "The Dike Marker," MRS.911, MACRIS.

[221] Michael F. Holt, *The Rise and Fall of the American Whig Party: Jacksonian Politics and the Onset of the Civil War* (New York: Oxford University Press, 1999), particularly 7 (internal improvements), 26–28 (1834 rise of the party), and 31 (Adams and Webster associations with party).

[222] "North River" entry in WPA card index (quoted), online at Scituate Archives website, citing town meeting direction of Nov. 4, 1822, at vol. C-9, page 15–16.

²²³ *Hingham Gazette*, August 3, 1832, 1, col. 2. It may be that Samuel A. Turner was part owner of property on Fourth Cliff, south of the John Tilden property, at least by 1850. See Joseph Northey to John Tilden Jr., deed, recorded August 13, 1850, PCRD 238/180 (30 acres on Fourth Cliff).
²²⁴ "Memorial of Inhabitants of Scituate, Pembroke, Hancock [sic], &c. in the State of Massachusetts, Praying for the Improvement of North River Channel," Doc. No. 266, May 5, 1828, https://www.govinfo.gov/, at https://www.govinfo.gov/content/pkg/SERIALSET-00174_00_00-044-0266-0000/pdf/SERIALSET-00174_00_00-044-0266-0000.pdf.
²²⁵ "Report on the survey of North River, Massachusetts. December 23, 1830. Printed by order of the [US] House of Representatives," Washington, DC, Library of Congress, https://www.loc.gov/item/2022696885/, or https://hdl.loc.gov/loc.law/llserialsetce.00206_00_00-017-0016-000, or https://purl.fdlp.gov/GPO/gpo178386; "Report of Viewing Committee on Sundry Petitions for the Improvement of the Navigation of North River," House Doc. No. 6, January 1843, 8 (quote), http://archives.lib.state.ma.us/handle/2452/750309, or https://hdl.handle.net/2452/749486, ("1843 report") then scroll down list of 97 documents to the sixth one.
²²⁶ Isaiah Rogers, memorial in support of removing obstructions on North River, House Doc. No. 9, January 1844, 4, State Library of Massachusetts, https://archives.lib.state.ma.us/server/api/core/bitstreams/ebd1c896-4a56-44f1-9f99-013e98da7043/content.
²²⁷ Holt, *Whig Party*, *supra*; "John Quincy Adams," Wikipedia article, https://en.wikipedia.org/wiki/John_Quincy_Adams, and "Internal improvements," Wikipedia article, https://en.wikipedia.org/wiki/Internal_improvements.
²²⁸ "Town Meeting" entry in WPA card index, citing town meeting of November 1, 1830, vol. C-9, page 137, with votes for Representative in US Congress for Plymouth District, of 141 for John Q. Adams out of 157.
²²⁹ John Quincy Adams, John Quincy Adams Digital Diary, 21 December 1831, Massachusetts Historical Society, http://www.masshist.org/digitaladams at https://www.masshist.org/publications/jqadiaries/index.php/document/jqadiaries-v38-1831-12-21-p313#sn=9. Adams soon followed up on the petitions. Adams, Digital Diary, 3 January 1832, at https://www.masshist.org/publications/jqadiaries/index.php/document/jqadiaries-v38-1832-01-03-p342#sn=22.
²³⁰ *Hingham Gazette*, August 3, 1832, 1, col. 2.
²³¹ See "The States of Massachusetts, Connecticut and Rhode Island From the best Authorities," pocket map (Hartford: Andrus & Judd, 1834), Barry Lawrence Ruderman Map Collection, Stanford University, https://exhibits.stanford.edu/ruderman/catalog/qj509hz2751, and https://purl.stanford.edu/qj509hz2751; Ben Berke, "If history were different, Cape Cod Canal might have flowed through Brockton," *Taunton Gazette*, July 13, 2020, https://www.tauntongazette.com/story/news/2020/07/13/if-history-were-different-cape-cod-canal-might-have-flowed-through-brockton/114513146/; discussion below about 1915 report.
²³² Adams, Digital Diary, 19 April 1834, at https://www.masshist.org/publications/jqadiaries/index.php/document/jqadiaries-v39-1834-04-19-p285#sn=31; see discussion below about 1915 report.
²³³ Adams, Digital Diary, 9 October 1839, at https://www.masshist.org/publications/jqadiaries/index.php/document/jqadiaries-v42-1839-10-09-p221.
²³⁴ See discussion in text about 1852 plan and 1854 report; Nyberg, *On a Cliff*, 21–27.
²³⁵ Adams, Digital Diary, 9 October 1839; Norwell First Parish Church, NRW.19 (built 1830), MACRIS; May Elms - May, Rev. Samuel Joseph House, 841 Main Street, NRW.35 (built c. 1786, J. Stetson owner), MACRIS.
²³⁶ Adams, Digital Diary, 9 October 1839; "Nathan Cushing," Wikipedia article, including ref. 1, https://en.wikipedia.org/wiki/Nathan_Cushing.
²³⁷ Adams, Digital Diary, 9 October 1839; DAR, *Old Scituate*, 221. Samuel A. Turner was a state representative, a highway surveyor, town moderator, and member of various town committees in the 1820s to 1840s. "Turner, Samuel A.," entries (about 30) in WPA card index, online at Scituate Archives website. His 1831 map (by Robbins & Turner) has a circle and an asterisk at what is now Old Oaken Bucket Pond and First Herring Brook, indicating a nail mill, and a double asterisk at Second Herring Brook, indicating a mill.
²³⁸ Adams, Digital Diary, 1 February 1840, at https://www.masshist.org/publications/jqadiaries/index.php/document/jqadiaries-v42-1840-02-01-p350#sn=47. Adams, evidently meticulous, followed up with a reminder he left at Poinsett's office. Adams, Digital Diary, 24 March 1840, at https://www.masshist.org/publications/jqadiaries/index.php/document/jqadiaries-v42-1840-03-24-p379#sn=48.

[239] A. Robbins and S. A. Turner, surveyors, "Plan of Scituate made by A. Robbins and S. A. Turner, dated 1831" (Boston: Pendleton's Lithography, 1831), Massachusetts Archives (#2095), *Digital Commonwealth*, https://ark.digitalcommonwealth.org/ark:/50959/25152m521; georeferenced raster version available from Harvard Map Collection, Harvard College Library, https://hgl.harvard.edu/catalog/harvard-matwn-3764-s322-1831-r6. It seems Turner was baptized in 1792, the son of Charles Turner, perhaps the one who authored the 1795 map of Scituate. *Vital records of Scituate, Massachusetts, to the year 1850*, Volume I - Births (Boston: New England Historic Genealogical Society, 1909), 382, https://archive.org/details/vitalrecordsofsc01newe/page/382/mode/2up. In 1829, the town began to consider hiring a surveyor for a plan of the town, as evidently required by the state. "Town Meeting" entry in WPA card index, citing town meeting of March 2, 1829, vol. C-9, pages 107–109, and see 111–113, and 128–131. I found no town approval to hire Turner, and he may have published the map privately. In late 1831, the town "instructed Selectmen to procure 500 copies of a Lithographic Map of Town, and sell them to inhabitants at cost." "Town Meeting" entry in WPA card index, citing town meeting of November 14, 1831, vol. C-9, pages 152–153. A plan of 1839 was prepared by "Samuel A. Turner, Surveyor," "Plan of the Homestead farm belonging to the Heirs of the late Deacon Thomas Cushing … ," April 4, 1839, PCRD plan book 1/79. The 1795 and 1831 maps are discussed in John R. Stilgoe, *Landscape and Images* (Charlottesville: University of Virginia Press, 2001, 2005, 2015 paperback ed.), in chapter "Jack-o'-lanterns to Surveyors: The Secularization of Landscape Boundaries" (from a paper published in 1976), 47 in 2005 book, https://books.google.com/books?id=OFFQBgAAQBAJ&source=gbs_navlinks_s.

[240] Adams, Digital Diary, 14 November 1839, at https://www.masshist.org/publications/jqadiaries/index.php/document/jqadiaries-v42-1839-11-14-p252#sn=3.

[241] Adams, Digital Diary, 14 November 1839.

[242] Ford's 1838 "Map of Marshfield." This was a big improvement over the same surveyor's 1831 map, a counterpart to the 1831 map of Scituate. John Ford, Jr., "Plan of Marshfield made by John Ford, Jr., dated 1831," Massachusetts Archives (#2088), *Digital Commonwealth*, https://ark.digitalcommonwealth.org/ark:/50959/25152h468.

[243] John Stetson Barry, *A Historical Sketch of the Town of Hanover, Mass., with Family Genealogies* (Boston: by author, 1853), 164–165, https://archive.org/details/townhanovermass00barrrich/page/164/mode/2up.

[244] Adams, Digital Diary, 24 April 1840, at https://www.masshist.org/publications/jqadiaries/index.php/document/jqadiaries-v42-1840-04-24-p413#sn=49.

[245] Adams, Digital Diary, 5 October 1840, at https://www.masshist.org/publications/jqadiaries/index.php/document/jqadiaries-v41-1840-10-05-p113#sn=53.

[246] Adams, Digital Diary, 5 October 1840, at https://www.masshist.org/publications/jqadiaries/index.php/document/jqadiaries-v41-1840-10-05-p113#sn=53.

[247] Briggs, *Shipbuilding*, 198 (quoted)/

[248] Charles Francis Adams, ed., John Quincy Adams, *Memoirs of John Quincy Adams, Comprising Portions of His Diary From 1795 to 1848, Vol. XI* (Philadelphia: J. B. Lippincott & Co., 1876), 25, https://archive.org/details/memoirsofjohnqui11cadam/page/n1/mode/2up; same, at Adams, Digital Diary, 11 October 1841, at https://www.masshist.org/publications/jqadiaries/index.php/document/jqadiaries-v41-1841-10-11-p481#sn=4.

[249] Quote from Isaiah Rogers, memorial in support of removing obstructions on North River, House Doc. No. 9, January 1844, Appendix, 11, State Library of Massachusetts, https://archives.lib.state.ma.us/server/api/core/bitstreams/ebd1c896-4a56-44f1-9f99-013e98da7043/content.

[250] Briggs, *Shipbuilding*, 198 (quoted).

[251] Adams, Digital Diary, 28 October 1841, at https://www.masshist.org/publications/jqadiaries/index.php/document/jqadiaries-v41-1841-10-28-p481.

[252] 1843 report.

[253] 1843 report, 4.

[254] Briggs, *Shipbuilding*, 212 (quoted).

[255] "MHC Reconnaissance Survey Town Report: Marshfield" (Boston: Massachusetts Historical Commission, 1981), 1, 5, https://www.sec.state.ma.us/mhc/mhcpdf/townreports/SE-Mass/mrs.pdf.

[256] 1843 report, 5–6.

[257] 1843 report, 6.

[258] 1843 report, 6.
[259] 1843 report, 7–9.
[260] 1843 report, 9-10. Soon thereafter, on March 7, 1843, the committee on the judiciary reported that the state legislature had authority to enact such improvements to the North River because the federal government had not passed conflicting legislation under its powers in the Commerce Clause of the US Constitution. "1843 House Bill 0076. Report Concerning Improvement Of North River," State Library of Massachusetts, ocm39986872-1843-HB-0076.pdf, URI http://archives.lib.state.ma.us/handle/2452/750379.
[261] *Hingham Patriot*, February 4, 1843, 3, and February 11, 1843, 3 (identical copies of petition); "Peleg Thomas Ford," https://ancestors.familysearch.org/en/MVR3-7QM/peleg-thomas-ford-1786-1873.
[262] Kezia Bacon, "120 Years Ago: The Portland Gale," NSRWA website, November 2, 2018 (1843), https://www.nsrwa.org/120-years-ago-portland-gale/. See Sarah Messer, *Red House: Being a Mostly Accurate Account of New England's Oldest Continuously Lived-In House* (New York: Viking Penguin; 1st ed., 2004; Kindle ed.), 155.
[263] Isaiah Rogers, "1844 House Bill 0009, Memorial of Isaiah Rogers, Of Marshfield, Relating To Improvement Of Navigation Of North River," House Doc. No. 9 (January 1844), State Library of Massachusetts, https://archives.lib.state.ma.us/server/api/core/bitstreams/ebd1c896-4a56-44f1-9f99-013e98da7043/content, or https://archives.lib.state.ma.us/items/69344c22-df07-4712-b5bc-4ac18c627517, URI http://archives.lib.state.ma.us/handle/2452/755610.
[264] "Isaiah Rogers," Wikipedia article, https://en.wikipedia.org/wiki/Isaiah_Rogers. John Ford's 1838 map of Marshfield shows an I. Rogers building at what seems to be on Old Main Street near its intersection with Prospect Street.
[265] Rogers, memorial, 6.
[266] Rogers, memorial, 6–7.
[267] Rogers, memorial, Appendix, 11.
[268] Briggs, *Shipbuilding*, 47 (forests), 76, 257–258 (the *Helen M. Foster*, launched in 1871, was the last vessel of any size built on the North River).
[269] Briggs, *Shipbuilding*; esp. vi, 197; Nyberg, *Summer Suffragists*, ch. 7, esp. 142–146; "Eagle Hill Historic District," BOS.JK (see Nyberg Continuation Sheet of September 2020), MACRIS; "East Boston Inner Harbor Industrial Area," BOS.RP, MACRIS; Nyberg, "Smith, Sylvanus and Judith Winsor McLauthlin House," BOS.14278, MACRIS; Nyberg, "Shipyards of East Boston," website, https://www.lylenyberg.com/shipyards-of-east-boston.
[270] 1854 report, esp. p. 10 of report.
[271] Daniel Webster, Washington, to Honorable [Hannibal] Hamlin, letter, January 10, 1851, Mss 851110.2, Rauner Library Archives and Manuscripts, Dartmouth College, https://archives-manuscripts.dartmouth.edu/repositories/2/resources/2861. Tilden Ames (c. 1795–1867), whose family went back generations in Marshfield, built a farmhouse at Holly Hill in 1855. "Tilden (Eames) Ames (abt. 1795 - 1867)," WikiTree, https://www.wikitree.com/wiki/Eames-450; W. Ray Freden, "Hatch's Hill, Governor's Hill aka Holly Hill Part 2," April 5, 2023, https://wrayfreden.com/2023/04/05/hatchs-hill-governors-hill-aka-holly-hill-part-2/.
[272] Tower, "Plan of Scituate Harbor and North River."
[273] DAR, *Old Scituate*, 239 (1851 storm), as quoted in Nyberg, *On a Cliff*, 22. The Driftway is clearly shown on the 1831 Robbins & Turner map, which Tower appears not to have consulted. In addition, the 1831 map names the numbered cliffs, not "bluffs."
[274] Tower, "Plan of Scituate Harbor and North River." The note in red could have been added by the National Archives. The author of the plan, Maj. Tower, later worked on defenses of San Francisco during the Civil War. See Z. B. Tower letter to Brigadier General G. Wright, August 18, 1863, Civil War website, Chapter LX at 575-, https://www.civilwar.com/official-record/951-pacific-part-ii/252623-575-series-i-volume-l-ii-serial-106-pacific-part-ii.html. It seems that Tower had fortified the city's Alcatraz island (formerly La Isla de los Alcatraces, or the Island of the Pelicans). "From1853–59 the Corps of Engineers fortified the island under the direction of Major Zebulon B. Tower and the superintendence of Lieutenant Henry Prince." Ron Field, *Forts of the American Frontier 1776–1891: California, Oregon, Washington, and Alaska* (New York: Osprey Publishing, 2011), 29 (with photo of Maj. John G. Barnard on page 30), https://books.google.com/books?id=szW3CwAAQBAJ&source=gbs_navlinks_s.
[275] My calculations.
[276] 1854 report. My book *On a Cliff*, 25–26, discussed this 1854 report in more detail. At the time, I was unaware of Tower's 1852 plan, which reveals much detail not included in the 1854 report. The 1852 plan seems

to confirm that Jesse Dunbar established his second dam, proposed in 1801, to intercept Main Creek. See Nyberg, *On a Cliff*, 23, n.89.

[277] 1854 report (584 of 624), at 10 (report of Henry P. Andrews) (9 of 149 online).

[278] Deane's 1831 *History of Scituate*, 23, mentions past efforts to cut a ship channel here. In 1841 or 1843, a renegade group working at night tried to dig a cut here, unsuccessfully. Galluzzo, *North River*, 84–85; "US Air Force Recreation Area," NSRWA website, https://www.nsrwa.org/listing/us-air-force-recreation-area/. The Portland Gale of 1898 cut through at this place, creating the present mouth of the North River.

[279] William G. ("Cap'n Bill") Vinal files ("Vinal files"), Norwell Historical Society, reviewed August 2024. Vinal wrote that Scituate Historical Society had these files. See also Vinal, "Down to the Sea in Ships With Cap'n Bill Vinal," *Scituate Herald*, May 3, 1956, 14.

[280] Vinal files.

[281] William "Cap'n Bill" Vinal, "The North River Looking Back so as to Look Forward," typewritten manuscript (for speech?) (1970), in Vinal files.

[282] Merritt, *Old Time Anecdotes*, 72, in "Eaton's Hotel and Fourth Cliff House" chapter.

[283] Merritt, *Old Time Anecdotes*, 72. Deane, *History of Scituate*, 290, suggests that Thomas Hyland and his descendants occupied Fourth Cliff since 1633 until at least the publication of Deane's book in 1831. An 1887 book confirms that a Merritt operated the Fourth Cliff House. *The Old Colony, Or, Pilgrim Land: Past and Present* (Fall River Line and Old Colony Railroad, 1887), table at end, https://books.google.com/books?id=QTRFAQAAMAAJ&source=gbs_navlinks_s.

[284] For photos of the beach, see Nyberg, *On a Cliff*, 78–79, and below in discussion of 1870 report.

[285] Joseph Northey to John Tilden Jr., deed, recorded August 13, 1850, PCRD 238/180 (30 acres on Fourth Cliff).

[286] Unnamed correspondent of the *Plymouth Rock*, "A Sea-Side Ramble," *Hingham Journal*, February 11, 1859. Similar rambles were published in the 1950s by Willard deLue in the *Boston Globe*. "John Tilden also had charge of a house of refuge near Fourth Cliff," about 1869, according to John Galluzzo, "Cradle of the Coast Guard: History shows origins of service spawned on South Shore," *Weymouth News*, July 29, 2005, https://www.wickedlocal.com/story/weymouth-news/2005/07/29/cradle-coast-guard-history-shows/37714260007/.

[287] See Joseph Northey to John Tilden Jr., deed, recorded August 13, 1850, PCRD 238/180 (30 acres on Fourth Cliff); John Tilden to Gilbert A. Tapley of Danvers, deed, recorded October 3, 1872, PCRD 393/100; Gilbert A. Tapley to John Tilden, mortgage, recorded October 5, 1872, PCRD 393/110; "Mortgagee's Sale of Real Estate," *Hingham Journal*, September 26, 1877, 3, col. 6; John Tilden to Nathaniel P. Merriam, foreclosure deed, recorded October 20, 1877, PCRD 433/284; *Directory of Cohasset, Scituate, Marshfield, Duxbury and Norwell* (Quincy, MA: J. H. Hogan Co., 1894), 155, on file, SHS, and online, https://archive.org/details/directoryhistory00quin. Note Deane, *History of Scituate*, 290, says Thomas Hyland and descendants had a farm on Fourth Cliff.

[288] Norwell Open Space and Recreation Committee, "Norwell Open Space & Recreation Plan 2005–2010," 6 (quote), Town of Norwell website, https://www.townofnorwell.net/sites/g/files/vyhlif1011/f/uploads/openspaceplan.pdf; "Marshfield Pastimes: The final boat," *Marshfield Mariner*, August 6, 2010 (with extensive details based on an old paper at the Marshfield Historical Society), https://www.wickedlocal.com/story/marshfield-mariner/2010/08/06/marshfield-pastimes-final-boat/40398785007/; Merritt, *Narrative History*, 173 (detailed history of ship with photo), 3 (65 tons, 500 tons). Early on, a Chittenden owned the Chittenden Yard, which operated from 1690 to 1871, according to Briggs, *Shipbuilding*, ch. XIV.

[289] Merritt, *Narrative History*, 175 (quote); "Joseph F. Merritt Dies In Norwell," *Scituate Herald*, August 18, 1944, 7 ("Veteran Town Official" and "Norwell's Historian"); Merritt, *Old Time Anecdotes*.

[290] Briggs, *Shipbuilding*, 257; Merritt, *Narrative History*, 174–175.

[291] James S. Brust and Lee H. Whittlesey, "Thomas J. Hine: One of Yellowstone's Earliest Photographers," *Montana the Magazine of Western History* (Summer 1999), 14, Montana Historical Society, https://mhs.mt.gov/education/docs/CirGuides/Brust-Yellowstone.pdf.

[292] "Norwell, Massachusetts," Wikipedia article (using US Census records for 1870), https://en.wikipedia.org/wiki/Norwell,_Massachusetts.

[293] Janet Watson, Society Archivist, "150 Years Ago: the Final Launching of a North River Shipyard Schooner," *North River Packet*, Norwell Historical Society, December 2021, 1 (quote), https://norwellhistoricalsociety.org/newsletters%3A-2020-2024.

[294] "Marshfield Pastimes: The final boat," *Marshfield Mariner*, August 6, 2010 (quoted). The launch was at the end of Chittenden Lane, per Galluzzo, *North River*, 45, 104. The classic photo includes an inset for the ship's builder, was made by J. H. Williams, and appeared in Briggs, *Shipbuilding*, xii and 257.

[295] Carl W. Mitman, ed., *Catalogue of the Watercraft Collection in the United States National Museum*, Bulletin 127, (Washington, DC: US National Museum, 1923), 165 (dimension quote), Cat. No. 76,046 U.S.N.M., https://repository.si.edu/handle/10088/10158, DOI https://doi.org/10.5479/si.03629236.127.1; Howard I. Chapelle, *The National Watercraft Collection, United States National Museum*, Bulletin 219 (Washington, DC: Smithsonian Institution, 1960), 206–207 (successful), https://repository.si.edu/bitstream/handle/10088/10043/USNMB_2191960_unit.pdf.txt.

[296] "Notable Stones: First Parish Cemetery has many notable headstones and remarkable people who were buried here." First Parish Cemetery Association website, https://firstparishcemeterynorwell.org/notable-stones; "Helen Foster Merritt," FindaGrave, https://www.findagrave.com/memorial/146048510/helen_merritt; Massachusetts Archives, "Search for Citations to Vital Record (1841 - 1910)," (d. 1910), https://www.sec.state.ma.us/vitalrecordssearch/VitalRecordsSearch.aspx.

[297] Thanks to Archives of Norwell Historical Society for finding these documents. Merritt's *Narrative History* has a detailed discussion of the *Helen M. Foster*, starting at 173, including a photo of its launching that is very similar to the one in Briggs' book.

[298] "Among Our Churches," *The Christian Leader*, December 22, 1928, page 1626, https://books.google.com/books?id=E7DmAAAAMAAJ&source=gbs_navlinks_s.

[299] "Persis Madeleine (Wallace) Coons," FindaGrave [Google Translate] (buried in Church Hill Cemetery), https://www-findagrave-com.translate.goog/memorial/170393258/persis-m-coons?_x_tr_sl=fr&_x_tr_tl=en&_x_tr_hl=en&_x_tr_pto=sc; Richard R. Sherburne to Quentin L. Coons of Pembroke, deed, October 1, 1942, PCRD 1837/298, referring to February 24, 1896, plan by Harrison L. House, probably plan 2/289, sheet 1, showing dwelling house on five-acre lot surrounded by stone walls, similar plan 1/210, sheet 2; see Town of Norwell to Quentin L. Coons, deed, March 28, 1973, PCRD 3877/108.

[300] Town of Norwell Annual Report for 1960, various, https://archive.org/details/townofnorwellann1960unse/page/n2137/mode/2up?q=persis; Prof. Quentin L. Coons, in "Stetson, Cornet Robert and Honor Tucker House," 8 Meadow Farms Way, NRW.7, MACRIS.

[301] NRW.7, MACRIS; Norwell Historical Society website, https://norwellhistoricalsociety.org/where%2C-what-%26-who-1; "William G. Vinal," Wikipedia article, https://en.wikipedia.org/wiki/William_G._Vinal.

[302] "Old-Time New England," bulletin of SPNEA, Summer 1970, https://hne-rs.s3.amazonaws.com/filestore/1/2/9/9/2_0cc20d0fe584577/12992_64469f45e66ef17.pdf.

[303] Town of Norwell Annual Report for 1976, opposite title page (thanking Persis), 119 (quoted, with photo of Quentin and committee members), https://archive.org/details/townofnorwellann1970unse/page/118/mode/2up.

[304] Copy attached to Janet Watson email, April 18, 2024.

[305] Janet Watson emails, April 18, 2024, and January 5, 2025.

[306] "Church Hill and Vicinity before 1880, Compiled from Deeds, Grants and Histories of Scituate and Hanover by Anne Bonney Henderson 1961," map, 18 x 25 in., on file, Scituate Historical Society, map drawer 5, file 1; and Norwell Public Library, Local History Room, 911.744NO. [Author reference IMG_7810-12, and SHS 6-7-24.]

[307] "William Delano House," NRW.12, MACRIS; "The Delano Mansion," in DAR, *Old Scituate*, 130–133; "Delano family," Wikipedia article, https://en.wikipedia.org/wiki/Delano_family; *Vital Records of Scituate Massachusetts to the Year 1850, vol. I — Births* (Boston: New England Historic Genealogical Society, 1909), 136, https://archive.org/details/vitalrecordsofsc01newe; *Vital Records of Scituate Massachusetts to the Year 1850, vol. II — Marriages and Deaths* (Boston: New England Historic Genealogical Society, 1909), 383, https://archive.org/details/vitalrecordsofsc02newe/; Briggs, *Shipbuilding*, 226; "Wanton Shipyard," NSRWA website, https://www.nsrwa.org/listing/wanton-shipyard/; "William Delano," FindaGrave memorial, https://www.findagrave.com/memorial/135624515/william-delano; "Sarah Hart Delano | First Parish Cemetery Comes Alive," video (Marybeth Shea as Sarah Delano), 2023, Norwell Spotlight TV, http://72.93.231.20/CablecastPublicSite/show/2790?channel=2; Brad MacKenzie, "370 River Street, Norwell," property offering (2013), https://activerain.com/blogsview/3765338/370-river-street--norwell; Norwell Historical Commission, "Norwell: 1636-present," booklet, available from commission website, https://www.townofnorwell.net/historical-commission.

[308] Caleb Estabrooks, "North River Historical Association," NSRWA website, April 24, 2019, https://www.nsrwa.org/north-river-historical-association/; Lori Wolfe, "Sites of the Old North River Shipyards – Part 1," NSRWA website, June 12, 2019, https://www.nsrwa.org/sites-of-the-old-north-river-shipyards-part-1/; Audrey Cooney, "Volunteers working to restore North River's shipbuilding history for another 100 years," *Patriot Ledger*, October 29, 2019, https://www.patriotledger.com/story/news/2019/10/29/volunteers-working-to-restore-north/2417644007/.

[309] 1870 report, 19–27 (quotes from 19–20).

[310] 1870 report, particularly 71 (Whiting).

[311] Summary based on Herschel's 1872 proposal, discussed below in text. The shipyard mentioned was probably the "Barstow & Waterman" yard at Fox Hill in Hanover busy well into the 1860s, discussed in Briggs, *Shipbuilding*, 131 (Fox Hill Yard, "Scarcely a mile below North River Bridge"), 144–145.

[312] Nancy S. Seasholes, "Gaining Ground: Boston's Topographical Development in Maps," ch. 7, at 132, 136, in Alex Krieger and David Cobb with Amy Turner, *Mapping Boston* (Cambridge: MIT Press, A Norman B. Leventhal Book, paperback ed., 2001).

[313] 1870 report, 70 (Peirce).

[314] Image (with impressive muttonchops [sideburns]) at MIT Museum website, https://mitmuseum.mit.edu/collections/person/mitchell-henry-14963; *Fifth Annual Catalogue of the Officers and Students … 1869–70* (Boston: MIT, 1870), 6, https://dome.mit.edu/bitstream/handle/1721.3/82713/AC0598_001870.pdf?sequence=1&isAllowed=y; and http://hdl.handle.net/1721.3/82713. Thanks to Coleen Smith of the Association of MIT Alumnae (AMITA) for these references.

[315] *Fifth Annual Catalogue … 1869–70* (Boston: MIT, 1870), 6.

[316] 1870 report, 21, 69 (Mitchell); H. A. Marmer, "Biographical Memoir of Henry Mitchell, 1830–1902," *Biographical Memoirs, vol. XX – Third Memoir (National Academy of Sciences, 1938)*, https://harvardforest.fas.harvard.edu/sites/default/files/7-HenryMitchell-Bio.pdf.

[317] MIT President's Report (Boston: MIT, 1872), 2, http://hdl.handle.net/1721.3/62033.

[318] "Introduction to Volume 1: 1857-1866," sec. 1, in Peirce Edition Project, eds. (1982-), *Writings of Charles S. Peirce: A Chronological Edition* (Bloomington: Indiana University Press), https://peirce.indianapolis.iu.edu/writings/v1/v1introx.htm; "Benjamin Peirce," Wikipedia article, https://en.wikipedia.org/wiki/Benjamin_Peirce; Rossiter Johnson; John Howard Brown, *The Twentieth Century Biographical Dictionary of Notable Americans… , Vol. VIII* (Boston: The Biographical Society, 1904), 269, https://books.google.com/books?id=ve0UAAAAYAAJ&pg=PT269#v=onepage&q&f=false.

[319] "Nathaniel Bowditch," Wikipedia article, https://en.wikipedia.org/wiki/Nathaniel_Bowditch.

[320] Mark Monmonier, *Coastlines: How Mapmakers Frame the World and Chart Environmental Change* (Chicago: University of Chicago Press, 2008, updated edition), 150 (pioneer); "Notes on Henry Laurens Whiting," https://harvardforest.fas.harvard.edu/sites/default/files/8-Whiting-Notes.pdf; *The Boston Directory* (Boston: Sampson, Davenport, & Co., 1870), 695 (709/1202), https://catalog.hathitrust.org/Record/000499337.

[321] 1870 report, 24 ("peculiar"); *The Boston Directory* (1870), 474 (488/1202). See discussion below in text about Mitchell.

[322] Committee on Public Buildings, Massachusetts Historical Society, *The City Hall, Boston: Cornerstone laid, Monday, December 22, 1862. Dedicated, Monday, September 17, 1865.* (Boston: City Council, 1866), 109 (125/180), [page not numbered] (151/180) (corner office, although it is not clear if it was meant for the US or the state harbor commissioners, or both), https://catalog.hathitrust.org/Record/001262079; *The Boston Directory* (1870), 883–884 (869–870/1202), Koppmann entry on 410 (1202); 1870 report, 36 (commissioners); "Old City Hall," BOS.1977, MACRIS; Historic American Buildings Survey, Library of Congress, https://www.loc.gov/item/ma0445/. The building was listed on the National Register of Historic Places and was designated a US National Historic Landmark in 1970. By 1878, the Harbor Commissioners' Office was at 8 Pemberton Square, Boston, a peaceful square a few blocks from the old City Hall. Mitchell to Peirce, letter, October 19, 1878, MS Am 2368 (Box 9: Mitchell, Henry), Houghton Library, Harvard University; "Pemberton Square" (before court house was built there in 1885), https://en.wikipedia.org/wiki/Pemberton_Square; *Sanborn Fire Insurance Map from Boston, Suffolk County, Massachusetts* (New York: Sanborn Map Company, 1885), Vol. 1, sheet 13 (image 28 of 58), map, Library of Congress, https://www.loc.gov/item/sanborn03693_002/.

[323] *The Boston Directory* (1870), 883 (869/1202).

[324] *Fifth Annual Catalogue … 1869–70* (Boston: MIT, 1870), 6.

[325] "Hub of the Universe Origin," Celebrate Boston, http://www.celebrateboston.com/culture/the-hub-origin.htm.

[326] "Otto Hilgard Tittmann," Wikipedia article, https://en.wikipedia.org/wiki/Otto_Hilgard_Tittmann; Letter, To: Dr. Tittmann From: E. H. Shackleton, September 28, 1909, Digital Library@Villanova University, https://digital.library.villanova.edu/Item/vudl:682954#?xywh=-879%2C132%2C3646%2C1205; Letter, To: Dr. O. H. Tittmann From: R.E. Peary, December 9, 1910, Digital Library@Villanova University, https://digital.library.villanova.edu/Item/vudl:682941#?xywh=-1020%2C1146%2C3646%2C1205&cv=. In 1892, a US House of Representative panel listed salaries of Wm. H. Dennis, H. L. Whiting, and O. H. Tittmann in a report critical of funding the Coast Survey. *Congressional Record – House*, May 10, 1892, 4146, https://www.govinfo.gov/content/pkg/GPO-CRECB-1892-pt5-v23/pdf/GPO-CRECB-1892-pt5-v23-4.pdf.

[327] "History of Coast Survey," NOAA website, https://www.nauticalcharts.noaa.gov/about/history-of-coast-survey.html.

[328] Monmonier, *Coastlines*, 2, referring to Fig. 1.1, 1969 (USGS), Fig. 1.2, 1970 (US Coast & Geodetic Survey).

[329] S. [Samuel] Lambert (Salem), "Massachusetts Bay," nautical chart, 1812, NOAA #00-00-1812, https://historicalcharts.noaa.gov/, or direct, https://www.historicalcharts.noaa.gov/image.php?filename=00-00-1812.

[330] "What is hydrography?" NOAA website (both definitions), https://oceanservice.noaa.gov/facts/hydrography.html. You might trace the field to the astronomical information for sailing developed at the Greenwich Observatory starting in 1676. "Why is there an Observatory in Greenwich?" Royal Museums Greenwich, https://www.rmg.co.uk/royal-observatory/history. For an illuminating exploration of this field, see Stephen J. Hornsby, *Surveyors of Empire: Samuel Holland, J.W.F. Des Barres, and the Making of The Atlantic Neptune* (Montreal: McGill-Queen's University Press, 2011).

[331] "The Coast Survey," *Boston Globe*, October 17, 1873, 2 (quoted); Monmonier, *Coastlines*, ch. 4.

[332] Monmonier, *Coastlines*, particularly ch. 9.

[333] 1870 report, 34.

[334] 1870 report, 26 ("finely executed"), 70 (Whiting maps).

[335] Wm. H. Dennis, Sub Asst, under the direction of A. M. Harrison, Asst, "Map of Part of North River Massachusetts," 1858, scale 1:10,000, map 719a, US Coast Survey, University of Alabama, https://alabamamaps.ua.edu/historicalmaps/Coastal%20Survey%20Maps/massachusetts.htm/; O. H. Bittmann, Asst, under the direction of H. L. Whiting, Asst, "North River Mass." 1870, map (sheet 1 of 2), scale 1:5,000, Register No. 1251,a., US Coast Survey, University of Alabama., https://alabamamaps.ua.edu/historicalmaps/Coastal%20Survey%20Maps/massachusetts.htm/. These maps have much more detail viewed online. Another example is an 1857 Coast Survey map of Green Harbor River, used in an 1876 Harbor Commissioner map, both at 1:10,000, copied in the text below (Fig. 84). For a great discussion and examples of map scales, see Monmonier, *Coastlines*, ch. 1.

[336] O. H. Tittmann, H. L. Whiting, et al. US Coast Survey, *Sketch of North River, Mass.*, map, scale 1:40,000 (n.p., 1870), Digital Commons at Salem State University, http://digitalcommons.salemstate.edu/maps_massachusetts/4/. The map names four MIT students, three of whom were listed as alumni in 1904. *Register of Graduates*, 1903–1904 (Boston: Massachusetts Institute of Technology, 1904), 16 (William E. Hoyt, 1868), 17 (Albert H. Howland, 1871), 18 (Charles F. Stone, 1871), https://babel.hathitrust.org/cgi/pt?id=njp.32101058494251&seq=24.

[337] Henry Francis Walling, "Map of the County of Plymouth" (Boston: D. R. Smith & Co, 1857), Library of Congress, https://www.loc.gov/item/2012592354/, also at Yale University Library, https://collections.library.yale.edu/catalog/15654642?child_oid=15662609; Briggs, *Shipbuilding on the North River*, rarely mentions the "Waterman & Barstow" yard, mostly calling it the "Barstow & Waterman" yard or Barstow's yard, at Fox Hill (Sunset Hill) in Hanover, just east of Hanover Four Corners, east of the North River Bridge, and just east of Third Herring Brook. See Briggs, *Shipbuilding*, 29, 82–83 (map), 131, 258.

[338] 1870 report, 43 (Mitchell). See also Kezia Bacon, "The 1871 North River Dam," NSRWA, March 4, 2025, https://www.nsrwa.org/the-1871-north-river-dam/.

[339] 1870 report, 20–21 (quoted). Whiting's appendix to the 1870 report says, at 74–75, the marshes of the North River comprised 3,074 acres including mud flats, and about 1,506 acres for the Green Harbor River marshes.

[340] Briggs, *Shipbuilding*, 143–145 (1860s).

[341] 1870 report, 74.

[342] 1870 report, 20.

[343] 1870 report, 24.

[344] Nyberg, *On a Cliff*, 77–79; Deane, *History of Scituate*, 20. The 20 rods matches, or may have been taken from, Turner's 1795 map.

[345] 1870 report, 48–58; anonymous, "To accompany report of H. Mitchell on the Reclamation of Tide Lands [probably from Mitchell, H., Appendix No. 1869 - 5. pp. 75–104, US Coastal Survey]," from House document 53 of 1871, *5th Annual Report of the Massachusetts Board of Harbor Commissioners*, State Library of Massachusetts, call no. "Map Mass. Marshfield 1870–1," ("1871 Mitchell sketch"), https://archives.lib.state.ma.us/items/55730738-3015-4647-add5-b9d81b229f0c, URI http://hdl.handle.net/2452/48555. The 1871 sketch and the 1870 map were also included in Mitchell's 1872 US Coast Survey report, cited below.

[346] 1871 Mitchell sketch, Fig. 9; "Chesil Beach," Wikipedia article, https://en.wikipedia.org/wiki/Chesil_Beach. Both Mitchell's 1870 report and Herschel's 1872 report dwelled at length on shingle beaches.

[347] 1870 report, 48.

[348] 1870 report, 57; Patrick Browne, "The Tragic Story of Minot's Ledge Lighthouse," Historical Digression website, October 30, 2015, https://historicaldigression.com/2015/10/30/the-tragic-story-of-minots-ledge-lighthouse/; letter from Col. Swift, agent for Col. J. J. Abert, Chief Topographical Engineer, in "The Minot Ledge Light-house," *The Daily Union* (Washington, DC), May 11, 1851, 2, col. 2 (quoted), Library of Congress, https://chroniclingamerica.loc.gov/lccn/sn82003410/1851-05-11/ed-1/seq-2/.

[349] *Richmond Enquirer* (VA), April 22, 1851, 1, col. 5, Library of Congress, https://chroniclingamerica.loc.gov/lccn/sn84024735/1851-04-22/ed-1/seq-1/; *Vermont Watchman* (Montpelier), April 24, 1851, 2, col. 4, Newspaper Archive via BPL. In Boston, due to the gale, there was five feet of water at the State House (probably the Custom House given the accompanying illustration), according to John Horrigan, "The New England Lighthouse Storm and the Yankee Gale," https://www.historylecture.org/lighthousestorm.html.

[350] 1870 report, 57.

[351] 1870 report, 60, 69.

[352] "Humarock Beach," NSRWA, https://www.nsrwa.org/listing/humarock-beach/.

[353] 1870 report, 48 (Mitchell, levee), 57 (Mitchell), 69 (Mitchell).

[354] See Nyberg, *On a Cliff*, 78–79, for which historian Cynthia Krusell provided a photo of the shingle beach, similar to the one shown below in text.

[355] Nathaniel J. Stebbins, ""Barrier beach with transverse scallops [and] drumlin cliffs, Scituate, Mass.," Gardner Collection, Harvard, http://id.lib.harvard.edu/images/olvwork419445/catalog (Fig. 74). A blip atop the hills at the far left may be Eaton's Hotel. It was built about 1873, 150 feet above sea level next to the new railroad station. Another Stebbins photo has a better view of the station and hotel.

[356] Harvard, Gardner Collection. The hut, or at least its site before the 1898 Portland Gale, is marked on the Richards 1903 map, plate 31, along with other houses at the southern end of Third Cliff along Water Street, then the name of the Driftway. The Gardner photos show a surprisingly large number of buildings there, even before the start of the Rivermoor summer colony about 1906. E. Parker Welch owned this land and sold a few lots in the 1890s for summer cottages, shown as Young, Hanks, and Flaherty on the Richards 1903 map. But a close examination of deeds and the 1894 directory reveal that these lots were equivalent to 16 Collier Road ("Lamprey") and 18 Collier Road, near the top of the cliff. That would not seem to explain all the houses shown in the Gardner photos.

[357] George Augustus Gardner et al. George Augustus Gardner Collection of Photographs, Harvard University, HOLLIS number olvwork419446, https://id.lib.harvard.edu/alma/990114204590203941/catalog. As to Stebbins, see William Johnson & Susie Cohen, "Nathaniel L. Stebbins (1847–1922) Early Work," Hold History in Your Hand/VintagePhotosJohnson, April 25, 2024 (unbelievably detailed biography of Stebbins, noting "his father had studied theology for a Doctor of Divinity degree at the Harvard Divinity School"), https://vintagephotosjohnson.com/author/vintagephotosjohnson/; "Stebbins, Nathaniel L. (1847–1922) USA," (with photo), http://america-scoop.com/index.php/en/; "Nathaniel L. Stebbins photographic collection," Historic New England, https://www.digitalcommonwealth.org/search/commonwealth-oai:nv935j69t, and https://www.historicnewengland.org/nathaniel-l-stebbins-photographic-collection/; Jill, "The Unexpected Joys of Quarrying," a landscape lover's blog, November 26, 2012, https://landscapelover.wordpress.com/2012/11/26/the-unexpected-joys-of-quarrying/.

[358] 1870 report, 25. See 1870 report, 54–55 (Mitchell). The opening of the channel was 1843, per Kezia Bacon, "120 Years Ago: The Portland Gale," NSRWA website, November 2, 2018, https://www.nsrwa.org/120-years-ago-portland-gale/.

[359] 1870 report, 65, 58.

[360] 1843 report, 6, 12.

[361] "Henry Mitchell Papers, 1864–1900," MS259, Nantucket Historical Association, https://nantuckethistory.org:443/permalink/?key=6000_coll185.

[362] Henry Mitchell, "Tides and tidal phenomena: for the use more particularly of U.S. naval officers," Navy scientific papers, no. 2 (Washington: Bureau of Navigation, Navy Department, 1868), incl. 6 (rules), 22 (Orion's Belt), 36 (rivers), https://lccn.loc.gov/25020106, and http://catalog.hathitrust.org/Record/001687026; Henry Mitchell, "On the reclamation of tide-lands, and its relation to navigation" (Washington: US Coast Survey, 1872), 32 p., 2 maps 29 x 23 cm., https://lccn.loc.gov/06009861.

[363] 1870 report, 69 (Mitchell, quoted), 71 (Whiting mentions Herschel).

[364] "Clemens Herschel," Wikipedia article, https://en.wikipedia.org/wiki/Clemens_Herschel; "Flow measurement," Wikipedia article, https://en.wikipedia.org/wiki/Flow_measurement. Mark A. Vargas, "Guide to the Papers of Clemens Herschel," MIT ArchivesSpace, https://archivesspace.mit.edu/repositories/2/resources/750; "History of Water Measurement and Water Meters," 2019, Asia-Pacific Legal Metrology Forum (APLMF), https://www.aplmf.org/uploads/5/7/4/7/57472539/b_-_the_history_of_water_meters.pdf; Clemens Herschel, "Ueber Bestimmung des Querschnitts und der Höhenlage von Entässerungsschleusen (Sielen), etc." [On determining the cross-section and elevation of drainage locks (sluices)] in *Zeitschrift für Bauwesen* [Journal of Construction] *Ausgabe* XXI (Berlin: Ernst, 1871), 457–470, https://digital.zlb.de/viewer/image/15239363_1871/244/. For this reference to Herschel's 1871 Berlin paper, thanks to an anonymous marginal note in a copy of DAR, *Old Scituate*, 238, https://archive.org/details/oldscituate00mass_0/. Herschel's papers at MIT do not seem to include the North River project; thanks to Amanda Hawk for her research there. For much more detail, see Walter G. Kent, *An Appreciation of Two Great Works in Hydraulics, Giovanni Battista Venturi, born 1746, Clemens Herschel, born 1842* (London: Blades, East & Blades, 1912), https://archive.org/details/appreciationoftw00kentrich/page/4/mode/2up. This note is the source for the text accompanying the photo of Herschel, which was in Kent, *An Appreciation*, 20 (and Kent quote on 7, and 85 turbines on 23), and photo from Wikipedia, https://en.wikipedia.org/wiki/File:Clemens_Herschel_1906.jpg, public domain.

[365] Holyoke Gas & Electric (HG&E) website (Shad Derby), https://www.hged.com/community-environment/recreation/shad-derby.aspx; and HG&E website (photo), https://www.hged.com/about/default.aspx; Ashley Shook, "Thousands of American shad migrate upstream along Connecticut River in Holyoke," WWLP website, May 7, 2024 (noting the fishway is closed for maintenance), https://www.wwlp.com/news/local-news/hampden-county/thousands-of-american-shad-migrate-upstream-along-connecticut-river-in-holyoke/; "Holyoke Dam," Wikipedia article (ASME recognition), https://en.wikipedia.org/wiki/Holyoke_Dam.

[366] 1870 report, 71 (Whiting).

[367] 1870 report, 70 (Whiting).

[368] 1870 report, 71–72 (Whiting).

[369] See discussion in text below about the 2022 report. See also comments by scientist Dorothy Peteet on the value of salt marshes and the need for marsh grasses to have sediment nourishment and deep roots, in article by *NY Times*' Christopher Maag, "Armed with Saran Wrap, she sinks in the muck to save the planet," *Boston Globe*, August 3, 2024, https://www.bostonglobe.com/2024/08/03/nation/armed-with-saran-wrap-she-sinks-muck-save-planet. It appears the North River salt marshes are a good cushion against the "occasional excessive floods of salt water" that Whiting found to be "injurious" to the marshes.

[370] 1870 report, 73, 75 (Whiting).

[371] "Ecology," Wikipedia article, https://en.wikipedia.org/wiki/Ecology; "ecology," Britannica article, https://www.britannica.com/science/ecology. The 1870 report, 64–65 (Mitchell) briefly discusses economic value of these lands.

[372] 1870 report, 26–27.

[373] 1915 report.

[374] 1870 report, 74 (Whiting).

[375] "Draining of North River," *Hingham Journal*, April 14, 1871, 2, available from Hingham Public Library website, https://www.hinghamlibrary.org/. A transcript of the article is available on the author's website, https://www.lylenyberg.com/copy-of-1915-map-of-north-river.

[376] For a later review of the New Jersey marsh reclamation projects, see Kimberly R. Sebold article cited in Nyberg, *Ditching the Marshes*: Kimberly R. Sebold, "From Marsh to Farm: The Landscape Transformation of Coastal New Jersey" (Washington, DC: National Park Service, 1992), https://irma.nps.gov/DataStore/DownloadFile/484754, and https://archive.org/details/frommarshtofarm100sebo.

[377] 1870 report, 27; see also 65 (Mitchell), 73 (Whiting).

[378] 1870 report, 27.

[379] "Draining of North River," *Hingham Journal*. The towns would soon try to disentangle themselves from the railroad debt, and the Great Boston Fire of November 1872 would destroy wealth and cool interest in investing in property development.

[380] 1871 Scituate town report, 33, https://archive.org/details/annualreportofto1848scit/page/n519/mode/2up. The financing of this part of the rail line, the Duxbury & Cohasset Railroad Company, is explained in *History of the Old Colony Railroad* (Boston: Hager & Handy, 1893), 82, 105–108, https://ia801901.us.archive.org/28/items/historyofoldcolo00bost/historyofoldcolo00bost.pdf.

[381] Ch. 287, *Acts and Resolves Passed by the General Court* (Boston : Secretary of the Commonwealth, 1871), 635, https://archive.org/details/actsresolvespass1871mass/page/634/mode/2up?q=287.

[382] Minutes of town meeting, March 4, 1872, vol. C-10, p. 392, town archives; also cited in a WPA entry for North River. Israel H. Sherman was a town official (highway surveyor and fence viewer), according to the WPA card index, and a long-time shipbuilder, according to Briggs, *Shipbuilding*, 102.

[383] S. N. Gifford and W. S. Robinson, ed., *A Manual for the Use of the General Court (1872)*, (Boston: Massachusetts General Court, 1872), 163, 289, 310–313, State Library of Massachusetts, ocm01251790-1872.pdf, URI http://hdl.handle.net/2452/40650.

[384] "The North River Marshes," *Boston Globe*, August 15, 1872, 8.

[385] William "Cap'n Bill" Vinal, "Our Vanishing Landscape," *South Shore Mirror*, December 21, 1961, 12.

[386] Clemens Herschel, Civil Engineer, "To the Town of South Scituate, Thomas J. Tolman, and others, owners of North River Marshes," letter, 15 June 1872, on file, Scituate Historical Society, with copy on file with Norwell Historical Society (Cap'n Bill Vinal files). The letter is hereinafter called the Herschel plan. A transcript is available on the author's website, https://www.lylenyberg.com/copy-of-1915-map-of-north-river.

[387] "The North River Marshes."

[388] Herschel plan, 1.

[389] "The North River Marshes."

[390] 1870 report, 48 (Mitchell, levee), 57 (Mitchell), 69 (Mitchell).

[391] "The North River Marshes."

[392] Herschel plan, 6.

[393] "The North River Marshes;" 1870 report, 69.

[394] Herschel plan, 7.

[395] See Stilgoe, *Alongshore*, 87–90, and Nyberg, *On a Cliff*, 22, 27.

[396] "The North River Marshes" (summary); Herschel report, 11–12. A random page from the 1872 Valuation List (page 59) shows John Tilden owning 10 acres of salt marsh (possibly on Fourth Cliff), valued at $100 ($10/acre); also, other owners with 5 acres at $66 ($13/acre), and 1 acre at $35. Evidently, value depended on location.

[397] Herschel plan, 11.

[398] Copy of poster from North River Commission.

[399] "Reclamation of North River Marshes," *Hingham Journal and South Shore Advertiser*, December 27, 1872, 2.

[400] Nyberg, *On a Cliff*, generally, esp. 54; "Edmond [Edmund] Parker 'E Parker' Welch," FindaGrave memorial, https://www.findagrave.com/memorial/147426539/edmond_parker_welch.

[401] "Thomas Jones Tolman," Ancestry, https://www.ancestry.com/genealogy/records/thomas-jones-tolman-24-pc7d5d; *Vital Records of Scituate, Massachusetts, to the Year 1850, Vol. I – Births* (Boston: New England Historic Genealogical Society, 1909), 363, https://archive.org/details/vitalrecordsofsc01newe/page/362/mode/2up; *Vital Records of Scituate, Massachusetts, to the Year 1850, Vol. II – Marriages and Deaths* (Boston: New England Historic Genealogical Society, 1909), 330 (plane maker, marriage to Mary Willcutt), https://archive.org/details/vitalrecordsofsc02scit_0/page/n659/mode/2up; see "Thomas J. Tolman," FindaGrave memorial (inaccurate wife's name), https://www.findagrave.com/memorial/142765605/thomas_j_tolman; Thomas J. Tolman, "No. 16,412 – Adjusting the Size of the Mouth In Planes," Handplane Patents Database (for 1857), http://www.handplanepatents.com/tag/1857/; *Hingham Journal*, April 2, 1868, 2, col. 4. Examples of ownership of property and mills in Scituate (incl. South Scituate) and Hanover include: Philip Foster, Adm., to Thomas J. Tolman, PCRD 251/24, rec. 1/22/1853; Charles W. Sylvester to Thomas Tolman, PCRD 258/558, rec. 6/1/1854; Thomas Tolman to South Scituate Savings Bank, mortgage, PCRD 290/218, rec. 12/4/1858; Josiah W. Chamberlain to Tolman & Merritt, PCRD 334/83, rec. 3/24/1866. See Anne Bonney Henderson map of Church Hill before 1880 (1961). Thomas Tolman's house, no longer there, would have been at about

360 River Street, according to the 1857 Walling map of Plymouth County. He and his father are buried in the First Parish Cemetery, Norwell, as is William Delano of 370 River Street, discussed earlier in text.

[402] Author analysis. See Briggs, *Shipbuilding*. Based on Merritt's *Narrative History*, I count Nash, Tolman, Tolman, and Litchfield for South Scituate. Welch, Oakman, and Weatherbee are profiled in *Biographical Review, Vol. XVIII*, 398 (Welch, with photo), 431 (Oakman), 492 (Weatherbee, with mention of Elisha W. Hall).

[403] Nyberg, *Ditching the Marshes*.

[404] 1915 report, 9 (Waterman), 12 (White's Ferry).

[405] See 1879 Walker atlas, page 32, with T. J. Tolman and W. C. Tolman houses along unnamed River Street, and T. Tolman just north of center on inset for Village of South Scituate; Merritt, *Narrative History*, 37–38.

[406] Comments on "Scituate MA South River bridge clearance," The Hull Truth - Boating and Fishing Forum, 2018, https://www.thehulltruth.com/northeast/961701-scituate-ma-south-river-bridge-clearance.html; "Humarock Beach tide charts and tide times for this week," https://www.tideschart.com/United-States/Massachusetts/Plymouth-County/Humarock-Beach/Weekly/.

[407] Probable tide datum is Mean Lower Low Water (MLLW); see "Datums for 8445138, Scituate, Scituate Harbor, MA," NOAA Tides & Currents, https://tidesandcurrents.noaa.gov/datums.html?id=8445138.

[408] S. A. Talke, A. C. Kemp, J. Woodruff, "Relative Sea Level, Tides, and Extreme Water Levels in Boston Harbor From 1825 to 2018," *Journal of Geophysical Research: Oceans* (JGR), American Geophysical Union (AGU), June 1, 2018, vol. 123, issue 6 (June 2018), https://doi.org/10.1029/2017JC013645, and https://agupubs.onlinelibrary.wiley.com/doi/full/10.1029/2017JC013645. See also Lauren Hinkle, "Boston's High Waters," EAPS News, May 3, 2018, MIT Center for Global Change Science, https://cgcs.mit.edu/bostons-high-waters.

[409] See Crawford website, https://www.melonseed.com/crawford-boat-building, and blog, https://spritrig.wordpress.com/.

[410] 1870 report, 57. See Christopher McFadden, "13 Dams That Are Marvels of Engineering," June 28, 2023, #4 (Hoover Dam) and #6 (Tarbela Dam), Interesting Engineering, https://interestingengineering.com/lists/13-of-the-worlds-most-fascinating-dams.

[411] Acre-feet calculations based on 1870 report, 61 (only average 5 foot depth at shoalest place), 65–66 (32,920,470 square foot area or 756 acres).

[412] "National Inventory of Dams" (NID), https://nid.sec.usace.army.mil/#/; see also "Map Layer Info: Major Dams of the United States," https://web.archive.org/web/20090814080910/http://nationalatlas.gov/mld/dams00x.html, and Army pamphlet, https://www.publications.usace.army.mil/Portals/76/Publications/EngineerPamphlets/EP_360-1-23.pdf.

[413] NID.

[414] NID and Army pamphlet, cited above. There appears to have been a dam on the Neponset River in 1634. "The Neponset River, One of the First in New England to be Harnessed for Power," Neponset River Watershed Association, https://neponset.org/historic-resources-dams/.

[415] Tata & Howard, "The 7 Most Interesting Dams in the United States," #6. Dworshak Dam, https://tataandhoward.com/the-7-most-interesting-dams-in-the-united-states/.

[416] 1870 report.

[417] Stilgoe, *Alongshore*, 115–118 (118 quoted).

[418] Stilgoe, *Alongshore*, 118.

[419] Stilgoe, *Alongshore*, 119–120.

[420] *Twenty-Third Annual Report of the Secretary of the Massachusetts Board of Agriculture for 1875* (Boston: Commonwealth of Massachusetts, 1876), 238 at 243, and see 247, https://catalog.hathitrust.org/Record/007905215.

[421] "Abstract of Returns of the Agricultural Societies of Massachusetts. 1877." In *Twenty-Fifth Annual Report of the Secretary of the Massachusetts Board of Agriculture for 1877* (Boston: Commonwealth of Massachusetts, 1878), 80 [506 of 648] ("new soil"), 78 (White), https://catalog.hathitrust.org/Record/007905215.

[422] "About the Homestead Act," National Park Service, https://www.nps.gov/home/learn/historyculture/abouthomesteadactlaw.htm; "Homestead Act (1862)," National Archives, https://www.archives.gov/milestone-documents/homestead-act; Table 4, General Tables of Agriculture, 1870 census, "The Statistics of the Wealth and Industry of the United States," US Department of Agriculture, https://agcensus.library.cornell.edu/census_year/1870-census/.

[423] Nathaniel Southgate Shaler, "Inundated Lands of Massachusetts," in Massachusetts Board of Agriculture report for 1891, *Thirty-Ninth Annual Report of the Secretary of the Massachusetts Board of Agriculture*, Pub. Doc. No. 4 (Boston: Commonwealth of Massachusetts, 1892), 377–390 at 379 (quoted) and, with marine marsh discussion starting at 385 (almost poetical description, concluding that, on 387, "marine marshes afford an earth which is

of a permanent and high order of excellence"), State Library of Massachusetts, URI http://hdl.handle.net/2452/205469.

[424] Shaler, Inundated, 388–390.

[425] Stilgoe, *Alongshore*, 122.

[426] "Storm Stopped State Work," *Boston Globe*, December 3, 1898, 5.

[427] *Hingham Journal*, August 8, 1902, 4, col. 1. A rather uninformative photo of the area is, "Reclaimed Marshes, Green Harbor, Mass., [Looking North] from Dyke," 1911, Gardner Collection, Harvard University, Cabot Science Library GCP0740, http://id.lib.harvard.edu/images/olvwork420862/catalog.

[428] "The Dike Marker," MRS.911, MACRIS.

[429] "Wetland Cover Type Map," and "Green Harbor River Hydraulics Report," available from Marshfield website, https://www.marshfield-ma.gov/departments/town_hall/conservation/green_harbor_river_studies.php#outer-310. See also MACRIS Maps-Dyke Road, Marshfield 02050-Overlay Layer-Prime Farmland; "Green Harbor Navigation Project," US Army Corps of Engineers, New England District Website (project completed 1969), https://www.nae.usace.army.mil/Missions/Civil-Works/Navigation/Massachusetts/Green-Harbor/; Kezia Bacon, "Paddle the Green Harbor River," October 15, 2015, NSRWA, https://www.nsrwa.org/paddle-the-green-harbor-river/. The dam (dike) is not listed in the National Inventory of Dams.

[430] See discussion below in "Marshes Compared," which includes Marshfield marshes.

[431] Shaun Roche (who provided the 1906 article), Visitor Service Manager at the Stewart B. McKinney National Wildlife Refuge, "Salt Marsh Haymaking," Menunkatuck Audubon Society (CT) presentation, 2022, at 34:04, https://www.youtube.com/watch?v=4bhoojpdhkQ; Shaun Roche email, November 18, 2024; "The Great Marshes," The History of Lordship, Stratford, Connecticut website, archived March 20, 2018, at https://web.archive.org/web/20180320052016/http://www.lordshiphistory.com/, and https://web.archive.org/web/20180424090109/http://www.lordshiphistory.com/GREATMEADOWSwebpage.html. Hollister was the Dean of the Winona Agricultural Institute in 1906. "Opportunities," *The Sandersville [GA] Herald*, June 7, 1906, 4, https://gahistoricnewspapers.galileo.usg.edu/lccn/sn85034106/1906-06-07/ed-2/seq-4/.

[432] "Great Meadows Unit," Stewart B. McKinney National Wildlife Refuge, https://www.fws.gov/refuge/stewart-b-mckinney/visit-us/locations/great-meadows-unit-. See also Lauri Munroe-Hultman, "Stratford's Great Meadows Salt Marsh Gets a $4M Refresh," US Fish & Wildlife Service, August 30, 2022, https://www.fws.gov/press-release/2022-08/stratfords-great-meadows-salt-marsh-gets-4m-refresh; Mary Lawrence Young, "Restoration of the Great Meadows Marsh," StoryMap, March 1, 2023, https://storymaps.arcgis.com/stories/24e64d93a2704efabb404abac4ecd2d3. Maps and aerial photos of the site show extensive ditches and dikes.

[433] Merritt, *Old Time Anecdotes*, 71 (109/166), "Eaton's Hotel and Fourth Cliff House" chapter; "Financial Panic of 1873," US Department of the Treasury, https://home.treasury.gov/about/history/freedmans-bank-building/financial-panic-of-1873; "Panic of 1873," Wikipedia article, https://en.wikipedia.org/wiki/Panic_of_1873. See also Lee Coppock chart in John Arnold post on X, March 14, 2024 (179 months in recession, 1870–1899), https://x.com/johnarnoldfndtn/status/1768290299380449285, and in Jacob Zinkula and Madison Hoff, "Younger generations might not have to worry about recessions as much as their elders. It would be great news for their job security and stock portfolios," *Business Insider*, May 6, 2024, https://www.businessinsider.com/when-will-next-recession-hit-us-healthy-economy-financial-security-2024-5.

[434] Without going into detail, consider the deeds from these grantors, recorded February 18, 1873 (PCRD book/page): Charles Vinal (385/177), Daniel S. Jenkins (385/178), Caleb W. Prouty (385/179, for Front Street wharf and buildings), Barnabas W. Briggs (385/180).

[435] 1875 Valuation List, pages not numbered, copied March 2024, and author's calculations.

[436] Nyberg, *On a Cliff*, 55.

[437] "Important Land Sale in Marshfield Highlands – A Large Crowd and a Partially Successful Sale," *Boston Globe*, August 22, 1873, 8.

[438] "Important Land Sale;" Old Colony Railroad ad, *Boston Globe*, June 21, 1885, 11 (excursion rate to Sea View).

[439] "Important Land Sale."

[440] "Important Land Sale."

[441] Ray Freden, email, November 3, 2023. See his wonderful website posts, "Hatch's Hill, Governor's Hill, aka, Holly Hill, Part 1: The Mansion on Holly Hill, Seaview, Marshfield MA," March 21, 2023 ("Over 500 acres of hill, 150 feet high, that commands a view of 180 degrees overlooking Massachusetts Bay, from Rockport to Provincetown, to Plymouth's White Cliffs"), https://wrayfreden.com/2023/03/21/hatchs-hill-governors-

hillaka-holly-hill/; and "Hatch's Hill, Governor's Hill aka Holly Hill Part 2," April 5, 2023, https://wrayfreden.com/2023/04/05/hatchs-hill-governors-hill-aka-holly-hill-part-2/.

[442] S. L. Minot, "Plan of Building Lots at Marsfield [sic] Highlands, Scale 200 ft. to an inch," August 1873, PCRD plan book 1, page 41, sheet 3 of 7, received May 13, 187x, recorded June 9, 1879. Sizes are author's estimate; Ray Freden, email, November 7, 2023. The same sheet shows a 4th Cliff house to the North, probably the Fourth Cliff House mentioned elsewhere. This would place the island shown on the plan as the southernmost, rather elliptical one, just north of White's Ferry, shown on the 1831 Robbins & Turner map (see Fig. 46). It may also be the one shown on the Minot plan.

[443] Ray Freden, emails, November 4 & 5 (roads), 2023; Nyberg, *Summer Suffragists*, 157–159.

[444] Various deeds recorded in 1872, PCRD. See Merritt, *Old Time Anecdotes*, 71–72.

[445] Stephen M. Allen to Horace P. Flint, deed, February 8, 1873, PCRD 390/51; Flint to Allen, mortgage, February 8, 1873, PCRD 392/145 and 397/52; Allen to Flint, partial release, October 13, 1873, recorded January 8, 1874, PCRD 400/207. That is the only partial release I found. Horace P. Flint is probably the Horace Phillips Flint of Essex County, born in 1844, who served in the Civil War, and whose father was an "Importer and dealer in hardware, Boston." See pages 88–89 in John Flint and J H. Stone, *A Genealogical Register of the Descendants of Thomas Flint* (Andover, MA, 1860), https://ia802809.us.archive.org/24/items/genealogicalregi00flin/genealogicalregi00flin.pdf. In the mortgage, the word Howard appears to be a typo for Horace. The parties recognized the mortgage was still in effect in the October 13, 1873, partial release.

[446] Flint to Martha D. Luce, deed, October 25, 1873, PCRD 402/100, and 402/101; calculations by Lyle Nyberg based on deeds recorded at PCRD.

[447] Nyberg calculations.

[448] Marginal note of conveyance to Deshon, June 23, 1873, on Flint to Allen mortgage, February 8, 1873, PCRD 392/145 and 397/52; Deshon to Currall, May 14, 1881, PCRD 472/19; Currall to Emery, May 14, 1881, PCRD 472/20.

[449] Flint to Flint, deed, October 17, 1874, recorded October 19, 1874, PCRD 408/40. I found no further deeds involving Thomas Flint recorded in Plymouth County.

[450] *Hingham Journal*, September 10, 1875, 2, available at https://hingham.advantage-preservation.com/.

[451] See discussion below on Reed's North River plans of 1875, PCRD 1/52, sheet 3 of 7.

[452] *Boston Globe*, January 29, 1877, 6, and October 6, 1877, 7; *Insurance Company v. Stinson*, 103 U.S. 25 (1881). Ray Freden, "Hatch's Hill, Part 2," says "There was a rumor that a hotel was once built on the Hill."

[453] Ray Freden, email, June 22, 2024. I try to run rumors to the ground.

[454] "Ferry Hill Thicket," NSRWA website (also includes later history), https://www.nsrwa.org/listing/ferry-hill-thicket/; Ray Freden, "Ferry Hill's Early Days," March 5, 2023, https://wrayfreden.com/2023/03/05/ferry-hills-early-days/.

[455] "George W. Emery," Wikipedia article, https://en.wikipedia.org/wiki/George_W._Emery; Samuel L. Gerould, *Biographical Sketches of the Class of 1858, Dartmouth College* (Nashua, NH: Telegraph Publishing Co., Printers, 1905), 40 (with photo, born 1835, owned 500 acres), https://books.google.com/books?id=iiVPAAAAYAAJ&source=gbs_navlinks_s; *Biographical Review*, Vol. XVIII, 486 (Medford, married 1866); author search of Plymouth County Registry of Deeds; Ray Freden, emails, November 4 & 12, 2023; Currall to Emery, May 14, 1881, PCRD 472/20 (170 acres on Hatch's Hill). For more on the Hall family, see Nyberg, *Summer Suffragists*, and website at https://www.lylenyberg.com/shipyards-of-east-boston; D. Hamilton Hurd, *History of Plymouth County, Massachusetts: with Biographical Sketches of Many of its Pioneers and Prominent Men* (Philadelphia: J. W. Lewis & Co., 1884), 1168, https://archive.org/details/historyofplymout01hurd/page/n775/mode/2up.

[456] *Biographical Review*, Vol. XVIII, 489–490. Emery's estate is also shown in the distance in a photo in Cynthia Hagar Krusell and Betty Magoun Bates, *Marshfield: A Town of Villages 1640-1990* (Marshfield Hills: Historical Research Associates, 1990), 137. For a detailed description of the estate, stating that Emery was a president of the Marshfield Fair, see Freden, "Hatch's Hill, Part 1," https://wrayfreden.com/2023/03/21/hatchs-hill-governors-hillaka-holly-hill/. For later history of the estate, see Freden, "Hatch's Hill, Part 2," https://wrayfreden.com/2023/04/05/hatchs-hill-governors-hill-aka-holly-hill-part-2/.

[457] Gerould, *Sketches*, 42; "[Gov.] Brackett at Marshfield," *Boston Globe*, September 12, 1890, 2.

[458] 1000 Ferry Street, Marshfield, MRS.46, MACRIS; emails to and from Ray Freden, June 24–26, 2024.

[459] J. E. Judson, *Topographical Atlas of Surveys: Plymouth County together with the town of Cohasset, Norfolk County, Massachusetts* (Springfield, MA: L. J. Richards & Co., 1903), plate 27, State Library of Massachusetts, Massachusetts Real Estate Atlas Digitization Project, https://www.mass.gov/info-details/massachusetts-real-estate-atlas-digitization-project-by-the-state-library.

[460] USGS topographical maps from National Geologic Map Database, https://ngmdb.usgs.gov/topoview/viewer/; Freden, "Ferry Hill's Early Days."
[461] See Walter Crossley, "Storms Change Face Of Marshfield," *Marshfield Mariner*, August 17, 1972, 2. Scituate boundaries included the flats, even though they were more than halfway across the river to Marshfield, according to Turner's 1795 map, Chas. Turner, *A Plan of the Town of Scituate, in the County of Plymouth, taken in Conformity to Resolve of the General Court, which passed June the 26th 1794*, map, 200 rods to an inch, 1795, Massachusetts State Archives, No. 1242 "Maps and Plans," copy on file at Scituate Historical Society. The map shows an island here, but not with the later distinctive shape of the Great Green Island.
[462] 1843 report, 7.
[463] Emails from Town Archivist Jody McDonough, May 1, 2024.
[464] Bangs, *Town Records*, 1:14-15; Deane, *History of Scituate*, 111 (thatch, 1668); "Ancient Documents Relating to the Town of Scituate," *Hingham Journal*, April 20, 1877, 2 (quoted).
[465] "Great Green Island" in WPA card index, including summaries of town records of July 11, 1733, vol. C-3, p. 116, and separate records on 136 and 138 ½ (which could not be located). See also Norwell Conservation Commission, "Norwell Open Space and Recreation Plan 2005–2010" (2005), 45 (quoting 1849 deed from Scituate, with explanation of likely purposes), https://www.townofnorwell.net/sites/g/files/vyhlif1011/f/uploads/openspaceplan.pdf.
[466] Commissioners on Fisheries and Game, "A Report Upon the Mollusk Fisheries of Massachusetts" (Boston: Commonwealth of Massachusetts, Jan. 15, 1909), 165 (decline), 201, 202, https://www.gutenberg.org/files/48195/48195-h/48195-h.htm.
[467] *Hingham Journal*, November 29, 1907, 1, col. 3.
[468] "Clam Digger Fined," *Boston Globe*, October 28, 1908, 4.
[469] Walter Crossley, "Mudslinging For Profit Years Ago," *Marshfield Mariner*, July 26, 1973, 2,
[470] Town of Scituate to Town of South Scituate, deed, April 18, 1849, conveying property including the Salt Meadows or Flats of the North River, PCRD 231/192. The WPA card index notes that the conveyance of Great Green Island was "Recorded by Town Clerk, Jan. 15, 1876," but the reference (vol. 15, page 221, of Jan. 7, 1876) could not be located. This was probably a copy of the plan, recorded January 7, 1876, at the Plymouth County Registry of Deeds, rather than a new confirmatory deed.
[471] Town of Scituate deed, April 18, 1849.
[472] H. G. Reed, "Great Green Island," plan, probably June 1, 1875, recorded January 7, 1876, PCRD plan book 1/52, sheet 4 of 7 (and see other sheets); "Danforth – William S.," WPA card index. See "Reed, Horatio Gates House," SCI.1090 with continuation sheet, MACRIS. Reed's key role in bringing the railroad to Scituate and other towns is described in *History of the Old Colony Railroad*, 105–108.
[473] Merritt, *Old Time Anecdotes*, 72; "Fourth Cliff Today" (Fourth Cliff House was on Silver Road), https://fourthcliff.com/fourth%20cliff%20today.html. On Reed's plans, 1/52, see sheet 2/7 for a sketch of a larger house on Fourth Cliff in Scituate, probably the Fourth Cliff House discussed above in the text, and 3/7 for "Chimney of Hotel in Marshfield" (seems grand, 6+ bays). The hotel is probably the Webster House being built in Sea View that burned in September 1875, before it opened, as discussed elsewhere.
[474] See, generally, Nyberg, *On a Cliff*, which includes a history of the Welch homestead. Nyberg, *On a Cliff*, 20, 39. See also Day/Anderson map of 1829, copied above, which seems to depict the Welch house and barn.
[475] Maps cited elsewhere; 1902 atlas, sheet 1; Bangs, *Town Records*, 1:2 [12 of 552].
[476] Walter Crossley, "Old Men On The north River," *Marshfield Mariner*, June 15, 1972, 2.
[477] For example, see Briggs, *Shipbuilding*, 105, which says Barstows built the *Oeno*, a whaling vessel, in 1821 on the North River. In 1825, the vessel struck a reef and broke up in the Fiji islands. The crew landed but natives soon massacred all 21, except for William S. Cary, a Nantucket boy. He survived nine years among cannibals of the South Sea islands and returned to record a journal of his experiences. William S. Cary, *Wrecked On The Feejees* (Nantucket: The Inquirer and Mirror Press, 1949, orig. 1887), https://archive.org/details/feejees00_images/mode/2up. Thanks to Caleb Estabrooks for finding this.
[478] Briggs, *Shipbuilding*, 231–232.
[479] Bangs, *Town Records*, 1:161 (171:552). See Bangs, *Town Records*, 3:194, recording a 1682 agreement between Scituate and Marshfield to divide "Green Island," evidently different from "Great Green Island."
[480] See later discussion of these wetlands, now known as the English Salt Marsh and owned by the Commonwealth of Massachusetts.
[481] Snow, *Fantastic Folklore and Fact* (New York: Dodd, Mead, 1968), as described in Lowell Ames Norris, "South Shore Byline," *South Shore Mirror*, December 12, 1968, 30.
[482] Walter Crossley, "… Or Self Restoration," *Scituate Mariner*, March 1, 1979, 4.
[483] John B. Howard, email, February 2, 2025; conversations at NSRWA, February 4, 2025.

[484] John B. Howard, "Trouants Island: Reflections on Splendid Massachusetts Summers by Jack Howard [1875–1971]," post, September 22, 2024, https://substack.com/home/post/p-149238050; John B. Howard, "Borrowed Memories of Island Life," post, November 13, 2024, https://substack.com/home/post/p-149711464; see Donald M. Emery et al. to Frank Howard, lease, July 15, 1949, PCRD 2052/190; John Brooks Howard photos, Maine Memory Network,
https://www.mainememory.net/search/?entity=Howard%2C+John+Brooks.

[485] John Howard email, September 30, 2024 (quoted); John Howard email, November 13, 2024. See later discussion of the English Salt Marsh, which surrounds Trouant Island.

[486] "Junk Cars, Night Shooting Demand Board's Attention," *South Shore Mirror*, September 9, 1965, 1; John S. Keating, "The Spit: Paradise, battlefield, or both?" *Scituate Mariner*, August 7, 2014, 10. The 1965 article speaks of the probable effect of the Coastal Wetlands Bill, then close to enactment by the state, which provided for federal taking of "2300 acres on the North River of which over 60% would be in Scituate and Marshfield." The Bill was not analyzed in writing this book. The Trouant Island cottages are shown in a 1934 aerial photo, mentioned elsewhere in this book (Fig. 102).

[487] Morgan B. Salathé, "From the banks of Trouant's Island," (M.A.L.S. diss., Dartmouth College, 2016); Erin Kayata, "On the Market: A Marshfield Home on a Private Island," *Boston Magazine*, April 14, 2021, https://www.bostonmagazine.com/property/2021/04/14/marshfield-private-island/.

[488] See description in Messer, *Red House*, 257.

[489] "Humarock Beach," NSRWA, https://www.nsrwa.org/listing/humarock-beach/.

[490] Maria Ellis (Baker) Thomas (born 1859), diary entry for late November or early December 1898, courtesy of Phyllis Haskell, copy on file with author and at Scituate Historical Society. See also sources in Nyberg, *On a Cliff*, note 350.

[491] Coast Chart 109, "Boston Bay and Approaches," scale 1:80,000, updated version ("Corrections from surveys by Corps of Engineers, U.S.A. to Sept., 1903) (Washington, DC: Treasury Department, Office of the U.S. Coast and Geodetic Survey, July 1902, reissued Dec. 1904), from NOAA's Office of Coast Survey, Historical Map & Chart Collection, https://www.historicalcharts.noaa.gov/image.php?filename=109-12-1904; Fred Freitas and Dave Ball, *Warnings Ignored!: The Story of the Portland Gale of 1898* ([Scituate?], 1998, 2007).

[492] Galluzzo, *North River*, 84–85; 1902 atlas, sheet 1 (map, still naming it North River down to the old mouth, same as on sheet 22, corner 65), http://hdl.handle.net/2452/47879. A good view of the area is available from Open Street Map, https://www.openstreetmap.org/#map=4/38.01/-95.84. Humarock would then have been a junior version of Plum Island on Boston's North Shore, which is about eight miles long.

[493] John F. Smith letter, June 13, 1954, as reported in Fred Freitas, *Humarock: Hummocks, Humming Rocks, and Silver Sands* (Scituate: by author/Converpage, 2019), 69–71 (see Willard deLue columns in *Boston Globe*, May 30, May 31, and June 25 [14 or 19, depending on issue], 1954); 1902 atlas ("but the corner (65) is assumed to be where the old mouth of the river was located" and see sheet 22 detail, Fig. 106); "Which Town Owns the Beach," *Boston Globe*, December 18, 1903, 4 ("at present there are no signs whatever" of the old mouth); "New Maritime Highway, Along the Massachusetts Coast, Will Come Into Being With Completion of the Cape Cod Canal," *Boston Globe*, June 26, 1910, 67, cols. 3–4 (with photos) ("lagoon"); Richards 1903 map, plate 27, and plate 31, saying "Old Outlet (closed)."

[494] 1843 report, 6; 1870 report, 65, 58. See also 1871 Mitchell sketch, Fig. 10 (Fig. 73), and Stebbins photo (Fig. 74).

[495] Jim Glinski, "Salt Marsh Ditches of the South Shore," NSRWA website, Part 1 posted November 1, 2022, https://www.nsrwa.org/salt-marsh-ditches-of-the-south-shore-part-1-1/, and Part 2 posted November 4, 2022, https://www.nsrwa.org/salt-marsh-ditches-of-the-south-shore-part-2/; email from Jim Glinski, January 17, 2023 (quoted); [W. Bert Cunningham], "North River PILOT" series in *Scituate Herald*, January 5, 1945, 6 (Question No. 4) (quoted).

[496] Walter Crossley, "Growing Up On The North River," *Marshfield Mariner*, June 1, 1972 (quote); Sara Grady, presentation, "Making Salt Marshes More Climate Resilient - Zoom event," February 22, 2023, NSRWA, https://www.nsrwa.org/event/making-salt-marshes-more-climate-resilient-zoom-event/; "Salt Marsh Sentinels," https://www.nsrwa.org/get-involved/citizen-science/salt-marsh-sentinels/.

[497] DAR, *Old Scituate*, 238. But the market for salt hay had already declined. Vinal, *Salt Haying*, as referenced in Galluzzo, *North River*, 71–72.

[498] See Nyberg, *On a Cliff*.

[499] See Richards 1903 map; *Seacoast Scituate by Air*, 39. The "gates" swung open slowly. The 1939 Sanborn Map shows only a minor "flip" of the tip of Third Cliff (the "Spit"), which may understate the migration of the two tips. Sanborn Map for 1939, image 1, Library of Congress, http://hdl.loc.gov/loc.gmd/g3764sm.g038411944. By 1952 there is not much change, per the MacConnell aerial photos,

https://credo.library.umass.edu/view/full/mufs190-1952-dpt5k109-i001. They got bigger by 1968, with the tip of Fourth Cliff starting to "flip" inwards (upriver), https://www.lylenyberg.com/copy-of-aerial-photos. On a current Google Maps view, the tips are even longer.

[500] See Nyberg, *On a Cliff*, front cover (adaptation of Meteyard painting), 90, 162, 280 n. 355 (citing exhibition catalogs), 299 n. 600; Meteyard paintings, including "Scituate – Fourth Cliff from Second Cliff [Third Cliff?]," 1884–1900, Mark Murray Fine Paintings, https://www.markmurray.com/thomas-buford-meteyard-paintings-for-sale.

[501] See discussion about Fourth Cliff House, above; Nyberg, "Gunners at the Shore," in *On a Cliff*, 88–90 (with photo); various books about the North River; John B. Howard, "Trouants Island: Reflections on Splendid Massachusetts Summers by Jack Howard [1875–1971]," post (quoted), September 22, 2024, https://substack.com/home/post/p-149238050.

[502] "1915 report, 7–15.

[503] 1915 report, 1, 7–15. Walter Crossley observed the boulder removal process and reported on it in "Boating On The North River," *Marshfield Mariner*, June 22,1972, 2 (at 16).

[504] 1915 report, 7–15, 11–12 (quote).

[505] 1915 report, 7–15, 12 (quote).

[506] 1915 plan, cited above in full.

[507] 1915 plan; 1915 report, 12.

[508] The 1915 plan is available from North River Commission in lower resolution, http://www.northrivercommission.net/. Higher resolution copies were not available from State Library of Massachusetts, Massachusetts Department of Conservation and Recreation, Plymouth County Registry of Deeds, or other sources. Thanks to work by Caitlin Ramos, State Archives, and the amazing Bill Keegan, higher resolution copies of the odd-numbered sheets were found and made. They are available from my website, with explanatory information, at https://www.lylenyberg.com/copy-of-aerial-photos-1. These should be helpful for historical and ecological research.

[509] 1915 report, 8–9. The Waterman factory is shown in text (Fig. 18).

[510] 1915 report, 8–9.

[511] 1915 report, 9.

[512] HNV.903/PEM.900, MACRIS.

[513] 1915 report, 9.

[514] 1870 report, 65.

[515] Walter Crossley, "Growing Up On The North River," *Marshfield Mariner*, June 1, 1972 (quote); "Pembroke," *Scituate Herald*, July 4, 1941, 3 (camp); "Walter Edmund Crossley," memorial, https://www.findagrave.com/memorial/205928427/walter-edmund-crossley. Crossley was called "officiando of the North River" when interviewed in 1984. "What is polluting river?" *Scituate Mariner*, August 16, 1984, 1 (1906). Crossley articles in the *Marshfield Mariner*, including his early 1970s series, "As I Remember," do not seem to have been digitized, although photocopies are available and were used for this book, and excerpts can be found on W. Ray Freden's blog.

[516] 1915 report, 9.

[517] 1915 report, 11.

[518] 1915 report, 13.

[519] 1915 report, 10.

[520] HNV.903/PEM.900 (1904 bridge), MACRIS.

[521] 1915 report, 10.

[522] 1915 report, 13; Galluzzo, *North River*, 44. See also Winfield M. Thompson, "North River Has a New Birth," *Boston Globe*, January 9, 1910, 63 (with photos); Freitas, *Humarock*, 139 (1894-1920), 162 (smaller boat building).

[523] 1915 report, 15; https://www.amortization.org/inflation/; "Taunton River Project," *Boston Globe*, October 16, 1915, 10; "Liquor Cut Off From Dry Towns," *Boston Globe*, March 30, 1916, 3 (withdrawal of petition for Taunton-North River waterway). See discussion in text on 1839–1841 Federal Petitions; Board of Harbor and Land Commissioners of Massachusetts, "Plan of location of projected ship canal from Taunton River to Boston Harbor, through Weymouth Fore River ... Frank W. Hodgdon, engineer," map (Boston: The Commissioners, 1902), *Digital Commonwealth*, https://ark.digitalcommonwealth.org/ark:/50959/js956k17g.

[524] Courtesy of Massachusetts Department of Transportation. Photos by Fairchild Aerial Surveys (FAS) are in collections at University of California, Santa Barbara, https://www.library.ucsb.edu/geospatial/airphotos/fairchild-aerial-surveys-fas); and Boston Public Library, https://www.digitalcommonwealth.org/search/commonwealth:8k71nz834 (click on FAS link). A list of other older aerial photos of southeastern Massachusetts seems focused on Buzzards Bay. "Historical Aerial Surveys

SE Mass," Buzzards Bay National Estuary Program, https://buzzardsbay.org/technical-data/gisdownload/using-georeferencing-historical-aerials/historical-aerial-surveys-se-mass/. Other aerial photos are available in the MacConnell Collection, UMass Amherst, discussed elsewhere in this book (from 1951–1952, etc.), and on the author's website (including 1968 and 1978), including under Marshes tab, https://www.lylenyberg.com/copy-of-seacoast-by-air. The 1934 photos are under the River tab, https://www.lylenyberg.com/copy-of-aerial-photos-2.

[525] See Nyberg, "Aerial Photos," https://www.lylenyberg.com/copy-of-ditches.

[526] See Nyberg, *Seacoast Scituate By Air*, https://www.lylenyberg.com/copy-of-ditches.

[527] John D. Fiske, Clinton E. Watson, and Philip G. Coates, *A Study of the Marine Resources of the North River*, Monograph Series No. 3 (Division of Marine Fisheries, Department of Natural Resources, The Commonwealth of Massachusetts, 1966), 52 pages, on file at State Library of Massachusetts, Scituate Historical Society ("North River" file), and other places. A copy may be downloaded from the author's website, https://www.lylenyberg.com/copy-of-links-suffrage-1. Shad are covered at 23 and 29, lobsters at 39. At 21, the study notes that researchers conducted 525 interviews of sport fishermen. For a bit more on salt marsh species, with a discussion of crabs, see Duncan Oliver, "Cape Cod Salt Marshes – Asset or Swamp?" Historical Society of Old Yarmouth, December 18, 2022, https://www.hsoy.org/blog/2022/12/13/the-cape-cod-salt-marsh. This book does not go into detail into salt marsh species and habitats, but more is available in Nyberg, *Ditching the Marshes*.

[528] Fiske, *Marine Resources*, 1, 13. In recent years, Rockland's effluent has caused the closure of North River clam beds, since it enters a tributary of the North River. Lori Wolfe, "Clam Flat Closures," January 26, 2024, NSRWA website, https://www.nsrwa.org/clam-flat-closures/.

[529] Fiske, *Marine Resources*, 4–7.

[530] Fiske, *Marine Resources*, 14–16.

[531] Fiske, *Marine Resources*, 39–50 (47 quoted).

[532] Fiske, *Marine Resources*, 44 (quoted)–46.

[533] "History of Audubon in Florida," https://fl.audubon.org/about-us/history; "The History of Audubon and Bird Conservation," https://www.audubon.org/about/history; Shaun Roche, Visitor Service Manager at the Stewart B. McKinney National Wildlife Refuge, "Salt Marsh Haymaking," Menunkatuck Audubon Society (CT) presentation, 2022, https://www.youtube.com/watch?v=4bhoojpdhkQ. The Roche presentation is an outstanding and comprehensive discussion of salt marshes and salt haying, with reference to the Great Meadows salt marshes in Connecticut, and video of hay poling and haying from Newbury (MA).

[534] Mish, *Almanac*, 34, 37, 38; later pages contain a comprehensive running commentary on local and state environmental actions.

[535] Galluzzo, *North River*, 93–94 (NSRWA).

[536] "Environmentalism in music," Wikipedia article, https://en.wikipedia.org/wiki/Environmentalism_in_music; Martin Chilton, "Best Earth Day Songs: 30 Save The Environment Classics," https://www.udiscovermusic.com/stories/best-earth-day-songs/; Richard L. Wallace, "List of Songs Related to Climate Change and Human Impact on the Environment," Ursinus College Environmental Studies Program, 2009, https://conbio.org/images/content_groups/SSWG/climatechangesongs.pdf;

[537] National Estuarine Pollution Study: Proceedings of the Public Meeting held at Boston, Massachusetts, October 8, 1968, and Written Statements Concerning Tidal Waters of Massachusetts" (Boston: Federal Water Pollution Control Administration, Northeast Region, US Dept. of the Interior, 1968) [this was before the EPA was created], 212 pages, National Service Center for Environmental Publications (NSCEP), doc. 950R68008, https://nepis.epa.gov/. The North River on the South Shore is mentioned at 127 and discussed starting at 161, a long letter by Dr. William Vinal.

[538] William "Cap'n Bill" Vinal, "The North River Looking Back so as to Look Forward," typewritten manuscript (for speech?) (1970), in Vinal files, Norwell Historical Society.

[539] Dan Neumann, "The Battle for the North River," *North River Packet*, Norwell Historical Society, summer 2023, https://norwellhistoricalsociety.org/newsletters%3A-2020-2024; Jim Glinski, "NSRWA: The Origin," in "NSRWA 50th Anniversary (Part 1)," https://www.nsrwa.org/nsrwa-50th-anniversary-part-1/; Mike Beatrice, "Justice Douglas To Speak At Conservation Meeting," *Boston Globe*, September 16, 1964, 53; Elizabeth Sullivan, "Elections Uppermost This Week," *Boston Globe*, October 25, 1964, 64, col. 3; "Douglas Dined on No. River Clams," and "Large Crowd At Scituate High Hears Douglas Support No. River Project," *South Shore News*, October 15, 1964, 1 [Sec. II, incl. *Scituate Herald* edition] (the latter with extensive quotes from speech).

[540] "Opposition Has Delayed Sewage Plant at Least Year," *Scituate Herald* edition of *South Shore News*, 1, Sec. II (with discussion of three plans); William G. "Cap'n Bill" Vinal, "The Old Scituate Landscape," *South Shore*

News, July 7, 1966, 3 [Sec. II] (Rockland sewage plant ground breaking; "It is not necessary to inflict a poison program on neighbors.").

[541] Neumann, "Battle;" Douglas P. Hill, "Coastal Wetlands in New England," *Boston University Law Review*, 52:4 (Boston: Boston University Law Review, fall, 1972), 724.

[542] Reed F. Stewart, "The Humarock Question: Restoration At Great Cost …" *Scituate Mariner*, March 1, 1979, 4; Walter Crossley, "… Or Self Restoration," *Scituate Mariner*, March 1, 1979, 4; "Dr. Reed F. Stewart," Massachusetts Studies Project, https://www.msp.umb.edu/Reedbio.html; "Reed's Obituary," https://www.macdonaldfuneralhome.com/obituary/reed-stewart.

[543] "What is polluting river?" *Scituate Mariner*, August 16, 1984, 1 (Walter Crossley: "I'm afraid we're going to lose it [clamming]. I only hope we get the river back.").

[544] See Annie Proulx, *Fen, Bog and Swamp: A Short History of Peatland Destruction and Its Role in the Climate Crisis* (New York: Scribner, 2022); Lyle Nyberg, Gary Banks, Bill Richardson, *Seacoast Scituate By Air* (Scituate: by author, 2022); Nyberg, *Ditching the Marshes*.

[545] M. Margaret McKeown, *Citizen Justice: The Environmental Legacy of William O. Douglas—Public Advocate and Conservation Champion* (Sterling, VA: Potomac Books, 2022), 49–50, 91–93, 127–30 ("ecology" and "environmental").

[546] *Sierra Club v. Morton*, 405 U.S. 727, 741–43 (US Supreme Court, 1972), as quoted in Liam H. McMillin, "Where is Nature in Our Constitution? Part II," *University of Cincinnati Law Review* (2023), https://uclawreview.org/2023/10/17/where-is-nature-in-our-constitution-part-ii/. See also Nicholas Monck, "Who Will Speak For the Trees: A Modern Day Lorax?" *Medium*, July 16, 2023, https://nicholasmonck.medium.com/who-will-speak-for-the-trees-a-modern-day-lorax-7c8f1869223c.

[547] Judge M. Margaret McKeown, author of *Citizen Justice: The Environmental Legacy of William O. Douglas—Public Advocate and Conservation Champion* (Sterling, VA: Potomac Books, 2022), interviewed on "We the People," in National Constitution Center, December 1, 2022 [00:21:18], https://constitutioncenter.org/media/files/Justice_William_Douglas_Public_Advocate_Conservation_Champion_transcript.pdf.

[548] Cody Peluso, "What are the Rights of Nature?" Population Media Center, August 18, 2023, https://www.populationmedia.org/the-latest/what-are-the-rights-of-nature. See also Mauricio Guim & Michael A. Livermore, "Where Nature's Rights Go Wrong," *Virginia Law Review* 107:1347, November 29, 2021, https://virginialawreview.org/articles/where-natures-rights-go-wrong/; Shanthi Van Zeebroeck, "Nature Rights: What Countries Grant Legal Personhood Status to Nature And Why?" Earth.org, October 6, 2022, https://earth.org/nature-rights/; McKeown, *Citizen Justice*, 157–158.

[549] Rod Barnett, "Utu in the Anthropocene," *Places* journal, August 2021, https://placesjournal.org/article/redesigning-colonial-landscapes/; Isabella Kaminski, "For the First Time, Part of the Ocean Has Been Granted Legal Personhood," *Hakai* magazine, September 6, 2024, https://hakaimagazine.com/news/for-the-first-time-part-of-the-ocean-has-been-granted-legal-personhood/.

[550] "New Zealand grants human rights to a mountain," *Boston Globe*, January 31, 2025, A3.

[551] But see Josh Dawsey and Maxine Joselow, "What Trump promised oil CEOs as he asked them to steer $1 billion to his campaign," *Washington Post*, May 9, 2024, https://www.washingtonpost.com/politics/2024/05/09/trump-oil-industry-campaign-money/.

[552] See Nyberg, *Ditching the Marshes*; Maag, "Armed with Saran Wrap," at end (Stony Creek project); "Habitat of Potential Regional or Statewide Importance, Town of Scituate, MA," sample CAPS map, UMass Amherst, http://umassdsl.org/masscaps/DEPmaps/CAPS_DEP_SCITUATE.pdf, and https://umasscaps.org/data_maps/massdep-maps.html.; "Scituate Priority Habitats and Estimated Habitats," map, Massachusetts Division of fisheries & Wildlife, effective August 1, 2021, https://s3.amazonaws.com/eea-public/fwe/nhesp/atlas/Atlas15th_SCITUATE.pdf, and https://www.mass.gov/info-details/regulatory-maps-priority-estimated-habitats. In upper Manhattan, next to Inwood Hill Park is a one-acre *created* wetland. Devon Kennedy, "Muscota Marsh: the recent return of a wetland habitat in upper Manhattan," The City Atlas, July 15, 2014, https://newyork.thecityatlas.org/lifestyle/muscota-marsh-the-recent-return-of-a-wetland-habitat-in-upper-manhattan/.

[553] "Highlights from America's Biggest Conference on Coastal Restoration," in Conserving the Nature of the Northeast, Medium.com, February 14, 2017, https://medium.com/usfishandwildlifeservicenortheast/highlights-from-americas-biggest-conference-on-coastal-restoration-6a89a590f8a6.

[554] Paul McCarthy email, May 8, 2024.

[555] Kleinfelder Associates, "Sea Level Rise Study. The Towns of Marshfield, Duxbury, Scituate, MA" (Towns of Marshfield, Duxbury, Scituate, MA, July 18, 2013),

https://www.town.duxbury.ma.us/sites/g/files/vyhlif10506/f/uploads/south_shore_sea_level_rise_study_kleinfelder_2012x.pdf; Kristi Funderburk, "Marshfield panel examines threat of sea level rise," *Marshfield Mariner*, May 21, 2014, https://www.wickedlocal.com/story/marshfield-mariner/2014/05/21/marshfield-panel-examines-threat-sea/37296073007/.

[556] Climate change seems to be unfolding faster than expected, faster than models predicted, and faster than scientists can keep up. Zoë Schlanger, "Climate Models Can't Explain What's Happening to Earth," *The Atlantic*, January 6, 2025, https://www.theatlantic.com/science/archive/2025/01/climate-models-earth/681207/.

[557] Rapinel, S., Panhelleux, L., Gayet, G., Vanacker, R., Lemercier, B., Laroche, B., Chambaud, F., Guelmami, A., & Hubert-Moy, L. (2023), "National wetland mapping using remote-sensing-derived environmental variables, archive field data, and artificial intelligence," *Heliyon*, 9(2), e13482, https://doi.org/10.1016/j.heliyon.2023.e13482, and https://pmc.ncbi.nlm.nih.gov/articles/PMC9929292/. A comprehensive and enlightening report.

[558] The National Wetlands Inventory can be viewed in online maps on the mapper available at https://www.fws.gov/wetlands-month/national-wetlands-inventory, and https://www.mass.gov/info-details/massgis-data-national-wetlands-inventory.

[559] "The World's Tidal Marshes Are Finally on the Map."

[560] Kerstin Wasson email, December 31, 2024; Cheyenne Ellis, "Partnering Agencies and NGOs Join Effort to Restore the Great Meadows Marsh. Find Out How You Can Get Involved Too!" Long Island Sound Study, October 25, 2021, https://longislandsoundstudy.net/2021/10/partnering-agencies-and-ngos-join-effort-to-restore-the-great-meadows-marsh-find-out-how-you-can-get-involved-too/.

[561] "What is a geographic information system (GIS)?" USGS, updated November 27, 2024, https://www.usgs.gov/faqs/what-a-geographic-information-system-gis.

[562] "MassGIS Data: 2021 Aerial Imagery, Spring 2021," MassGIS, https://www.mass.gov/info-details/massgis-data-2021-aerial-imagery; "MassGIS Data: Digital Orthophoto Index," MassGIS, https://www.mass.gov/info-details/massgis-data-digital-orthophoto-index. Aerial images of Massachusetts are also available in the viewer at "Rhode Island STORMTOOLS," RI Coastal Resources Management Council (CRMC), https://stormtools-mainpage-crc-uri.hub.arcgis.com/. That site says "STORMTOOLS is a method to illustrate and display storm inundation, with and without sea level rise, for different types of storms that could occur along Rhode Island's coast line."

[563] Holmquist, J.R., Windham-Myers, L, "A Conterminous USA-Scale Map of Relative Tidal Marsh Elevation," *Estuaries and Coasts* 45:1596–1614 (2022), https://doi.org/10.1007/s12237-021-01027-9, and https://link.springer.com/article/10.1007/s12237-021-01027-9.

[564] Erin Douglas, "Whipsawed and washed out in Vt.," *Boston Globe*, August 18, 2024, A1; Marianne Mizera, "'Historic' flooding in Conn. Kills 2," *Boston Globe*, August 20, 2024, B1; Erin Douglas and Chris Gloninger, "From modest disturbance to fierce '1,000 year storm,'" *Boston Globe*, August 22, 2024, B1.

[565] Denise Chow, "Hurricane Milton's downpour around Tampa Bay was a 1-in-1,000-year rain event," NBC News, October 10, 2024, https://www.nbcnews.com/science/science-news/hurricane-milton-rain-1-in-1000-year-event-rcna174838.

[566] "Ellicott City, MD: A City on Edge, The Weather Channel, July 7, 2020, https://features.weather.com/ellicott-city-md-a-city-on-edge/; Kevin Crowe, Shannon Osaka, and John Muyskens, "Federal flood maps underestimated risk in areas hit hardest by Hurricane Helene," *Washington Post*, October 13, 2024, https://www.washingtonpost.com/weather/2024/10/13/fema-flood-maps-hurricane-helene/. An excellent general discussion of flood risks and how FEMA maps attempt to show them is in Mark Monmonier, *Coastlines: How Mapmakers Frame the World and Chart Environmental Change* (Chicago: University of Chicago Press, 2008, updated edition), particularly Chapter 9, "Calibrating Catastrophe," which includes an extensive analysis of flood mapping for Lee County, FL, starting at 127 (original edition). Lee County is home to Fort Myers and is just southeast of Tampa Bay. Both were hit by Helene and Milton in 2024.

[567] Crowe et al. "Underestimated."

[568] Michael J. Coren, Naema Ahmed, and Kevin Crowe, "Insuring your home has never been harder. Here's how to do it." *Washington Post*, December 16, 2024 (nice graphics for US costs by state), https://www.washingtonpost.com/climate-environment/interactive/2024/home-insurance-climate-change-premiums-strategies/; Zoë Schlanger, "Are You Sure Your House Is Worth That Much? Climate risk is still not being priced into American homeownership." *The Atlantic*, August 22, 2024, https://www.theatlantic.com/science/archive/2024/08/climate-change-risk-homeowners-housing-bubble/679559/.

[569] Will Steinfeld, "In the Wake of the Water," *Places Journal*, December 2024, https://placesjournal.org/article/in-the-wake-of-the-water/.

[570] New England Flood Information is available at a USGS website, https://www.usgs.gov/centers/new-england-water-science-center/science/new-england-flood-information.

[571] "Neighborhood Level Flood Inundation Maps: Transforming NWS Water Prediction across the U.S.," NOAA, https://www.weather.gov/media/owp/operations/2024_NWS_OWP_FIM_Rollout_Flyer.pdf.

[572] US Office of Water Prediction, https://water.noaa.gov/gauges/BATM3; "!NEW! - National Water Prediction Service (NWPS)," and "!NEW! - Flood Inundation Mapping (FIM) Services," accessed December 17, 2024, https://www.weather.gov/owp/operations.

[573] "Viewing Flood Inundation Mapping on the National Water Prediction Service," NOAA Office of Water Prediction, https://www.weather.gov/media/owp/operations/Viewing_FIM_NWPS.pdf; and NWPS map of the US: https://water.noaa.gov. "A commonly used layer is the NWM Medium-Range High Water Arrival Time Forecast." National Viewer Quick Start How-To Guide (2023), NOAA, https://www.weather.gov/media/owp/operations/nws_fim_viewer_instructions.pdf. Notes: "This map shows approximated flood inundation extent based on modeled river discharge and contains inherent uncertainty."

[574] "Coastal Ecosystem Mapping," Global Coastal Wetlands Lab, https://www.globalcoastalwetlands.com/our-research. The lab's work is discussed elsewhere in this book.

[575] "Weekend Coastal Flooding Expected September 20–21, 2024," Scituate Emergency Management bulletin, September 19, 2024 (moderate coastal flooding; "Areas prone to flooding, including Cole Parkway, Front Street, Edward Foster Road, Cedar Point, and Central Ave in Humarock, may be particularly vulnerable." https://www.scituatema.gov/home/news/a-message-from-scituate-emergency-management-0. Nicholas Kusnetz (InsideClimate News), "Homeowners of Humarock," December 16, 2017, The Weather Channel, https://features.weather.com/us-climate-change/massachusetts/. For coverage of a 2018 coastal storm's effect on Scituate, see Andrew MacFarlane, "Never the same every year," The Weather Channel, August 1, 2018, https://features.weather.com/exodus/chapter/never-the-same-every-year/.

[576] Daniel Wolff and Dorothy Peteet, "Why a Marsh," *Places Journal*, May 2022, https://placesjournal.org/article/the-deep-history-and-uncertain-future-of-a-marsh-on-the-hudson/.

[577] Kate D. Ramsayer, Kathryn Cawdrey, "NASA Scientists Map Global Salt Marsh Losses and Their Carbon Impact," NASA, December 7, 2022, https://www.nasa.gov/missions/landsat/nasa-scientists-map-global-salt-marsh-losses-and-their-carbon-impact/. See also "The World's Tidal Marshes Are Finally on the Map" (2024).

[578] Wolff & Peteet, "Why a Marsh."

[579] Chris Mooney, John Muyskens, Brady Dennis, with images by Ricky Carioti, "Where the sea wall ends," *Washington Post*, September 23, 2024, https://www.washingtonpost.com/climate-environment/interactive/2024/galveston-sea-level-rise-condo-development/; "Galveston, Texas," Wikipedia article, https://en.wikipedia.org/wiki/Galveston,_Texas. In 1909, a sea wall was proposed along Humarock beach to protect what were then about 28 cottages. Shaw, Wilson, "Concrete Sea Wall at Humarock Beach," MIT thesis, last sketches. Sea walls were probably built around 1923, according to the NSRWA, "Humarock Beach," https://www.nsrwa.org/listing/humarock-beach/. Humarock has struggled with rising sea levels, as described in a 2017 article. Nicholas Kusnetz, "An American Beach Story: When Property Rights Clash with the Rising Sea," *Inside Climate News*, https://insideclimatenews.org/news/16122017/beach-erosion-sea-level-rise-property-rights-massachusetts-government-storm-nourishment-project/.

[580] "Outer Banks," Wikipedia article, https://en.wikipedia.org/wiki/Outer_Banks; Brady Dennis, "One block on the Outer Banks has had three houses collapse since Friday," *Washington Post*, September 25, 2024, https://www.washingtonpost.com/climate-environment/2024/09/24/obx-erosion-house-collapse-ocean-sea-levels/.

[581] For example, David Abel and Dharna Noor, "On Cape Cod, the latest barrage of wind and waves, exacerbated by climate change, turns concern to desperation," *Boston Globe*, updated January 31, 2022, https://www.bostonglobe.com/2022/01/31/science/barrage-wind-waves-weekends-storm-pummeled-coast-cape-cod/; Emily Sweeney, " Nantucket beach homes come close to auction," *Boston Globe*, December 22, 2024, B2 ($2M homes selling for $200,000).

[582] Osland, M.J., Chivoiu, B., Grace, J.B. et al. "Rising seas could cross thresholds for initiating coastal wetland drowning within decades across much of the United States," *Communications Earth & Environment* 5, 372 (2024), https://www.nature.com/articles/s43247-024-01537-x, and https://doi.org/10.1038/s43247-024-01537-x; Brady Dennis and Chris Mooney, "A 'collapse' is looming for Louisiana's coastal wetlands, scientists say: Scientists say the overwhelming majority of the state's wetlands — a natural buffer against hurricanes — are in a state of 'drowning' and could be gone by 2070," *Washington Post*, updated February 15, 2024,

https://www.washingtonpost.com/climate-environment/2024/02/15/louisiana-coastal-erosion-swamp-wetland-loss/.

583 See Holly Binns & Joseph Gordon, "11 Facts About Salt Marshes and Why We Need to Protect Them: These coastal habitats help wildlife, ecosystems, and economies thrive," Pew Charitable Trusts, March 1, 2021, https://www.pewtrusts.org/en/research-and-analysis/articles/2021/03/01/11-facts-about-salt-marshes-and-why-we-need-to-protect-them.

584 Joseph Gordon & Holly Binns, "6 Types of Wildlife and Plants That Thrive in Salt Marshes," Pew Charitable Trusts, March 22, 2021, https://www.pewtrusts.org/en/research-and-analysis/articles/2021/03/22/6-types-of-wildlife-and-plants-that-thrive-in-salt-marshes; Sue Pike, "Mummichogs are stout little fish found in salt marsh pannes," *Foster's Daily Democrat* (Portsmouth, NH), June 26, 2018, https://www.fosters.com/story/lifestyle/2018/06/26/nature-news-mummichogs-are-stout-little-fish-found-in-salt-marsh-pannes/11874242007/; "Elkhorn Slough," WHSRN (Western Hemisphere Shorebird Reserve Network, with executive office in Manomet, MA), https://whsrn.org/whsrn_sites/elkhorn-slough/. See 1966 study, discussed above.

585 See "Shellfish classification areas," Massachusetts Division of Marine Fisheries, https://www.mass.gov/info-details/shellfish-classification-areas. The North River is covered by Growing Area Code MB5. The map shows extensive marsh/wetland, and salt marsh. Currently, harvesting is conditionally approved only for an area from the Rte. 3A bridge east for about a mile along the river, not necessarily streams. For more detail, see the shellfish classification layer in the GIS viewer, Aquaculture Siting Tool MA-ShellfAST.

586 *NY Times*? Christopher Maag, "Armed with Saran Wrap, she sinks in the muck to save the planet," *Boston Globe*, August 3, 2024, https://www.bostonglobe.com/2024/08/03/nation/armed-with-saran-wrap-she-sinks-muck-save-planet.

587 Wolff & Peteet, "Why a Marsh."

588 Tatum McConnell, "Protecting nature's best carbon sink: Peatlands," Scienceline, January 7, 2022, https://scienceline.org/2022/01/protecting-natures-best-carbon-sink-peatlands/; Kimbra Cutlip, "For the World's Wetlands, It May Be Sink or Swim. Here's Why It Matters," *Smithsonian Magazine*, January 13, 2016, https://www.smithsonianmag.com/smithsonian-institution/worlds-wetlands-it-may-be-sink-or-swim-heres-why-it-matters-180957808/; both quoted in Nyberg, *Ditching the Marshes*, 37.

589 "Peatlands store twice as much carbon as all the world's forests," UN Environment Programme, February 1, 2019, https://www.unep.org/news-and-stories/story/peatlands-store-twice-much-carbon-all-worlds-forests. See also Proulx, *Fen, Bog and Swamp*.

590 "Why soil carbon sequestration is overrated," Wageningen University & Research, January 18, 2023, https://www.wur.nl/en/research-results/research-institutes/environmental-research/show-wenr/why-soil-carbon-sequestration-is-overrated.htm; "The ocean – the world's greatest ally against climate change," United Nations Climate Action, https://www.un.org/en/climatechange/science/climate-issues/ocean; David Malmquist, "VIMS study: Sea-level rise is double-edged sword for carbon storage," William & Mary's Virginia Institute of Marine Science, April 3, 2023, https://news.wm.edu/2023/04/03/vims-study-sea-level-rise-is-double-edged-sword-for-carbon-storage/; Sarah Raza, "How an antacid for the ocean could cool the Earth," *Washington Post*, January 3, 2025, https://www.washingtonpost.com/climate-solutions/2025/01/03/ocean-carbon-removal-alkalinity-enhancement/.

591 Bobby Bascomb, "Marshes are cost-effective for protecting coasts: Study," Mongabay, October 31, 2024 (quoted), https://news.mongabay.com/short-article/marshes-are-cost-effective-for-protecting-coasts-study/; David Chandler, "Study: Marshes provide cost-effective coastal protection," *MIT News*, October 23, 2024, https://news.mit.edu/2024/study-marshes-provide-cost-effective-coastal-protection-1023; Lee, E.I.H., Nepf, H, "Marsh restoration in front of seawalls is an economically justified nature-based solution for coastal protection," *Commun Earth Environ* **5**, 605 (2024). https://doi.org/10.1038/s43247-024-01753-5, and https://www.nature.com/articles/s43247-024-01753-5.

592 "Elkhorn Slough Salt Marshes: Past, Present and Future," Elkhorn Slough (summary of investigation from 2009–2012), https://elkhornslough.org/reserve/research/elkhorn-slough-salt-marshes-past-present-and-future/. A description and history of the reserve is at "Elkhorn Slough Reserve," Nature Conservancy, https://www.nature.org/en-us/get-involved/how-to-help/places-we-protect/elkhorn-slough/.

593 Annie Ropeik and Kate Cough (of *The Maine Monitor*), "Development and rising seas threaten Maine's salt marshes, a key carbon sink," WBUR, https://www.wbur.org/news/2024/09/17/maine-salt-marsh-development-climate-change.

594 "Time to Invest in Marshes Is Now," National Estuarine Research Reserve Association (NERRA), April 15, 2024, https://www.nerra.org/time-to-invest-in-marshes-is-now/.

[595] Frederick T. Short, ed., *The Ecology of the Great Bay Estuary, New Hampshire and Maine: An Estuarine Profile and Bibliography* (Durham, NH: NOAA et al. 1992), 156, https://coast.noaa.gov/data/docs/nerrs/Reserves_GRB_SiteProfile.pdf.

[596] Charlie Endris, Suzanne Shull, Andrea Woolfolk, Laura S. Brophy, Daniel R. Brumbaugh, Jeffrey A. Crooks, Kaitlin L. Reinl, Roger Fuller, Denise M. Sanger, Rachel A. Stevens, Monica Almeida, Kerstin Wasson [project lead], "Lost and found coastal wetlands: Lessons learned from mapping estuaries across the USA," *Biological Conservation*, 299:110779 (November 2024), https://doi.org/10.1016/j.biocon.2024.110779, and https://www.sciencedirect.com/journal/biological-conservation/vol/299/suppl/C, and https://nerrsscienceollaborative.org/sites/default/files/resources/Lost%20and%20found%20coastal%20wetlands-%20Lessons%20learned%20from%20mapping%20estuaries.pdf ("2024 NERRS study").
Reports for individual reserves are collected at "Estuary Changes," https://experience.arcgis.com/experience/ef3df91f750d467d9bdad3f9fbd3c54a/page/Homepage/#data_s=id%3AdataSource_2-18b4eb99b15-layer-10%3A6%2Cid%3AdataSource_2-18c1dd070ef-layer-21%3A3.

[597] Charlie Endris et al. "Estuarine habitats at Elkhorn Slough NERR, California: Past, present, and future," National Estuarine Research Reserve System and the Institute for Applied Ecology (2023), https://www.nerra.org/estuary-change. See also Jane Caffrey, Martha Brown, W. Breck Tyler, and Mark Silberstein, eds., *Changes in a California Estuary: A Profile of Elkhorn Slough* (Moss Landing, CA: Elkhorn Slough Foundation, 2002), 124, https://coast.noaa.gov/data/docs/nerrs/Reserves_ELK_SiteProfile.pdf; "Tidal Wetland Program," Elkhorn Slough, https://elkhornslough.org/reserve/tidal-wetland-program/.

[598] Wolff & Peteet, "Why a Marsh;" "Piermont Marsh," HRNERR (& NYState DEC), https://hrnerr.org/visit/piermont-marsh/; "Pilot Shoreline Resilience Project at Piermont Marsh," HRNERR (278 acres), https://hrnerr.org/shore-protection-piermont/. Other estuarine research reserves may be found at https://coast.noaa.gov/nerrs/. Each reserve page has vital statistics, most including tidal range.

[599] "Pilot Shoreline Resilience Project at Piermont Marsh."

[600] "Restoring Padilla Bay's Vital Tidal Marsh," NOAA Office for Coastal Management, https://coast.noaa.gov/states/stories/vital-tidal-marsh.html; "Finding Common Ground on Padilla Bay," NERRA, February 1, 2024, https://www.nerra.org/finding-common-ground-on-padilla-bay/.

[601] Anna Phillips, "Why cranberry country is turning into wetlands," *Washington Post*, November 26, 2024, https://www.washingtonpost.com/climate-environment/2024/11/26/cranberries-bogs-wetlands-farmers/; Erez Ben-Akiva, "Mattapoisett Bogs reopen," *Sippican Week*, November 17, 2024 (Quintal), https://sippican.theweektoday.com/article/mattapoisett-bogs-reopen/72813; "The Bogs," Buzzards Bay Coalition, https://www.savebuzzardsbay.org/places-to-go/the-bogs/.

[602] Waquoit Bay National Estuarine Research Reserve (WBNERR), https://waquoitbayreserve.org/about/.

[603] Margaret A. Geist, Waquoit Bay National Estuarine Research Reserve (NOAA et al. 1996), III-12, https://waquoitbayreserve.org/wp-content/uploads/reserve-waquoit-site-profile.pdf. An excellent detailed study of salt marshes and other estuarine features.

[604] Herb Heldt MapWorks, "Town of Marshfield Conservation Map 2002," https://cms3.revize.com/revize/marshfield/Documents/Departments/Town%20Hall/Conservation/Conservation%20Land%20Trail%20Maps/town_of_marshfield_conservation_map.pdf; "Marshfield Open Space," available from town's Conservation Commission site, https://www.marshfield-ma.gov/departments/town_hall/conservation/conservation_lands.php.

[605] "English Salt Marsh WMA," MA Division of Fisheries and Wildlife, https://www.mass.gov/info-details/english-salt-marsh-wma; Heldt, "Marshfield Conservation Map 2002." The Marshfield assessor's parcel number is G-19-01-02C.

[606] "Marshland given to state," *Scituate Mariner*, August 3, 1995, 2; "State receives 177-acre gift," *Boston Globe*, August 5, 1995, 15; author's research on website of Plymouth County Registry of Deeds, including Trouant's Island Club, Inc. to Clayton F. English, PCRD deed, May 15, 1954, 2395/101; Clayton F. English to William S. English, PCRD, deed, 1974, 3983/552-555 (saying Trouant's Island was "now known as Rum Island Trust"); William S. English to Commonwealth of Massachusetts, PCRD deed, rec. 12/27/1994, 13337/282. The deeds mentioned no plans (drawings), and most referred to deeds in the 1800s and in 1903. The names Hall and Rogers appeared frequently in the older deeds. Some of them referred to ditches running directly to the North River, marking property boundaries (see Christopher Tilden to Joshua Jacobs, PCRD deed, rec. 9/19/1749, 40/110).

[607] "Sturtevant Mill Chairman," *Boston Globe*, July 6. 1961, 18; Sturtevant Inc. website, https://sturtevantinc.com/about/.

[608] *Scituate Herald*, August 28, 1931, 5, col. 1; *Boston Globe*, March 28, 1934, 19 (Laura Sturtevant engaged to "Clayton F. English, son of Mr and Mrs. William English of Jamaica Plain and Scituate"); "Yacht Club Has

Capacity Crowd For Officers," *South Shore Weekly Mirror*, July 19, 1956, 9; "William English and Bride Take Cruise Along East Coast," *Boston Globe*, "July 8, 1962, 93; Oliver W. Woodburn, "The Scituate Harbor Yacht Club: A Perspective on Its Fiftieth Anniversary," [1990], http://shyc.net/files/pdfs/SHYC_History.pdf, recovered from
http://web.archive.org/web/20120214073806/http://shyc.net/files/pdfs/SHYC_History.pdf.

[609] "Tracking Estuary Change: Informing Conservation Decision Making through Historical and Elevation-based Mapping," NOAA, National Estuarine Research Reserve System Science Collaborative, 2024, and sources listed, https://nerrssciencecollaborative.org/project/Wasson20; 2024 NERRS study (quoted). The study with its appendices is available at
https://www.sciencedirect.com/science/article/pii/S0006320724003410?via%3Dihub#s0130.
A webinar about this research, "Estuaries Past, Present and Future," November 30, 2023, was recorded and is on YouTube at https://www.youtube.com/watch?v=cDw4OwKL2OU. It is great and engaging. The research project was also called History and Topography to Improve Decision-making for Estuary Restoration (HiTIDER). See also "Using Historical and Elevation-based Mapping to Understand our Estuaries,"
https://www.youtube.com/watch?v=L8AhvVd0qo4.
An excellent StoryMap about this research is "Our Changing Estuaries,"
https://storymaps.arcgis.com/stories/3cd864fcb3ef478fb6ee3bcd6dfd8ed7.

[610] Tom Wheatley, "New Study Reveals True Size of Many U.S. Estuaries," Pew Trusts, November 21, 2024, https://www.pewtrusts.org/en/research-and-analysis/articles/2024/11/21/new-study-reveals-true-size-of-many-us-estuaries.

[611] My approach differed from that of the NERRS study. I did not consider the NWI. I did not georeferenced or digitize the 1870 map. That map had a scale of 1:40,000, rather than T-sheets of 1:10,000. However, the 1870 map covered a whole river, more than 12 miles, rather than the T-sheet's typical thin slice of shore, perhaps one mile. Also, the 1870 map was supported by detailed published reports, rather than surveyors' notes. Finally, I am no expert in Photoshop or GIS; I did not explore "tidal prism" or "morphometry;" and I did not develop precise numbers for marsh loss or gain over the years considered.

[612] Tom Bell, PhD PG, WaterWatch Lecture Series 2023, session 7, NSRWA, February 22, 2023, https://www.nsrwa.org/event/making-salt-marshes-more-climate-resilient-zoom-event/; "2023 WaterWatch Lecture - Making Salt Marshes More Climate Resilient," YouTube,
https://www.youtube.com/watch?v=RaZDvrZ_bsg. See Data Access Viewer – Elevation/Lidar, NOAA, https://coast.noaa.gov/dataviewer/#/. The 2023 lecture was very informative. Bell's calculations of channel widening from 1952 to 2015 match the annual rate from 1870 to present in the Yellen et al. 2022 study.

[613] Bell, 2023 WaterWatch lecture.

[614] The town of Scituate purchased much of the Scituate marshes in the 1970s. I hope to cover that in another book.

[615] Harvard University, "1771 Massachusetts Tax Inventory,"
https://legacy.sites.fas.harvard.edu/~hsb41/masstax/masstax.cgi. The data is based on the work of Bettye Pruitt, Philips Exeter Academy, who used original tax lists in the Massachusetts Archives.

[616] Mish, *Almanac*, 22.

[617] Wolff & Peteet, "Why a Marsh."

[618] "The Neponset River changes radically as it merges with the Neponset Estuary," Neponset River Watershed Association, https://neponset.org/neponset-estuary/.

[619] "Salt Marshes," On the Coast, The Trustees of Reservations, https://www.onthecoast.thetrustees.org/salt-marshes-22.

[620] Peter Phippen, "The Great Marsh: An Introduction To A Magical Place," The Cricket, January 13, 2022, https://www.thecricket.com/stories/the-great-marsh-an-introduction-to-a-magical-place,6184; "Great Marsh ACEC," Mass. Dept. of Conservation & Recreation, https://www.mass.gov/info-details/great-marsh-acec.

[621] Olivia Gieger, "Setting salt marsh standards: How a Parker River restoration project models lessons for an entire coast," US Fish & Wildlife Service, https://www.fws.gov/story/setting-salt-marsh-standards; Michelle Lockhart, "Building Great Marsh Resiliency from the Bottom-Up: Biologists heal man-made scars from colonial-era farming and 20th century mosquito control," October 5, 2020, US Fish & Wildlife Service, https://www.fws.gov/story/2021-08/building-great-marsh-resiliency-bottom.

[622] Belen Delgado Mio and Nancy Pau, "Case Study by CART: Salt Marsh Habitat Restoration on Parker River National Wildlife Refuge," June 24, 2024 (very informative),
https://storymaps.arcgis.com/stories/30bd30a7bb3d445dac7a16c42e4426fd, and https://arcg.is/LD0WG.

[623] Brian Yellen, Jonathan D. Woodruff, Hannah E. Baranes, Simon E. Engelhart, W. Rockwell Geyer, Noa Randall, Frances R. Griswold, "Salt Marsh Response to Inlet Switch-Induced Increases in Tidal Inundation,"

Journal of Geophysical Research: Earth Surface (JGR), American Geophysical Union (AGU), December 22, 2022, vol. 128, issue 1 (January 2023), https://doi.org/10.1029/2022JF006815, and https://agupubs.onlinelibrary.wiley.com/doi/10.1029/2022JF006815.

[624] Yellen et al. "Salt Marsh Response," Abstract.

[625] Yellen et al. "Salt Marsh Response," 4.4, 5.2.

[626] Yellen et al. "Salt Marsh Response," 5.1. See also Nyberg, *Ditching the Marshes*.

[627] "WaterWatch Lecture Series 2024," NSRWA, https://www.nsrwa.org/event/waterwatch-lecture-series-2024/; "WaterWatch Lecture 2024 Ep7: North and South River Marshes and the Legacy of the 1898 Portland Gale," YouTube, https://www.youtube.com/live/1mONc_yMtXs. See "Salt Marshes and Estuaries with the Experts Tour" (May 21, 2022), NSRWA, https://www.nsrwa.org/event/salt-marshes-and-estuaries-with-the-experts-tour/.

[628] Yellen et al. "Salt Marsh Response," 5.3; Brian Yellen email, March 4, 2024.

[629] Lori Wolfe, "Balancing Streamflow for Fish with Seasonal Water Demands in Scituate," NSRWA website, March 22, 2024, https://www.nsrwa.org/balancing-streamflow-for-fish-with-seasonal-water-demands-in-scituate/.

[630] Deane, *History of Scituate*, 20.

[631] Neumann, "Battle;" North River Commission website, https://www.northrivercommission.net/. The North River Protective Order is almost impossible to find. Try the Plymouth County Registry of Deeds (PCRD) website, https://www.plymouthdeeds.org/home/pages/search-records. For example, in "Business of Name," enter SCITUATETOWNOF and in "Advanced" features, limit search to ORDR, and maybe 1978–1979. The Order was filed against a number of private and public owners. See PCRD book 4639, page 278, document 12727, 56 pages, going town by town, with listing of unknown owners (see page 56, after Pembroke, listing 190 acres "directly south of river, west of Herring Brook [in Pembroke].), recorded 4/11/1979, referencing Plan Book 20, Page 869, 10 pages, recorded 4/11/1979. The plan is "Scenic River Corridor North River, Scale 1:5000" prepared by Clarks Engineering Collaborative, Inc., etc., certified by the state 10/13/1978, hearing 12/20/78, approved 3/22/79. The plan starts with an aerial photo of Fourth Cliff, followed by more aerial "ortho" photos, certified by William I. Morse, R.L.S., provided by James W. Sewall Company of Bangor, ME. Their photos are archived at University of Maine, and copies may be in local archives of the North River towns affected by the Order.

[632] "The North & South Rivers Watershed Association," presentation, undated, Massachusetts Real Estate Bar Association, https://www.reba.net/UserFiles/files/docs/river/PP_Woods_compressed.pdf.

[633] For a history of mills along these streams, see Kezia Bacon, "The Power of Water: Milling and Manufacturing in the North River Valley," Nature blog post, April 22, 2008, http://keziabaconbernstein.blogspot.com/2008/04/power-of-water-milling-and.html.

[634] Especially in my 2000 BMW Z3 sports car.

[635] "Dams," WPA card index, summarizing town records at vol. C-9, page 70; "Dam Railing Committee," WPA card index, summarizing town records at vol. C-9, page 138, November 1, 1830.

[636] "Guard Rails, Repairing of," WPA card index, summarizing town records at vol. C-12, page 356.

[637] Hanson Town Hall (1872), HNS.1, MACRIS.

[638] "Nathanial Thomas Mill," NSRWA website, https://www.nsrwa.org/listing/nathaniel-thomas-mill/.

[639] "Nathanial Thomas Mill," NSRWA (quoted); Margaret Kitchenham, "Nathaniel Thomas Mill History" (2019), https://archive.org/details/1hansonbicentennialcommittee1973nathanielthomasmillwithphotos/page/2/mode/2up.

[640] Benno M. Forman, "Mill Sawing in Seventeenth-Century Massachusetts," *Old-Time New England*, vol. 60, no. 220 (Boston, Mass.: Society for the Preservation of New England Antiquities, 1970), 109, https://hne-rs.s3.amazonaws.com/filestore/1/2/8/0/0_743f3ba38c50e98/12800_43708f204bfc452.pdf. Forman cites Bishop's history, discussed below.

[641] *History of the Town of Hanson* (Hanson: Town of Hanson Historical Committee, c. 1959), ch. 2, p. 2. https://archive.org/details/historyoftownofh00sn/page/n81/mode/2up.

[642] A fuller quote is: "North river, rising from ponds in Pembroke, gives it a good water power. For more than 40 years after the settlement at Plymouth, this town contained the only sawmill in the colony." *New England Gazetteer*, as quoted in *Boston Globe*, March 3, 1909, 10, cols. 3–4; the 1841 gazetteer is available online, https://books.google.com/books?id=Aa8TAAAAYAAJ&printsec=frontcover#v=onepage&q&f=false.

[643] J. Leander Bishop, *A History of American Manufactures from 1608 to 1860*, 2 vols. (Philadelphia: Edward Young & Co., 1861, 1864), 1:97, https://babel.hathitrust.org/cgi/pt?id=hvd.hneg7u&seq=5.

[644] Herbert L. Osgood, *The American Colonies In the Seventeenth Century* (New York: The Macmillan Company), probably vol. 3 (1926), as quoted in "Samuel Maverick: The Restoration and the Royal Commission of 1664," http://samuelmaverick.blogspot.com/2012/03/restoration-and-royal-commission-of.html; Louis Jordan, "Chronological Listing of Documents and Events relating to the Massachusetts Mint" (at events of 1664) in The Coins of Colonial and Early America project (c. 2022), University of Notre Dame, https://coins.nd.edu/colcoin/colcoinintros/MAMintDocs.chron.html.

[645] Bishop, *Manufactures*, 1:97.

[646] Bangs, *Town Records*, 156; see Nelson M. Stetson, *Book No. 6, Sketch of Cornet Robert Stetson: The Veteran Cornet of the Plymouth Colony Troopers, 1658 [etc.]* (Campello, MA: The Stetson Kindred of America [or by author, who was the association's Secretary], c.1923 [see page 126]), 52, 77 (see note), and other pages, https://archive.org/details/sketchofcornetro00stetiala. This detailed account bears careful study.

[647] Stetson, *Book No. 6, Sketch*, 52 ("decay"), 77 (see note), and other pages.

[648] Stetson, *Book No. 6, Sketch*, 18–21.

[649] "Herring Run Park – Pembroke," NSRWA, https://www.nsrwa.org/listing/herring-run-park-conservation-area/.

[650] Alexandra Weliever, 'It feels like home': Hanover family-owned shop Myette's celebrates 50 years," *Patriot Ledger*, October 19, 2021, updated October 24, 2021, https://www.patriotledger.com/story/news/2021/10/19/myettes-country-store-celebrates-its-50th-anniversary-hanover/8477835002/.

[651] "Indian Head River Trails," NSRWA, https://www.nsrwa.org/listing/indian-head-river-trails/; Indian Head River Coalition, "Indian Head River Trail Map," https://www.hanson-ma.gov/sites/g/files/vyhlif3231/f/pages/ihr_trail_map_brochure.pdf.

[652] "Indian Head River Restoration," NSRWA website, https://www.nsrwa.org/protect-our-waters/healthy-rivers/dam-removals/indian-head-river-restoration/.

[653] The park on the Hanover side is owned by the Town of Hanover. Abraham Starr to Town of Hanover, deed, March 30, 1950, recorded April 17, 1950, PCRD 2087/296 (all land in Hanover "conveyed to me by the E. H. Clapp Rubber Company, by Receivers, by deed dated January 10, 1935"); Assessor parcel 72-33 (PID 4905) (13.75 acres). The 1935 deed refers to plans by W. G. Ford, C. E., including "Plan of Land in Hanover and Pembroke Owned by E. H. Clapp Rubber Co.," October 26, 1934, PCRD plan book 5, page 328 (and see 329 and 330).

Starr likewise conveyed the former Clapp land in Pembroke to the Town of Pembroke, March 30, 1950, PCRD 2087/297. It seems the park is now owned by Wildlands Trust, Inc. See Harold M. Tucker to Plymouth County Wildlands Trust Inc., PCRD certificate of title 85738, December 28, 1993; Assessor parcel B13-3 (3,422,945 sq. ft., almost 79 acres); "Tucker Preserve – Pembroke, MA," Wildlands Trust, https://wildlandstrust.org/tucker-preserve: "Donated to Wildlands Trust in 1993 by Sidney Tucker and Harold M. Tucker."

[654] Barbara Barker, "Early Industries at Luddam's Ford in Hanover," June 1998, *Focus on History*.

[655] "Indian Head River Restoration," NSRWA website, https://www.nsrwa.org/protect-our-waters/healthy-rivers/dam-removals/indian-head-river-restoration/.

[656] For example, see Ernst Halberstadt, "Dam showing fish ladder," photograph, April 23, 1973, *Digital Commonwealth*, https://ark.digitalcommonwealth.org/ark:/50959/8336kj80s.

[657] "Indian Head River Restoration," NSRWA website.

[658] Stetson, *Book No. 6, Sketch*, 53–54.

[659] 1832 Valuation List, 138; John Grove Hales. "Plan of Hanover made by John G Hales, dated 1831," map, 1831, Norman B. Leventhal Map & Education Center, https://collections.leventhalmap.org/search/commonwealth:25152m18q; Dwelley and Simmons, *History of Hanover*, 194 (Stockbridge), 195; "The Tack Factory," Wikipedia article, https://en.wikipedia.org/wiki/The_Tack_Factory (1834); "The Tack Factory," NRW.5, MACRIS (1834, based on Merritt); Merritt, *Narrative History*, 157 (photo before 155); Samuel Salmond Papers, Baker Library, Harvard Business School, Mss:733 1816-1853 S172, Collection Overview, https://id.lib.harvard.edu/ead/bak01755/catalog; Briggs, *Shipbuilding*, 33.

[660] Dwelley and Simmons, *History of Hanover*, 195; Barbara Barker, "A Beautiful Old Hanover House," June 1998, *Focus on History* (quoted; a very good discussion of families and home on Washington Street); "Smith, Albert and Anne Lenthal Eells - Salmond, Samuel and Elizabeth Smith House," 128 Washington Street, Hanover, HNV.192 (source of birth and death dates), MACRIS; "Historic Sylvester Field" (across from Samuel Salmond house), NSRWA, https://www.nsrwa.org/listing/historic-sylvester-field/.

[661] Email about event held on September 14, 2024.

[662] "Welcome to River House," Andrew and Jaime Sullivan Family Foundation, https://sullivanfamilyfoundation.org/about-us/; "River House 1715," booklet, https://sullivanfamilyfoundation.org/wp-content/uploads/2023/06/RiverHseBro7x10-Web-6-5-2023.pdf; "Turner, Thomas House" ("The River House"), 2 Washington St, Pembroke, PEM.9, MACRIS.

[663] HNV.903/PEM.900, and HNV.911/PEM.9xx (tablets), MACRIS. The 1930 Columbia Road bridge is documented at HNV.901/PEM.902, MACRIS.

[664] Frank Perrotta, "New map charts rivers," *Boston Globe*, May 5, 1991, 306/G12 South.

[665] University of Massachusetts Amherst, Department of Forestry and Wildlife Management, Plymouth County: aerial photograph (dpt-10k-202), August 19, 1952, William P. MacConnell Aerial Photograph Collection (FS 190), Special Collections and University Archives, University of Massachusetts Amherst Libraries, https://credo.library.umass.edu/view/full/mufs190-1952-dpt10k202-i001. As stated in "MacConnell Aerial Photos Index (1951–1952)," https://www.arcgis.com/home/item.html?id=50545e378c7d407b883d730dd9de2c89, the MacConnell Collection is based on "black-and-white aerial photographs captured in 1951–52 across the state of Massachusetts at an approximate scale of 1:20,000. The flights were commissioned by the US Department of Agriculture and flown by Robinson Aerial Surveys, Inc., out of Newark, NJ. For more information on this photo program, see the National Archives." See Record Group 145.8 Cartographic Records (General), 1935–52, https://www.archives.gov/research/guide-fed-records/groups/145.html; and "Domestic Aerial Photography, Special List 25," NARA, https://www.archives.gov/research/cartographic/aerial-photography/domestic-photography.

[666] Nyberg, *Summer Suffragists*, ch. 7, and website at https://www.lylenyberg.com/shipyards-of-east-boston; PEM.16 continuation sheet, MACRIS; "Judith Winsor Smith Bridge Dedication," Town of Pembroke website, https://www.pembroke-ma.gov/council-aging/events/453476.

[667] Mish, *Almanac*, 14.

[668] "Block House Yard," NSRWA website (quoted), https://www.nsrwa.org/listing/block-house-yard/; Briggs, *Shipbuilding*, 260. See discussion in text about the *Helen M. Foster*, launched from Chittenden Yard in 1871.

[669] "Second Church Graveyard at Wilson Hill," Norwell Cemetery Dept, https://norwelldpw.com/historical-cemeteries-in-norwell/second-church-graveyard-at-wilson-hill. This seems a bit far from the earlier reports.

[670] "Norris Reservation," Trustees website, https://thetrustees.org/place/norris-reservation/; "Norris Reservation," NSRWA website, https://www.nsrwa.org/listing/norris-reservation/.

[671] News clipping with photo and notes in "Mills" file, Scituate Historical Society.

[672] Erin Douglas, "In the Berkshires, an effort to corral climate change, one stream at a time," *Boston Globe*, July 7, 2024, 1, and July 2, 2024, https://www.bostonglobe.com/2024/07/02/science/massachusetts-berkshires-culverts-bridges-stormwater-climate-change/.

[673] Douglas, "In the Berkshires;" "Massachusetts Stream Crossings Handbook" (Commonwealth of Massachusetts, 2d ed., 2012), https://www.mass.gov/doc/massachusetts-stream-crossing-handbook/download; "Massachusetts River & Stream Crossing Standards" (River and Stream Continuity Partnership, 2006, corrected 3/8/12), 10, https://www.nae.usace.army.mil/Portals/74/docs/regulatory/StreamRiverContinuity/MA_RiverStreamCrossingStandards.pdf. The standards are designed to protect passage of wildlife and fish, including shad.

[674] "Steadman, Isaac - Russell, George Grist Mill [Stockbridge Grist Mill], SCI.45, MACRIS; "Stockbridge Grist Mill," NSRWA website, https://www.nsrwa.org/listing/stockbridge-grist-mill/; "The Stockbridge Grist Mill, 1650," Scituate Historical Society website, https://scituatehistoricalsociety.org/historic_property/grist-mill/; "Old Stockbridge Grist Mill," Wikipedia article, https://en.wikipedia.org/wiki/Old_Stockbridge_Grist_Mill; signs at mill.

[675] Charles C. Lincoln, *Through the Years with the Old Grist Mill* (Scituate: by author, 1950) (hand-written on lined paper), on file at Scituate Historical Society (974.482 Lincoln) with excerpts in "Mills" file, Scituate Historical Society (quoted).

[676] Lincoln, *Through the Years*; Annette Langley Markward, "The Early Millers of Greenbush," booklet in color (with many old photos) (2007), in "Mills" file, Scituate Historical Society.

[677] *Explore South Shore Recreation Guide Map* (Norwell, MA: North and South Rivers Watershed Association, 5th ed., 2019).

[678] "Highest and best use," https://en.wikipedia.org/wiki/Highest_and_best_use; "Valuation matters - Appraisers apply four tests to determine highest and best use," Elliott Davis, September 23, 2019. https://www.elliottdavis.com/insights/valuation-matters-appraisers-apply-four-tests-determine-highest-best-use.

INDEX

Note: Images are noted by page numbers in *italics*.

A
Accord Pond, 26
Adamowicz, Susan, 182
Adams, John Quincy, 20–21, 67, 73, *73*, 74–81, 85
Allen, Stephen M., 144
Ames, Tilden, 85–86
Anderson, John, 71
Astor House (New York), 84
Audubon Society, 176

B
Bache, A. D., 104, 106
Bacon, Kezia, 33
Bangs, Jeremy Dupertuis, 7
Barnard, J. G., 89
Barry, John, 78
Barstow, Elijah, Jr., and J. B., 78
Bates, Joseph A., 78
Bear Island, *163*, 166, *219*
Bell, Tom, 194
Belle House Neck, 6
Birch Pond Dam, 134
Block House, 59, *59*
bog shoes, 50–51, *51*
Boston, 2, 103–105, *104*, 141
Bowditch, Nathaniel, 103
Bradford, William, 207
Brant Rock, 11, *11*, 138
Bridgewaye Inn, 110, 132
Briggs, L. Vernon, 6, 30, 34, 36, 45, 55, *56*, 64–67, 155
Brown, Calvin, 83, 115, 162
Bryant, J. Fox, *104*
Bryant, John, 21
Bryant-Turner Mill, 214

C
Cape Cod Canal, 74
Charles River, 12, 102
Chittenden Landing, 93, 95, 99, *100*
City Hall Building (Boston), 103, *104*
Clapp Rubber Mill, 30–33, *31–32*
climate change, 10, 178, 183–186, 189
cod, 36
Cohasset, 20, 36, 38, 64, 80, 122
Collamore, Anthony, 81
Colman's Landing, 51
common field system, 7–8
Concord, 7, 134
Concord River, 22

Conley, Cort, 134
Connecticut River, 17, 22, 28, 35–36, 117
Coons, Persis, and Quentin, 97–98
Cornet's Mill, 205
"Countess, The" (Whittier), 52
cranberry bogs, 181, 191
Crossley, Walter, 16, 47, 58–59, 152, 154, 156, 162, 178
Cross Street Dam, *206*
Cudworth Barn, 45, *46*, 47, *47*
Currall, George G., 145
Curtis, Edward, 78
Cushing, Nathan, 60, 76
Cushing, William, 76

D
dams, 21–35, *23–24, 27, 31–33*, 102, 110, 122, 126, 131–134, *132–133*, 171, 202, 205, *206–208*
Danforth, William S., 152
Davis, Charles H., 104
Deane, Samuel, 23, 110, 199
DeBrusk, Skip, 17–18
Delafield, Richard, 104
de Lannoy, Philippe, 99
Delano, William, 99
Dennis, William H., *107*, 108
Denton, Sherman Foote, 38–39
Derby, Shad, 117
Deshon, James, 144
development, 141–158
dikes, 112, 115, 126–127, 135–138
Donahue, Brian, 7
Donahue, John, 165
Douglas, William O., 177–179
Drinkwater River, 205

E
Elkhorn Slough, 190
Elm Street Bridge, *207*
Emery, George, 145–146, *146–147*, 148
English, Clayton, 192–193
English Salt Marsh, 192–193
environmental awareness, 176–178
environmental frontiers, 178–180

F
Factory Pond, 205
Ferry Hill, 126, 145–146, *149*
First Herring Brook, 1, 19, 22, *23*, 34, 51, *65*, 76, 209, 216, 219, *219*
First Parish Church of Norwell Unitarian Universalist Church, 22

269

fishing, 9, 15–16
   cod, 36
   herring, 36–38, *37*
   salmon, 36
   shad, *17*, 17–21, *20*
Flint, Horace P., 144
Flint, Thomas, 145
flooding, 88, 106, 127, 184–186, 215
Ford, Peleg, 83
Forge Pond, 205
Forman, Benno, 204
Foster, Helen M., 94, 96
Founding Fish (McPhee), 38
Fourth Cliff, 5, 66, 69, 71, 73, 79–81, 83, *88*, 89, 91–92, 109, 150, 153, *158*, 159, 164, 178. *See also* Humarock
Fourth Cliff House, *91*, 91–92
Freden, Ray, 142–143, 147, *147*

G
Gaffney, John P., 151–152
Galluzzo, John, 173
Garside, Jeanne, 96, 98
George Moore's Pond, 34
Glinski, Jim, 162
Great Boston Fire, 141, 144
Great Green Island, 109, 150–152, *153*, 154–155
Great Marsh, 196
Great Meadow, The (Donahue), 7
Green, Seth, 18
Green Harbor, 11, *11*, 138
Green Harbor River, 12, 70, 118, 121, 131, 134–139, *135*, 137–138
gundalows, 51–54, *52–54*, 61
Gunderway, Jerry, *61*, 61–62
Gunderway, Richard, 61

H
Haeckel, Ernst, 119
Halberstadt, Ernst, 207
Hall, Marcia, 146
Hanover, 2, 19, 23, 101, 205–207, 209–214
Hanover Bridge, 170–172, 211, *212*, 213
Hanover Four Corners, 55, 109, 129, 173, 205, 209–210, 213, *213*
Hanson, 2, 21, 77, 134, 199, 201, *201–203*, 201–206
Hatch, George, 92
Hatch Tilden house, *59*
Hatherly, Timothy, 6
haying, 9, *41*, 41–54, *43*, *46–54*
haystacks, 46–49, *48–49*
Heade, Martin Johnson, *48*, 49
Helen M. Foster (ship), 93–96, *94*, 110, 121
Hemenway, Augustus, 176
Henderson, Anne Bonney, 99

Henderson, Harry P., 15
Henderson, Lloyd B., 15
herring, 36–38, *37*
Herschel, Clemens, 116–118, *117*, 118, 125–127, 221
History of Shipbuilding on North River (Briggs), 55, 66–67
Holly Hill, 148, *149*
Holyoke Dam, 117–118
Howard, Frank, *157*
Howard, Helen, *157*
Howard, Jack, 156
Howard, John Brooks, *157*
Hudson River, 22
Humarock, 5, 101, 108, 126, 131–132. *See also* Fourth Cliff
hydrography, 105–106

I
Indian Head Brook, 21
Indian Head River, 1, 12–13, 21, 30, *65*, 170, 206, *206*, 209, 213
Ireland, George, 145

J
Jackson, Andrew, 73
Jackson, William Henry, 93
Jamestown, Virginia, 4
Jenkins, Cumings, 74
Jones, Ezekiel, 74
Joseph, Nancy, 15

K
King Philip's War, 214

L
Lawlor, Dennison J., 95–96
laws, dam, 24–28, *27*
Lester, Allen, 97
Limburg, Karin, 35
Lincoln, Charles, 216–217
Little's Bridge, 1, 51, 57, 80, 92, 171, *172*
Lowell, James Russell, 52
Luce, Martha D., 144
Ludden, James, 207
Ludden's Ford, 13, *14*, 21, 33–34, *65*, 171, 201, 206–207, *207–208*
Lunt, George, 50
Lynn, 134

M
Macomber, Charles W., 81
Marguerite house, 165, *165*
Marshfield, 2, *2*, 3, 10, 66, 78–81, 91, 138, *143*, 161, *161*, 175, 192–193
Massachuset, 1
Massachusetts Wetlands Protection Act, 178

Massaugetucket, 9
Mattakeeset, 15
Mattapoisett Bog, 191
May, Samuel J., 60, 75, *76*
Mayflower, 4, 41–42
McCarthy, Paul, 182
McKay, Donald, 85
McPhee, John, 19, 34–36, 38
meadow shoes, 50–51, *51*
Merchants Exchange (Boston), 84
Merritt, Charles, Charles H., 63–64
Merritt, Joseph Foster, 45, 61, 91, 93, 96–97
Merritt, Joseph Foster, Jr., 98
Merritt, William O., 91
Meteyard, Thomas Buford, 164, *164*
Mill Dam (Scituate), 202
Mills, William E., 61
Minot's gale, 88, 112
Mitchell, Henry, 102–103, 106, 110–113, 115–116, *116*, 131, 133
Monmonier, Mark, 105
Myette's Corner Store, 206

N
Narragansett Bay, 74
Nathaniel Thomas Mill, *203*
Newton, James, *43*
New York City, 5
Norris Reservation, 61
North and South Rivers Watershed Association (NSRWA), 13, 21, 31, 38, 64, 113, 159, 177, 198, 205
North River, 1–4, *2*
    in 1900s, 167–180
    improvement of, 69–123
    length of, 12
    settlement of, 5–6
    slope of, 12
    tides, 3, 5–6, 12–15, *14–15*
    vital statistics on, 10–15, *11, 14–15*
    watershed, 10–11
North River Bridge, 170
Norwell, 2, *2*, 3, 19, 61, 93–94, 96, 98, *98*, 99, *99*, 177, 214–215
Norwell Center, 22, 75

O
Oak Island Site, 16
Old Lyme, Connecticut, *50*
Old Oaken Bucket Pond, 22, 34, 134, 199, 202, 216, 218
Old Oaken Bucket Pond Dam, 134
Onion Island, 154
Otis, Cushing, 76

P
Padilla Bay, 191

paintings, of shad, 38–39
Panic of 1873, 141
Pau, Nancy, 196
Peakes, William, 28
Peggotty Beach, 12, 173
Peirce, Annie Foster, 45–46
Peirce, Benjamin, 102–103, *103*, 106–107
Peirce, Silas, II, 45–46
Peirce, Silas, III, 45–46
Pembroke, 2, 19, 24, *24*, 37, *37*, 64, *65*, 85, 206–207, 211, 213
Pembroke Center, 205
Peteet, Dorothy, 187, 189
Phillips, Daniel, 80
Piermont Marsh, 191
Plum Island, 137
Plymouth, 4, 16
Plymouth Colony, 6–8, 19, 21
Portland Gale of 1898, 3–5, 9, 69, 137, 154, 159–166, *160–161, 163–165*
Potato Island, 154
Previte's Marketplace, 209
"public trust" doctrine, 8
Pudding Brook, 209

R
Randall, William, 65
reclamation, 101, 109–110, 113, 116, 125, 127–131, *128*, 181
Reed, H. G., 152–153
Rexhame, 5
Reynolds, Florence A., *54*
Rights of Nature, 179
Rio de Janeiro, 4
River House, 211
rivers, in colonial history and context, 4–5
Rogers, Clift, 80
Rogers, Isaac, 84
Rogers, Isaiah, 84–85
Rogers, Luther, 77, 80–81
Rogers' Wharf, 81, 101, 108, 109, 112, 126, 127, 131
Roosevelt, Franklin Delano, 99
Roosevelt, Theodore, 176

S
Salem, 189
Salisbury, 20
salmon, 36
Salmond, John, 210
Salmond, Samuel, 210
Salmond, William, 210
salt marsh haying, 9, *41*, 41–54, *43, 46–54*
Schuylkill River, 22
Scituate, 2–3, 7, 24–25, 29, 49, 64, 66, 69, *75*, 155–156, 161, *161*, 186, 216–219

Scituate Harbor, 5, 11, *11,* 22, 69, 73, 83, 85–86, *87–88,* 89
Scothorne, Donald G., 16
sea levels, 13, 119, 133, 183, *186,* 190
Sea Street Bridge, 131–132, *132–133*
Sea View, 10, 142–143, 145–146, 148, *149*
Second Herring Brook, 19, 22, *23,* 61, 76, 214, *215–216*
Second Parish Church, 214
seines, 28–29
settlement, by English, 5–6
shad, *17,* 17–21, *20*
Shad Creek, 20
Shaler, Nathaniel, 136–137
shingle beach, 110–115, *111–114*
shipbuilders, 64–67, *65*
shipbuilding, 9, 70, 93–96, *94,* 99
Shipbuilding on North River (Briggs), 6, 9, 155
Shirley, William, 42, 44
Sierra Club v. Morton, 179
slope, 12
Smith, John F., 162
Smith, Sylvanus, 85, 214
Snow, Edward Rowe, 156
South River, 4, *11,* 12, 120, 195–197
South Shore, 2, *11*
staddles, 46–49, *48*
Stage Beach, 86
Stebbins, Nathaniel Livermore, *113–114,* 115, 164
Stedman, Isaac, 21
Stetson, Cornet, 214
Stetson, Joshua, 56–58
Stetson, Robert, 21, 204–205
Stewart, Reed F., 178
Stilgoe, John, 45, 135
Stinson, William B., 145
Stockbridge, John, 21
Stockbridge Mill, 22, 202, 205, 210, 216–217, *217–218*
Sturtevant, Laura, 192–193
Susquehannah River, 22
Sylvester Field, 210, *210*

T
Talbot, Zephaniah, 210
Taunton River, 16, 66, 74
Taylor, Brian, 13
Third Cliff, 5, 22, 51, 66, 69, 71, 79–81, 88, *88,* 89, 92, 101, 109, 114, 127, 150, 153, 159, *160,* 164, *165*
Third Herring Brook, 19, 21, 23, *23, 65,* 204–205, 209, *209,* 210
Thomas, Nathaniel, 202, *203*
tides, 3, 5–6, 12–15, *14–15,* 45, 106, 110, 115–116, *133,* 171
Tilden, John, 92
Tilden, Robert, 157

Tilden, Wales, 70
Tilden, William, 59–60, 164
Tittmann, O. H., 105, *107–108*
Tolman, Joseph Robinson, 63
Tolman, Thomas Jones, 63–64, 125, 129
Tolman Family, *62,* 62–64
Tower, John, 56, 89
Tower, Z. B., 86
Treasure Island, *54*
Tremont House, 84
Tripp, Joseph, 60
Trouant Island, *149,* 155–158, *155–158,* 192
Turner, Charles, 22, 29, 76, 156
Turner, Daniel, 65, 69
Turner, Humphrey, 65, 76
Turner, Samuel A., 70, 74, 76, *76,* 77, 88

U
Union Bridge, *2,* 51, 59, *59, 107,* 172

V
Valdespino, Stephen R., 7
Vassall, William, 6–8, 42
Vinal, Abe, 94
Vinal, William Gould, 45, 49, 90, 97, 125, 177

W
Wampanoag, 1
Wampatuck, Josias, 7
Wampatuck Pond Dam, 134
Waquoit Bay, 191–192
Waterman & Barstow, *108,* 130
Waterman's Tack Factory, *33,* 33–34
Watson, Janet, 97–98
Webster, Daniel, 77, 86, 148
Webster House (hotel), 91, 145
Weir River, 26, *27*
weirs, 16
Welch, E. Parker, 129, *129,* 141, 151
Welch, George, 129
Welch, Michael, 88, 141
West Barnstable, *48*
Weymouth River, 74
White, Edward, 136
White's Ferry, 81–82, *82,* 101, 110, 131
Whiting, Henry L., 102–103, 106–108, *108,* 118–120
Whittier, John Greenleaf, 52
William Delano House, 99, *99*
Williams, James H., 93, *94*
Wills' Island, 49, 57
Winthrop, John, 207
Wolff, Daniel, 187
Wood Island, 151
Woodruff, Jon, 197

Y
Yellen, Brian, 197–198

Acknowledgments

Thanks to:

My wife Kathleen and family, for patience, support, and hard work editing
My parents, whose love of books, maps, and travel flowed down to us children
Jim Conroy and Roy Harris, friends-writers-advisers on becoming a writer and author
Janet Paraschos, for providing clarity in writing
Alix Stuart, for wisdom, support, and overall perspective on the subject
My late brothers-in-law for their many gifts, including Photoshop and lessons in history and ecology that helped make this book what it became
Ray Freden, for help on Sea View history
Tom Whalen, for advice on publishing and for the Tolman toolmakers' stories
Jim Glinski, for raising and helping to answer questions of history
Brian Yellen and Jon Woodruff, for their research and help on environmental science
John Howard, for sharing historical family photos of life at Trouant Island
Gary Banks and Bill Richardson, for being such great people with such great photos
John Roman, artist, mapmaker, author
Susannah Green, designer and adviser
Nancy Seasholes, David Dixon, Bob Gallagher, and others, for critiquing my work and making it better
Prof. John Stilgoe, an inspiration, and a landmark in landscape history
My friends at Scituate Town Archives and Scituate Historical Society, who are great resources, as well as great people
Scituate Town Library, for answering all those special requests
NSRWA, for inspiring lectures, complete guides to the river, and ecology help
Neighbors on Third Cliff, present and past
Those whose names I forgot to mention (please excuse me), and those whose help flowed into the text, quotes, photos, captions, endnotes, and spirit of this book, including Skip & Carolyn DeBrusk and Sally Rossi-Ormon

I tried to be as accurate as possible. But in a work like this, with a human being like me, it is only natural for mistakes to occur. They are my responsibility. Let me know and I will try to fix them.

About the Author

Lyle Nyberg was born near the River Plate (*Rio de la Plata*), grew up near the Mississippi River, went to college next to the Connecticut River, went to law school next to the Charles River, worked in view of the Potomac River and later the Delaware River, and now lives near the North River in Scituate, Massachusetts.

Lyle graduated from Dartmouth College and Boston University School of Law. He retired as a lawyer and turned independent scholar and historian. He wrote and published books on historical topics. They include *Summer Suffragists* (2020), *On a Cliff* (2021), *Ditching the Marshes* (2022) and (with Gary Banks and Bill Richardson) *Seacoast Scituate By Air* (2022). His writing has been published in scholarly and other journals, as well as in a state database, where he documented more than 50 historical buildings in the greater Boston area.

He is a member of the Scituate Historical Society, the Massachusetts Historical Society, and the New England Historical Association.

He can be reached at www.lylenyberg.com.

www.ingramcontent.com/pod-product-compliance
Lightning Source LLC
Chambersburg PA
CBHW061123170426
43209CB00013B/1657